FREEDOM SUMMER

FREEDOM SUMMER

The Savage Season
That Made Mississippi Burn and
Made America a Democracy

BRUCE WATSON

VIKING

VIKING

Published by the Penguin Group

Penguin Group (USA) Inc., 375 Hudson Street, New York, New York 10014, U.S.A.

Penguin Group (Canada), 90 Eglinton Avenue East, Suite 700,

Toronto, Ontario, Canada M4P 2Y3 (a division of Pearson Penguin Canada Inc.)

Penguin Books Ltd, 80 Strand, London WC2R 0RL, England

Penguin Ireland, 25 St. Stephen's Green, Dublin 2, Ireland (a division of Penguin Books Ltd)

Penguin Books Australia Ltd, 250 Camberwell Road, Camberwell,

Victoria 3124, Australia (a division of Pearson Australia Group Pty Ltd)

Penguin Books India Pvt Ltd, 11 Community Centre, Panchsheel Park, New Delhi–110 017, India

Penguin Group (NZ), 67 Apollo Drive, Rosedale, North Shore 0632,

New Zealand (a division of Pearson New Zealand Ltd)

Penguin Books (South Africa) (Pty) Ltd, 24 Sturdee Avenue, Rosebank,

Johannesburg 2196, South Africa

Penguin Books Ltd, Registered Offices: 80 Strand, London WC2R 0RL, England

First published in 2010 by Viking Penguin, a member of Penguin Group (USA) Inc.

10 9 8 7 6 5 4 3 2 1

LIBRARY OF CONGRESS CATALOGING IN PUBLICATION DATA

Watson, Bruce, date.

Freedom summer : the savage summer that made Mississippi burn

and made America a democracy / Bruce Watson.

p. cm.

Includes bibliographical references and index.

ISBN 978-0-670-02170-3

1. African Americans—Civil rights—Mississippi—History—20th century. 2. African
Americans—Suffrage—Mississippi—History—20th century. 3. Civil rights movements—
Mississippi—History—20th century. 4. Civil rights workers—Mississippi—History—
20th century. 5. Mississippi—Race relations—History—20th century. I. Title.

E185.93.M6W285 2010

323.1196'0730762—dc22   2009047211

Printed in the United States of America

Set in Times New Roman

Designed by Francesca Belanger

For all the teachers and the volunteers
giving of their time, compassion, and spirit

A dream is not a very safe thing to be near, Bayard. I know; I had one once. It's like a loaded pistol with a hair trigger: if it stays alive long enough, somebody is going to be hurt. But if it's a good dream, it's worth it.

—William Faulkner, "An Odor of Verbena"

Contents

FREEDOM SUMMER

By the summer of 1961, Herbert Lee was a wealthy man by local standards—local black standards. After thirty years of farming in the deepest corner of the Deep South, Lee had a small dairy farm, a modest home, nine children, and a road or two that did not seem like a dead end. So one day that scorching summer, when a young, bespectacled black man from New York showed up on his porch wearing bib overalls and speaking softly about his right to vote, Lee decided he could take a few risks. He agreed to drive the stranger around Amite County. To friends and family, Lee's decision suggested a death wish.

Blacks did not vote in Mississippi—never had as long as anyone could remember. "Niggers down here don't need to vote," one cop said. "Ain't supposed to vote." Entire counties where black faces far outnumbered white had not a single black voter. Seventy-some years had passed since Mississippi had crafted a clever combination of poll taxes, literacy tests, and other legalistic voodoo that, within a decade, slashed black voting rolls from 190,000 to just 2,000. Ever since, whenever a Negro had dared to register, terror had taken care of him. A trip to the courthouse registrar landed his name in the newspaper. Soon the "uppity nigger" was beaten, fired, thrown off a plantation, or left trembling in the night by a shotgun fired into his shack. Herbert Lee knew the risks, but when he decided to face them, he did not know he was risking his life.

On the morning of September 25, 1961, Lee was rattling along dusty back roads toward the tiny town of Liberty, Mississippi. Looking in the rearview mirror of his old pickup, he saw a newer truck. Lee pulled into the parking lot of a cotton gin. The other pickup, its tires popping the gravel, pulled alongside. Lee recognized the driver, a burly white man with jug ears and a broad, shiny forehead, pink from the summer sun. Lee had known "Mister Hurst" all his life, had even played with him as a boy. The two men's farms were not far apart. Perhaps Mister Hurst just wanted to talk. Then Lee spotted the .38 in his neighbor's hand.

Through the window of his pickup, Lee shouted, "I'm not going to talk to you until you put the gun down!" Hurst said nothing, just bolted out of his truck. Lee frantically slid across his seat and scrambled out the passenger door. Hurst circled, gun waving.

"I'm not playing with you this morning!" the hulking white man said. Before Lee could run two steps, Hurst put a bullet in his left temple. Lee fell facedown in the gravel. The new pickup sped away. The parking lot fell silent. The body, encircled by onlookers, lay in a pool of blood for hours beneath the sizzling sun. Blacks were afraid to move it, and whites refused.

No one knew how many black men were murdered in Mississippi in 1961. No one could remember the Magnolia State ever convicting a white man of killing a black man. At the coroner's inquest, Hurst spun a story about a tire iron Herbert Lee had brandished. His gun, Hurst said, had gone off by accident. A witness was coerced into swearing he saw the tire iron, too, the same one "found" under Herbert Lee's body. State legislator E. H. Hurst never went to trial. But the bullet that killed Herbert Lee set off a string of firecrackers that clustered in a single summer, a season so radically different, so idealistic, so savage, so daring, that it redefined freedom in America.

BOOK ONE

Crossroads

And the problem of living as a Negro was cold and hard. What was it that made the hate of whites for blacks so steady, seemingly so woven into the texture of things? What kind of life was possible under that hate? How had this hate come to be?

—Richard Wright, *Black Boy*

Prologue

In the fall of 1963, America was suffused with an unbearable whiteness of being. Confident and assertive, the nation rode an unprecedented wave of prosperity. The engines of the American economy were at full bore; the young, handsome president was well liked and respected. The enemy was unmistakable—a mushroom cloud, a bald bully banging his shoe at the United Nations, a worldwide threat that had to be contained. Americans drove two-thirds of the world's cars and held half the world's wealth. Cars were big and beefy, with fins, flamboyant taillights, and loud engines under expansive hoods. Jars of Miracle Whip and loaves of Wonder Bread were in most kitchens; Marlboros and Kents were advertised on TV, and half of all adults smoked a pack or more a day. Only one or two cities had enclosed malls. Ninety-nine percent of homes had TVs—almost all black and white—yet none received more than seven channels. These featured "a vast wasteland" of Westerns, medical shows, and silly sitcoms. Not a single program showed a dark face in any but the most subservient role. In the halls of Congress and in city halls across the nation, all but a few politicians were as white as the ballots that elected them. Yet from this ivory tower, the future could be spotted.

That fall in Southeast Asia, American advisers sent back discouraging reports, causing President Kennedy to consider ending involvement in Vietnam. College students strummed folk songs, their younger siblings danced to syrupy pop music, but off in England a shaggy-haired rock band was riding a wave of frenzy that would soon sweep across the Atlantic and sweep away old mores. Across the South, blacks were marching into police dogs and fire hoses, demanding decency and human rights. But the most significant

signpost in the autumn of 1963 arose in the nation's poorest state. There, on
a November weekend shortly before events in Dallas began to change everything, thousands of bone-poor citizens gave America a long-overdue lesson
in democracy.

Mississippi's official ballot listed Republican and Democratic candidates
for governor. Yet in a southern state still voting as if Lincoln headed the GOP,
the election was never in doubt. Everyone knew Democrat Paul B. Johnson,
following in his father's footsteps, would be the next governor. White voters
admired how, as lieutenant governor, "Paul Stood Tall Last Fall," blocking
a black man's entry to the state university. White voters relished Johnson's
sneers at the most hated politicians in Mississippi, Jack and Bobby Kennedy,
whose federal troops, so the story went, had incited the integration riots at
"Ole Miss." White voters sniggered at Johnson's joke that NAACP stood
for "Niggers, Alligators, Apes, Coons, and Possums." And on November 5,
white voters comfortably elected "Tall Paul." But that Tuesday, whites were
not the only voters in Mississippi.

From the buff sands of the Gulf Coast to the cotton fields of the Delta,
a parallel election was held, a black election, a "Freedom Election." In little
wooden churches with majestic names, whole congregations rose from
the pews. While gospel choirs chanted—"We-ee shall not, we shall not be
moved"—men and women slipped "Freedom Ballots" into wooden boxes. In
cafés sweetened by the smell of cornbread, withered hands marked Xs beside
"Aaron Henry—Governor" and "Reverend Edwin King—Lt. Governor." On
teetering porches, black men in overalls and black women in gingham spoke
with students from Yale and Stanford recruited for this prelude to "Freedom Summer." Nodding politely, calling their clean-cut guests "sir," lifelong
sharecroppers learned that voting did not have to remain "white folks' business." And thousands, forging raw democracy out of Mississippi's red clay,
cast "Freedom Votes" in beauty parlors and grocery stores, in barbershops
and pool halls. Yet thousands more were far too terrified to risk anything so
dangerous as voting.

Throughout that weekend, fear had quickened the pulse of Mississippi.
Much more than a governorship was being decided. In a "closed society"
where segregation ran as deep as the fertile soil of the Delta, black and white
agreed on little, yet both knew that voting equaled power. Elsewhere in the
South, blacks had begun to register—44 percent in Georgia, 58 percent in

Texas, 69 percent in Tennessee—but in Mississippi just 6.7 percent could vote. So long as they remained "second-class citizens," blacks knew they would remain powerless. And whites knew that if "our colored" registered en masse, or worse, if they were led to courthouses by "goddamned NAACP Communist trouble makers," all the nightmares recounted by grandparents would return. Just as during Reconstruction, "Niggers, Alligators, Apes, Coons, and Possums" would run Mississippi, sweeping away white power and all the peculiar institutions of segregation on which it rested. "Citizens," remembered an unrepentant Klansman, "not only have a right but a duty to preserve their culture." In 1963, no one needed to explain this in Mississippi. The brutality that fall weekend was swift, spontaneous, and as blunt as a fist in the face.

On Halloween night, a Yale student stopped for gas in Port Gibson. A century earlier, Union troops had entered Mississippi through this same small town whose gorgeous mansions General Ulysses Grant found "too beautiful to burn." Now in the eyes of locals, another invasion had begun. The "goddamn Yankee" was easy to spot—a white blond-haired stranger in the same car as a black man and woman. Ordering the white man out of the car, four men pummeled him to the pavement, then circled, fists coiled, kicking, pounding. Heads turned, but no one intervened. When the bloodied man climbed back in the car, the thugs followed it for miles along dark roads. Two days later, the same strangers—the men only—were spotted again.

On a warm Saturday morning, the two Freedom Election workers headed north out of Natchez to distribute campaign fliers. Suddenly, a shiny green Chevy Impala pulled behind them. In his rearview mirror, the driver saw two white faces. He made a U-turn, but the Chevy followed, riding his bumper. Heading south past farms and fields, the two cars sped up. Twice the Chevy pulled alongside, but twice the lead driver, who had raced hotrods in high school, roared ahead. The Chevy stayed right on his tail. Engines groaning, gravel flying, the cars soon topped one hundred miles an hour. Finally, the Chevy pulled even and forced the strangers' car into a ditch. This time the locals had a gun. Ordered out of his car, the driver paused—then punched the accelerator. The car lurched back onto the road. A bullet shattered the rear window. Another tore into a side panel. A third grazed the rear tire. Running red lights, weaving into oncoming traffic, slowing as the tire lost air, the driver finally ducked down a side road as the Chevy roared past.

All that weekend, similar welcomes met "agitators" throughout Mississippi. Up north in Tate County, shots narrowly missed a Freedom Election worker. Down south in Biloxi, a rock-throwing mob broke up a Freedom Election rally. In Yazoo City, gateway to the Delta, cops closed down another rally. Before the weekend ended, seventy election workers had been arrested. Charges ranged from disturbing the peace to driving cars too heavy for their license plates. Roughed up or just told to get out of town, the students got a strong taste of how the law worked in Mississippi in 1963.

The terror nearly succeeded. Organizers had hoped 200,000 blacks would cast Freedom Votes. Not counting ballots confiscated by cops, 82,000 did. Organizers hoped to use the parallel ballots, legally binding under a Reconstruction-era law, to challenge the official election. No one expected the challenge to succeed, but each Freedom Vote signaled a change in Mississippi. Centuries of bowing and scraping, centuries of pleasing "Mr. Charlie," centuries of "yassuh" and "nossuh," had come to their final days. But the Freedom Election also stirred embers as old as the Civil War, or as it was still called in Mississippi, "the War for Southern Independence." Come 1964, Mississippi would be swept by a racial firestorm. The long and vicious year centered around what organizers called the Mississippi Summer Project. The rest of the nation came to call it Freedom Summer, and it would pit the depth of America's bigotry against the height of America's hopes.

Ten weeks before Mississippi elected its new governor, a quarter million people had flocked to Washington, D.C., to hear Martin Luther King Jr. speak of his dream. As the multitude gathered near the Lincoln Memorial, pollsters had fanned out across the country. The Harris Poll on race, taken during a summer of shocking violence across the South, suggested how remote King's dream remained. Along with the stark income gap—blacks earning just 56 percent of what whites earned nationwide—a sizable majority of whites disliked, distrusted, and struggled to distance themselves from blacks. Some were cautious: "It's a rotten, miserable life to be colored." Others were blunt. "We don't hate niggers," a smiling San Diego woman said. "We just don't want them near us. That's why we moved from Chicago."

While King's soaring baritone described his dream that "one day the sons of former slaves and the sons of former slave owners will be able to sit down together at the table of brotherhood," 71 percent of whites said, "Negroes smell different." While crowds cheered King's hope that someday his children would "not be judged by the color of their skin but by the content of their character," half of those polled claimed, "Negroes have less native intelligence." And as King rose to a crescendo, dreaming of a time when "all of God's children—black men and white men, Jews and Gentiles, Protestants and Catholics—will be able to join hands," 69 percent said, "Negroes have looser morals," three of every four said, "Negroes tend to have less ambition," and 90 percent said they would never let their daughter date a Negro.

"Negroes are oversexed," a Nevada man said. "They're wild."

"I don't like to touch them," a Pennsylvania woman admitted. "It just makes me squeamish."

Revealing prejudice from sea to shining sea, the poll also documented what northerners loved to crow about—that racism ran rampant in the South. There, 73 percent thought blacks less intelligent, 88 percent thought they "smelled different," and 89 percent thought they had "looser morals." The numbers were not broken down by southern state, but everyone knew where the deepest prejudice festered. When Medgar Evers was gunned down in Mississippi that June, the head of the NAACP had not even feigned surprise. "There is no state with a record which approaches that of Mississippi in inhumanity, murder, brutality, and racial hatred," Roy Wilkins said. "It is absolutely at the bottom of the list."

For all its natural beauty, its proud heritage, its subsequent racial progress, Mississippi in 1963 was a mean and snarling state, run by tight-lipped politicians, bigoted sheriffs, and cops "not playing with" anyone who crossed them. Mississippi's mounting brutality had disgraced many of its own citizens. "During the past ten years," native son and novelist Walker Percy wrote, "Mississippi as a society reached a condition which can only be described, in an analogous but exact sense of the word, as insane." Across America, Mississippi had become a symbol of racial terror. Singer Nina Simone crooned, "Everybody knows about Mississippi, goddamn," and nightclub comedian Dick Gregory never missed a chance to mock the state. Seems he was fired from a Chicago post office, Gregory told audiences, for putting letters to Mississippi in a sack marked "Foreign Mail."

In the twenty-first century, the joke would fall flat. Modern Mississippi, having achieved a racial reconciliation to rival South Africa's, has more black elected officials than any other state. Even its former Klan enclaves boast black city councils, black mayors, black police chiefs. But in 1963, for nearly a million blacks too broke, too rooted, or too beaten down to follow Highway 61 north, life in Mississippi was no joke. Before Freedom Summer and the changes it jump-started, Mississippi was a place where a black body floating in a muddy river was "as common as a snake"; spies and informers working for the state kept dossiers on 250 organizations and 10,000 individuals backing integration; black sharecroppers picked cotton from "kin to cain't"— from sunup, when you "kin see," to sundown, when you "cain't"—for three dollars a day; civil rights workers were routinely arrested and beaten while cops laughed off charges of "police brutality"; and the slightest tremor of racial equality unleashed shock waves of raw brutality.

The violence had most recently touched down in Greenwood, a small city in the cotton fields that boasted of being "the long staple cotton capital of the world." Though the majority of Greenwood's residents were black, whites owned 90 percent of everything. Fine mansions and stately oaks earned Greenwood's Grand Boulevard the title "America's Most Beautiful Street." But rows of decrepit shacks stood on "the other side of the tracks," and all public facilities—pools, drinking fountains, even popcorn stands—were segregated. A tired joke said that Greenwood had one black voter, but no one could find him. In the summer of 1962, enraged whites beat back a voting drive with mass arrests, drive-by shootings, and Molotov cocktails torching black homes. When dozens continued marching to the courthouse, when no number of cops flailing nightsticks could stop them, county officials used a more elemental weapon—hunger. As winter approached, they seized federal allotments of rice, flour, and dried milk that helped many sharecroppers survive the lean season. Across Leflore County, as temperatures plunged below zero, thousands were left "neckid, buck-barefoot, and starvin'." Only a "Mississippi airlift," activists driving tons of food into the Delta, averted a famine. Still, one infant died of starvation, and two sharecroppers froze to death. As spring approached in 1963, blacks marched to the courthouse in greater numbers. Whites fired point-blank into cars. Firebombs gutted the movement's headquarters. A snarling police dog tore into a line of marchers. By summer, with just thirteen new voters to show for all the arrests, all the violence, the Greenwood movement stalled.

Mississippi stood at a crossroads. Years of peaceful protest had been met with bombings, beatings, and simple murder. And the rest of America did not seem to care. With Martin Luther King focusing attention on southern cities, Mississippi remained a neglected outpost of civil rights, too removed, too rural, too simmering with hatred to offer the slightest hope. In the wake of the fall's Freedom Election, a new tactic was needed. The election's architect, a man so saintly he was often compared to Jesus, labored to find that tactic. The Freedom Election, Bob Moses said, "makes it clear that the Negroes of Mississippi will not get the vote until the equivalent of an army is sent here." Finally, the idea blossomed.

What if, instead of Mississippi's black folk struggling in isolation, hundreds of college students from all across the country poured into the state? Wouldn't America pay attention then? And what if, along with registration drives, these volunteers staffed Freedom Schools, teaching black kids subjects their "separate but equal" schools would never teach? Black history. Black literature. The root causes of poverty. What if, in the spirit of America's new Peace Corps, this "domestic Peace Corps" set up Freedom Houses all over Mississippi, with libraries, day cares, and evening classes in literacy and voting rights? And what if, at the culmination of the summer, delegates from a new Freedom Party went to the Democratic National Convention to claim, beneath the spotlight of network news, that they, not Mississippi's all-white delegation, were the rightful representatives from the Magnolia State? "Before the Negro people get the right to vote, there will have to be a massive confrontation," said twenty-four-year-old John Lewis, chairman of the Student Nonviolent Coordinating Committee, "and it will probably come this summer. . . . We are going to Mississippi full force."

The idea haunted a state still haunted by the Civil War. Mississippi had long been a land of stark contrast—red clay and green grass, mansions and shacks, folks as pleasant as flowering magnolias, folks as mean as swamp snakes. But Freedom Summer, while it brought out the best in America, brought out the worst in Mississippi. When word of the summer project leaked, it sparked rage and resentment not seen in America since Reconstruction. Mississippi newspapers warned of an "invasion." Governor

Johnson denounced the "invaders" and their "dastardly scheme." "We are going to see that law and order is maintained," the governor said, "and maintained Mississippi style." The capital city of Jackson beefed up its police force with shotguns, teargas, and a tank, a six-ton armored vehicle with room for a dozen cops. "This is it," Mayor Allen Thompson said. "They're not bluffing, and we're not bluffing. We're going to be ready for them. . . . They won't have a chance." Rural residents also steeled themselves, Mississippi style.

In small towns with lilting names—Holly Springs, Picayune, Coffeeville—people proud of their southern hospitality seethed at the thought of summer. How dare these "beatniks," ignoring their Harlems and their Roxburys, invade Mississippi to tell the entire state how to deal with race! In tranquil town squares, where skinny men in suspenders sat on storefront benches, where women in sunglasses and sundresses promenaded beneath covered sidewalks, the majority of whites believed Mississippi had no "Negro problem." "We give them everything," Greenwood's mayor said. "We're building a new swimming pool. We work very close with the nigger civic league. They're very satisfied." For nearly a decade, white Mississippi had watched with dread as integration came to Montgomery, Little Rock, Greensboro, Nashville . . . And now this army of northerners was poised to overrun their state, to change "our way of life." Word had it the "invaders," including white women, would be *living in Negro homes!* Visceral fears of "wild" Negroes, of "carpetbaggers," of the "mongrelization" of black and white, brought generations of hatred bubbling to the surface.

In Mississippi's most remote hamlets, small "klaverns" of ruthless men met in secret to discuss the "nigger-communist invasion of Mississippi." They stockpiled kerosene, shotguns, and dynamite, then singled out targets—niggers, Jews, "nigger lovers." One warm April night, their secret burst into flames. In some sixty counties, blazing crosses lit up courthouse lawns, town squares, and open fields. The Klan was rising again in Mississippi. Like "White Knights," as their splinter group was named, the Klan planned a holy war against the "dedicated agents of Satan . . . determined to destroy Christian civilization." The Klan would take care of business, a recruiting poster said. "Get your Bible out and PRAY! You will hear from us." Finally, as swamplike humidity spread and the noonday sky seemed to catch fire, summer arrived.

Before it was over, all of America would focus on Mississippi. TV and newspapers would tar and feather the state. Hundreds of doctors, lawyers, and clergymen would come to help student volunteers. Folksingers, Hollywood stars, and Martin Luther King himself would flock to Mississippi, where whiplash violence was shredding the social contract. Thirty-five churches would be torched, five dozen homes and Freedom Houses bombed, and Mississippi would become synonymous with murder. The FBI would give a code name to its investigation, one that eventually named a movie whitewashing the agency's role—"Mississippi Burning." But Freedom Summer was more than the sum of its violence.

That summer, the complexion of America began to change. President Johnson signed the landmark Civil Rights Act, and slowly, grudgingly, "Whites Only" signs vanished across the South. Urban riots ended racial complacency in the North. The Gulf of Tonkin Resolution plunged America deeper into Vietnam. And at summer's end, a black sharecropper taking the microphone at the Democratic National Convention nearly ended the political career of the president of the United States. Meanwhile in Mississippi, several hundred students and their host families showed Americans, black and white, how to treat each other with uncommon decency.

That summer, whites hosted in black homes marveled at people who, after lifetimes of degradation, openly shared faith, food, and hope. That summer, Mississippi blacks met whites who shook their hands and spoke to them as equals. "Nobody never come out into the country and talked to real farmers and things . . . ," Fannie Lou Hamer remembered. "And it was these kids what broke a lot of this down. They treated us like we were special and we loved 'em." Waking each morning to a rooster's cackle, the smell of biscuits baking, the sizzle of something frying, suburban students discovered "the other America," the neglected nation of dirt roads and distended bellies, of tumbledown shacks and outhouses askew. Teaching in makeshift classrooms, volunteers learned the human cost of racism. Canvassing voters porch by porch, they tested their faith in democracy. And when it was over, shaken by violence, inspired by courage, aged years in just one season, veterans of the summer project went home to face down the nation they thought they had known.

"Mississippi changed everything for anyone who was there," volunteer Gloria Clark remembered. Most were quick to say they were not heroes, not when compared to those who risked their lives just to vote. The volunteers merely dropped in for a summer, then went home to question America. Some would spearhead the events that defined the 1960s—the Berkeley Free Speech Movement, the antiwar movement, the women's movement. Others, spreading ideals absorbed in Mississippi, would be forever skeptical of authority, forever democrats with a small *d*, and forever touched by this single season of their youth. But first, they had to survive Freedom Summer.

You who live in the North: Do not think that Mississippi has no relevance to you. . . . My Mississippi is everywhere.

—James Meredith

CHAPTER ONE

"There Is a Moral Wave Building"

School was out and summer was making promises across America when three hundred people descended on a leafy campus in Oxford, Ohio, not far from the Indiana border. All were Americans, most were under twenty-five, and all felt their country changing in ways they could not ignore. Beyond these traits, they had little in common.

They came in two distinct groups. The first—mostly white—had just finished another year at Harvard, Yale, Oberlin, Berkeley. . . . Guitars slung over shoulders, idealism lifting their strides, they piled out of cars sporting a Rand McNally of license plates. California. Massachusetts. "Land of Lincoln." They wore the *American Bandstand* fashions of 1964—polo shirts and slacks for men, capris and sleeveless blouses for women. Talking of LBJ, Bob Dylan, the civil rights bill struggling in the Senate, they found their way to dorms, met roommates, and settled in to learn about the daring summer they had chosen.

The second group—mostly black—brought no guitars and had little idealism left to pack. They did not wear slacks and polo shirts but denim overalls and white T-shirts. Many sported buttons depicting hands, black and white, clasped above the letters SNCC. And although most were the same age as the students, instead of sharing college stories, they arrived with stories of being beaten, targeted, tortured. Like the students, they sometimes spoke of recent reading—of Kant and Camus, James Baldwin and *The Wretched of the Earth*. But they did not read for grades; they read to arm themselves against the world. And their world was not sunny California, quaint Massachusetts, or the Land of Lincoln. This second group had come less from a state than from a state of war. They had come from Mississippi.

On Sunday afternoon, June 14, when the two groups met on the campus of the Western College for Women, the Mississippi Summer Project began. But the scene suggested the end of summer rather than the beginning. As if it were September, boxy Corvairs and humpbacked VWs braked in front of Gothic, ivied dorms. From them stepped two, three, or four people, stretching legs and casting glances. Across courtyards strewn with students, an occasional transistor radio blared a hit—"My Guy" or "She Loves You"— yet many students, goateed men or women with long, ironed hair, sat beneath trees strumming guitars, making their own music. Within a few hours, they would learn stirring hymns of freedom, but most only knew one such song now, and now seemed too soon to boast of overcoming someday.

Over dinner in the dining hall, where the food was surprisingly good, students talked about their hopes for the summer. Few harbored even postcard images of the South. Most had been in grade school during the Montgomery bus boycott, slightly older when federal troops desegregated Central High in Little Rock, in high school when spontaneous sit-ins desegregated lunch counters across the South and Freedom Rides made headline violence. The previous year, they had seen the appalling images on TV—attack dogs and fire hoses tearing into blacks in Birmingham, dead children, their dark legs dangling, carried from the rubble of the First Baptist Church. And now they were headed to the South, the Deep South. Most could conjure up only fleeting imagery. "At Oxford, my mental picture of Mississippi contained nothing but an unending series of swamps, bayous, and dark, lonely roads," one student later wrote. Some thought they knew the South. It was the fabled land of Faulkner's doomed families, the bittersweet nostalgia of *Gone with the Wind*, the hokum of TV's top show, *The Beverly Hillbillies*. Few had ever seen a spreading live oak dripping in Spanish moss or sweated in the steambath of a Mississippi summer. Even fewer had set foot in a sharecropper's shack, seen a pickup with a gun rack, used an outhouse, been in jail, heard a shotgun blast echo and die in the darkness. They had six days to prepare.

To help them, the denim-clad group from the Student Nonviolent Coordinating Committee (SNCC) arrived in Oxford with a simple plan—tell the truth. The Mississippi Summer Project was a death-defying roll of the dice. In a state where a sassy comment could get a Negro killed or a white battered, it was one thing to risk your own safety; it was another to ask hundreds of strangers to risk theirs. And so, like sergeants in boot camp, SNCC trainers felt duty bound to turn innocent idealists into anxious, even terrified realists. But only after singing.

The Freedom Songs began after dinner. Standing in the cool twilight beside a circle of trees, volunteers were introduced to songs fired in the crucible of "the Movement." On beyond "We Shall Overcome," they learned "Wade in the Water," "Oh, Freedom," and "Ain't Gonna Let Nobody Turn Me Around." Early that evening, a stocky black woman in a floral dress, her arms thick from a life in the cotton fields, limped to the stage, threw her head back, and belted out song after song, lifting the entire ensemble.

> *Ohh—ohhhhhhh*
> *This little light of miii-iiine,*
> *I'm gonna let it shiii-iiine*

Soon volunteers and staff were holding hands. Arms crossed, they swayed to the harmonies of songs they would sing all summer without ever tiring of them. Some songs were as feathered as lullabies, others as strident as marches. SNCC veterans stood with eyes closed, heads rolled back, their suffering pouring through the timeless melodies. Volunteers struggled to keep up, fell a syllable behind, then joined in as if they had known the songs since childhood. As the sun set and stars glittered above, the singing continued. The songs made hair stand on end, made souls sink in sorrow and rise again in triumph.

In the coming days, the Mississippi veterans would do their best to scare some sense into the students.

Tuesday: "I may be killed and you may be killed."

Thursday: "They—the white folk, the police, the county sheriff, the state police—they are all watching for you. They are looking for you. They are ready and they are armed."

Friday: "They take you to jail, strip you, lay you on the floor and beat you until you're almost dead."

On Sunday evening, however, songs kept terror at bay.

> *Who's that yonder dressed in red?*
> *Let my people go*
> *Must be the children that Moses led*
> *Let my people go-oooo.*

As the week progressed, the truth about Mississippi would sober the volunteers, but it would not send more than a few home. Youthful idealism is more tensile than any truth. Just seven months had passed since John Kennedy had been cut down in Dallas, and his spirit—"Ask not . . ."—suffused the Ohio campus. The summer project reminded many of Kennedy's Peace Corps and had begun with the same call to commitment. "A great change is at hand," Kennedy had told the nation in announcing his civil rights bill the previous June. "Those who do nothing are inviting shame as well as violence. Those who act boldly are recognizing rights as well as reality." Throughout the spring of 1964, SNCC speakers touring colleges across the country had recruited the bold. Their horror stories from Mississippi captivated entire auditoriums. Was this America?

By late May, more than seven hundred students had chosen to forgo internships, opt out of summer jobs, let Europe's cathedrals wait, and instead spend a summer in Mississippi. Cynical friends told them they would be "cannon fodder for the Movement," yet they saw a higher purpose. Filling out applications, some had quoted the Constitution, the Emancipation Proclamation, or Jesus. But many had cited Kennedy, the need to "honor the memory" and "carry out the legacy." Sarcasm, burnout, the intense self-consciousness of an entire generation—these would come later in the 1960s. In this crystalline moment on a campus in Ohio, while hundreds of young voices sang of freedom, there seemed nothing trite in SNCC's founding statement: "Through nonviolence, courage displaces fear; love transforms hate. Acceptance dissipates prejudice, hope ends despair. Peace dominates war, faith reconciles doubt."

For all their sincerity, dozens failed their interviews. Guidelines for interviewers were explicit. Each volunteer was asked whether working under black leadership would be difficult. Each had to "possess a learning attitude toward work in Mississippi" and recognize "that his role will be to work *with* local leadership, not to *overwhelm* it." Those displaying a "John Brown complex" were not welcome. "A student who seems determined to carve his own niche, win publicity and glory when he returns home can only have harmful effects on the Mississippi program." Anyone expressing the slightest interest in interracial sex was rejected. Once accepted, volunteers were divided into two groups: Freedom School teachers, who would show up for training the following week, and these first arrivals, whose summer would take them from shack to shack registering voters. But although their jobs would be distinct, Freedom Summer volunteers who made the cut and made it to Ohio presented a group portrait of American idealism.

As volunteers took over the campus, the *New York Times* saw in their faces "an unmistakable middle-class stamp." Yet their average family income was 50 percent above the national norm. Just two-fifths were female. As with the whole of America in 1964, 90 percent were white. All but a few were in college, almost half from Ivy League or other top schools. Many were the sons and daughters of success, the children of lawyers, doctors, CEOs, even a congressman, but just as many were the children of teachers, social workers, union organizers, and ministers. Taken together, they were the offspring of the entire nation. While four dozen came from metropolitan New York, three dozen from the San Francisco Bay Area, and two dozen from Southern California, the rest came from every corner of the country. From Flint, Michigan, and What Cheer, Iowa. From Tenafly, New Jersey, and Prairie City, Oregon. From Americus, Georgia, and Peoria, Illinois. From Del Rio, Texas, and Vienna, West Virginia. Raised amid Cold War consensus, the vast majority were true believers in America. Some had been jaded by the Bay of Pigs or darkening reports from Vietnam, yet all clung to the hope that whenever America fell short of its ideals, young Americans could restore them.

Accepted for the summer, volunteers were told to bring $150 in expenses, $500 for bail, and three publicity photos. They were to show up in Oxford, Ohio, for a week of training starting June 14 for canvassers, June 21 for teachers. Applicants under twenty-one needed parental permission. Some had received it grudgingly. "I don't see how I have any right to stop you," a mother in Manhattan told her son. She then went in the kitchen, did the dishes, and wept. Others had met resistance. One woman got letters from her grandfather saying, "You've deserted us for the niggers." And a few applicants ran into stone walls. "Absolutely mesmerized" by the recruiter on her campus, a student called home to share her summer plans. "My Mom starts crying. Then my Dad gets on and starts yelling about how he's not paying $2,000—or whatever my tuition was—for me to run off to Mississippi; that I'm there to get an education and that if I have anything else in mind he'll be glad to stop sending the check. End of discussion." Most parents, however, could not argue with ideals that shone so brightly. "Surely, no challenge looms larger than eradicating racial discrimination in this country," one man wrote on his application. "I want to do my part. There is a moral wave building among today's youth and I intend to catch it!"

As a high school senior in Amherst, Massachusetts, Chris Williams would have understood the surfing metaphor, but he preferred rhythm and blues to the Beach Boys. Lean and wisecracking, with a rebellious streak and a lust for adventure, Chris welcomed any challenge to the status quo, especially the racial status quo. He had seen racism's ugly face at an early age. While living in Washington, D.C., Chris had befriended the children of the maid who helped his mother care for his four younger siblings. Neighbors began throwing stones, shouting, "Nigger lover!" The Williams family soon moved north, but Chris never forgot. From the first headlines out of Montgomery, he was drawn to the civil rights movement. "You didn't run into many situations where there was a clear right and wrong," he remembered. "In this case, 'right' seemed very obvious."

In the spring of 1964, Chris was of medium height, with a Boy Scout face but brown hair long enough—over his ears, even—to get him suspended from school. During his spring break, he had followed local ministers to Williamston, North Carolina, to picket a courthouse. A melee on Easter Sunday saw one man hit with a baseball bat; Chris was merely arrested. Finding jail more exhilarating than depressing, he whiled away three days listening to Top 40 radio and joking with fellow protesters, black teenagers who, amused by his hair, called him "Ringo." Bailed out, Chris headed home, vowing to return. The opportunity was not long in coming. At nearby Smith College, he sat in on a civil rights rally that ended with two Yale students describing the Mississippi Summer Project.

Parental permission came readily. Chris's father understood restlessness. Schafer Williams had dropped out of Harvard in 1928 to bum around America, working in sawmills and pipe gangs. When the adventure wore thin, he had returned to college, earning a Ph.D. in medieval history. Now, having grown skeptical of the generation he taught at the University of Massachusetts, he saw the summer project as a way for his son "to actually do something worthwhile." Chris's mother was more apprehensive. "The Birmingham church bombing had occurred the previous fall," Chris remembered. "Medgar Evers had been assassinated—in Mississippi. She knew the danger." Still, Jean Williams told local papers that too many Americans considered teenagers "do-nothings." "American students have finally come around to support something that must be done."

On fire with his summer plans, Chris did not wait to graduate. In early June, he got a crew cut, handed in his schoolbooks, and hitchhiked back to North Carolina. In Williamston, he passed out leaflets, sat in on boisterous church meetings, and ate collard greens with his host family. Then, as the training in Ohio approached, he stuck out his thumb and hitched west. Picked up by cops, he was questioned "like I was the nation's most wanted criminal." Forced to call home to prove he was not a runaway, he cited Thoreau in his journal—"That government which governs best is the government which governs least." He crossed the Blue Ridge Mountains, riding with farmers and soldiers, then waited hours while big, brawny cars roared past, leaving him in the twilight—alone, eighteen, and in love with the road. Somewhere along the way, he lost his wallet and was penniless. But finally, more rides came—from "a homosexual," "a car full of hoods," and two off-duty cops drinking beer and throwing the cans out the window. Through Appalachian hollows, across the rolling farmland of southern Ohio, he slowly made his way to the campus, "and the whole Mississippi adventure began."

Like others at the training, Chris thought he had come solely for the summer. That fall, he expected to enter the University of Pennsylvania. He did not know that in the coming months he would be shot at, smell tear gas, and meet people who would forever become his measure of humanity. He did not know he would meet the woman he would marry. And although he signed up for just a few months, come September he would give up his slot in the Ivy League to continue organizing in rural Mississippi. "I realized Mississippi was more educational than anything I was going to get at Penn. There was a sense that this was not some crazy escapade—this was history in the making. This was going to be written down, talked about. This was a sea change in the United States."

When the singing ended that Sunday night, SNCC staff stayed up late. Released from Mississippi's constant terror, some drank, others debated. Many were already anxious about the volunteers. These "kids" seemed so naive, so vulnerable, so maddeningly certain of themselves. The thought of throwing them into the hellhole of Mississippi terrified those who bore its bruises and bullet wounds. How much truth should the kids be told? Could Yale and Harvard students feel the agony of Mississippi? Could they understand what it was like to drive on a dark road and suddenly see headlights flash in the rearview mirror, see a car coming up fast, ramming your bumper at sixty, seventy, eighty miles per hour? Could they know what it was like to hit the floor if the car pulled around and passed? To know that when terror loomed, when a mob gathered, when a sheriff took you in, there was no one to call? Not the cops who would watch as some "good ol' boy" knocked your teeth out. Not the Justice Department, who cared little. Not the FBI, who cared less. In six days, 250 students would leave for places like McComb, Mississippi, where five black men had been killed and fifty flogged since the first of the year. Would they panic? Flaunt their northern superiority? Could they meet violence with nonviolence? The time had come, as Chris Williams noted in his journal, for "the hairy stories."

On Monday morning, as students talked and joked in a spacious auditorium, a white man in a minister's collar stepped before them. The previous evening, the Reverend Edwin King had conducted a memorial for Medgar Evers. From throughout the hall, volunteers had seen the large white bandage on King's jaw, which had been shattered in a car crash when he was run off the road near Jackson. Now the minister called Mississippi a "police state." Every institution, he told volunteers, would be against them. The government, the courts, the newspapers, the cops, the wealthy businessmen, the small merchants, and especially the poor whites would stop at nothing—not arson, torture, not even murder—to keep Negroes "in their place." King described the relentless intimidation, the routine police brutality, the "disappearance" of black men, and the juries that acquitted murderers in less than an hour.

But the reverend's scenario was tepid compared to stories that followed. One by one, black men in their denim and T-shirts described terrors witnessed or endured. Some told of the notorious prison called Parchman Farm, where they were drenched with water on cold nights, left to swelter in the "hot box" on blistering afternoons. Others described the police dog unleashed on marchers in Greenwood, recent beatings in Canton and Natchez, shotguns fired into black homes in almost every town. Volunteers raised to believe that "the policeman is your friend" now heard about cops in Mississippi. "When you go down those cold stairs at the police station," said Willie Peacock, beaten in police custody just the week before, "you don't know if you're going to come back or not. You don't know if you can take those licks without fighting back because you might decide to fight back. It all depends on how you wanna die." One tall SNCC staffer did not have to say anything. The bullet holes in his neck were clearly visible above his white T-shirt. Finally, the same stout woman whose singing had lifted the congregation on Sunday evening described a June night in 1963. Ordered away from a whites-only lunch counter, Fannie Lou Hamer had been led to a cell and forced to lie down as guards handed an inmate a blackjack. "That man beat me till he give out." The blows had smashed her head, her back, her bare feet. Hamer's booming voice now chilled the volunteers. "Don't beat me no more! Don't beat me no more!" Across the crowded auditorium, hands went to mouths, eyes were averted, tears held back. This was Mississippi—where they would be on Sunday.

At dinner that second evening, the mood on campus resembled that of a prison camp more than a summer camp. Over food that now seemed taste-less, students imagined being battered, shot, killed. White faces seemed whiter somehow. Smiles were gone. Freedom Songs were forgotten. "It just scared the crap out of us," Chris Williams wrote. Some vented their fears in letters home.

> Monday night
> June 15
>
> I turned down a chance to work in the southwest part of the state, the most dangerous area. I talked to a staff member covering that area for about fifteen minutes and he told me about the five Negroes who have been taken into the woods and shot in the last three months. . . . I told him that I couldn't go in there because I was just too scared. I felt so bad I was about to forget about going to Mississippi at all. But I still wanted to go; I just didn't feel like giving up my life. . . .

Chris found another way of coping. At midnight on Monday, he donned gym shorts and went for a shirtless, barefoot run. Across dewy lawns, beside softly lit dorms, past SNCCs partying in their office, he ran and ran, recon-sidering his "Mississippi adventure." "I just ran until I was really tired and then I wasn't scared anymore."

Throughout Tuesday, as workshops focused on Mississippi politics, geography, and history, tensions between the two groups tightened. Some students felt lectured; others lamented the racial divide: "We don't know what it is to be a Negro, and even if we did, the Negroes here would not accept us. . . . In their eyes we're rich middle or upper-class whites who've taken off a summer to help the Negro." Yet many were beginning to idolize the Mississippi veterans.

Wherever students met on campus, stories circulated about this organization called SNCC (pronounced "Snick"). How in 1960, a brave and brilliant black woman named Ella Baker, active in civil rights since the 1930s, had gathered dozens of college students fresh from the "sit-ins" that had sprung up at lunch counters in southern cities. How Baker had forged them into the Student Nonviolent Coordinating Committee, a political force designed to earn blacks "more than a hamburger." How SNCC soon had chapters on campuses across the country and how its members had kept the Freedom Rides going. (In May 1961, thirteen Freedom Riders—seven blacks and six whites—rode buses into the South, daring the federal government to enforce laws desegregating interstate travel. Freedom Riders were arrested in North Carolina, beaten by mobs in South Carolina, and saw their bus fire-bombed in Alabama. Unprotected by police, they abandoned their ride in Birmingham. But SNCC members soon came from Nashville to continue the Freedom Rides into Mississippi, where they were rounded up in Jackson and sent to Parchman Farm Prison.) The Freedom Rides made SNCC the "shock troops" of the Movement, its members pitting Gandhian pacifism against kneejerk brutality, singing through weeks of "jail—no bail," surviving on spaghetti and hamburgers, talking into the night about love, compassion, and nonviolence. In small projects from Georgia to Arkansas, SNCC members met poor blacks on their porches, slept on cots or floors, ventured into Klan territory, all for a salary of $9.64 a week, after taxes.

Even among daring civil rights workers, SNCC staffers—often just called "SNCCs"—stood out. SNCCs were cooler, braver, feisty to a fault. "They would argue with a signpost," member Joyce Ladner recalled. Though they waxed eloquent about creating a "beautiful community," "a circle of trust," SNCC jargon made the Movement sound like World War II. They spoke of "cracking Mississippi," of establishing "beachheads," of working "behind enemy lines." Historian Howard Zinn, who traveled with SNCC, wrote: "To be with them, walking a picket line in the rain in Hattiesburg, Mississippi . . . to see them jabbed by electric prod poles and flung into paddy wagons in Selma, Alabama, or link arms and sing at the close of a church meeting in the Delta—is to feel the presence of greatness." And in their presence in Ohio, most volunteers were in awe. The training changed her life, one later said, "because I met those SNCC people and my mouth fell open."

Disdaining the celebrity status of Martin Luther King, SNCC fostered "group-centered leadership," no member more important than another, all decisions made by consensus hammered out in meetings that seemed to last for days. SNCC became its own university as members shared books or talked in jail cells—about overcoming fear, about philosophy, mathematics, or sometimes just about women. Seeing themselves not as leaders but as organizers, SNCCs empowered locals to stifle fear and organize the Movement in their own communities. Group-centered leadership meant that while every volunteer in Ohio knew of Dr. King, few recognized the pantheon of future civil rights icons in their midst. In one corner stood James Forman, the suave, pipe-smoking air force veteran who had grown up in Mississippi so poor he had sometimes tried to eat dirt, but who returned from college to forge SNCC's ragtag revolutionaries into a white-hot force. Elsewhere was John Lewis, the shy son of Alabama sharecroppers who was SNCC's chairman and would later serve in Congress. Also on campus were other future leaders of this brave new generation of African Americans—Julian Bond, Fannie Lou Hamer, Stokely Carmichael, Victoria Gray, Marion Barry. . . . But even in this remarkable gathering, one SNCC stood out, no matter how hard he tried not to.

With his bib overalls, glasses, and thick, furrowed brow, he looked like a wise sharecropper, and his small stature helped him slip unnoticed through crowds. But when he spoke, he gave himself away. "He is more or less the Jesus of the whole project," one volunteer noted. This was the man the press recognized as the mastermind, the Negro with "the Masters' degree from Harvard." Who left a cushy job teaching math at a New York prep school. Who went to Mississippi in 1960, when no other civil rights leader dared to. Who went there alone. Frequently arrested and attacked, he had developed an icy calm that astounded everyone in his presence. How could one comprehend the courage it took to enter an office just ransacked by a mob, set up a cot, and take a nap? And his name, as if chosen by more than chance, came straight from the Freedom Song they had sung the night before. This was Moses. Bob Moses.

Before he came to Mississippi, there was little in Robert Parris Moses' life that suggested he would be a leader, let alone a legend. Raised in Harlem, one of three sons of a hardworking janitor, he had excelled in school, earning scholarships to Stuyvesant High, Hamilton College, and finally a doctoral program at Harvard. There he studied mathematical logic, earning his master's in 1957. The following year, however, his mother died of cancer, and his father, overcome with grief, wound up in a mental institution.

Moses left Harvard and went home, taking odd jobs to support the family
and his father's eventual recovery. One job, tutoring the teen crooner Frankie
Lymon ("Why Do Fools Fall in Love?"), took Moses to ghettos around the
country, where he pondered the fate of blacks who had fled the South for "the
promised land." Feeling the hopelessness Harvard had helped him escape, he
began seeking answers. Then on February 1, 1960, four black men took seats
at an all-white lunch counter in Greensboro, North Carolina.

Moses studied newspaper photos of that first sit-in, studied them for
weeks. Seated at the counter, the four seemed so serene, so confident.
"Before, the Negro in the South had always looked on the defensive, cring-
ing," he recalled. "This time they were taking the initiative. They were kids
my age, and I knew this had something to do with my own life. . . . This was
the answer." While in college, Moses had worked in Quaker summer camps
in Europe and Japan, building housing for the poor, talking with new friends
about pacifism and its power. His favorite author was Albert Camus, whose
novels portrayed ordinary men ennobled by their opposition to evil, whose
essays convinced him that "words are more powerful than munitions." Four
months after the Greensboro sit-ins, Moses, then twenty-four, put Camus's
philosophy and his own to the test, heading south.

While visiting his uncle, an architect in Virginia, Moses picketed in Newport News. The simple protest brought him great relief. After a lifetime of
stifling resentment, of "playing it cool," he was finally, as Camus would have
said, *engagé*. Heading on to Atlanta, he worked for Martin Luther King's
Southern Christian Leadership Conference (SCLC), stuffing envelopes at
an old desk and discussing Kant with a coworker. The intense newcomer
unnerved some in the SCLC office. Julian Bond recalled many thinking the
somber, intellectual Moses had to be a Communist. "We were immensely
suspicious of him," Bond remembered. "We had tunnel vision. . . . Bob
Moses, on the other hand, had already begun to project a systematic analy-
sis; not just of the South, but of the country, the world." When SNCC needed
someone to go to Mississippi to recruit for a conference, Moses volunteered,
paying for his own bus ticket. Armed only with his passport and the names
of local NAACP leaders, he crossed Alabama and headed for America's
poorest region, the land of sprawling cotton fields flanked by sharecroppers'
shacks, the land whose sorrows birthed the blues, the land known simply as
the Delta.

In the flat, sun-baked town of Cleveland, Mississippi, Moses met NAACP organizer Amzie Moore. The Harvard Ph.D. candidate and the owner of a Delta gas station became instant friends. Moore saw in Moses the quiet courage black Mississippi needed to "uncover what is covered." And to Moses, the stout, stocky Moore suggested the old spiritual, "a tree beside the water" that would not be moved. Amzie Moore wasn't interested in sit-ins, Moses learned. Sharecroppers earning $500 a year could not afford to eat at lunch counters. Voting, Moore said, was the key to change in Mississippi. Blacks outnumbered whites two to one in the Delta, but only 3 percent could vote. Since World War II, even the smallest registration campaigns had sparked shattering violence. As they talked in the fading light, Moses noticed the loaded rifle Moore kept at his side and the bright lights outside protecting him from the drive-by shooting, the sniper, the firestorm in the night. And as they talked, Moses drafted a plan for voter registration to begin the following summer. Moore soon drove his young protégé around the Delta, talking of local politics, explaining how a burdened people moved and survived—a black ocean, deep and serene, encircling human volcanoes. Moore had Moses speak to church groups, watching to see how Delta folk responded. "There's something coming," Moses told the tired faces in each tiny church. "Get ready. It's inevitably coming your way whether you like it or not. It sent me to tell you that." Most people lowered their eyes, but some softly said, "Amen." With these few, a handful of seeds in each terrified town, Moses and SNCC would sow the Movement in Mississippi.

Reluctantly, Moses returned to New York for a final year in his teaching contract. In the summer of 1961, he headed south again. He would stay in Mississippi nearly four years. By the time he left, embittered, exhausted, but somehow still alive, Mississippi would be swarming with voting campaigns, Freedom Schools, and change that had been centuries in coming.

At the Ohio training, volunteers quickly recognized Moses' inner strength, and some tried to copy him, walking and speaking slowly, wearing bib overalls. But because he was too self-effacing to share his own tales of terror, few yet knew them. Later they would learn how, in August 1961, Moses had set up voter registration classes in the backwoods hill country of southwest Mississippi, a place he described as so "rural, impoverished, brutal that [it] hardly seemed a part of America." They would hear of him leading blacks to courthouses, walking right up to sour-faced registrars, answering their hatred with gentle words. And how curious clerks had dropped into one registrar's office to see this "New York nigger," and how a highway patrolman had pulled him over on his way out of town.

"You the nigger that came down from New York to stir up a lot of trouble?"

"I'm the Negro who came down from New York to instruct people in voter registration," Moses corrected. Then he began to take down the cop's badge number.

"Get in the car, nigger!"

Taken to the police station, Moses was allowed the customary phone call. Cops listened as he asked the operator to call the Justice Department in Washington, D.C. Collect. He then detailed the violations of civil rights laws in Amite County. Startled cops asked Moses to pay just five dollars in court costs. He refused and spent two days in jail. The NAACP finally bailed him out, but not before a local asked him, "Boy, are you sure you know what you're about?"

Within weeks, word spread. Blacks heard that "Dr. King and some other big people" were in the area. Teenagers Hollis Watkins and Curtis Hayes went searching for King, found Moses, and joined SNCC. Meanwhile, whites heard that some "nigger from New York" was stirring up trouble, and the name Bob Moses soon topped a Klan hit list. The hit was not long in coming. In late August, as Moses led three people to the squat brick courthouse in Liberty, a man pounced, smashing his head with a knife handle. With blood streaming down his face, Moses led the trembling applicants up the courthouse steps. The registrar's office was closed. After getting nine stitches, Moses then did another thing blacks simply did not do in Mississippi in 1961—he pressed charges. Before a courtroom packed with shotgun-toting farmers, Moses coolly testified about the beating, then let the sheriff escort him to city limits. His assailant was acquitted—self-defense. The terror soon escalated, culminating in the murder of Herbert Lee. Fear crippled the Movement, and SNCC pulled out of southwest Mississippi, but stories about Bob Moses inspired more to join him in SNCC's new beachhead—the Delta. By 1964, Moses was little known outside civil rights circles but a legend within. Still, those few volunteers who had heard of him must have been surprised when they heard him speak.

In a voice as soft as silk, Moses spoke briefly on Sunday night, then periodically throughout the week. He broke every rule of elocution. He often looked at his feet. He never repeated himself, rarely told stories, never smiled. And yet, because in the timeless tradition of genuine leaders he spoke truth to power, he had everyone's attention.

"No administration in this country is going to commit political suicide over the rights of Negroes," Moses told volunteers. "This is part of what we are doing . . . getting the country involved through yourselves." Convinced that only a bold move would change Mississippi, Moses had lobbied heavily for the summer project, overcoming strong objections by Movement veterans. But now he did not seem so sure: "Don't come to Mississippi this summer to save the Mississippi Negro," he told volunteers. "Only come if you understand, really understand, that his freedom and yours are one. Maybe we're not going to get very many people registered this summer. Maybe, even, we're not going to get very many people into Freedom Schools. Maybe all we're going to do is live through this summer. In Mississippi, that will be so much."

Sighing as if the world were on his shoulders, Moses told volunteers about the murder of Herbert Lee. But he did not tell them about his nagging concerns. By Tuesday afternoon, he was very worried. Despite all the "hairy stories," no one had gone home. In long, soul-searching discussions, volunteers had aired their doubts. Weren't they being egocentric? Masochistic? Did they have Messiah complexes? As whites raised in America, weren't they also steeped in racism? Volunteers quoted Gandhi, Tolstoy, and James Baldwin, yet none took the commonsense option of leaving. Moses' concern was shared by other SNCCs.

"It's not working," said Charles McLaurin, still nursing bruises from a recent beating. "It's really not working. They're really not getting through to each other." Sitting through sessions that ranged from the character of southern whites to the history of slavery, volunteers seemed studious, solemn. But when released from workshops, they played touch football or strummed "Blowin' in the Wind," acting as if headed for summer at the seashore. Students read SNCC's security handbook: "No one should go *anywhere* alone, but certainly not in an automobile and certainly not at night. . . . Try not to sleep near open windows; try to sleep at the back of the house. . . . Do not stand in doorways at night with the light at your back." But just as Mississippi's strange savagery was sinking in, the naïveté resurfaced. During a frank discussion on sex, one woman asked, "We have talked about interracial dating. Is there a policy you'd like for us to follow?" SNCC staffers were incredulous. A *policy*? Had anyone heard of Emmett Till? Beaten to a pulp, shot in the head, tied to a fan, and thrown in the Tallahatchie River for just whistling at a white woman? Emmett Till was fourteen years old. It wasn't working. Further proof came Tuesday night.

After dinner, volunteers watched *Mississippi and the Fifteenth Amendment*. The CBS documentary detailed how the Magnolia State had defied the Constitution by disenfranchising its black populace. The federal government had filed lawsuits, but Mississippi judges had stonewalled, nitpicked, thrown most out of court. Volunteers seethed or sat disgusted. But then the camera fell on a hideously fat man in a white shirt and horn-rimmed glasses. Laughter rippled through the auditorium. SNCC staffers fumed. This was no comical stereotype. This was Theron Lynd, registrar in Forrest County, who had never registered a Negro until hit by a lawsuit. The audience quieted as a black man onscreen told of a shotgun fired into his home, wounding two little girls, but when his wife came on in a funny hat, some giggled. Several SNCCs stormed out. When the documentary ended, another jumped onstage. "You should be ashamed! You could laugh at that film!"

"The flash point," as one volunteer called it, had arrived. Across the auditorium, whispers and stares punctuated an aching silence. A few volunteers stood and spoke, calling SNCC staffers distant, arrogant, patronizing. They acted superior to anyone who had not shared their suffering. In one corner, Bob Moses stood with his arm around his wife, Dona, a recent University of Chicago philosophy grad. Both were stone-faced. Other SNCCs let the tension linger, as in their own meetings, before finally lifting it. They told of the fat registrar—"We know that bastard." The previous January, Theron Lynd had been the target of Hattiesburg's Freedom Day. Hundreds had picketed in the rain. Moses was arrested, one marcher was beaten in jail, and here these kids were, safe in Ohio, laughing. Another SNCC erupted: "Ask Jimmie over there what he thinks about Mississippi. He has six slugs in him, man, and the last one went right through the back of his neck. . . . Ask Jesse here—he's been beaten so we couldn't recognize him, time and time and time and time again. If you don't get scared, pack up and get the hell out of here because we don't need any people who don't know what they're doing." The confrontation went on until 2:00 a.m. When it was over, everyone joined hands and sang SNCC's mournful anthem, "Never Turn Back," written in memory of Herbert Lee. Volunteers slowly filed back to their dorms, but staff again stayed up, talking, drinking, more worried than ever. Bob Moses and his wife were near tears, but one volunteer, crying as he wrote home, noted: "The crisis is past, I think."

On Wednesday, a workshop turned into a heated debate. The Reverend James Lawson, who had written SNCC's lofty mission statement on nonviolence, argued with Stokely Carmichael, who would later take SNCC into the realm of Black Power. As rapt volunteers watched, the tall, gangly Carmichael said nonviolence had once worked because it was new and made news. But having been beaten in jail and tortured in Parchman Farm, he considered nonviolence useless against vicious racists. Lawson admitted goodness had its price. "When you turn the other cheek," he said, "you must accept the fact that you will get clobbered on it." Many volunteers remained uncertain. Wasn't violence sometimes justified? In self-defense? Finally, one of the few white SNCC staffers spoke up. Alabaman Bob Zellner had been the lone white in a peaceful protest in McComb in 1961. Singled out by a mob, he was clubbed, beaten, and had his eyes gouged while he gripped a railing, holding on for his life. "You must understand that nonviolence is essential to our program this summer," Zellner told the group. "If you can't accept this, please don't come with us." Again, no one left.

After lunch, an outdoor workshop beneath a bright blue sky taught volunteers how to take a beating. Near a tree pinned with a sign— "Courthouse"—students became a mob, shouting "Nigger!" and "Commie bastard!" swarming around their new friends, lashing out, knocking some to the ground. Volunteers learned to fall, roll in a ball, absorb the blows. "Your legs, your thighs, your buttocks, your kidneys, your back can take a kick or a billy club. So can your arms and your hands. Your head can't. Your neck can't. Your groin can't." Some students shuddered at the viciousness of the "mob." One attacker, twenty-year-old Andrew Goodman, seemed to lose himself in the moment, shouting, screaming, then looking slightly sheepish at the anger within. Yet this faux Mississippi still seemed surreal—college kids playing at violence on a green lawn in Ohio. College kids who would be in Mississippi in just four days.

That Wednesday afternoon, a call came to SNCC's campus office. The long-distance line was scratchy, but the voice had an unmistakable drawl. No one ever found out how the caller got the number. "I got me a twen'y foot pit out bay-ack," the voice said. "Y'all just come on down." SNCC did not tell volunteers about the call, but the following afternoon, staffers shared hate mail that had come to the campus. Phrases from one letter leaped out: "morally rotten outcasts of the White race. . . . 'White Negroes' are the rottenest of the race-mixing criminals. . . . it will be a long, hot, summer—but the 'heat' will be applied to the race-mixing TRASH by the <u>DECENT</u> people who do not believe in racial mongrelization through racial prostitution."

Volunteers listened, sickened by the hatred. But for one black woman, the hate mail was just more information to be filed under "Survival." Like other volunteers, Muriel Tillinghast had come to Ohio straight from another campus. Two weeks earlier, she had graduated from Howard University, where she had majored in sociology and political science but spent most of her time with NAG, Howard's Non-Violent Action Group. "We were renegades," Muriel recalled with pride. "Within the black community of Washington, D.C., we were an alienated group. We looked different, we talked differently, we hung together." Centered around Stokely Carmichael, then a Howard philosophy student, NAG's "Weekend Warriors" held endless late-night discussions, talking, passing a hat to send someone out for cold cuts, talking more. Protesting on weekends, NAG members kept pressure on segregated Maryland, Delaware, and D.C. In Cambridge, Maryland, Muriel had survived "NAG's local Mississippi," when marchers confronted the Maryland National Guard. With bayonets fixed, guardsmen laced the streets with tear gas, sending Muriel, Carmichael, and others coughing, vomiting, burning in retreat.

Savvy, street-smart, and fiercely independent, Muriel Tillinghast was the latest incarnation of the rock-solid women who helped generations survive slavery. When gripped by fear, she was sometimes overwhelmed, yet able to summon deep rivers within. When despair surfaced, a quick and sarcastic wit kept her going. And when these resources failed, she fell back on her family. "I did not come out of a family where you played the victim," she said, "but from multi generations of people who fought back." The Tillinghasts, intensely involved in the Lutheran church and "about eighty other groups," had long been an "organizational family." Even in 1964, they still shared the story of how, sometime around 1900, Muriel's grandmother had left a Texas plantation and *walked* to Washington, D.C. There Gloria Carter had married a "race man." Muriel's grandfather was "no bigger than a match stick" but, widely traveled and defiantly self-educated, he shared a household where books were cherished, college was mandatory, and children "spent time in meetings from when we could walk."

Growing up in D.C., Muriel rarely encountered the dark racism of the Deep South. But she remembered a visit to Florida where she was told not to even touch the clothes in a department store, and *never* to try them on. And closer to home, she had often met racism's lighter-skinned cousin. Like the old spiritual turned into SNCC's anthem, she had been "'buked and scorned" more times than she cared to count. Her sophomore class had been the first to integrate D.C.'s Roosevelt High School, facing down the hatred of the principal and student body. Each affront gave Muriel a steely strength hidden in a slight frame. By the time she reached Howard, meticulous and driven, she was a natural for NAG's nonviolent protests. But as an urbanite who knew the Deep South only in legend and in Movement lore, was she ready for Mississippi? As a woman who had not yet learned to drive, was she prepared for harrowing chases down back roads? And as a black woman who chose not to straighten her hair, instead letting it grow into an Afro long before the style became popular, could she stand up to the relentless bigotry she was about to encounter?

Muriel knew Mississippi only as "a distant well of human woe," yet human woe had been beckoning. During the winter of 1963, when Delta officials cut off federal food allotments, she had collected enough clothes and food to fill half a semitruck, then found a teamster willing to arm himself and drive it to Leflore County. A year later, she had again reached out to Mississippi when NAG members began calling isolated SNCCs there, offering solidarity, friendship, human contact. Muriel recognized one name on the list—Charlie Cobb in Greenville. Cobb had been a fellow Howard student and NAG member. His aunt had also been Muriel's fifth-grade teacher, so she called him up unannounced. Cobb soon became her "Sunday call." "He would tell me about what they were doing, their daily work which was mostly staying alive." As plans for the summer solidified, Cobb began telling this kind female voice on the phone about the upcoming project.

Some volunteers had agonized about going to Mississippi. Others had leaped at the chance. For Muriel, Mississippi was simply the next logical step. Her mother, having taught school in Mississippi, was "beside herself" over her daughter's decision, but Muriel did not consider it a decision. "At NAG meetings, I was informed around February that something was going on in

Mississippi that summer and the attitude was, 'You're going, aren't you?' As we got into May, it was, 'The bus is leaving at such and such a time—you're going to be on it, right?'" On June 12, NAG members left Washington, D.C., for Ohio. Seated beside her battered blue suitcase filled with more books than clothes, twenty-two-year-old Muriel Tillinghast was on the bus.

Once on the Ohio campus, Muriel did not concern herself with the tension between staff and recruits. As she had all her life, she got down to business. Her experience with NAG immediately moved her from volunteer to SNCC staffer, privy to all the endless meetings, strategies, and concerns. Becoming "a sponge" of information, she pestered Charlie Cobb and other veterans for survival tips. She learned how she would have to walk in Mississippi—a slow rural pace that did not call attention to her. She learned how she would have to address people, and how she could organize small, quarreling communities into cohesive armies united in the fight. SNCC's horror stories "brought us to the stark reality that some of us were not going to come back," but Muriel tried not to think about that. Instead, she called on her inherited strength, her organizational skills, the solidarity she had learned at Howard, and prepared to take them south. Courage had nothing to do with it. "It was *esprit de corps*. These were my friends and they were going and I was going with them."

Suddenly there were just two days till departure. Volunteers wrote to President Lyndon Johnson, asking, "As we depart for that troubled state, to hear your voice in support of those principles to which Americans have dedicated and sacrificed themselves." Bob Moses had already written LBJ requesting federal protection for the project. Neither Moses nor volunteers heard from the president.

Buses would head south on Saturday afternoon, entering Mississippi on Sunday under cover of darkness. As if to highlight the danger, the media began to swarm over the campus. Final workshops unfolded before TV cameras. Volunteers were interviewed again and again. "Are you scared?" "Do you really think it will do any good?" "You *are* scared, aren't you?" Besieged by reporters, volunteers tried to explain their motives. "Part of it is the American dream, you know, and part is shame," one told the *Saturday Evening Post*. "I feel a very real sense of guilt. But I hope I'm not going down there to get my little red badge of liberalism." Berkeley student Mario Savio told the *Los Angeles Times*, "The injustices to the Negro in Mississippi are also an infringement upon my rights." Newspapers alerted the country— Mississippi was in for "a long, hot summer," a "racial explosion." Syndicated columnist Joseph Alsop feared "guerilla war."

Muriel Tillinghast barely noticed the media, but Chris Williams was incensed. "The guy from *Life* was a real jerk," he wrote in his journal. "The TV men were a pain in the neck as well with their big grinding cameras. They loved Non-Violent Workshops because that was where the action was. It was the closest thing to actual violence they could find. Sadists!" Volunteers wrote to parents, telling Mom and Dad to look for them in print or on TV. "*Look* magazine is searching for the ideal naïve northern middle-class white girl," one wrote. "For the national press, that's the big story. And when one of us gets killed, the story will be even bigger." Two days left.

On Thursday, volunteers learned of their legal rights and how little they would mean that summer. Chris met attorney William Kunstler, later famous for defending the Chicago Seven, who was handling his case in North Carolina. Kunstler's daughter, Karin, was among the volunteers. That morning, a graying man puffing a cigar stepped before the group. Jess Brown, one of four black lawyers in Mississippi, pointed a bony finger at the sweep of faces before him. "Now get this in your heads and remember what I am going to say!" Brown began. Mississippi sheriffs, cops, and highway patrolmen already knew their names, their hometowns, their full descriptions. "All I can do is give you some pointers on how to stay alive. If you are riding down the highway—say, on Highway 80 near Bolton, Mississippi—and the police stop you and arrest you, don't get out and argue with the cops and say, 'I know my rights.' You may invite that club on your head. There ain't no point in standing there trying to teach them some constitutional law at twelve o'clock at night. Go to jail and wait for your lawyer." In Mississippi, Brown warned, they would be classified into two groups—"niggers and nigger-lovers. And they're tougher on nigger-lovers." That night, Muriel Tillinghast gathered more survival tips; Chris Williams took another midnight run.

On Friday morning, volunteers heard from the Department of Justice. In the field of civil rights, John Doar was as close to a hero as anyone at the federal level. As assistant attorney general in the Justice Department's Civil Rights Division, Doar had filed lawsuits against the fat registrar in Forrest County and elsewhere. He had worked closely with Bob Moses, taking his collect call from jail in Liberty, coming to Amite County to investigate threats against Herbert Lee, only to learn back in D.C. of his murder. At

Medgar Evers's funeral in Jackson, Doar had helped calm angry marchers, averting a riot. Now he praised the volunteers as "real heroes." But when someone asked, "What are you going to do to enable us to see the fall?" Doar answered, "Nothing. There is no federal police force. The responsibility for protection is that of the local police." Boos filled the auditorium. Shouts erupted. "We can protect the Vietnamese, but not the Americans, is that right?" Finally, Moses stepped beside his friend. "We don't do that," he cautioned. The room fell silent. Doar was just being honest, Moses said. The session left volunteers feeling more vulnerable than ever. Back in Massachusetts, Jean Williams felt her son's fears in a letter arriving that afternoon.

Dear People at home in the Safe, Safe North,

June 17

Mississippi is going to be hell this summer. We are going into the very hard-core of segregation and White Supremacy. . . . I'd venture to say that every member of the Mississippi staff has been beaten up at least once and he who has not been shot at is rare. It is impossible for you to imagine what we are going in to, as it is for me now, but I'm beginning to see. . . .

Love,
Xtoph

On the last night in "the Safe, Safe North," the singing again began after dinner. Crossing arms and holding hands, volunteers sang the songs they now knew well, songs of jail, of picket lines, of endurance. Despite all the truth told about Mississippi, idealism still trumped fear. SNCC staffers had a term for such spirit—"freedom high"—and it kept the singing going till midnight. Between songs, some shared the news they had just heard on the radio. LBJ's civil rights bill had finally passed the Senate. Now the South would be forced to desegregate. And they would be in Mississippi to see history happen. After midnight, most volunteers tried to sleep. A few stayed up drinking beer, talking, trying to imagine the mysterious places they were headed—Tchula, Mississippi. Moss Point. Itta Bena. At 3:00 a.m., a station wagon crammed with two trainers and six volunteers left for Mississippi to investigate a church burning in Neshoba County. No one saw them drive away.

Saturday: packing, a lingering lunch, long good-byes. At makeshift barbers' chairs, lines were three deep as men had hair trimmed, beards shaved.

"Before You Leave Oxford," a sign announced, "Write Your Congressmen Asking Them to Act to Insure Your Safety." The afternoon was as bright and sunny as the day the students had arrived. Beside green lawns, two rattletrap charter buses waited, but no one seemed eager to board. Encircled by TV cameras and reporters, volunteers and staffers again joined hands and sang. They had been two groups when they arrived; they were one now.

Finally, the call came to depart. Black and white sang one last chorus of "We Shall Overcome." Then volunteers piled duffel bags, suitcases, and guitars in the back of each bus and crammed into seats. Some hung out windows to clasp hands with staffers who were staying to train the next group. Others just stared blankly, eyes fixed straight ahead. From inside the buses came sad voices singing SNCC's woeful anthem, "We'll Never Turn Back":

We have walked through the shadows of death,
We've had to walk all by ourselves.
We have hung our head and cried
For those like Lee who died. . . .

And the buses pulled away.

Across the cornfields of southern Ohio, where fugitive slaves had first tasted freedom, the singing continued. In the Cincinnati bus terminal, charter buses were exchanged for Greyhounds while students sang "Freedom Train." Filled with song, two buses crossed the Ohio River into Kentucky. Volunteers stopped for dinner in Louisville, saw a livid red sun disappear behind the hills, and continued into Tennessee. Nashville, then through the warm night to Memphis. Looking out the bus window, Chris Williams spotted the "little guy" from *Life* and knew the press was still following. He tried to read but fell asleep. In the bus farther ahead, Muriel Tillinghast was wide awake. All her confidence, all her take-charge spirit, were beginning to wither. In the black southern night, she felt fear mounting. Leaving Memphis, Muriel's bus was still rocking, singing. "We hit the Mississippi state line at midnight," she recalled, "and the bus went *silent*. There was no turning back now." Through windows, some volunteers spotted a billboard depicting an antebellum mansion, a sailboat, and a flowering magnolia beside tall pines. Above the bucolic scene were the words "Welcome to Mississippi." Beyond the billboard, lined up along the highway, stood several highway patrol cars. A welcoming committee.

Ours is surely the black belt. It is all very well for Cheyenne or Schenectady or Stockholm or Moscow, where a black-faced visitor is a day's wonder, to exclaim: "There is no race problem! Southerners are barbarians and brutes." There never is a race problem until the two races living in close contact approach numerical equality.

—William Alexander Percy, *Lanterns on the Levee*

CHAPTER TWO
"Not Even Past"

Shortly after rain clouds parted on a spring day in '61, Confederate troops marched through downtown Jackson. Five thousand proud Rebels, their double-breasted topcoats starched, their Enfield rifles shouldered, their mustachioed faces as stiff as statues, tramped along the glistening streets. Brass bands blared out sparkling renditions of "Dixie," and teeming crowds sang along. Women in long floral dresses blew kisses from beneath parasols. Boys could not take their eyes off the officers on horseback, the glint of bayonets, the unfurling stars and bars. Flanking the governor's mansion, where the governor waved from between white pillars, the troops marched on in a rippling ribbon of gray. Confederate flags were everywhere, waving in defiance of the Union. The parade, said to be the largest in the history of Mississippi, continued for hours. Then everyone got in their cars and went home. For this Confederate glory, this celebration of Mississippi's secession from the United States of America, took place not in 1861 but in 1961.

The old cliché about history—that it is "written by the winners"—has always been, as Henry Ford said of history itself, "more or less bunk." Countries defeated in war always write their own versions of history, versions that turn defeat into a noble cause and suffering into martyrdom. These unofficial versions soothe consciences and salve war wounds, yet with tragic regularity, they lead to more violence. Consider Germany after World War I. France after its revolution. The Balkans. The South.

"The past is never dead," William Faulkner wrote. "It's not even past." Faulkner was not referring to the rest of America, where time gradually turned the butchery of the Civil War into a period piece. In the North, where a single town in Pennsylvania had seen the face of battle, the war was remembered in aging monuments, in daguerreotypes, in medals displayed on mantels but finally stored in attics. Yet across the former Confederacy, and especially in Mississippi, the War for Southern Independence was woven into the fabric of life. Every southern boy, Faulkner wrote, could easily summon the dreamlike moment at Gettysburg just before Pickett's Charge, before the war became a slaughterhouse and defeat became inevitable. Faulkner wrote this in 1948, eighty-five years after Gettysburg. He wrote it in the present tense. And he wrote it in Mississippi, where the war, living on in laments, eulogized by sons and daughters of Confederate soldiers, still defined every reaction. Such was the century-long enshrinement of the Civil War in Mississippi, a state invaded, occupied, driven to its knees.

From the moment Northern troops crossed its border in 1862, Mississippi spearheaded Confederate suffering. It was the first Confederate state to be looted and burned, the first under siege, the first to see its capital destroyed. Northerners could not deny Mississippi's bravery. "Mississippians," one said, "don't know, and refuse to learn, how to surrender." After routing Grant at Holly Springs, Mississippi soldiers defeated Sherman at Chickasaw Bluffs. At Vicksburg, they held off Grant again, making the entire South salute. But after a forty-eight-day siege that saw townspeople burrow into caves and survive on dead dogs and rats, Vicksburg fell, and total war swept across the land. William Tecumseh Sherman, before he cut his famous path through Georgia, practiced his savagery on Mississippi, where his men burned mansions and cotton fields, sacked small towns, and tortured the earth. After tearing up Meridian, Sherman boasted, "Meridian, with its depots, storehouses, arsenal, hospitals, offices, hotels, and cantonment, no longer exists." Battleground Mississippi saw its rivers patrolled by Union gunboats, its railroad depots crammed with rotting corpses, and its capital so devastated that survivors called it "Chimneyville." The day Vicksburg fell, news came from Gettysburg, where the proud Mississippi Greys, 103 students from Ole Miss, had led Pickett's Charge. Every last one had been killed. And when the war was over, Mississippi had achieved another first. Its 78,000 soldiers—the Benita Sharpshooters, the Oktibbeha Ploughboys, the Tullahoma Hardshells, and others—had suffered 28,000 dead and 31,000 wounded, the highest per capita casualty rate in either South or North. In 1866, one-third of Mississippi's budget was spent on artificial limbs.

Before the war, Mississippi had been America's fifth wealthiest state— although most of that wealth was measured in muscle, the monetary value

of 436,631 slaves, more than half the state's population. In the wake of the
war Mississippi became, and has been ever since, the nation's poorest state.
Rising from the ashes of Carthaginian destruction, Mississippians made a
vow—*never* to forget. Yet for every Civil War horror, more painful memories
followed. Wartime battles had been brief compared to the struggle to repel
the occupation historians term Reconstruction and Mississippians came to
call "The Tragic Era." Here, too, Mississippi led the South—in resistance.
Ranging from simple election fraud to a full-blown race war, the reaction
tainted American democracy right through to Freedom Summer. Following
four years of total war and a dozen of occupation and guerilla fighting, moderation in Mississippi became like snow, something occasionally in the air,
especially farther north, but which vanished whenever the heat was turned
up. As one freed slave observed, "Things was hurt by Mr. Lincoln gettin'
kilt."

Lincoln was barely in his grave when the power struggle began. Four
months after Appomattox, Mississippi crafted a constitution that would
earn readmittance to the Union. But the hastily drawn accord, coupled with
"Black Codes" denying freed slaves any vestige of citizenship, did not fool
Congress. Refused statehood, Mississippi was occupied as part of the Fourth
Military District. Only in 1870 did the Magnolia State again become a state.
With former slaves voting freely, Mississippi sent America's first black
senator to Washington, D.C. Freedmen never dominated Mississippi politics, but an ex-slave was elected mayor of Natchez, another became police
chief in Vicksburg, and still others served as judges, sheriffs, even secretary
of state. At one point, nearly half the legislature was black. In less than a
decade, the social system of an entire state had been plowed up, turned over,
and replanted with the flimsiest of roots. The uprooting was soon termed
"redemption," and like the war, its ennobled savagery would scar Mississippi
for a full century.

In Mississippi, redemption began in 1871, when members of the upstart
Ku Klux Klan turned the streets of Meridian into a shooting gallery. After
killing two black politicians, whites roamed the countryside, hunting and
lynching Negroes. Thirty were racked up before federal troops arrived. The
Meridian riot inspired congressional "Ku Klux" laws. Seven hundred Mississippi Klansmen were indicted, yet in a state whose remote jungle landscape gave it a Wild West lawlessness, rebellion was not confined beneath
white hoods.

Over the next four years, raw violence "redeemed" Mississippi. The battles of Reconstruction were not as costly as those of the war, but they were battles nonetheless. The Second Battle of Vicksburg started on July 4, 1874, with gunshots in the streets. Enraged by a recent interracial marriage, whites took over the town and began slogging through alligator-infested bayous to hunt down terrified blacks. During elections that August, terror kept blacks from voting, allowing whites to rule unopposed. The taking of Vicksburg turned the coming election year into a vigilante campaign to slaughter democracy. Pitched fighting between black and white broke out in Clinton, Yazoo City, Clarksdale. . . . Fearing "a war of races," Governor Adelbert Ames, a former Union officer whites despised as a "carpetbagger," begged President Grant to send troops. This time Grant refused. "The whole public are tired out with these annual, autumnal outbreaks in the South," the president wrote back. "The great majority are ready now to condemn any interference on the part of the government."

Come Election Day in 1875, the shotgun, the noose, and the mob ended black political power in Mississippi. "Democrats Standing Manfully by Their Guns!" the *Atlanta Constitution* boasted. "Mississippi Redeemed at Last!" Governor Ames, impeached and driven from the state, lamented: "A revolution has taken place—by force of arms—and a race are disenfranchised—they are to be returned to a condition of serfdom—an era of second slavery." Over the next two years, inspired by "the Mississippi plan," other southern states wore down northern will to fight for the Negro and brokered a deal that removed federal troops from the South.

Reconstruction was over—a mistake in the eyes of all but ex-slaves, who had tasted political power only to have it stolen by mob rule. Mississippi's second black senator lost the next election. He was the last African American in the U.S. Senate until 1966. In 1890, as black laborers cleared the Delta of bears, wildcats, and snake-infested canebrake taller than a man, Mississippi's new constitution legalized what mobs had set in motion. Literacy tests and poll taxes, fully sanctioned by the U.S. Supreme Court, ended black voting. By 1900, blacks comprised 62 percent of Mississippi, the highest percentage in the nation. Yet the state had not one black elected official. Meanwhile, the sharecropping system, under which ex-slaves picked cotton and harvested mounting debt to "the boss man," kept 90 percent of Mississippi blacks mired in the "era of second slavery." Ex-slaves were free, all right— free to pick cotton from "kin to cain't," free to live in tarpaper shacks, free to send their children to decaying schools where "we could study the earth through the floor and the stars through the roof." Jim Crow had settled in to stay, tamping down an entire people. Black subjugation was ingrained at all levels, from the all-white university to "Whites Only" signs to the very nursery rhymes children sang:

Naught's a naught,
Five's a figger.
All fer de white man,
None fer de Nigger.

From top to bottom, segregation was enforced by custom as much as law. And custom—imposed whenever blacks stepped off the sidewalk as a white approached, whenever a black man was called "boy," whenever "Nigger!" was spit into the face of a child—made Mississippi, as one Delta woman noted, "jus' as different here from other places as tar from biscuit dough."

Having redeemed its politics, Mississippi set about redeeming its honor. History written by the defeated does not often become the official version, yet as an American apartheid spread from Texas to the Mason-Dixon line, historians rewrote Reconstruction. In an era of minstrel shows, weekly lynchings, and calls to "Take up the White Man's Burden," North and South suddenly agreed: freed slaves had been slothful politicians, Klansmen were liberators, and vigilantes had been not white but black. Popular books such as *The Clansman* and *The Negro: A Menace to American Civilization* sold white supremacy to the whole nation. Northerners, the *New York Times* noted in 1900, no longer denounced the suppression of black voting because "the necessity of it under the supreme law of self-preservation is candidly recognized." Reconstruction soon became "The Tragic Era."

The nationwide best seller by that name recounted "the darkest days in Mississippi," when the legislature was "one of the most grotesque bodies that ever assembled. A mulatto was Speaker of the House, a darker man was Lt. Governor." Evil carpetbaggers and traitorous scalawags had labored to "inflame the Negroes," causing them to attack white women. "Rape," *The Tragic Era* noted, "is the foul daughter of Reconstruction." Riding to the rescue, as Klansmen did in the popular film *Birth of a Nation*, the Klan "was organized for the protection of women, property, civilization itself." Revisionism did more than justify Jim Crow—it pacified the North and solidified the South. In his landmark study of race, *An American Dilemma*, Gunnar Myrdal observed, "The South needs to believe that when the Negro voted, life was unbearable."

The generations came and went. The price of cotton rose and fell. The Mississippi River did likewise. Through sweltering summers and gray, bone-chilling winters, descendants of Confederates and descendants of slaves shared a volatile truce. Segregated yet strangely intertwined, the two cultures coexisted—tar and biscuit dough, cordial, edgy, neither separate nor equal. White folks had their side of town and all the twentieth century could add—fine and finer homes, Model Ts, shopping trips to Memphis or New Orleans. And black folks had their side of town and what little they could scrape together—a few barnyard animals, perhaps a mule, and a shack barely big enough for two, let alone the eight or ten crammed inside. Life in white Mississippi was intensely social, based on kinship and the camaraderie of cotillions and hunting trips. But life in black Mississippi was more hopeless than any other in America. In 1903, W. E. B. Du Bois wrote, "The problem of the twentieth century is the problem of the color line." Among the "colored" of Mississippi, the problem was Mississippi itself, where "Mr. Charlie" cheated sharecroppers at annual "settlements," where dresses had to be made out of flour sacks, where submission was ground into the soul.

During World War I, blacks fled north to factory jobs. So many left that those left behind joked, "What are the three largest cities in Mississippi?" Hint: none were actually *in* Mississippi. Back home, a few blacks in each town inched ahead, bought a little land, opened a barbershop or funeral parlor, kept up modest homes. But the vast majority, serfs under the feudal rule of King Cotton, lived for Saturday-night revelry at "juke joints." When that turned violent—over women, usually—some ended up in Mississippi's own corner of hell, Parchman Farm Penitentiary, whose bestial murders, rapes, and tortures made it "worse than slavery." Those who survived Saturday night repented on Sunday in churches where the spirit was barely contained within wooden walls. And then came Monday, when hordes of blacks rose at dawn and headed again for the fields, not to return till dusk.

In the 1920s Harlem hosted a Renaissance of art, jazz, and literature. In Mississippi, blacks sat on swaybacked porches playing beat-up guitars with bottlenecks and table knives. To some their music sounded like fingernails on a blackboard, to others like human anguish distilled into song. It came to be called the Delta blues. By the 1930s, textile mills dotted the upper

South. Atlanta was a bustling city, Birmingham a steel town. But Mississippi remained a state of rural hamlets, zoned by race and railroad tracks, surrounded by snarled backwoods and linked by dirt roads. This gave the state a quaint charm locals loved—you could still hunt, fish, live as your granddaddy lived. Yet to "outsiders" riding the Illinois Central through the Delta, it seemed the twentieth century had yet to come downriver from St. Louis. Even into the 1940s, sprawling plantations were tended by blacks in overalls stuffing cotton into bulging sacks. Even into the atomic age, Baptist tent revivals drew the devil out of sinful small-towners. And the generations came and went. The price of cotton rose and fell. The river did likewise.

Justifying the economics was an ideology, also in black and white. In *The Mind of the South,* W. J. Cash explored how the Civil War shaped the thinking of an entire region. Refusing to repent for their secession, southerners romanticized the antebellum world the war had rendered "gone with the wind." Slavery had not been one of the worst crimes in history but a humane, paternal system. "Never was there happier dependence of labor and capital on each other," recalled Confederate president and Mississippian Jefferson Davis. The slave system had protected white women—"the loveliest and purest of God's creatures"—from lustful black men. And not a word was said about why some Negroes had lighter skin. A genteel culture with cotillions and calling cards preferred to talk about acts of kindness— and there were many—between black and white. Yet the same culture also required savage retaliation against any black who through "reckless eyeballing" dared to offend whites, especially white women. Atrocities, including the lynching of more than five hundred Mississippi Negroes—more than any other state—were ennobled as righteous. Lynching went unpunished, murder was "self-defense," and many towns announced their meanness in a road sign—"Nigger, Don't Let the Sun Go Down on You Here." Whites who disapproved learned to keep quiet. Criticism of Jim Crow became disloyalty to be dealt with, Cash noted, by "making such criticism so dangerous that none but a madman would risk it."

Yet until the 1950s, criticism was marginal. All but a few northerners dismissed "the Negro problem" as a southern problem, and all but a few southerners chose not to see a problem. Understanding is a two-way street, but it ran one way through Greenwood, Jackson, and Liberty, Mississippi. Black women cleaned and cooked in white homes, cared for white children, were often "a part of the family." They knew too well how whites lived. Yet whites, though they might play with blacks as children, never went to "Nig-gertown" and rarely compared their own comforts to those of their maids and cooks. Blacks smiled a lot, therefore they must be happy. "When civil rights came along, a lot of us were shocked," said one Natchez woman. "I was shocked to find black people we knew participating in the marches, because we didn't know they were unhappy." And when Freedom Summer focused the eyes of America on Mississippi, many whites there would not recognize the state others saw. Seemed they had never been to black Mississippi, even though it was just across town.

To sidestep the minefield of class, Mississippi politicians played the race card expertly. Because Mississippi was a one-party state—almost no one voting for the party of Lincoln—incumbent congressmen held their seats for generations, becoming the most powerful men on Capitol Hill. And when-ever an election was at risk, politicians found a convenient whipping boy in the Negro. James K. Vardaman, Mississippi governor: "The Negro is a lazy, lustful animal which no conceivable amount of training can transform into a tolerable citizen." Vardaman's successor to Mississippi's power elite, a bald-ing little bigot named Theodore G. Bilbo, was more blunt. Toward the end of his long and corrupt career, Senator Bilbo announced, "I am calling upon every red-blooded American who believes in the superiority and integrity of the white race to get out and see that no nigger votes . . . and the best time to do it is the night before."

Bilbo's call to arms came in 1946 when, home from World War II, blacks in Mississippi were beginning to clamor for citizenship. Things were finally changing, thanks in part to technology. Late in the war, the first mechanical cotton picker was demonstrated on a Delta plantation. The cost of picking a bale of cotton by hand was $39.41; the cost by machine was $5.26. In the decade following the war, 315,000 blacks displaced by automation headed north, and Mississippi's racial lava cooled. A new generation of black lead-ers began speaking out. Small NAACP chapters began meeting in lamplit churches. Lynching, in decline since the 1930s, stopped. Several thousand Negroes registered to vote, and no one shot into their homes. Few spoke of universal Negro suffrage, but stagnation seemed at an end. "Segregation will never end in my lifetime, of course," many said, "but my children will see its end." Yet those who remembered the great Mississippi flood of 1927, which spread the river across the Delta for a hundred miles, knew how stealthily disaster could come.

Levees do not break as dams do—with a roar and rush. Instead, the relentless pressure of rising water forms "boils," small geysers that bubble through softer soil. Sandbag each boil, and you can hold back the floodwaters, but if enough boils bubble through, the whole levee goes. For Mississippi and the entire South, the first boil surfaced on May 17, 1954.

Mississippians, their governor announced, were "shocked and stunned." Senator James Eastland, owner of a huge Delta plantation, flailed his fists and proclaimed, "We are about to embark on a great crusade to restore Americanism." A Mississippi judge bemoaned "Black Monday." The Monday in question was the day the U.S. Supreme Court ruled on *Brown v. the Board of Education of Topeka, Kansas*. Influenced by psychological studies of black children, the court ruled that "to separate them from others of similar age and qualifications solely because of their race generates a feeling of inferiority as to their status in the community that may affect their hearts and minds in a way unlikely ever to be undone." Separate schools, the court unanimously declared, were "inherently unequal." Alarm was still rippling across the South when, late in 1955, Rosa Parks refused to give up her seat on a bus in Montgomery, Alabama.

As in resisting Reconstruction, Mississippi led resistance to the civil rights movement. Two months after the *Brown* decision, planters, lawyers, and other prominent Delta men met in Indianola to form the White Citizens' Council. The council often clothed its policies in the garb of "states rights," but one pamphlet succinctly defined its purpose: "The Citizens' Council is the South's answer to the mongrelizers. We will not be integrated! We are proud of our white blood and our white heritage. . . . If we are bigoted, prejudiced, un-American, etc., so were George Washington, Thomas Jefferson, Abraham Lincoln, and other illustrious forebears who believed in segregation." Within a year, Citizens' Council chapters had sprung up throughout Mississippi. Within two years, similar councils were meeting across the South.

Sometimes called "the uptown Klan," Mississippi's Citizens' Councils used a variety of tactics. They held high school essay contests on "Why Separate Schools Should be Maintained for the White and Negro Races." They sent volunteers house-to-house to survey racial attitudes. Their list of subversive organizations—those backing integration—ranged from the Methodist and Episcopal churches to the Elks Club, the YWCA, and the U.S. Air Force. The Citizens' Council's primary weapon was the mimeograph machine, churning out some five million pages of pamphlets and press releases to rally "right thinking" Mississippians. Many spouted the familiar tenets of white supremacy; others served up a more mendacious venom. In 1956, the South was deluged with mimeographs of a speech by Professor Roosevelt Williams of Howard University. At an NAACP meeting in Jackson, Williams claimed that white women yearned for black men and any black man could get any white woman he wanted. The speech was widely quoted until a Georgia journalist found there was no Professor Roosevelt Williams of Howard University. The "speech" had been distributed by the Citizens' Council in Mississippi. But as the Citizens' Council gained enough power to elect Governor Ross Barnett—"God was the original segregationist"—disinformation proved a mild tactic compared to economic warfare. Blacks who dared register to vote, who joined the NAACP, who signed petitions demanding school integration, quickly had their credit cut off, their taxes audited, their insurance canceled. Soon the phone threats started. For most "agitators," these were enough. They stopped fooling around with "dat Brown mess." Those who persisted were handled by citizens not quite so "uptown."

Rednecks. Peckerwoods. White trash. By whatever degrading name, the impoverished whites of Mississippi kept one rung up on the social ladder by beating down the blacks below them. Shunned by better-off whites, they carved out hardscrabble lives in shacks and hovels where, living close to the unforgiving earth, they absorbed its cruelty. Growing up in Yazoo City, writer Willie Morris knew them well. "And then there were the redneck boys," Morris wrote.

> Almost all of them were rough and open, and you learned early to treat them with a diffident respect; they were bigger and often older, from failing a grade or from having to stay out of school, sometimes for days at a time, during picking season. . . . Pity the poor colored child who walked past the schoolhouse when they were outside. There would be cries of "coon" or "nigger baby," followed by a barrage of rocks and dirt clods. When I was a grown man and saw the deputy sheriffs and the mobs pummeling Negro demonstrators on television, I needed no one to tell me they had been doing the same thing since the age of eight.

The "redneck boys" hung out in packs where they hardened each other with a junkyard meanness passed down from father to son. Bottled up throughout boyhood, it exploded when mixed with moonshine and a mob mentality, especially when blacks tried to climb the ladder.

In May 1955, George Lee, a minister who had urged fellow blacks to register, was driving through Belzoni when shots rang out. His face blown off, Lee died en route to the hospital. The murder was reported in Jackson papers as an "odd accident." That August, a black veteran was gunned down on a crowded courthouse lawn in Brookhaven. Two weeks later, teenager Emmett Till, having come from Chicago to visit relatives, flirted with a white woman in Money, Mississippi (pop. 55). No African American of "the Emmett Till generation" would ever forget the photo of Till's monstrously mangled face in the casket his mother left open to let "the world see what they did to my boy." More than one hundred reporters sat in the segregated courtroom where the sheriff greeted the black press—"Good morning, niggers"—and where the defense urged the jury, "every last Anglo Saxon one of you," to find the killers not guilty. The jury complied in just over an hour. William Faulkner observed, "If we in America have reached that point in our desperate culture when we must murder children, no matter for what reason or what color, we don't deserve to survive, and probably won't." A less eloquent white man proved more prophetic. "There's open season on Negroes now," he said. Within four years, ten more Mississippi blacks were murdered by whites; no guilty verdicts were rendered. The reign of terror also revived lynching. In the tiny town of Poplarville, Mack Parker, accused of rape, was dragged from jail and later found in chains, drifting in a logjam on the Pearl River. But the Emmett Till murder galvanized blacks more than whites. "From that point on," Bob Moses' mentor Amzie Moore remembered, "Mississippi began to move."

And when it moved, the movement came from the bottom up. "It was the so-called dumb people," a Holmes County farmer remembered. ". . . The school teachers, the educated people, they ain't did a damn thang! The preachers ain't neither. The so-called dumb people open the way for everybody. See, the table was set." The Mississippi movement began with common laborers whose dignity would not be denied and with self-employed farmers whites could neither fire nor frighten. A chapter of the NAACP or the Regional Council of Negro Leadership, a place to meet, and a coalition of the brave—these were the sparks. And Emmett Till's face, printed in *Jet* magazine and passed from hand to hand, was the fan reminding blacks that little had changed in Mississippi, and that everything had to.

When vigilantes and the Citizens' Council could not contain the movement, the state stepped in. In the wake of *Brown*, prospective voters were required not just to read but to *interpret* part of the Mississippi constitution, a document, as Senator Bilbo noted, "that damn few white men and no niggers at all can explain." The state constitution had 285 sections. Each "interpretation" was left open to the registrar. No appeal was allowed. Black teachers, doctors, and Ph.D.s routinely "failed" the test most whites did not have to take, and statewide black voting rolls fell from 22,000 to 8,000. In 1956, state legislators declared *Brown* "invalid, unconstitutional, and not of lawful effect." The vote was 136–0. After voting, legislators sang "Dixie." That same year, the legislature created Mississippi's own KGB, the State Sovereignty Commission. Chaired by the governor, funded by taxpayers and private donations, the Sovereignty Commission spied, paid informers, tapped phones, and convinced newspaper editors to plant false stories and kill factual ones. The commission's most extreme actions now seem comical, such as when investigators examined a baby born out of wedlock, checking its hair, nose, and fingernails to discover if he was part Negro. But other tactics seemed more appropriate for Khrushchev's Soviet Union than for Eisenhower's America.

During its first five years, the Sovereignty Commission spent much of its time fielding letters of support from segregationists across the nation. But members also found time to stir things up in Mississippi. The commission used black informers to imprison a man who tried to integrate the University of Southern Mississippi. It investigated NAACP leaders. Who were their friends? Were they Christian? What sexual habits might lead to their disgrace? Commission reports on racial violence inevitably blamed blacks and exonerated whites. Then Bob Moses came to Mississippi. An investigator interviewed Moses and concluded he was "working hand-in-glove with Communist sympathizers if not out-right Communist agitators. It is my opinion that Moses is himself a Communist." Moses and SNCC deepened the siege mentality that set in across the state when, several years after the Montgomery bus boycott, the civil rights movement finally took hold in Mississippi.

By the summer of 1962, SNCC was building a "beachhead" in the most impoverished and explosive spot in America—the Mississippi Delta. Meanwhile in Jackson, blacks were boycotting segregated stores, sitting in at lunch counters, going limp as cops dragged them into paddy wagons. And across

Mississippi, from the Delta south to the Piney Woods, blacks were lining up
to register at county courthouses.

In Mississippi, the courthouse was more than a symbol of law and
order—it was the heart of white society. Situated at the hub of each county
seat, framed by a tidy town square, each courthouse was the oldest and
best-preserved building for miles around. Each stood with towering cupola
and an ornate brick facade. And on each courthouse lawn, a stone soldier
stood atop a pedestal chiseled with the roll call of the Confederate dead.
Every white birth, death, and marriage was recorded in the courthouse. And
now as blacks came en masse to register, it was as if they were tearing a hole
in these nostalgic portraits of the Old South. Because terror alone could not
stop them, Mississippi barred its doors, locked its mind, and clung to the past
that was not even past.

But preserving the status quo in the 1960s was not as easy as it had once
been. A new invader, television, threatened to spread northern ideas about
integration. Even if most Mississippi towns had just one or two TV channels, they had to be controlled. When novelist James Baldwin appeared on
the *Today* show, he was not seen in Mississippi. NBC affiliates statewide
showed an old movie. When NAACP lawyer Thurgood Marshall spoke on
TV, WLBT in Jackson flashed the sign "Cable Difficulty." The announcement "Sorry, Cable Trouble" soon became common on Mississippi TV.
Newscasts were often preceded by a warning: "The following program is
Northern-managed news." Such control depended on media monopoly. The
manager of WLBT was a Citizens' Council director. So were the station's
owners, the Hederman family, which also owned Mississippi's two statewide
dailies, the *Jackson Clarion-Ledger* and the *Jackson Daily News*. As with
the rest of Jim Crow, opposition to "northern" media sometimes reached
absurd heights. In the spring of 1964, rumors that the hit Western *Bonanza*
would feature a "Negro cow-girl" led to a boycott of the show and its sponsors. A few months later, Mississippi's ABC affiliates protested the new sitcom *Bewitched*, arguing that a show about a man marrying a witch might be
seen as "a veiled argument for racial intermarriage."

Blackouts, spies, vigilantes, cops cracking down, Citizens' Council chapters lobbying the "right thinking"—all turned Mississippi into "The Closed
Society." And when Ole Miss history professor James Silver coined the term
in 1963, he too became a target. Denounced by the governor, investigated

by the university, Silver began sleeping with a shotgun by his bed. He never drove at night. Other moderates faced similar harassment. At Ole Miss, speakers were screened for their views on integration. The campus director of religious life was forced to leave. His crime? Hosting a black journalist. Protesting "intellectual straight-jacketing," professors resigned one after another until a quarter of the faculty had quit. Clergymen also felt the pressure. In January 1963, twenty-eight Methodist ministers signed a statement urging church integration. Within a year, half had left the state.

Dick Gregory once joked that a Mississippi moderate was someone "who will lynch you from a low tree." But despite the dangers, a few voices of reason remained, courageously crying out in what one called "The Magnolia Jungle." Hazel Brannon Smith, publisher of the *Lexington Advertiser*, waged a one-woman campaign against the Citizens' Council and its "private Gestapo," the Sovereignty Commission. In her front-page column, "Through Hazel Eyes," Smith observed: "Today we live in fear in Holmes County and in Mississippi. It hangs like a dark cloud over us dominating every facet of public and private life. None speaks freely without being afraid of being misunderstood. Almost every man and woman is afraid to try to do anything to promote good will and harmony between the races."

Smith was ostracized in her small town. Advertising dried up, her name was linked to Communists, her husband lost his job, and she was found guilty of libel for denouncing a white cop who had shot a black man. Yet Smith kept speaking out, and a month before Freedom Summer, she became the first woman to win the Pulitzer Prize for editorial writing. Farther south, in Petal, Mississippi, P. D. East, editor, publisher, ad salesman, reporter, and typesetter for the *Petal Paper*, denounced the spreading "assdom." East ran mock Citizens' Council ads asking readers to "Join the Glorious Citizens Clan . . . the Bigger and Better Bigots Bureau." Like Hazel Brannon Smith, East was boycotted. The *Petal Paper* survived only on out-of-state sales. And still farther south, in the shipyard town of Pascagoula, publisher Ira Harkey Jr. had the audacity to remove the labels "nigger" and "colored" from his newspaper, then editorialize against local "goons" and "Hateists." They responded by shooting into his house and burning a cross on his lawn. The hatred hardened, finally bringing on Mississippi's greatest fear—the return of northern troops.

Mississippians thought they knew how to handle any Negro who tried to enroll at Ole Miss. The first, in 1958, was sent to a mental institution. But in 1962, James Meredith's pending enrollment threw the charming old town of Oxford into an uproar. "Dixie" blared on radio stations. Confederate flags flew. Rebel yells sounded in the streets, and whites from as far south as the Gulf Coast poured into Oxford armed for battle. Federal marshals arrived on troop trucks. On September 30, as darkness descended on campus, bricks smashed cars and windows. Mississippi highway patrolmen withdrew, enraging Attorney General Robert Kennedy, who sent in more marshals. All night the rioting continued, leaving two dead, twenty-eight shot, hundreds beaten, cars burned, buildings gutted. The next morning, federal troops escorted Meredith through the rubble and into class. "We hate violence," one student said, "but we are determined to keep our way of life. Nobody can take it away from us, and I would die for it."

Federal troops stayed on the Ole Miss campus until the following August. Come 1964, three years after the centennial secession parade, the Civil War remained an open sore, the Oxford "occupation" had rekindled smoldering hatreds, and Mississippi had become a pressure cooker. In March, news of the summer project sent tremors through the state. Freedom Summer planners announced, again and again, that volunteers coming to Mississippi would not march, sit in, or protest. In a letter to all county sheriffs, planners explained, "The project is concerned with construction, not agitation." Yet that spring, the Mississippi legislature passed a spate of laws doubling the number of state police and banning picketing, leafleting, and assembly.

While the state legislature met in emergency session, Mississippi's KGB made its own preparations for Freedom Summer. Throughout April and May, the State Sovereignty Commission held clinics for sheriffs and cops, advising them of new state laws for handling the incoming wave of "communists, sex perverts, odd balls, and do-gooders." The agency also hired two black spies it called Informant X and Informant Y. X's job was to travel with civil rights workers. "It will be a long hot summer in Mississippi," X reported back, "because they are going to demonstrate in the streets of Jackson until the 'walls of segregation' come tumbling down." Attending the Ohio training, X reported, "The white girls have been going around with the Negro boys and Negro girls going with the white boys." While X traveled, Y infiltrated the Jackson headquarters of the Council of Federated Organizations (COFO), an umbrella group of civil rights agencies in Mississippi.

COFO headquarters would be the nerve center of Freedom Summer. Located on Lynch Street in the black section of Jackson, COFO shared a low brick building with the Streamline Bar and Billiards. As Freedom Summer approached, the office was far busier than the adjacent bar. Phones rang incessantly. Women sat at typewriters clacking out letters, lists, solicitations, and a stream of reports on all aspects of the summer project. Meetings in smoke-filled back rooms went on past midnight. Boxes of books and clothes—donations from around the country—piled up in corners. Moving freely through the clutter was Informant Y. Along with stealing key documents, including lists of all volunteers with their home addresses, Y also sent fanciful reports to the Sovereignty Commission. Apparently the COFO office was thick with Communists and even a "queer." Photos of Khrushchev and Lenin adorned the wall, Y reported, Marxist literature was everywhere, and talk was of a new world "where black and white will walk together and where Communism will dominate. They do not talk of love but only of sex to satisfy the body." As the summer unfolded, Informant X would continue to file dry reports while Informant Y would tell the State Sovereignty Commission just what it wanted to hear.

By June 1964, Mississippi's past was digging in against the onslaught of the present. All but a few moderates had been silenced or exiled. Pascagoula publisher Ira Harkey had sold his crusading paper. Frank Smith, the lone Mississippi moderate in Congress, had been defeated for reelection. P. D. East had moved to Alabama, and William Faulkner was dead. Unfettered, Confederate pride resurged with a vengeance. Reconstruction-era insults— "carpetbagger" and "scalawag"—were common. The *Jackson Clarion-Ledger* was running a Civil War column—"This Week in 1864"—recounting atrocities by Union troops. Behind the scenes, softer voices pleaded for understanding. "I know we've had a hundred years," a Hattiesburg doctor said. "I know that, and I'm ashamed to ask it, but we need more time. If we had more time, we'd work it out." To most Mississippians, however, it was too late for pleas. "In my life span, I have never felt so compelled to stand up for God and our country," a Jackson man wrote the *Clarion-Ledger*. "I ask both white and colored not to let Mississippi turn into a small New York."

With Freedom Summer just a week away, rumors verged on panic. Not just a few hundred but thirty thousand "invaders" were on their way! In Jackson, word that Negro gangs were "forming to rape white women" led to a run on gun shops. Mississippi police stockpiled tear gas, riot guns, and electric cattle prods. Cops took riot training. The Klan announced it had 91,000 members in Mississippi and was actively recruiting. In this spreading alarm, violence became common currency.

Early one June evening, two cars stopped in front of COFO headquarters in Jackson. Two young white men stepped out. Each calmly pulled out a gun, aimed at the office, and fired. Windows shattered. Screams came from inside. The men drove off. Six days later, a bomb hit the Freedom House in Canton. That same day in volatile southwest Mississippi, whites mauled three journalists. "This is just a taste of what you Northern agitators will get," one attacker said.

With the days melting away, Mississippi braced for the "long, hot summer." Chambers of commerce shared strategies. Stay calm. Discourage the Klan in your area. Trust the police. Stonewall the press. In southwest Mississippi, two new organizations began meeting. The Americans for the Preservation of the White Race urged peaceful defiance. "Don't do no violence," a preacher told the group. "The day we kill three or four, they'd be martial law in Mississippi." In McComb, the neighborhood watch group Help, Inc. organized block captains and mailed out "Guidelines for Self-protection and Preservation." Among them: "Know where small children are at all times. . . . Look before unlocking door to anyone. . . . Learn alarm codes. . . . Temporary alarm to be three blasts from a shotgun or car horn." And in klaverns dotted throughout Mississippi, Klansmen steeled themselves. "This summer, within a very few days, the enemy will launch his final push for victory here in Mississippi," the Klan's shadowy Imperial Wizard announced. "We must use all of the time which is left to us in these next few days preparing to meet this attack. Weapons and ammunition must be accumulated and stored. Squads must drill. . . . And a solemn, determined spirit of Christian reverence must be stimulated in all members."

On the last day of spring, as volunteers boarded buses in Ohio, Jackson's huge armored tank waited at police headquarters. Nearby, the county fairgrounds had become a holding camp big enough to house thousands of prisoners. After months of rumors and threats, Mississippi hunkered down for the worst. In Jackson, Eudora Welty wrote a friend, "I hear that this summer all hell is going to break loose." The State Sovereignty Commission reported "increased activity in weapon shipments." From towns carved out of the clay to those rising from cotton fields, Mississippi waited. Then shortly after midnight on the first day of summer, young men and women rode buses south from Memphis, singing as they approached the state line. When a blood-red sun rose that Sunday, Mississippi was again engulfed in the wars—between white and black, between North and South, between tolerance and intolerance—that had never really ended.

"Why doesn't everybody love each other?"

"Do what?"

"Love each other. Why don't they love each other?"

"Say, what are you anyhow? Some kind of a nut?"

—Shelby Foote, Jordan County

CHAPTER THREE

Freedom Street

The land was a pool table of green, the sky was bigger than Montana's, and the asphalt was long, straight, and empty when eight volunteers and two SNCC staffers were dropped by the side of a highway somewhere in Mississippi. They knew the date—June 21, 1964. They knew the time—5:00 a.m. But where were they?

The last sign had read, "Batesville—Corp Limit," but there was no town in sight. Other than the felt fields and skinny two-lane, there was nothing in sight except a vacant Greyhound bus station and, across the highway, a squat brick building stamped with the words "Mississippi Highway Patrol." Chris Williams, still bleary from the bus ride, found this "unpleasant, to say the least." Where the hell was Batesville? Back in Ohio, they had learned the rudiments of Mississippi geography—the Delta cotton fields, the low central hills, the matchstick Piney Woods farther south—but standing by the road near Batesville, the group saw no cotton, no hills, no woods, just a sweep of emptiness filling them with a vague terror that something had gone very wrong.

Someone was supposed to meet them. Someone had met the dozen people dropped an hour earlier at the small college in Holly Springs. But no one was there now, just the highway patrolman across the street. Sitting in his car. Sunglasses glinting. Volunteers talked among themselves, trying to remain calm, but they had been warned to expect the worst, and it looked as if they had been dumped right into it. Wherever they might be in Mississippi, it seemed far from any America they knew. A billboard farther back had read "Impeach Earl Warren." Gorgeous white magnolias burst from roadside greenery while lush vines strangled telephone poles, fences, and trees. Even the morning sun was so blinding it hurt. Scattered houses seemed buried in an impoverished past, their faded clapboards barely rising above piles of old refrigerators, rusted sedans, and decaying pickups. The last gas station had advertised "Ethyl—29.9¢/gal," but it looked as if no one had filled up there since World War II.

SNCC staffer Tillman McKellar, having been to Mississippi, quickly took charge. McKellar walked to a phone booth at the bus depot to call their contact, then returned to the highway to flag down the first passing black driver. The highway patrolman revved his engine, followed, and pulled the car over. The cop seemed to be lecturing—McKellar later said the cop told him they would all end up at the bottom of the Tallahatchie River. Then both cars drove off, leaving nine people by the roadside, alone—but not for long.

June was "hospitality month" in Mississippi, and on Route 6 the hospitality started with mosquitoes. Mississippi "skeeters," locals joked, were "so big they could stand flatfooted and fuck a turkey." As they swarmed, their piercing whines and stinging bites made the rising sun feel hotter, the sky more like a pot's lid than open space. June bugs followed—nasty brown lumps buzzing ears and eyes. Then came the human pests. A pickup roared past, followed by Chevys and Fords, their souped-up engines rumbling through hot-rodders' glass packs. Each muscle car was filled with "redneck boys" doing their best to look like Elvis. Hair was Brylcreemed, beefy biceps hung out open windows. Some men just sneered. Others bellowed.

"We're gonna give you a hard time, goddamn it!"

"We ought to kill these bastards right now!"

The volunteers were stunned. Had these stellar specimens of humanity gotten up at 5:00 a.m. to threaten them? Had they stayed up all night? Wasn't there anything better to do in Batesville—wherever it was? Cars and pickups kept passing. Nine volunteers stood slapping at mosquitoes, their suitcases and duffel bags in a heap, their hopes on hold. Someone had better come soon, someone said.

The opening day of Freedom Summer began with volunteers stranded on Mississippi Route 6. What followed was a day like few others, a day when it seemed possible to believe there were no barriers between black and white, a day when history seemed forgiven and the future worth the wait. Some 250 Americans had come to the poorest, most explosive state in the nation, and even if they were seen as "invaders," they shrugged off the label and went to work. Back in Ohio, Bob Moses had told them to get busy right away to show "that you did not come down to organize any sit-ins . . . marches or demonstrations." But it was Sunday, the first day, and their only work was simply to be there, whites walking through the black side of town, eating in black homes, introducing themselves in black churches, sitting on porches where no whites had ever sat before. The day would end ominously, but one woman later recalled its beginning, the first meetings: "Their demeanor, how they treated us, how they approached you, how they were courteous and polite, and how they didn't talk down to you. There was no fear associated in talking to them. There was no consciousness of *your place* with them." This was why, despite all the warnings, the fears, the skepticism about what little they could accomplish, they had come to Mississippi, after all.

On the road somewhere near Batesville, volunteers waited another ten strange minutes. Insect swarms tormented them. More cars and pickups zoomed into view, revved their fury, and roared down the road. A police car passed, then the sheriff. The sun climbed the simmering sky. Finally toward 5:30 a.m., an old white panel truck pulled up. The driver introduced himself as Mr. Miles, their contact, and with a palpable sense of relief, the whole group piled in the back. The highway patrolman quickly pulled the truck over and gave Mr. Miles a ticket for running a stop sign he had not run, but he was allowed to go on. Within minutes the truck had crossed the railroad tracks, had taken a U-turn onto a frontage road, and was approaching a modest house behind the deep drainage ditch that ran the length of Tubbs Street. As they entered Robert Miles's home, volunteers noted several bullet holes in the white side paneling. Inside they spotted rifles and shotguns behind doors. But the breakfast, served by a middle-aged black woman still in her bathrobe, was all anyone could ask for.

Over eggs, spicy sausage, and the first grits most had tasted, volunteers met the Miles family. Dressed most often in white shirt and tie, fifty-year-old Robert Miles exuded confidence, though whites called it "arrogance." "He thinks out his moves carefully and doesn't take any crap from the white man," Chris Williams wrote home. Since returning from World War II, Miles had been a civil rights pioneer. In the late 1950s, he had cofounded the Panola County Voters League, which had sued the county to open up voter registration. For his courage, Miles had seen his home shot into and a cross burned on his lawn. Violence, he had long ago decided, was "something I had to live with . . . we weren't going anywhere, we didn't have anywhere to go."

At the breakfast table, volunteers smiled at eight-year-old Kevin Miles and his younger brother Vernon who, if they were startled to see white faces at their table, did nothing more than giggle. Later that week volunteers would learn why Mrs. Miles—Mona—seemed on edge. A few years earlier, a town marshal had badly beaten her niece "on account of your father being a smart NAACP nigger!" Bullets later blasted into Mona's brother's house and a cross was burned on his lawn, causing him to move to Detroit. The stress had left Mrs. Miles with a "nervous condition." She spoke freely, read widely, but lived in her bathrobe, never going outside. Still, she managed to temper the constant danger with humor. "I don't see why they don't let us swim in seg- regated pools," she often said. "It's been proven that we don't fade." When talk at the table turned to farming, Mr. Miles—volunteers would always call him that—spoke of his six hundred acres of wheat, soybeans, cotton, and corn. After breakfast, "Junior," the Mileses' oldest son, recently graduated from Alcorn A & M, took the group around the farm. Chris was amazed by the pigs, especially an eight-hundred-pound sow buried to its snout in mud to escape the heat that by 10:00 a.m. already topped 90 degrees. A tour of the discolored old barn filled the remaining time until church.

West Camp Baptist Church stood just a few blocks from the Miles home, but it was a world away from any church Chris or the others knew. There were no soaring ceilings, just one small room filled with people in their "Sunday best." Little girls wore cotton-candy dresses, boys chafed at coat and tie, men and women were decked out as if for a wedding. When the hymns began, the music burst from every soul. The preacher's exhortations were punctuated by calls of "Amen!" or "Tell it!" that filled the room with power and purpose. At the close of the service, "Deacon Miles" introduced the volunteers. Each stood, shyly offering a name and hometown. Baltimore. Ann Arbor. Amherst, Massachusetts. Hastings-on-Hudson, New York. Then their host warned the congregation. "Y'all gonna hear a lot of different sto- ries from white folks about what these people are and why they're down here," Robert Miles said. "White folks are gonna tell you they're agitators. You know what an agitator is? An agitator is the piece in the center of a washing machine that spins around to get dirt out. Well, that's what these people are here for. They're here to get dirt out." After parting handshakes and pleased-to meet-you's, it was back home for lunch. While volunteers ate, then sat out sweltering hours beneath a tree, Robert Miles was on the phone arranging last-minute housing.

Meanwhile across Mississippi, a century of Jim Crow began its long, slow thaw. For this one day, at least until sunset, a sense of wonder drowned all sense of foreboding. Host families took volunteers around "the quarters," showing them off like prized possessions. "Have you seen my girls yet?" Old women stopped young "girls" and touched their skin, calling them "skinny" or "pretty." Children fingered their hair. Hands waved from porches, smiling faces leaned out of windows. Everywhere volunteers walked on that sultry afternoon, down dirt roads leading deeper into labyrinths of shacks, along dust-deviled streets teeming with children, past stoop-shouldered old men sitting and staring, they noticed themselves being noticed. Strangers came out to greet them. Careful to say "Yes, sir" and "No, sir," they were unfettered in their gratitude.

"We're mighty glad the good Lord sent you to us."

"It's a right fine Christian thing, a fine thing that you all have come here."

Children ran to the newcomers, asking their names, or stood shyly in the background, whispering behind cupped hands: "There they is!" And from every soul crushed into the Mississippi soil, the same feeling emerged. "I've waited eighty years for you to come," the gray-haired son of a slave told one volunteer. Pressing a dollar into the white hand, he added, "I just have to give you this little bit to let you all know how much we appreciate your coming. I prays for your safety every night, son. God bless you all."

They had been told to expect the worst—beatings, blackjacks, shotguns. But none of the horror stories in Ohio had prepared them for this. They had been warned about white Mississippi, but on this first day, black Mississippi overwhelmed them. Along with swarms of well-wishers, sounds swirled around them—the drone of insects, the rumble of passing trains, a baby's cry from a shack that looked empty and abandoned. Savory odors of fried food mixed with the foul stench of outhouses. Sights from a distant past surprised them: washed-out ads for Camels and Lucky Strikes painted on splintering wood; women bent over washboards; laundry on a line. They were charmed by the folk art of poor folk desperate for finery. Ornate hubcaps were nailed to walls. Blue milk-of-magnesia bottles hung glittering from trees. Rotting porches were graced with pink geraniums in rusted tin cans. This new world also attacked their skin. Mosquito bites were nothing new, but what were these things called chiggers? Why couldn't you even see them? How could anything itch so much? And if the sun was this mean in

June, what oven temperatures awaited in July, what furnace would fire up come August?

But despite the heat, the bugs, the swarm of sounds, nothing startled the volunteers as much as the destitution all around them. Raised in "the affluent society," where poverty had supposedly been conquered, they walked that day into its shadows. Most were appalled; some were enraged. Where was the pavement? The plumbing? The streetlights? Their hosts, with their modest two-bedroom homes, were rich compared to those living in the shacks just down the gravel road and around the corner. "There are people here without food and clothing," one volunteer wrote home. "Kids that eat a bit of bread for breakfast, chicken necks for dinner. Kids that don't have clothes to go to school in. Old old people, and young people chop cotton from sun up till sundown for $3 a day. They come home exhausted, it's not enough to feed their family on. It's gone before they earn it." Many children running to greet volunteers had open sores on their limbs. In doorways of the more desperate shacks, some infants were too weak, too bloated, to run at all. Ancient black hands reaching out to shake a white hand—for the first time—were callused or crippled. For every smiling face, another on some distant porch was vacant, broken, defeated. On the newcomers walked, past homes "I could kick down with my feet and a small hammer." Some shacks had raw sewage out back. Others, propped on cinder blocks, seemed sunken in their own stench. This was America, many had to remind themselves. This was "the most appalling example of deprivation ever seen." Against these odds, what could one volunteer—or a thousand—hope to accomplish? And yet they were in Mississippi now; they had nothing else to do but try.

Returning to their homes, volunteers found everyday heroics. In the town of Itta Bena, in the heart of the Delta, two young men marveled at their hostess, a sixty-seven-year-old woman living alone beside the railroad tracks that ran along Freedom Street. Limping on a leg long ago broken and badly set, Rosa Lee Williams was "a fiery and fast moving old woman." A retired midwife, she had lost her children in the 1918 flu epidemic, her husband some years later. Happy to have the four dollars a week each volunteer paid her, she kept an immaculate house, constantly sweeping dust stirred by passing trains, battling horseflies with insecticides she sprayed from aerosol cans. When the men moved a bed into the living room, she was quick to put a can under it—for "spittin'." She chewed tobacco, didn't they?

Soon they would get used to Mississippi, sooner than black Mississippi expected. College students would sit at tables piled with fried chicken, collards, even "chitlins"—spicy pig intestines—and eat their fill. A woman from Long Island would plunge her chigger-infested legs into a bucket of gasoline, and the nasty bugs would be gone. "And the outhouse that we had to use?" remembered Greenwood author Endesha Ida Mae Holland. "I was really surprised because I said, 'Well, I know this white girl ain't gonna go use this outhouse like everybody else.' And the girl would use the outhouse like she was *born to it* and that made us all gang around them." Soon volunteers would take evening "showers" out back with buckets of cold water and wake the next morning to the assault of sounds—roosters and barking dogs and a radio blaring down the block—and not even complain . . . much. But on that Sunday, everything was new, exciting, something to write home about.

June 21, 1964

Dear People,

Greetings from Batesville, Miss. The Freedom Riders, as we are called by the locals, arrived here at 5 a.m. after leaving Oxford at about 2 p.m. Sat. . . . This morning as we waited to be picked up at Batesville, we were greeted by the police, sheriff, and members of the White Citizens Council. One heckler told us, "We're going to give you a hard time, goddamn it." Another fellow said to his companion, "We ought to kill these bastards right now." However, the Negro community assures us that this is the common bluff. The people here are very friendly and Panola County should be easy. Send mail to Rev. Robert Miles, Route 2, Box 20, Batesville, Miss.

Love,

Xtoph

Late that afternoon, Chris and other volunteers dropped in at Batesville's two juke joints. Dimly lit bars festooned with beer signs and Christmas lights, each had a soda fountain and general store up front. On Saturday nights, there would be live music, but it was Sunday afternoon down at the Thomas Sundry, and even if it looked like the kind of place their parents warned them against, Chris and other volunteers passed beneath the neon Coca-Cola sign and were inside. Moving deeper into a room that reeked of

barbecue sauce and kerosene, they found a bar, a pool table, and a jukebox
with the best R & B selection Chris had ever seen. The volunteers were soon
surrounded by dozens crowding in to meet "The Riders." After a half hour,
the crowd followed Chris and his new friends through the black section of
Batesville—little more than a drugstore, beauty parlor, and gas station—to
the H & H Café. There locals convinced Chris to try "some good old southern bourbon." Eager to oblige, amazed to be served hometown hooch in the
last dry state in America, the teenager had his first burning sip of moonshine. It was shaping up to be quite a summer.

No one is certain who dreamed up Freedom Summer. Some say Bob Moses,
some say Allard Lowenstein. A quixotic academic and Pied Piper of young
idealists, Lowenstein had brought Stanford and Yale students to the previous
fall's Freedom Election, then suggested a larger white influx the following
summer. But this much is agreed upon: "Had Moses not wanted it to happen, it wouldn'ta happened." And the summer project almost did not happen.
Hotly debated throughout the winter of 1963, the idea had seemed to Stokely
Carmichael "either an act of madness or a daring stroke of genius." Carmichael had not been the only skeptic. Many SNCC veterans felt theirs was
the rightful claim to any progress Mississippi might make. *They* had braved
Mississippi when no one else would. *They* still bore the scars—bloody welts,
broken bones, bullet wounds you could put your finger in. And now a bunch
of white college kids with names like Pam and Geoff were being invited to
Mississippi to gather headlines and plaudits for bravery. Mississippi natives
had other reasons to oppose the project. "We had worked so hard trying to
get local people to take initiative for their own movement," Hollis Watkins
recalled. "That process was beginning to take place. And I felt that bringing
a large number down from the North would snatch the rug right from under
the people in the local communities."

Yet as Carmichael noted, "This was Bob Moses talking." As the idea
gained credence, several in SNCC tried to limit white involvement. Hadn't
those arrogant Stanford and Yale students "taken over the Jackson office"?
Hadn't it been impossible to maintain SNCC's "beautiful community" when
every office had "a bunch of Yalies running around in their Triumphs"? But
how could SNCC reject whites? "If we're trying to break down the barrier
of segregation," Fannie Lou Hamer argued, "we can't segregate ourselves."
Others disagreed. "We don't have much to gain from Negroes meeting

whites," cautioned MacArthur Cotton, a Freedom Rider who had been hung by his thumbs in Parchman Farm Penitentiary. "We've got too much to lose if they come down here and create a disturbance in two or three months, and they're gone." Learning of the attempt to "get rid of the whites," Moses flatly declared he would not be part of anything "all black." Only when blacks in Mississippi were joined by whites, he argued, would civil rights be no longer a question of skin color but "a question of rational people against irrational people. . . . I always thought that the one thing we can do for the country that no one else could do is to be above the race issue."

The debate had continued in grueling meetings that began with eloquent arguments, rose to righteous anger, and ended with hands clasped, songs sung, and no agreement. As 1964 began, the summer project remained in doubt. "How large a force of volunteer summer workers should we recruit?" Moses asked in a memo. "100? 1,000? 2,000?" Had SNCC made this decision by consensus, the answer might have been zero. In late January, another meeting deadlocked. "Too difficult." The "huge influx" would overwhelm SNCC. Why waste an entire summer on "sociological research"? The turning point came a week later, prompted by another murder.

Nearly three years after Herbert Lee had been gunned down, the killing still tormented Moses. At Lee's funeral, his wife had approached Moses, screaming, "You killed my husband! You killed my husband!" Following the funeral, Moses and fellow organizers had gone looking for witnesses. Knocking on doors at night, they met a burly logger named Louis Allen who had seen it all. Herbert Lee had not brandished a tire iron, Allen assured Moses. He had been killed in cold blood. Allen had only testified otherwise after coming home to find his living room filled with white men toting shotguns. Later Allen told the FBI the truth and agreed to testify if he could get federal protection. None was offered. When word leaked of what Allen knew, locals stopped buying his logs. His credit was cut off. A sheriff stopped him, repeated his FBI testimony word for word, then broke his jaw with a flashlight. Hounded and harassed, Allen made plans to flee Mississippi. He did not want to die, he told his wife, because "when you're dead, you're dead a long time." On the evening of January 31, 1964, just hours before he was to leave for Milwaukee, Louis Allen pulled his pickup into his driveway and got out to open the barbed-wire gate. From inside his tarpaper shack, his wife heard three shots. The crack of a shotgun in Mississippi was nothing unusual, and Elizabeth Allen stayed inside watching TV while her husband lay in the driveway, clinging to life as the truck's headlights slowly dimmed. Shortly after midnight, her son found the body. That morning, Moses got a phone call.

"For me, it was as if everything had come full circle," he remembered. "I had started in Amite County, unable to offer protection or force the federal government to provide it. Herbert Lee had been killed; Louis Allen had witnessed it and now he was dead." In 1961, the fledgling SNCC had no power to respond to Lee's murder "other than to dedicate our own lives to what we were doing," Moses said. "But Louis Allen's murder happened at a moment in history when we had another option." Moses threw his full influence and reputation behind the summer project. "The staff had been deadlocked, at loggerheads with each other; this decided it."

The timing could not have been better. Nearly nine years had passed since the victorious Montgomery bus boycott had elevated Martin Luther King to national status and stirred so much hope. But by the spring of 1964, the civil rights movement was spinning its wheels. While lifting spirits and making headlines, the movement had changed few laws or customs. After years of foot dragging, John F. Kennedy had proposed his civil rights bill, but ten months later it remained stalled by a Senate filibuster. Few held out any hope that Lyndon Johnson, a southerner with no great track record on civil rights, would risk his reputation and power for the bill. "Whites Only" signs remained throughout the South, and Dixie politicians were getting attention and votes by denouncing integration in terms reminiscent of the Civil War. In the past year, shotguns and bombs had shaken the certainty of the most devoutly nonviolent. And the Klan was rising. Martin Luther King was soaring to new heights of eloquence, but for most whites outside the South, civil rights remained some distant struggle that concerned them little and their children even less. Freedom Summer, now that SNCC had finally made up its mind, would get everyone's attention and get the civil rights movement rolling again.

Once deciding on the project, SNCC was consumed by it. Meetings wore down even the most tireless talkers. SNCC staffers, like the grad students many later became, churned out reports: "Notes on Teaching in Mississippi"; "Techniques for Field Work—Voter Registration"; "The General Condition of the Mississippi Negro." SNCC staff in Atlanta turned much of their energy to Mississippi. The cautious NAACP warned that a summer of racial unrest in Mississippi might cause a white "backlash," putting Barry

Goldwater in the White House, yet SNCC forged ahead. Bob Moses fought off a power play by Allard Lowenstein. After recruiting students across the country, Lowenstein tried to put Stanford- and Boston-area volunteers under his aegis, then, fearing SNCC had been infiltrated by Communists, abruptly left the project, leaving Moses with precious little time to prepare. Working with staffers, Moses defined four strict jobs for summer volunteers: registering voters, teaching in Freedom Schools, running community centers (often called Freedom Houses), and a fourth task that would take Freedom Summer to the national stage.

The Mississippi Freedom Democratic Party, formed that spring, would be the beacon of Freedom Summer. Like the Freedom Election the previous autumn, the MFDP was an exercise in parallel democracy. Summer volunteers, SNCCs decided, would register as many voters as Mississippi's closed system might allow, but blacks unwilling to take the risk could safely register as Freedom Democrats just by signing a form. Moses envisioned 400,000 names on MFDP rolls, a massive outpouring that would prove that blacks were desperate to vote in Mississippi. Armed with these names, and their own delegates to be chosen that summer, Freedom Democrats would go to the Democratic National Convention in Atlantic City at the end of August. There they would plead their case—perhaps even on TV—telling the nation of beatings, drive-by shootings, and other outrages denying blacks the vote. With enough support, Freedom Democrats might even unseat Mississippi's all-white delegates and become the state's official delegation. But all that was for later in the summer. Throughout that spring, SNCC staff remained focused on the one ingredient—aside from idealism—essential to the coming summer.

Money was not merely the name of the Mississippi hamlet where Emmett Till had been killed. Money was the lifeblood of the summer project. Calculating a cost of $200,000, SNCC began fund-raising in February with a full-page ad in the *New York Times*. Campus-based "Friends of SNCC" chapters around the country held benefits. A speaker's bureau visited campuses from Smith to Stanford. Dick Gregory gave benefit performances, while the SNCC Freedom Singers drove an old station wagon from concert to concert, earning $5,000 a week. James Baldwin, then the most highly touted black writer in America, sent out a personal appeal to thousands, and the National Council of Churches agreed to bankroll two training sessions in Ohio. By the end of March, SNCC had raised $97,000. Yet some staffers were still going weeks without pay. More mailings were needed. More fund-raisers. More money.

SNCC's *New York Times* ad drew hate mail—"Niggers . . . Beatnicks . . . NIGGER LOVERS"—but it also tapped America's rising concern about a state long neglected or dismissed. For several years after the uproar over Emmett Till's lynching, hardly any news had come from Mississippi. But the bloody riots at Ole Miss, the shocking assassination of Medgar Evers, and the daring of the summer project had turned Mississippi into America's hotbed of civil rights. Even if most Americans felt Mississippi's problems were not their business, hundreds responded to SNCC's appeal. An interracial women's group in Harvey, Illinois, sent $25. A California woman sent a box of pencils, asking, "Would you please give these to Negro children under 10. . . . Tell them each one was touched with love and understanding." A Manhattan lawyer gave $25 "for the good work that you are doing." A clergyman from Yazoo City, a Mississippi town SNCC thought too dangerous to organize, sent five dollars. Those who could not give money sent books.

The previous October, a *Harper's* article on SNCC asked readers to send used books to "Robert Moses, 708 Avenue N, Greenwood, Mississippi." Within three months, enough arrived to open Freedom House libraries in Greenwood and Meridian. In the latter city, New Yorker Rita Schwerner and her husband, Mickey, working for the Congress of Racial Equality (CORE), were managing a library of ten thousand books. Kids were checking out fifty a day, Rita reported. Now, with more than two dozen Freedom Schools planned for summer, more books were needed. When another call went out, boxes of tattered books were shipped to Mississippi. A New Hampshire woman sent forty-five cartons, mostly histories and dog-eared copies of *Reader's Digest*. She also sent two dollars and an apology: "I'm sorry it isn't more but a relatively poor school teacher doesn't have too much." At the University of Minnesota, a teaching assistant persuaded his class to turn in their texts at term's end, then sent multiple copies of *Black Like Me* and *The Other America*. School committees in California, Arkansas, and the Bronx held book drives and sent the collections to Mississippi. By June, project offices overflowed with books, enough to fill every Freedom School library, assuming school buildings could be found. SNCC staffers began combing black communities for Freedom School sites, convincing church deacons to offer their small rectories or locating abandoned shacks that eager volunteers could refurbish into classrooms.

With money and books coming in, planners solicited other materials they would need that summer—typewriters, mimeograph machines, blackboards, bulletin boards, and office supplies. "It would be very difficult for us to get too much of anything," one appeal letter said. Next on the agenda was publicity. Though known as community organizers, SNCC staffers were also masters at public relations, or as they called it, "hooking people up." Media targets, national and local, were pinpointed. Each new press release was sent to the AP, UPI, the *New York Times*. . . . Before heading for Ohio, volunteers were urged to contact hometown papers—"The mass media are always interested in local angles." To ensure widespread publicity throughout the summer, each volunteer gave SNCC ten contacts likely to run news of a "local girl" or "area man" working in Mississippi. With publicity covered, SNCC then reached out to the power brokers of American culture.

In the year leading up to Freedom Summer, SNCC had convinced several celebrities to cancel appearances in Mississippi to protest its lockstep segregation. The "no-shows" were an eclectic group, including trumpeter Al Hirt, baseball player Stan Musial, the stars of *Bonanza*, and the entire lineup of ABC's folk music show *Hootenanny*. Come spring, SNCC continued its celebrity outreach, sending summer project brochures to big names known for supporting civil rights: Sidney Poitier, Leonard Bernstein, Frank Sinatra, Tony Bennett, the folksinger Odetta, Langston Hughes, Ella Fitzgerald, Sammy Davis Jr., Burt Lancaster, Van Cliburn, Lena Horne, Thelonious Monk. . . . Meanwhile COFO contacted more than a hundred professors and deans, "for we think it is important for the best minds in the country to know what is happening in Mississippi." The "best minds" were invited to observe Freedom Schools or advise research projects. Among the invited: author Irving Howe, *Lonely Crowd* sociologist David Riesman, black historian John Hope Franklin, southern historian C. Vann Woodward, and noted intellectuals Hannah Arendt, Bruno Bettelheim, Herbert Marcuse, John Kenneth Galbraith, and Harvard professor Henry Kissinger. None accepted the invitation, but SNCCs were accustomed to rejection. The outreach continued.

Early that spring, Bob Moses formed "Friends of Freedom in Mississippi." The ad hoc group of civil rights leaders and celebrities soon wrote President Lyndon Johnson. Calling Mississippi "a virtual police state," the Friends of Freedom warned of "a clear and present danger" of violence that summer, and urged federal protection for volunteers. Receiving no answer, SNCC took its appeal closer to the White House—within a few blocks.

On June 8, a distinguished panel gathered at the National Theater on Pennsylvania Avenue. Seated beneath the glittering chandeliers of the stately old theater, the panel included authors Joseph Heller and Paul Goodman, Harvard psychiatrist Robert Coles, and various educators. With grim faces, panelists listened to Fannie Lou Hamer recount her savage beating in jail. "I can say there will be a hot summer in Mississippi," Hamer said, "and I don't mean the weather." Elizabeth Allen, widow of Louis Allen, told of the murders of her husband and Herbert Lee. Panelists were shocked. Hadn't anyone been charged? "They don't arrest white people in Mississippi," Allen's widow replied. "They arrest Negroes, but they don't do anything to white people." A stocky farmer named Hartman Turnbow charmed the group with his sweet Mississippi drawl, then told how his house in Tchula was firebombed after he tried to register. Again, wasn't anyone arrested? "I was," Turnbow replied. Police had charged him with arson. After the hearing, the panel wrote to LBJ describing "incidents of brutality and terror we scarcely believed could have happened in the United States. . . . children beaten . . . people shot . . . men murdered for no other offense than seeking to vote." Citing threats to human life and to "the moral integrity of this country," panelists urged the president to send federal marshals, to hold hearings, to enforce voting rights. The president did not respond. In private, LBJ's special counsel mocked requests for protection, finding it "nearly incredible that those people who are voluntarily sticking their heads into the lion's mouth would ask for somebody to come down and shoot the lion." Freedom Summer planners, having expected little from the president, turned to each other for support.

Two days after the D.C. hearing, on a sweltering evening in Atlanta, SNCC convened a final meeting to discuss the looming summer. Everything seemed set. Money had come in and rolled out. Books were stacked up, ready to fill Freedom Schools. The "Sojourner Motor Fleet," dozens of beat-up old cars and a handful of new white Plymouths, was ready to drive volunteers from site to site. SNCC, COFO, and CORE, though they would quarrel over details all summer, had their territories—who would coordinate what in which region. (Martin Luther King's Southern Christian Leadership Conference approved of the summer project but was not involved. The NAACP still disapproved, its leader saying, "We're sitting this one out.") And despite threats of retaliation, hundreds of blacks across Mississippi had agreed to open their homes to volunteers. Now, two dozen people crammed into a basement around a table strewn with papers and pitchers of iced tea. For the next several hours, SNCCs wrestled lingering doubts to one last draw.

Faces at the table were anxious, worn, weighted with thoughts of mortality. This was new ground. The summer project was far scarier than anything SNCC had ever dared. What might go wrong? What had they not anticipated? Should they send volunteers to southwest Mississippi, where the Klan was most vicious? The danger had to be weighed against the "danger to local Negroes if we don't work there." Perhaps Natchez, they decided, but definitely not McComb. Not yet. Talk then turned to nonviolence. SNCC's founding faith—"through nonviolence, courage displaces fear; love transforms hate"—was breaking down. The Greenwood SNCC office, Bob Moses now learned, had a few guns. No one was preaching violence, but shouldn't an office firebombed and sprayed with bullets be able to defend itself? The argument lasted nearly an hour. Mississippi was explosive—blacks arming themselves, whites "more convinced than ever that they can kill a Negro and get away with it." Wasn't it time to fight back? How long would SNCC "lead people into the fire, then ask them to sing a song and return to church?" Long silences brought only one consensus—death would hover over Mississippi all summer.

Finally, a deeply religious woman many times jailed and once shot spoke up. All heads turned to the slight, somber Prathia Hall. "No one can be rational about death," Hall began. "For the first time we are facing that this may be the last time. We are fighting because we want life to be worth living. . . . When the kids in Birmingham were killed, I wanted to pick up a gun until I realized that by destroying lives we don't preserve them." The answer, Hall said, lay not just in nonviolence but in national awareness. "We must bring the reality of our situation to the nation. Bring our blood onto the White House door. If we die here, it's the whole society which has pulled the trigger by its silence." Consensus was finally reached. SNCC would not discourage locals from self-defense, which, Moses said, "is so deeply ingrained in rural southern America that we as a small group can't affect it." But SNCC staffers "have committed ourselves not to carry guns." Weapons in the Greenwood office would be removed. No SNCCs would be armed that summer.

The meeting lasted until early morning. Race proved the thorniest issue. Would white volunteers take over from locals? Should they be allowed any authority at all? "When whites come into a project," one man said, "the ego of Negroes is destroyed." But Ella Baker objected. Since forming SNCC in 1960, Baker had seen her lifelong ideals taken up by the young organizers she often called "the kids." But the kids were quarreling now, arguing over black and white. Believing in consensus, Baker usually let her protégés argue on, but now she spoke up. Might it be time, she suggested, "to take the revolution one step further?" "We have a responsibility to live up to an agreement," she added. "The agreement is not that the white volunteers are coming as emissaries to the white community. One of the reasons we're going into Mississippi is that the rest of the United States has never felt much responsibility for what happens in the Deep South. If we can simply let the concept that the rest of the nation bears responsibility for what happens in Mississippi sink in, then we will have accomplished something." The meeting concluded with a financial report. SNCC had $11,600 in the bank. Bills totaled $17,600. Everything—money, time, energy, and spirit—had been spent on the summer project. Eleven days later, on the first day of summer, volunteers had been welcomed beyond all expectation. Yet no amount of spending, planning, or caution could stop the night from coming.

Evening came late on the longest day of the year. Adults rose from porches. Children were called home from their games. Twilight lingered as if, like the old blues lyric, it hated "to see that evenin' sun go down." Finally just after 8:00 p.m., the last pink filaments faded over the Mississippi River, taking with them the last welcomes of the day. Fireflies startled volunteers from out west who had never seen whole fields glitter. Despite such magic, fear crept over volunteers' host homes and over their souls. Night had come to Mississippi. Night so far south and so rural was darker than any the volunteers had seen, darker and warmer—a muggy greenhouse heat that stifled any hope of a breeze. And then there was the symphony of a southern night, bullfrogs throat-singing and crickets humming as if 10,000 volts pulsed through the trees. The constant *screeee* of cicadas blasted like a referee's whistle until a low *whoo-whoo* interrupted. And then the crickets again, and the whistle and the frogs and the heat—on into the night.

Night had a reputation in Mississippi. Volunteers had heard much about it, and none of what they heard was comforting. Night was when "things happened" here, when "riders" meant not Freedom Riders but night riders, no longer on horseback but in pickups, yet still seeding the darkness with terror. SNCC's safety handbook was explicit about night: "Do not stand in doorways *at night*. . . . No one should go anywhere alone, but certainly not in an automobile and certainly not *at night*." None were likely to flout these rules, but the Mississippi night could easily enter their new homes, their "safe" homes, where streets were pitch-black, where their mere presence put a bull's-eye on each house. Night had come, all the welcoming people were off the streets, and who knew what type of people were out, fired by a century-old rage.

Across Mississippi, in villages dotting the darkening landscape, locals cleaned up from Father's Day suppers, then settled in to watch TV—*The Ed Sullivan Show, Bonanza, Candid Camera*. In Batesville, Chris Williams and others were in the Miles backyard, arms linked, singing Freedom Songs. "Get on Board, Children" and "We'll Never Turn Back" kept fear at bay, yet when the songs were done, Robert Miles and "Junior" went inside and came out with shotguns. Mounting a flatbed truck, they sat, ready to fire at any car entering the driveway without giving the signal—headlights blinked three times. The scene was mirrored in host homes across Mississippi—dark-skinned men with guns sitting in driveways, on porches, standing guard beneath a sparkling blanket of stars. From inside, volunteers parted curtains and peered into the blackness. Then, weary from the amazing day, they went to bed and tried, for all the mosquitoes, all the sticky heat, all the shrill sounds of night, to get a little sleep.

Night found Muriel Tillinghast upstairs in the project office in Greenville—alone. She was just eight blocks from the Mississippi River, but so far from home and so far south that it made her tremble. Since she had crossed into Mississippi on the midnight bus that turned from singing to silence, the quaking in her stomach had worsened. Riding south along Highway 61, the blues highway whose escape route she was traveling in reverse, she had watched others step off the bus and into the early morning. Town by town, winding through the Delta, she had said good-bye to old friends from Howard and new ones from Ohio. "It was so quick," she recalled. "Bye, see you later. Ummm, I hope I *will* see you later." Shortly after 8:00 a.m., her turn had come. The bus rattled through the empty streets of downtown Greenville, past churches and cafés, drugstores and parks, before reaching the "colored" section. As if she had crossed into another country, Muriel saw sidewalks cracked and broken, houses suddenly smaller, and a slipshod sadness pervading the streets. When she and a half dozen others were dropped off at 901½ Nelson Street, sheer terror sent Muriel straight upstairs into the

office. There she stayed, in cluttered rooms above a dry cleaner's—all day.
While other volunteers were welcomed into homes, Muriel huddled inside,
terrified by just being in "the black hole" of Mississippi.

White Greenville, a mile south along the mounded levee, was a thriving
city, but black Greenville was like no place Muriel had ever seen. Decades
earlier, Nelson Street had been the living, pulsing heart of the black community, attracting top blues singers and inspiring a song, the "Nelson Street
Blues." But by 1964 the street was just a shadow of itself, with just a drugstore, a few juke joints, and some boarded-up blues clubs clinging to life. To a
young woman from Washington, D.C., Nelson Street looked like a one-horse
town from an old Western movie. Muriel had seen poverty before. As part of
a Lutheran mission to Guyana, she had traveled into "the bush," met descendants of slaves living in bamboo huts, saw a child die of malnutrition. But
that was another country; this was her own. All her life she had heard about
the Mississippi her mother had fled, and now she was there. Gone were the
idealism, the solidarity that had sent her south. In their place was a primal
dread that recalled every tale of lynching she had ever read, every southern
horror she had ever heard. Greenville project director Charlie Cobb, the man
she had called each Sunday throughout the spring, might have calmed her,
but he was still in Ohio, preparing for the second training. And nothing any
fresh-faced volunteer said could convince Muriel to leave the office. "I was
petrified," she recalled.

Bob Moses had told her, "Mississippi can't be exaggerated." Now it did
not need to be. As night blackened office windows, as other volunteers went
to their homes, leaving her alone with a sleeping bag and a host of mice scurrying in the walls, her sense of alarm spiraled. Holed up in the office, she
asked herself hard questions. All right, she had always been the organizer,
the take-charge person. What now? How could she survive the summer?
How could she canvass door-to-door if she could not even force herself to
leave the office? Greenville, everyone assured her, was known for its moderation. Freshened by new people and new ideas that came along the river, it
had a reputation as "different." SNCCs said they would "rather get arrested
in Greenville than any town in Mississippi." Yet Muriel did not kid herself.

"Many Mississippi towns were predatory," she said. "Greenville was not
predatory, but it was reactionary. In West Hell the heat may not be boiling, but . . ." For a young black woman on her own a thousand miles from
home, accustomed to big cities with well-lit streets, regular traffic, pragmatic

people, night released inherited terrors. Night was when Muriel's grand-mother, walking from Texas to D.C., had taken refuge in barns to hide from the Klan. Night was when crosses were burned. Night had been her introduction to Mississippi, and now night had come again. "Mississippi has a black and inky night," she recalled. "Most of us were city kids. We'd never been in a rural area, certainly had never been in a southern area at night. I shed all the veneer of urban life and got down to basics—food, water, paying attention to even the smallest detail." All that first night alone in the office, the smallest details made her heart race. Each headlight flashing across a wall startled her. Each shout from the street sat her up. Each creak on the office stairs made her jump. Mississippi, it seemed, could be exaggerated.

To cope with the night, COFO had set up a warning system. All project offices were connected to the Jackson headquarters by a WATS (wide area transmission service) line. Long-distance calls in 1964 were expensive, reserved for emergencies, but the WATS line allowed unlimited calling for a monthly fee, enabling hourly check-ins from offices throughout Mississippi. Like a delicate spiderweb stretched across the state, COFO's phone network kept a vigil on the summer project, recoiling with each report of violence, relaxing with each report of calm. That first day, only minor flare-ups had been phoned in. Cops had detained a CBS camera crew in Ruleville. A Molotov cocktail exploded in a church basement near Jackson, causing minor damage. That was all. But night had just begun.

COFO's phone network also protected workers traveling through Mississippi. Anyone sent out from a Freedom House provided a precise return time and promised to phone in if delayed. If the hour came and went with no contact, calls went out to all area jails and police departments. Often these calls turned up a worker arrested and detained. Sometimes the call, alerting cops that someone was watching, prevented a beating. More often it did not. On June 21, as darkness fell, the alarm system was put to a test that justified the worst fears.

Shortly after noon that Sunday, three men had set out from Meridian, in the eastern part of the state, for the remote backwater of Longdale, Mississippi. These were the three who had left Ohio before dawn on Saturday to investigate a church burning in Neshoba County. Arriving in Meridian that Saturday night, they had slept, eaten breakfast, had their hair cut, then headed for the ash and twisted rubble that had once been the Mt. Zion Methodist Church. Before entering Neshoba County, a sparsely populated tangle of swamps and fields known to be thick with Klansmen, the group's leader had issued strict instructions. If they were not back by 4:00 p.m. that Sunday, the calls should begin. The hour came and went. The three did not return. Back in the Meridian office, a volunteer on her first day in Mississippi immediately called COFO in Jackson. But Bob Moses and all the rest were in Ohio, welcoming more volunteers. Without their seasoned fear as guide, the worker on the WATS line advised waiting an hour before calling jails. If the men had car trouble or had taken a longer route home, they would arrive soon. They would arrive soon.

During the endless hour that followed, the three men still did not return. At 5:00 p.m., the WATS line in Jackson rang again. The volunteer penciled phone numbers on paper.

Philadelphia Jail—656-3765
Meridian City Jail 485-9811
County 482-7262

Within minutes, phones rang in jails throughout Neshoba and surrounding counties. The men's names were Michael Schwerner, James Chaney, Andrew Goodman. None of the jail clerks admitted having the three in custody, nor any record of their arrest. Philadelphia police "said they knew nothing at all about the case," that the Neshoba County sheriff was visiting his wife in the hospital and could not be reached. The wait continued. Six p.m. Seven. Seven thirty. Night descended. More calls brought the same answers. The black ribbon roads of Neshoba County were quiet. Volunteers knew nothing about the disappearance, yet a mounting dread was spreading among staffers across the state.

Back in Meridian, Sam Block, whose courage in standing up to Greenwood cops was the stuff of SNCC lore, went to the local jail. Everyone knew Block would settle for no nonsense, but he returned with no news. Eight p.m. They would arrive soon. Pickups began circling the office. The grinding of engines and shouts of "Nigger lovers!" unsettled the steamy, disheveled rooms more than usual. The next hour was even longer. Volunteers and locals, black and white, sat on desks, on floors, waiting, waiting. Some played Ping-Pong in a back room, the click-clock of paddles only tightening the tension. A few walked down the street to get coffee. A volunteer just arrived from Massachusetts read *All Quiet on the Western Front*, its wartime terror seeming to fit the moment. Others just sat beneath a slow ceiling fan. Sweat darkened shirts and blouses. Nine p.m. Should they call Schwerner's wife, Rita, who was also in Ohio? They had to call someone. They called SNCC in Atlanta. Staffer Mary King began posing as an *Atlanta Constitution* reporter, making her own calls to county jails in Mississippi. Still no trace.

Shortly after 10:00 p.m., a law student taking over the WATS line phoned an FBI agent at his home in Jackson. The student gave the agent the three names and where they had been traveling, then demanded an immediate investigation. The agent said only, "Keep me informed of what happens." Half an hour later, the CORE office contacted the FBI in Meridian. The agent listened to frantic concerns, just listened. He listened during a second call at 11:00 p.m. and listened some more at midnight. Finally he said he was going to bed. The FBI was not a police force, he said. The wait continued.

Fears were deepening like darkness itself when the first day of Freedom Summer ended. Chris Williams was asleep in Batesville. Muriel Tillinghast was awake and alone amid the shifting shadows of the Greenville office. The rest of the volunteers, having enjoyed the most heartfelt welcome of their lives, were in host homes, asleep or else alert to each whisper of the night. None knew that three men they had seen back in Ohio just two days earlier were missing in Neshoba County. On into the early morning hours, the calls continued—to the Mississippi Highway Patrol, to the Justice Department in Washington, D.C., finally to fathers, mothers, a wife. No one offered any answers, any explanation. Michael Schwerner, James Chaney, and Andrew Goodman had vanished without a clue.

Before the sit-in, I had always hated the whites in Mississippi. Now I knew it was impossible for me to hate sickness. The whites had a disease, an incurable disease in its final stage. What were our chances against such a disease?

—Anne Moody, *Coming of Age in Mississippi*

CHAPTER FOUR
"The Decisive Battlefield for America"

A lone car trailing dust down a back road in Neshoba County could be seen for miles. Cars were common enough along the sunburned fields fifty miles inside the Alabama line, but not so common that a stranger's car would not be suspected. When a black man was driving, the suspicion doubled. And if he was a known civil rights worker, perhaps even driving with a white man, there was no way to measure the trouble ahead. So in the final weeks before he disappeared into the darkness of Neshoba County, James Chaney made his visits at night. Crossing the county line, he killed his headlights and punched the accelerator.

Neshoba County, its farmland framed by thickets, its gentle hills bottoming into bogs, had just 20,000 people spread over 570 square miles. Three-quarters were white, with less to fear from Negro voting than in the "black belt" of the Delta. Yet no Negro had registered in Neshoba County since 1955, and anyone who suggested it was time had several forces to reckon with. There was a big, beefy cowboy of a sheriff, elected on a campaign promise to "handle the niggers and the outsiders." There was the White Citizens' Council. There was the Klan, posting recruitment flyers and burning crosses that spring. And there were the good people of Neshoba County—merchants, laborers, teachers—all rather partial to the way things had been since their granddaddy's day.

Neshoba County's reputation reached far beyond its borders. Steeped in bootleg whiskey and the corruption it brought, Neshoba was known as "one of the wettest dry counties in the dry state of Mississippi." The county was also notorious as a backwater—provincial, hidebound, friendly to its own but just plain mean to strangers. Not many strangers came to "these parts," however. Growing up in Neshoba County, a native might pass a lifetime without meeting more than a few people from outside Mississippi. Whites who ventured north returned with stories of cold, crime-ridden cities where blacks were caged in ghettos, where "folks yah met on the street just didn't care whether yah lived or died." But blacks who fled north never came back, and those who stayed in Neshoba County learned to be invisible. "We don't bother no white folks and usually they don't pay no attention to us," one said. "We just live here and scratches it out." Blacks who thought differently had to keep quiet or keep moving.

Racing down dirt paths lit only by his parking lights and the moon, James Chaney often hit speeds of seventy-five or eighty. Though raised in adjacent Lauderdale County, Chaney knew Neshoba, knew every gully, every ditch, every shack where a black family was brave enough to "reddish to vote." Flying past swamps, skittering over rutted roads, Chaney's blue Ford wagon was a shadowy streak by moonlight. When he arrived at a dark cabin, Chaney cautiously stepped out and whistled. His white companion waited. A candle or kerosene lamp signaled that they had the right place. They entered and in the gloaming, talked about family, farming, and finally, voting. Leaving leaflets about registration classes in Meridian, they hopped in the station wagon and sped on. Throughout the spring of 1964, each night run continued for as long as Chaney could stand the tension. Then he would drive toward the county line as fast as fear could take him. Crossing into Lauderdale County, Chaney flipped on his headlights, slowed to a safe speed, and headed home.

In the nightmare hours of June 22, phone calls startled sleepers from Mississippi to Moscow. Three men were missing, vanished, gone. SNCC in Atlanta called the Justice Department three times. Each call deepened concern, until by morning John Doar gave the FBI power to investigate. But the FBI agent in Jackson still refused to act. On the Ohio campus, a stunned Rita Schwerner lay curled on a cot, making her own calls. In New York, CORE director James Farmer was awakened at 2:30 a.m. A few hours later, a call alerted attorney William Kunstler. "You don't know me," the caller said, "but my son, Mickey, told me to call you if he ever needed a lawyer." In Moscow, a UPI reporter phoned Dick Gregory. The comedian canceled his goodwill tour and headed for Mississippi, where phones were ringing all over the state. Another call to Meridian: no word of the three. A call to the Mississippi Highway Patrol—without a sheriff's order, no missing persons bulletin could be issued for seventy-two hours. More calls. To sheriffs. To Washington, D.C. To the FBI in Jackson . . .

At 6:55 a.m., the first breakthrough came with a follow-up call to the Neshoba County jail. The jailer's wife, having earlier denied seeing the three, now admitted they had been in custody. Brought in about 4:00 p.m. Sunday, James Chaney had been booked for speeding, Michael Schwerner and Andrew Goodman held "for investigation." But all three had been released at 6:00 p.m. The news sent shudders through COFO's phone network. Freedom Summer planners had expected something like this, but on the first day of the project?

Volunteers still did not know. In Greenville, Muriel Tillinghast, hollow-eyed from sleeping on the floor, welcomed others to the office she would refuse to leave all that week. In Batesville, Chris Williams had another down-home breakfast and, with orders come from COFO to "lay low," wondered when the work would begin. Meanwhile in Ohio, a second group of trainees was about to hear the most chilling of all SNCC stories from Mississippi. At 9:30 a.m. Bob Moses stood before an auditorium of fresh faces—Freedom School teachers—explaining Mississippi from a blackboard map. Calling the state "The Closed Society," he added, "Mississippi is closed, locked. We think the key is the vote." He paused, looked at his feet, then resumed. "There is an analogy to *The Plague,* by Camus. The country isn't willing yet to admit it has the plague, but it pervades the whole society." Just then, three SNCCs entered and called Moses over. When he returned to the stage, his voice was even softer, his manner still more grave.

"Yesterday morning, three of our people left Meridian, Mississippi, to investigate a church burning in Neshoba County. They haven't come back and we haven't had any word from them." The auditorium rippled with alarm. In the confusion, a waiflike woman with dark, closely cropped hair and black-rimmed glasses strode to the stage. Rita Schwerner asked volunteers to group by home states and send telegrams to their congressmen, demanding an FBI investigation. When someone asked how to spell the names of the missing, she strode to the blackboard and erased half of Mississippi. Then, as if it were not her husband but some stranger who had vanished, she calmly wrote the names in block letters. The clicking of the chalk could be heard to the back of the auditorium. Suddenly there was no need to "scare the crap" out of anyone. Each face bore a primal fear—this could happen to *me.* While volunteers grouped, Moses slipped outside and slumped down on a step overlooking a spreading lawn. Occasionally a friend approached to give him a hug. One whispered, "You are not responsible for this," but Moses sat there for hours.

Within a few days, three photos would be seen around the nation—Goodman posed with a choirboy innocence; Chaney, his kindly face tilted; Schwerner, goateed, with a wry smile. Seen over and over, the trio would soon seem familiar to volunteers, as if they knew these three well. Some would talk of meeting "Andy" in Ohio, having had dinner with Mickey, or hearing Chaney talk to their group. Yet this morning, there were no faces, no trace of the men—just names on a blackboard.

> JAMES CHANEY—CORE STAFF
> MICHAEL SCHWERNER—CORE STAFF
> ANDREW GOODMAN—SUMMER PROJECT VOLUNTEER
> NESHOBA COUNTY—DISAPPEARED

In his five months in Mississippi, some had come to revile Mickey Schwerner as "that Communist Jew Nigger lover." Yet those who knew him were struck by his kindness, his easygoing manner, his lack of hatred for anyone, black or white. He was "full of life and ideas," "the gentlest man I have ever known." A coworker in Meridian paid him the compliment he would have cherished most: "More than any white person I have ever known he could put a colored person at ease." Of average size and height, usually dressed in a gray sweatshirt, jeans, and black sneakers, Mickey Schwerner loved W. C. Fields, a good game of poker, and the hapless New York Mets. Raised by liberal parents—his father, a wig manufacturer, was a member of the War Resisters League—Mickey grew from a high school beatnik into a veterinary student before becoming a dedicated social worker with a degree from Cornell. By the summer of 1963, he was deeply involved in the social services of lower Manhattan. Each day he rose at 6:00 a.m. to work on civil rights with CORE. He spent afternoons helping teens in a social settlement on the Lower East Side. After dinner, he made home visits or attended meetings, often till midnight. His new wife, Rita, shared his dedication. While still a student at Queens College, she tutored middle school students, did her own work for CORE, and joined her husband on picket lines, where both were arrested for protesting segregated unions.

During the summer of 1963, as racial violence seared America, the civil rights movement captivated the Schwerners. That August, Mickey took teens to the March on Washington, yet it was not Martin Luther King but the Birmingham church bombing a few weeks later that drew him south. "I am now so thoroughly identified with the civil rights struggle that I have an emotional need to offer my services in the South," the twenty-four-year-old Schwerner wrote on his application for CORE in Mississippi. "I would feel guilty and almost hypocritical if I did not give full time."

In January 1964, Mickey and Rita Schwerner sublet their Brooklyn Heights apartment, left their cocker spaniel, Gandhi, with friends, and drove their '59 VW to Jackson. Within days, they were in Meridian, the first white civil rights workers to penetrate Mississippi's second largest city. Sleeping on cots, showering at a local black hotel, they lived less on their meager salaries than off the infinite energy of their ideals. Each day they tackled the job of turning a filthy old office into a Freedom House. Rita swept, cleaned, and sewed long, blue curtains while Mickey and an eager volunteer named James Chaney did repairs and built bookcases. By late February the house was bustling. A dozen or more kids showed up for Saturday story hours. On Tuesday and Thursday evenings, adults came to voter registration classes. Most afternoons, teenagers dropped by just to be with the Schwerners.

Mickey loved to joke and jive with the kids he called "Mississippi's best hope," taking them on drives in his VW and talking about freedom. Yet some blacks in Meridian were not ready for this northern couple's push on civil rights. A high school principal threw Mickey off campus, but he and Rita went back and leafleted a basketball game, drawing more teens to their Freedom House. When the Schwerners talked about removing "Colored Only" signs, CORE thought they were moving too fast, but they were allowed to organize boycotts of downtown stores that refused to hire black clerks. By April, they were fixtures on Meridian's black side of town. "We're actually pretty lucky here," Mickey told a reporter. "I think they're going to leave us alone."

But in "Whites Only" Mississippi, the Schwerners could not have aroused more outrage. They had only been in the state a few days when a cop told them, "I just want you to know you're about as welcome here as hair on a biscuit." Soon they were spotted as not just outsiders, not just Jews, but "mixers." Rita was even seen talking with black men. And although it would have fit well in Greenwich Village, Mickey's goatee was a red flag in the clean-cut South. He had shaved it before leaving Brooklyn, but grew it back in March, saying anyone who hated him would need no excuse. Black kids loved Mickey's goatee and called him "Mitch" after TV's bearded choral leader Mitch Miller, but the beard enraged some whites, providing the nickname Mickey first heard when arrested for picketing that May—"You must be that Communist-Jew nigger lover they call 'Goatee.'" By then, threats had become part of daily life. Callers to the Freedom House accused Rita of sleeping with Negroes. Others chanted, "That Jewboy is dead! That Jewboy is dead!" Electricity was cut off several times, water occasionally, and the Schwerners moved again and again when host families sensed their homes targeted. Mississippi's Sovereignty Commission had already given their license plate number to police departments throughout the state.

In late May, Mickey told his father he was "a marked man." A few days later, the Schwerners took their phone off the hook. Rita was sometimes homesick and convinced that if she got pregnant, they would leave, but Mickey was rooted. "I belong right here in Mississippi," he told a friend. "Nothing threatens peace among men like the idea of white supremacy. Nowhere in the world is the idea of white supremacy more firmly entrenched, or more cancerous, than in Mississippi. . . . So this is the decisive battleground for America, and every young American who wants to have a part in the decision should be here."

Anchoring the Schwerners' commitment was the commitment they inspired in others. James Chaney, shy and self-effacing, was as opposite the gregarious Mickey Schwerner as their skin color. Because James's middle name was Earl, his family called him J. E., but Schwerner always called him "Bear," and the two were inseparable. "Mickey could count on Jim to walk through hell with him," a Freedom House regular said. After the army rejected him for having asthma, Chaney had drifted, working odd jobs, spending months unemployed, then helping his father plaster houses. But when his father left home, the two fought, and Chaney stormed off the job. Committed to civil rights since high school, he found his way into the Schwerners' circle. It felt like coming home.

"Mama," he said, "I believe I done found an organization that I can be in and do something for myself and somebody else, too."

But Fannie Lee Chaney, raising five children on $28 a week, knew Mississippi better. "Ain't you afraid of this?" she asked.

"Naw, Mama, that's what's the matter now," Chaney said. "Everybody's scared."

By the time he started his night runs into Neshoba County, Chaney was a CORE staffer. At twenty-one, he was also on the verge of being a father, but he would not be around for the birth. The day his daughter was born, he was driving with Mickey and Rita to the Ohio training. There the three agreed that volunteer Andrew Goodman was the man they wanted to start a Freedom School in Neshoba County. And when they heard that the church set to host the school had burned to the ground, Schwerner and Chaney returned to Mississippi with their new recruit.

Before his face appeared on an FBI poster, twenty-year-old Andrew Goodman might have been a poster boy for youthful altruism. With passions ranging from drama to poetry to the Holocaust, Goodman was, his mother recalled, "a born activist." Like Mickey Schwerner, he had attended the progressive Walden School on Manhattan's Upper West Side. Like the Schwerners, the Goodmans were a liberal family. Their dinner guests included such McCarthy-era pariahs as Alger Hiss, Zero Mostel, and their own attorney, who had defended the blacklisted Hollywood Ten. While in high school, Andrew Goodman had taken a bus to Appalachia to report on impoverished coal miners. In college, he shifted majors and campuses until settling at Queens College to study drama. He was planning to spend the summer of 1964 building a school in Mexico, but when he heard Fannie Lou Hamer speak at his college, he came home and told his parents he just had to go to Mississippi.

When his father asked why, Goodman's idealism poured out: "Because this is the most important thing going on in the country! If someone says he cares about people, how can he not be concerned about this?" Carolyn Goodman, a psychologist, felt her son might as well have said, "I want to go off to war," but she managed to respond that Mississippi seemed like "a great idea." His father realized, "We couldn't turn our backs on the values we had instilled in him at home." Robert Goodman, a civil engineer, offered to provide the $150 in expenses, but Andy took a job loading trucks. Two months later, he was packing his duffel bag. As hopeful as his photo suggested, Goodman packed a sweater for a summer in Mississippi. "I'm scared," he told a friend. "I'm scared but I'm going." When he left for Ohio, Carolyn Goodman slipped iodine and bandages in her son's bag. In Ohio, Goodman was originally slated to work in Vicksburg but was recruited by the Schwerners. Once reassigned, he called his parents. "Don't worry," he told them, "I'm going to a CORE area. It's safer." And on June 21, when he awoke in Mississippi, he wrote home:

> Dear Mom and Dad,
>   I have arrived safely in Meridian, Miss. This is a wonderful town, and the weather is fine. I wish you were here. The people in this city are wonderful, and our reception was very good.
>   All my love,
>   Andy

At noon that Sunday, the three men set out for Neshoba County in the same blue Ford wagon Chaney drove on his night runs. Before they left, twelve-year-old Ben Chaney, whom Schwerner called "Cub," was crying and asking to go with his big brother. Chaney told Ben to be patient. When he came back that afternoon, they'd go driving. Ben began waiting.

By late Monday morning, the men had been missing for eighteen hours. In Jackson, word had just come from Philadelphia. Spotted in jail at 9:00 p.m. Sunday, the three men appeared bruised and battered. COFO again called the FBI. Hearing of the alleged brutality, the agent in Jackson finally acted— he called his New Orleans office. SNCC was growing desperate. What about an air search? Roadblocks? An all-points bulletin? Mississippi was heating up in ways that had little to do with the humidity. All that morning, project offices were besieged with angry calls—"Nigger Lover!"; "Communist!"; "Go to hell!" After their warm welcomes in black communities, volunteers were finding first encounters with whites strange and sinister. Several were approached by nattily dressed college students. Calling themselves the Association of Tenth Amendment Conservatives (ATAC), the students talked on and on about states' rights and the danger of minorities "issuing dictatorial orders." But other whites did more than talk. Volunteers crossing the tracks to the white side of town were drilled by hate stares and startled by the loathing they would endure all summer.

In Clarksdale, at the north end of the Delta, a volunteer from Los Angeles was talking to blacks when a cop pulled up.

"What're you doing here?"

"I'm helping to register voters."

"Don't you know that the niggers don't want any help? Don't you know you're not wanted here? What are you son-of-a-bitch bastards doing here anyway?" When the volunteer tried to answer, he was ordered into the police car, where two snarling men cursed him: "Your mother's not fit to work in a nigger whorehouse." Jailed, denied phone calls, the man was finally released and told to get the hell out of Mississippi. Clarksdale, the sheriff said, had a hundred deputized citizens armed with billy clubs, "just waiting for the signal to split some head open. . . . Some folks are going to get hurt, maybe some killed, but then things will settle down."

All that frantic Monday, despite mounting fear, the FBI in Jackson refused to investigate. SNCC was outraged but not surprised. Since Bob Moses had first come to Mississippi, SNCCs had knocked on federal doors, asking simply that the law be enforced. They were met with a palpable indifference. John F. Kennedy had no use for SNCC, considering its members "sons of bitches" who "had an investment in violence." Robert Kennedy, hoping to steer civil rights from the streets to the courts, had his Justice Department file some two dozen voter discrimination lawsuits in Mississippi, but all were tangled in appeals or overturned by Mississippi judges, one of whom ranted against "niggers on a voter drive." Frustrated at every turn, Moses had filed his own suit. *Moses v. Kennedy and Hoover* listed the long litany of brutality, demanding that the attorney general and FBI director "arrest any Mississippi law enforcement officer interfering with Negro voting." Moses lost the case and appealed.

The federal record on protecting civil rights workers was even worse. John Doar had investigated threats against Herbert Lee and Louis Allen but refused protection. And both had been gunned down. Robert Kennedy delayed protection for the Freedom Riders, even after their bus was fire-bombed. His request for a "cooling off period" became a SNCC joke. But SNCC reserved its deepest cynicism for the FBI. SNCCs often saw FBI agents on the fringes of some violent mob—taking notes. Taking notes while Bob Zellner was nearly killed by a mob in McComb, taking notes while a police dog tore at Bob Moses in Greenwood, taking notes while cops lashed out in Canton or Jackson. FBI director J. Edgar Hoover did not apologize. Convinced the civil rights movement was infused with Communists, Hoover was already eavesdropping on Martin Luther King, whom he considered "a true Marxist-Leninist from the top of his head to the tips of his toes." When pressed about the FBI's hands-off approach, Hoover declared, "We do not wet nurse those who go down to reform the South."

A year before Freedom Summer, SNCC's frustration had threatened to mar the elegiac mood of the March on Washington. Speaking before Martin Luther King, SNCC chairman John Lewis had planned to ask, "Which side is the federal government on?" Lewis was talked out of making the charge. By the time Freedom Summer began, a sign in SNCC offices throughout Mississippi summed up the cynicism.

> There is a street in Itta Bena called Freedom
> There is a town in Mississippi called Liberty
> There is a department in Washington called Justice.

SNCC and COFO had asked—pleaded—that summer volunteers receive federal protection. There had been no answer. And three men had vanished the first night. With hundreds of potential targets now in the state, who knew how many more would soon set out down some Mississippi back road and not come back?

Not until a full day after Goodman, Schwerner, and Chaney were due back in Meridian did federal inertia finally end. Toward 6:00 p.m. Monday, Robert Kennedy ordered a full FBI investigation under the provisions of the Lindbergh kidnapping act. President Johnson was alerted. The Mississippi Highway Patrol issued a missing persons bulletin, and journalists across America and Europe began checking maps, locating Neshoba County, and booking flights. At 6:30 p.m., Walter Cronkite broke the news to the nation: "Good evening. Three young civil rights workers disappeared in Mississippi on Sunday night near the central Mississippi town of Philadelphia, about fifty miles northeast of Jackson." While Cronkite spoke, FBI agents drove north from New Orleans. Mississippi had simmered for another day. Night had come again. The muggy blanket descended, the electric symphony crackled through the trees, and in one small town that would lead all of Mississippi in violence that summer, the night riders came out.

SNCC had decided not to send volunteers to McComb. After further discussion, Klan-infested Pike County, where blacks had been disappearing all spring, was deemed too dangerous. Shortly after 10:00 p.m., SNCC's decision suddenly seemed wise. Bolting upright in bed, a black woman looked out her front window to see a shiny new Chevy skid to a halt. A man jumped out and tossed a package. As the woman scrambled to the back of her house, the explosion leveled the porch, blew in the front door, and littered her bed with glass. Moments later, another bomb, then another, rocked homes of longtime civil rights supporters. The following morning, while blacks surveyed the rubble, the eyes of America turned to a remote corner of the Magnolia State and to a town whose name meant "Brotherly Love."

When it awoke on the last morning of its past, Philadelphia (pop. 5,017) looked much like any other Mississippi hamlet. Rising above a two-story sky-line, dozens of short, sharp steeples aimed at the heavens. Smokestacks from three sawmills belched black clouds. Downtown merchants pushed brooms outside the Ben Franklin Five and Dime, the A & P, and the Piggly-Wiggly. Along covered sidewalks, clusters of sun-shriveled old men sat on wooden benches, smoking, spitting, watching their town awaken. Pickups passed as if on parade. A farmer in overalls waved from a tractor. Mothers walked with crew-cut boys in tow. By 9:00 a.m. the sun baked the gravel streets, giving the old men no reason to believe June 23 would be different from any other Tuesday. Some may have seen network reports about the three men said to have disappeared in their county—more "Northern-managed news." Whatever the problem was, things would soon go back to normal. "Normal" in Philadelphia was as homespun as the upcoming Neshoba County Dairy Princess contest; "normal" was as timeless as the courthouse. With its Corinthian columns and Confederate statue, the brick building was the bedrock of the town some called "the other Philadelphia." Yet there was still another Philadelphia within this one.

Down a snaking dirt road and across the railroad tracks stood Independence Quarters. There, in tiny homes with boarded-up windows, Philadelphia blacks "scratched it out." Independence Quarters had its own school, its own churches, its own version of Mississippi. And when word spread that three men were missing in Neshoba County, few in "the quarters" doubted the story. Folks said it must have something to do with the burning of that church. The church that was supposed to host a Freedom School. The church that a young CORE worker had visited a few weeks back.

White Philadelphia had not heard of the church burning. A local bank president had convinced editors to kill the story, and it had not run in a single

Mississippi paper. Those few who knew considered it typical—niggers fighting over this or that, burning their own church. That, too, would all blow over. Things always did in Philadelphia, which, having no antebellum mansions, no battlefields or plantations, prided itself on its hospitality and its "fair-minded, Christian people." Yet that was about to change, starting with the people.

The old men spotted the invaders first. By 10:00 a.m., whichever way they looked, they saw strangers with sunglasses and briefcases, white shirts and skinny ties. Each man drove a dark sedan with a whiplike antenna, and each seemed nervous, scribbling notes, scanning the town square, avoiding eye contact. The old men huddled on benches, sharing fears instilled by grandparents, fears of Yankees, carpetbaggers, and a war that had never really ended. Now the nightmare was starting again. Now, in numbers no one in Mississippi could have imagined, the FBI had invaded Neshoba County.

All Tuesday morning, the FBI set up operations. At the Delphia Courts Motel, a right angle of dilapidated rooms fronting a concrete lot, Room 18 became FBI headquarters. Behind city hall, agents installed a communications center and began erecting an antenna on the wide, squat water tower. After establishing radio contact with Washington, they set out to visit the police, the courthouse, and the jail. The jailer told agents she had fined James Chaney twenty dollars and released the three at 10:30 p.m. Deputy Sheriff Cecil Price, a brawny, moon-faced man with an "aw shucks" smile, said he had arrested the men, all right. He had last seen them on Sunday night, heading south on Highway 19 toward Meridian. He had watched their taillights disappear over a hill. Agents were soon driving along the rolling two-lane, stopping to peer into swamps that seemed eerily still. But by noon, swamp waters rippled as FBI helicopters swooped low, flapping laundry on clotheslines, sending chickens scurrying.

Back in town, as the temperature hit 100, tempers flared. Enraged men, arms waving, mouths like open scars, confronted reporters outside the courthouse. Didn't they know they were being duped? It was all a hoax! Those three boys just took off! And if agents knew what was good for them, they'd damn sure do likewise. Going house to house, agents met stone walls. No one would talk. No one would even listen. A hoax. Then toward 3:30 p.m., bulletins broke into radio and TV nationwide. The blue Ford had been found, not south of Philadelphia, where Deputy Price said he had watched its taillights vanish, but near the Choctaw Reservation, fifteen miles *north* of town.

Choctaw Indians fishing in a creek had spotted the smoldering wreckage. The head of the reservation called the FBI, whose agents waded in to find the car, sizzling hot, protruding from a blackberry thicket at the edge of the Bogue Chitto swamp. The car's interior was as black as an oven. A rear wheel was missing, but the license—H25 503—checked out. Towed from the swamp, its muffler dangling, its windshield blown out, the charred vehicle was hauled into town. Within minutes, word reached the White House.

Lyndon Johnson had learned of the summer project back in April. "They're sending them in by buses in the hundreds from all over the country to help 'em register," Johnson told Georgia senator Richard Russell. "And they're gonna try to get 'em all registered in Mississippi. And there're gonna be a bunch of killings." Yet heeding his aide's advice, the president had ignored all pleas for protection. Johnson had other pressing problems that Tuesday. He had to replace his ambassador to Vietnam, screen vice presidential candidates, and plan the ceremony to sign the Civil Rights Act. But all morning and into the afternoon, Mississippi kept coming up—in his press conference, in phone calls, in bulletins. Johnson was outraged by suggestions that he was not doing enough to find the missing men. "I asked Hoover two weeks ago, after talking to the Attorney General, to fill up Mississippi with FBI men and infiltrate everything he could," the president said. "I've asked him to put more men after these three kids. . . . I'm shoving in as much as I know how." At 3:00 p.m., Johnson's archrival Robert Kennedy met with the Goodmans and Nathan Schwerner, but the president did not want to follow suit. "I'm afraid that if I start house mothering each kid that's gone down there and that doesn't show up, that we'll have this White House full of people every day asking for sympathy." Finally, Johnson asked Nicholas Katzenbach, deputy assistant attorney general, what he thought had happened to the three.

"I think they got picked up by some of these Klan people, would be my guess."

"And murdered?"

"Yeah, probably. Or else they're just being hidden on one of those barns or something . . . and having the hell scared out of them. But I would not be surprised if they'd been murdered, Mr. President. Pretty rough characters." Katzenbach agreed the president should not see the parents. "I think you'd have a problem of every future one. . . . This is not going to be the only time this sort of thing will occur, I'm afraid." Toward 4:00 p.m., Johnson was on the phone with Senator James Eastland, who was calling from his plantation in Ruleville.

"I don't believe there's three missing," Eastland told LBJ. "I believe it's a publicity stunt." No Klan was active in Neshoba County, the senator lied. "There's no white organizations in that area of Mississippi. Who could possibly harm them?" The conversation was interrupted by a call from J. Edgar Hoover.

"Mr. President, I wanted to let you know we've found the car. . . . Now whether there are any bodies in the car, we won't know until we can get into the car ourselves . . . but I did want you to know. Apparently what's happened—these men have been killed."

"Well now, what would make you think they've been killed?" the president asked.

"Because of the fact that it is the same car that they were in in Philadelphia, Mississippi . . . ," Hoover answered. "This is merely an assumption that probably they were burned in the car. On the other hand, they may have been taken out and killed on the outside."

"Or maybe kidnapped and locked up."

"Well, I would doubt whether those people down there would give them even that much of a break."

Hoover called back an hour later, but the conversation was cut short when Carolyn and Robert Goodman were escorted into the Oval Office. With them was Nathan Schwerner. Frazzled, red-eyed from lack of sleep, the parents had flown from New York that morning. Hearing the president mention the car, Carolyn Goodman wanted to leap over the huge desk, shouting, "Are they all right?" LBJ hung up, stepped around the desk, and, towering over the slim blond woman, took her hand and broke the news. The "three kids" were still missing, he said. All the powers of the Justice Department and the Department of Defense were being thrown into the search. After twenty minutes, the families left, impressed that the president, as Carolyn Goodman recalled, "changed from a public figure . . . to a human being genuinely concerned about the life of my son."

That afternoon in Neshoba County, heat melted into thundershowers, curtailing the FBI search, but aftershocks continued to ripple across America. TV bulletins interrupted soap operas and quiz shows: Robert Kennedy was canceling a trip to Poland. The president was sending former CIA director

Allen Dulles to Jackson. More FBI agents were on their way. When night fell again, COFO's WATS line recorded local shock waves. Every report of harassment, every call about a late volunteer, stirred panic. And for the third night in a row, the terror ratcheted up another notch. Shots hit a black minister's home and a Negro café in Jackson. A firebomb struck a meeting hall on the Gulf Coast. Rumors spread through the coastal town of Moss Point— two black children had eaten poisoned candy thrown from a passing car. One was dead. In the Delta, whites chased reporters out of Ruleville, then drove through "the quarters" hurling bottles and Molotov cocktails.

On Wednesday morning, photos of the charred station wagon jutting from a Mississippi swamp accompanied front-page headlines across the nation: "Burned Car Clue in Hunt for Three Men" (*Washington Post*), "Dulles Will Direct Rights Trio Hunt" (*Los Angeles Times*), "Wreckage Raises New Fears over Fate of Missing Men" (*New York Times*). By noon, marchers were picketing federal buildings in Chicago, New York, and the nation's capital. At the NAACP national convention in Washington, D.C., members walked out to join the protests. Robert Kennedy went with Myrlie Evers, Medgar's widow, to shake hands with demonstrators. Back at the epicenter, police with shotguns, automatic weapons, and riot clubs circled the Neshoba County courthouse. All along the street, all through shops and stores, all up and down covered sidewalks, locals seethed with rage and denial.

"They had no business down here."

"COFO must have burned their own car to make the hoax look convincing. They're probably far out of the county laughing."

"This wouldn't have happened if they had stayed home where they belong."

"How long do you think we'd last in Harlem?"

Swarming with reporters, invaded by the FBI, "the other Philadelphia" was just a shot away from a full-blown race war. Shortly after noon, the trigger was cocked when a caravan of cars approached the Neshoba County line.

Fluttering like a mirage as it rolled along Highway 19, the caravan carried black leaders—CORE's James Farmer; SNCC's John Lewis; Dick Gregory, just back from the Soviet Union—and teenagers ready to search for bodies. All had been warned about Neshoba County. "Farmer, don't go over there," the head of the Mississippi State Police said. "That's one of the worst redneck areas in the state." The caravan crossed the county line. Beneath the blazing sun, the cars passed swamps, farms, and Calvary crosses by the pebbled roadside. At the Philadelphia city limits, the cars halted before a scene out of a cheap Western. Like some posse, Sheriff Lawrence Rainey and several men with shotguns stood across the road. Rainey, an enormous, paunchy man in a cowboy hat, with a wad of tobacco bulging his cheek, strode up to the lead car and loomed over it. "Where do you think you're goin'?" he asked Farmer.

Like most in Neshoba County, the sheriff mocked the disappearance. The three men were "hid somewhere trying to get a lot of publicity out of it, I figure." After spitting on the asphalt, Rainey told Farmer he would only meet with four men. The rest would have to wait by the highway. Moments later, Rainey's patrol car led a lone sedan into town. At the courthouse, the black men walked past glaring white faces, then rode a silent elevator to the sheriff's office. Inside, a slow ceiling fan kept the temperature just below ninety. The black men bristled, tense and indignant, but Rainey and Deputy Price seemed delighted by the attention, smirking and joking while county attorneys handled all questions.

Farmer demanded to visit the burned-out Mt. Zion Church. He was told he would need a search warrant. John Lewis insisted on seeing the burned Ford wagon. He was refused, lest he "destroy evidence." So there had been a crime, Lewis countered. "*If* there has been a crime," the lawyer said with a smile. "Those boys may have decided to go up north or someplace and have a short vacation. They'll probably be coming back shortly." Farmer mentioned his young volunteers, ready to search. Heads shook. Private property. Water moccasins. Trespassing. "We don't want anything to happen to you down here." After several brittle minutes, the black men were escorted outside, past the shotguns and sour faces, to the cars waiting at city limits. All were certain the smug sheriff and his smiling deputy knew exactly what had happened to the missing men.

Back in Meridian, as thunder rattled rooftops, a mass meeting crackled with anger. Dick Gregory offered $25,000—just arranged in a call to *Playboy* publisher Hugh Hefner—to anyone finding the missing men and those responsible. That evening, rain clouds parted to reveal an eclipsing moon. In small towns across the state, "redneck boys" roared through "Niggertowns," shouting, throwing bottles, daring anyone to mess with Mississippi.

Someone had miscalculated. Someone had not recognized how times had changed. Time was when a murder in Mississippi had stayed in Mississippi, when few even heard about the crime, when the rest of America went about its business, distanced by culture and geography. But that time had passed. It was 1964, and when three men disappeared in the most remote corner of the South's most rural state, the whole nation heard the news the next day. Whoever knew the whereabouts of Michael Schwerner, Andrew Goodman, and James Chaney must have been surprised to see what an old-fashioned Mississippi lynching—if that's what it had been—had unleashed. Because never had a disappearance in the Deep South sent such tremors through the nation. The alarm also paid unwelcome tribute to the planners of Freedom Summer. Their cynicism had been dead on. All the blacks murdered in Mississippi since Emmett Till had scarcely raised concerns beyond state borders. The killing of Herbert Lee had been reported in just one major newspaper; the murder of Louis Allen was found only on back pages. But when *whites* were killed . . . "It's a shame that national concern is aroused only after two white boys are missing," John Lewis told the press. SNCCs had expected as much, but someone in Mississippi had not.

By Thursday, even the president of the United States was counting the days. "I imagine they're in that lake," Johnson told an aide that afternoon. "It's my guess. Three days now." The rest of the nation watched and waited. The concern was for more than just three men. Murder had always marred America's self-image, but it had been an especially disfiguring year. The previous twelve months had seen Medgar Evers gunned down in his driveway, four little girls killed in a Birmingham church, the assassination in Dallas, and the televised murder of the alleged assassin. A strangler was on the loose in Boston, throttling innocent women. In New York that spring, Kitty Genovese had been murdered in full view of dozens of neighbors, who had not even called the police. Now came this news from Mississippi. What was America becoming? "We are basically a law abiding nation," President Johnson reminded Americans that week. But so long as three men were missing in Mississippi, the jury was still out.

Although the FBI had begun to move, although two hundred sailors from the Meridian Naval Air Station were preparing to join the search, SNCC had little faith in any federal investigation. "We need the FBI before the fact," Bob Moses said. "We have them now after the fact." SNCC had to conduct its own search. Shortly after the news reached Ohio, two cars left the leafy campus. Taking different routes lest both be halted by police, the drivers planned to rendezvous that Tuesday afternoon in Meridian. Crossing into

Mississippi, each team phoned in on schedule. "No word yet." One car was delayed outside Holly Springs by ATAC students lecturing about the Tenth Amendment. Still, it arrived on time. The other was . . . missing. More panic swept through the Meridian office, panic that continued all night and into Wednesday morning. When Stokely Carmichael and Charlie Cobb finally showed up, they told of another near miss. Their old Buick had broken down in Durant, a town "knowed for mean." Cops had not bought their cover— that they were schoolteachers headed for a Florida vacation. Carmichael was held overnight, but Cobb was told—at 10:00 p.m.—that he could go free. He refused, was thrown out of jail, and spent a terrifying night in the car, clutching a tire iron and "praying for sunrise." The following morning, Cobb bailed out Carmichael and they drove to Meridian, ready to search.

Toward dusk on the third day after the disappearance, SNCC's search team snuck into Neshoba County. Making their way along back roads, they visited the ashes of the Mt. Zion Church, then found refuge in a shack filled with rifles. Over a dinner of collards and ham hocks, they heard what local blacks thought had happened. The three had surely been killed by "those same peckerwoods" who burned the church. "Ain't no telling where they done hid the bodies." The men waited until midnight, then set out for the swamps. Their hosts drove them as James Chaney would have, headlights out, slamming over rutted roads, clambering deeper into Klan territory, where a wrong turn would have meant a flogging or another disappearance. Piling out of pickups, they spread out into swamps and creeks, searched barns and wells, used long sticks to probe muddy ditches. The muggy night seemed alive with fear. Any moment they expected to hear the thud of stick against a shoulder or torso, but all they heard were snakes hissing, mosquitoes whining, and deerflies buzzing their ears. They trudged on, ankle deep, knee deep, waist deep. Vines snagged their clothes; brambles slashed their arms. The teams searched until the sky turned salmon pink, returned to cabins to sweat more than sleep, then searched again the following midnight, tracking down the latest rumors. "So and so said they saw something. . . . We heard tell. . . . So and so heard the white people talking about . . ." Finally, rumors said the Klan had learned of their presence, and the midnight searches were called off.

On Thursday afternoon, striding into those same swamps came the two hundred sailors ordered by President Johnson. All wore white sailor hats and grimy old shoes. The men taped pant legs to their ankles to keep leeches out.

Grabbing branches to fend off snakes, the sailors searched until dusk. Before plunging in, many noted how strangely evil a Mississippi swamp appeared. The waters were opaque, calm, and flat, with no clue to their depths. Dragonflies, like little blue helicopters, darted over floating logs. Heat hung like a shroud over the pea-green carpet, but nothing beneath it stirred. And then, every so often from the black water below, a bubble surfaced, popped, and was gone.

From Lyndon Johnson on down, federal officials thought they were doing everything possible to find the men. But what about preventing future disappearances? Congressmen were besieged by parents' calls and telegrams demanding that federal marshals protect their children. LBJ's men were unanimously opposed. Sending in troops, said Assistant Attorney General Burke Marshall, "would have an irretrievable effect for two or three generations." Robert Kennedy insisted Mississippi's smoldering violence was "a local matter for local law enforcement." Prominent law professors disagreed, issuing a statement citing the Justice Department's legal right to intervene. But intervene how? Protecting "a thousand of these youngsters going down there . . . living in the homes of the colored population" would be an "almost superhuman task," J. Edgar Hoover told Allen Dulles. With Klansmen in the Mississippi Highway Patrol, Klansmen among "the chiefs of police," even some sheriffs in the Klan, "you almost have got to keep an agent with them as they come into the state," Hoover said. In New York, Malcolm X offered members of his Muslim Mosque as protection. No one took him up on the offer.

Newspapers and Congress soon joined the debate. The *Washington Post* praised "this breathtakingly admirable group of youngsters" but said federal protection was "simply impossible." The *New York Times* outlined the risks of "a second Reconstruction." On the Senate floor, Mississippi's John Stennis was urging the president to issue "a firm, positive statement" to stop "this invasion" when New York's Jacob Javits leaped to his feet. Americans, Javits shouted, had the right to go anywhere they wanted. Stennis responded that any blood shed in Mississippi "will be on the hands of those who formed and led this invasion into a state where they were not welcome nor invited." Faced with pressure to do *something*, LBJ stood firm. He would send more FBI that weekend, but he would not be responsible for a "second Reconstruction." "I'm not going to send troops on my people if I can avoid it," he said. "And they got to help me avoid it."

Would Mississippi help? Overnight, the long-dreaded "invasion" had come to resemble an occupation. Sailors slogged through swamps. Reporters from across America as well as France, England, and Germany descended on Philadelphia. FBI agents were stopping cars at checkpoints. Aluminum skiffs were motoring along a coffee-brown river as agents dragged grappling hooks along its bottom. The occupation stirred deep resentments, bringing the sediment to the surface. Watching the search from a bridge, several young men lit up Marlboros and traded jokes: "We throw two or three niggers in every year to feed the fish," one yucked. Another told the FBI how to find James Chaney. "Why don't you just float a relief check out there on top of the water? That black sonofabitch'll reach up and grab it." A few sober voices spoke in private, but only a few. "You know damn well our law is mixed up in this," a Philadelphia man told the Rotary Club. "I can't see why we have to protect them." A local woman was appalled: "The idea of these people trying to defend murder!" The way things were going, many said, Mississippi would be under federal occupation by mid-July. And wasn't it a shame, one added, given that the whole affair "if it was boiled down to gravy there wouldn't be much to it, no how."

Suspicions of a hoax were spreading throughout Mississippi. The *Jackson Clarion-Ledger* claimed Andrew Goodman had been spotted boarding a bus in Baton Rouge. CORE, rumor had it, had phoned police on Sunday afternoon *before* the men came up missing. And the Schwerners' VW? Odd that it was nowhere to be found. Letters to editors "proved" the hoax; otherwise why would Andrew Goodman, whose boyish face networks were showing in footage from the Ohio training, have been filmed before he "disappeared"? And wasn't Mississippi getting a black eye on the nightly news? Walter Cronkite spoke of "Bloody Neshoba." NBC interviewed a Neshoba County man who said Sheriff Rainey was involved. ABC let Mississippians damn their state with callous denial: "I believe them jokers planned this and are sittin' up in New York laughin' at us Mississippi folk," one man said. A woman added, "If they're dead, I feel like they asked for it. They came here lookin' for trouble."

In contrast to Mississippi, the aggrieved families displayed uncommon grace. On Thursday afternoon, TV cameras jammed the Goodmans' stylish Manhattan apartment. While flashbulbs popped, Carolyn Goodman read an appeal "to all parents everywhere, particularly the parents of Mississippi who, like myself, have experienced the softness, the warmth and the beauty of a child whom they cherish and love and want to protect. I want to beg them to cooperate in every way possible in the search for these three boys." Graying Anne Schwerner then spoke about James Chaney, "a Negro, a friend, and a brother to my boy Mickey." Though she had never met Mrs. Chaney, she wished "I could take her in my arms." Back in Mississippi, Fannie Lee Chaney said little, even when a cross was burned on her lawn. This was not the first disappearance in her family. Decades earlier, her grandfather had refused to sell his land to a white man. Only his shoes, shirt, and watch were ever found. Now, head in her hands, the stunned woman told the press, "I'm just hoping and not thinking." Like President Johnson, most assumed the three men were dead. "For God's sake," Nathan Schwerner shouted at a reporter. "Don't you know we'll never see Mickey again?" An FBI agent confided, "We're now looking for bodies." Yet the mothers insisted their sons might be found in some jail, some barn, somewhere. While they held out hope, Rita Schwerner, whom some had thought too small and frail to work in Mississippi, returned to take on the entire state.

As the mothers spoke to the press, Rita flew into Jackson. Speaking to reporters at the airport, she announced, "I am going to find my husband and the other two people. I am going to find out what happened to them." Rita also issued several demands—"that scores of federal marshals be sent to Mississippi . . . that there be a full scale investigation of reports of the involvement of some law enforcement officers . . . that President Johnson's personal envoy Allen Dulles confer with those in Meridian who know precisely what is going on." "In a word," she concluded, "we demand 'freedom now.'" Accompanied by SNCC's Bob Zellner, Rita then headed for the capitol to speak to Governor Paul Johnson.

After listening to a clerk go on and on about the beauty of Mississippi, Rita finally learned the governor was at his mansion, greeting George Wallace. "I'm sure Wallace is much more important to Mississippi than three missing men," Rita said. Entering the mansion grounds, she found the two governors heading a receiving line. Stepping in line, she heard someone mention the missing men. And she heard Johnson joke, "Governor Wallace and I are the only ones who know where they are, and we're not telling." Moments later, when Johnson bent to greet Rita, Bob Zellner shook his hand and introduced her as the wife of Michael Schwerner. When Johnson recoiled, Zellner held tightly to his hand, asking if it was true "that you and Governor Wallace here know where the missing civil rights workers are?" Panic broke out as reporters shouted questions and state troopers yanked Zellner away. Wallace and Johnson retreated inside and slammed the door. Hustled off the grounds, Rita moved on to meet Allen Dulles. The president's envoy kept her waiting forty-five minutes, then spoke with her for five. When Dulles offered his sympathy, Rita replied, "I don't want your sympathy! I want my husband back!"

On Friday afternoon, Rita was in Philadelphia talking to FBI agents at the Delphia Courts Motel. Suddenly Sheriff Rainey pulled in to the concrete lot. Striding up to her, the tobacco chaw still in his cheek, Rainey barked, "What in the goddamn hell are you doin' here?" Rita stood her ground. She would not leave until she saw the station wagon. As a menacing crowd gathered, Rainey invited Rita into his patrol car to talk. Sensing the woman's mood, a highway patrol investigator warned Rita not to be too hard on the sheriff. His wife was in the hospital.

"Well, at least he still has a wife to be concerned about," Rita said. "I ask him only to do me the courtesy of telling me where my husband is."

"But the sheriff doesn't know that."

Rita persisted. "Sheriff Rainey, I feel that you know what happened. I'm going to find out if I can. If you don't want me to find out, you'll have to kill me."

Rainey's neck reddened. His fists clenched the steering wheel. "I'm very shocked," he said softly. "I'm sorry you said that." The sheriff then took Rita and Zellner to see the station wagon. While garage mechanics hooted Rebel yells, they eyed the blackened shell. Since the moment she heard the car had been found, Rita had known she would never see her husband again. Now she saw the proof. When she and Zellner left, a green pickup, the same one that had blocked the highway when they entered Philadelphia that morning, chased them out of town.

By week's end, Mississippi had become a national obsession. Only weeks earlier, all civil rights news had come out of St. Augustine, Florida, where Martin Luther King and others were braving the Klan and white mobs to integrate public pools and beaches. But suddenly, TV, radio, and newspapers turned to the Magnolia State, reporting on its alarming poverty and backwoods violence. James Silver's *Mississippi: The Closed Society*, calling the state "as near to approximating a police state as anything we have yet seen in America," hit best-seller lists. Folksingers from Judy Collins to Pete Seeger began scheduling summer concerts in Jackson, Greenville, and McComb. Dozens of doctors and lawyers signed up to spend July or August in Mississippi, and SNCC offices were flooded with calls from people hoping to volunteer, so many that Bob Moses spoke out: "A wave of untrained and unoriented volunteers into the project areas would serve only to disrupt what is now a well-controlled plan of operation throughout the state." That afternoon in Chicago, a black man pulled his car over near the Calumet Expressway, took out a rifle, and shot himself in the head. A policeman found his note: "This is for the three in Philadelphia. They wouldn't let me join the movement and I'm giving my brain this way."

Under the national spotlight, Philadelphia was at a breaking point. Appalled by reporters and FBI "swarm[ing] upon our land like termites on old lumber," people huddled on street corners, talking, whispering when strangers passed. Near the courthouse, a driver rammed a cameraman's car. When the cameraman stepped out, so did the driver, clutching a hunting knife. Police intervened. Angry whites trailed *New York Times* reporter Claude Sitton, who sought safety through a chance connection. It happened that the small town making national news was the hometown of the *Times*'s managing editor. Learning how his town was behaving, Turner Catledge had written a friend, "Where, oh where, are those decent people I used to know?" Now, as menacing whites approached Sitton, he and a *Newsweek* reporter ducked into the hardware store owned by Catledge's uncle. "Be frank with you, Sitton," the uncle said. "If you were a black man being whupped out here on the sidewalk, I might help you. But you got no business here. And I wouldn't lift a finger if they was stomping the hell out of you." As the two reporters drove toward their hotel, a car chased them to the county line.

On the fifth night of what everyone was now calling the "long hot summer," Mississippi erupted. In town after town, volunteers were hounded by pickups, taunted by obscenities, arrested on trumped-up charges. Beer cans flew, and a SNCC car's tires were slashed. In Hattiesburg, whites spread flyers through the black community warning: "Beware, good Negro citizens. When we come to get the agitators, stay away." Near Jackson, someone broke into a church, doused the floor in kerosene, and tossed a match. In the midst of this mayhem, the most startling news came from the Delta. On Thursday, two volunteers had been abducted at gunpoint—"Want us to do to you what they did over in Philadelphia?"—and held at a gas station awaiting a bus to

send them north. On the COFO log, it was just another in the lengthening list
of incidents, but the following evening, the FBI arrested three white men in
Itta Bena. SNCCs could barely believe the news. "You dig it?" a volunteer
wrote home. "They are in a Southern jail!" That night, warned that a church
would be bombed, Itta Bena cops surrounded it and kept all whites away.

Of all the Americans watching the news that week, none watched with greater
alarm than the volunteers in Ohio, bound for Mississippi. SNCC structured
its second training much like the first, yet volunteers found the mood on
campus "like a funeral parlor." From the first bulletins out of Neshoba
County, frantic parents began calling, begging their children to come home.
All week, psychiatrist Robert Coles met with anxious, terrified volunteers.
Diagnosing panic, "near psychosis," or just "character disorders," Coles sent
eight students home. But in the rest, he witnessed the power of idealism.
"Suddenly hundreds of young Americans became charged with new energy
and determination," Coles wrote. "Suddenly I saw fear turn into toughness,
vacillation into quiet conviction." Many volunteers found their way to the
chapel. Others crowded around TVs to watch Walter Cronkite, to see the
car towed out of the swamp, to watch the ABC special *The Search in Mississippi*. When the program ended, volunteers joined hands and sang. "You
know what we're all doing," one man told the group. "We're moving the
world."

The first volunteers, trained for voter registration, had arrived with the
confidence of young politicos. But this second group consisted of Freedom
School teachers. Accustomed to working with children, they now faced
the likelihood of being beaten, jailed, even murdered. All that week, they
struggled to explain to terrified parents why they would not turn back.

June 27

Dear Mom and Dad,

    This letter is hard to write because I would like so much to com-
municate how I feel and I don't know if I can. It is very hard to
answer to your attitude that if I loved you I wouldn't do this—hard,
because the thought is cruel. I can only hope you have the sensitivity
to understand that I can both love you very much and desire to go to
Mississippi . . .

Dear Folks,

   . . . You should know that it would be a lot nicer in Hawaii than in Mississippi this summer. I am afraid of the situation down there, and the beaches and the safety are very alluring. But I am perhaps more afraid of the kind of life I would fall into in Hawaii. I sense somehow that I am at a crucial moment in my life and that to return home where everything is secure and made for me would be to choose a kind of death. . . . I feel the urgent need, somehow, to enter life, to be born into it. . . .

On their last evening in the safe North, volunteers again filled the campus auditorium. A spectral déjà vu loomed over the meeting. The previous Friday night, the three missing men had sat in this same auditorium, sang these same songs, heard these same leaders. Now this second group would follow them down. First, however, they listened one last time to Bob Moses.

Sighing and starting in, Moses asked if anyone had read the book that was becoming trendy on campuses, Tolkien's *Fellowship of the Ring*. It had much to say about good and evil, he said. Then pausing, rubbing his eyes beneath his glasses, Moses said softly, "The kids are dead." He hesitated, letting his words sink in. "When we heard the news at the beginning I knew they were dead. When we heard they had been arrested I knew there had been a frame-up. We didn't say this earlier because of Rita, because she was really holding out for every hope. There may be more deaths. . . ." Across the auditorium, some looked at their feet, others remained riveted on the reluctant "Jesus of the movement." "I justify myself because I'm taking risks myself," Moses continued, "and I'm not asking people to do things I'm not willing to do. And the other thing is, people were being killed already, the Negroes of Mississippi, and I feel, anyway, responsible for their deaths. Herbert Lee killed, Louis Allen killed, five others killed this year. In some way you have to come to grips with that, know what it means. If you are going to do anything about it, other people are going to be killed."

Moses knew what some were saying—that the summer project was "an attempt to get some people killed so the federal government will move into Mississippi." Yet he saw a bigger, darker picture. "In our country we have some real evil, and the attempt to do something about it involves enormous effort . . . and therefore tremendous risks. If for any reason you're hesitant about what you're getting into, it's better for you to leave. Because what has got to be done has to be done in a certain way, or otherwise it won't get done." Volunteers sat, some faces streaked with tears, others just shining on Moses, pinning their faith in America, in humanity, on his words.

"I would have gone anywhere," one woman recalled. "I would have done anything he asked me to do, I trusted him so much."

After a few more comments, Moses slowly walked out. No one said a word, no one took the stage. Volunteers sat in the stillness. Finally from the back of the auditorium, a lone woman sang:

> They say that freedom
> is a constant struggle
> They say that freee-dom
> is a constant struggle.

Across the auditorium, people crossed arms, held hands, joined in.

Many stayed up all night. A laundry room discussion lasted until 4:00 a.m. Others just wandered. A few stood in phone booths, arguing with parents. "If someone in Nazi Germany had done what we're doing," one woman shouted, "then your brother would still be alive!" A Long Island woman heard her father yell, "You're killing your mother! Do you know what it takes to make a child?" But all Heather Tobis could think was, "Do you know what it takes to make a child in Mississippi?" The following evening, Tobis was on one of two buses heading south. Songs again paced the miles through Kentucky and into Tennessee. The buses reached Memphis at 5:00 a.m. Sunday. And there was Bob Moses to help them make connections to Greyhounds stopping in Clarksdale, Vicksburg, Ruleville. . . .

A hot, syrupy haze hung above a sea of knee-high cotton when, at 2:00 p.m., the Greyhound pulled into Ruleville. On that crawling Sunday, the Delta town of 2,000 slumbered, but when twenty volunteers stepped out with luggage, boxes, and bedrolls, Ruleville awoke in a foul mood. Across from the bus station, several brawny white men, beer cans in hand, stared down the newcomers. Seconds later, a woman wearing pink hair curlers drove past the bus and waved her middle finger. The sheriff's pickup pulled up with a German shepherd in back, snarling, tearing at his cage. Next came the mayor, a short, jowly man stepping from his car, wearing a straw hat. When several black families drove up, another standoff looked likely, but then Fannie Lou Hamer strode onto the scene. The sturdy woman directed host families to take everyone to her house. There they met volunteers who had arrived the previous Sunday. All enjoyed an enormous lunch, then cooled off beneath the billowing pecan tree out front. Filling Hamer's lawn, fanning themselves in the shade, newcomers learned that voter registration was under way. Canvassers had been chased out of the "tough town" of Drew, but some locals had already gone to the courthouse in Indianola. And fifty kids had signed up for Freedom School.

That evening, volunteers and locals gathered at the Williams Chapel, just around the corner from Hamer's house. Four days earlier, a Molotov cocktail had charred the small church, but flames somehow missed plastic sacks of gasoline laid around the perimeter. The Ruleville fire department put out the blaze, leaving blackened concrete and a congregation feeling blessed. By the time Sunday's mass meeting began, a hundred people were crammed into a single room. Bare bulbs cast thin shadows on a photo of Jesus and a banner reading "We Shall Overcome."

"Be strong and of good courage," the preacher urged. "God sometimes likes us to feel we can't go any further . . ."

"Yes, yes."

"That's because God only helps us with the impossible things we can't achieve by ourselves . . ."

"Yes, yes."

When the preacher finished, a volunteer from Illinois announced the FBI arrests in Itta Bena. The FBI had not acted "because it wanted to," he said. "They did it because they had to. . . . The whole nation is watching you and admiring you, and you must keep on and you must stand up." Then came the songs, swelling and surging. Uplifted faces, black and white, glistened as they sang.

Nearly five hundred volunteers were now in Mississippi. A few would be gone within a week, leaving in terror or despair. The rest would stay on for what would be either a breakthrough summer or, as the *New York Times* now feared, a "racial holocaust." That Sunday morning in Neshoba County, black parishioners prayed in makeshift pews beside the rubble of the Mt. Zion Church. FBI agents again piled into skiffs to drag the Pearl River. In Philadelphia, agents were preparing to question Sheriff Rainey. Posters with mug shots of Goodman, Schwerner, and Chaney below the words "Missing—Call

FBI" were now posted all over the South. Rita Schwerner was on her way to meet President Johnson, while mayors throughout Mississippi talked of heading to Washington, D.C., to protest "the invasion." At dusk, a candlelight vigil for the missing men marched in silence outside the White House. Back in Mississippi, a few more volunteers, having driven their own cars from Ohio, arrived in their towns. All the way down, one kept saying, "I don't know what all the fuss is about. It's still the United States of America."

> Integrity can be neither lost nor concealed nor faked nor quenched nor artificially come by nor outlived, nor, I believe, in the long run, denied.
>
> —Eudora Welty

CHAPTER FIVE

"It Is Sure Enough Changing"

On his first full day in Mississippi, Fred Winn tore down an outhouse and turned it into bookshelves.

The outhouse stood behind a two-room shack on a dusty road skirting Ruleville's cotton fields. The road divided black sections of town whose names—Jerusalem and Sanctified Quarters—spoke of spirit, not scenery. The flatness of the Delta made the shack, the quarters, and the railroad tracks nearby seem like some tabletop model train set. Like many Mississippi shacks, this one looked as if no one had lived there since the birth of the blues. Four sunflowers leaned alongside a sagging porch. When the front door creaked open, cockroaches bigger than pecans scurried for cover. Inside lay musty rooms strewn with broken bottles, splintered furniture, and rusted box springs. Cobwebs draped corners. Walls wept with mildew. And out back stood the outhouse, angled like some ancient sundial in the morning glare.

Twenty volunteers traipsed through the house that Monday morning, in shock or dismay. This was to be Ruleville's Freedom School? *This?* But in a scene mirrored throughout Mississippi that week, women tied their hair back, men stripped off shirts, and all began swarming over the house like the insects swarming around them. Bearing brooms, buckets, and bottles of Lysol, they revived the dying shack. Women carried white rags inside, only to emerge holding shredded scraps as black as Delta topsoil. Men slick with sweat brought out armloads of debris. Soon several black women, their heads wrapped in bright bandannas, came with their own cleaning solutions. And sometime that morning, someone delivered boxes of books. Volunteers tore open the cardboard, finding childhood favorites or, to their dismay, college texts. The books were stacked in piles—"History," "Reference," "Language," "Crud"—and the piles were still small when Fred Winn began talking about bookshelves. Local kids roamed the quarters, bringing back two-by-fours but no planks. Finally Winn, a short, burly man with a mustache and horn-rimmed glasses, noticed the outhouse. With the help of several laughing kids, he rocked and rocked until it toppled with a crash. The smell was paralyzing, but the boards were not as old as they looked, not once Winn grabbed a plane from his toolbox and skinned them clean.

By the time a late-afternoon thunderstorm rumbled across the Delta, the Ruleville Freedom School was ready for classes. The rooms were still musty and the floorboards still creaked, but walls were tacky with fresh paint. A crib headboard found in the attic and spray-painted green had become a blackboard, and fully stocked bookshelves lined both classrooms. Walking through their new school, volunteers could hardly believe what they had accomplished, yet similar miracles were taking place in Vicksburg, in Clarksdale, in Hattiesburg . . . Ruleville's Freedom School was scheduled to open that Friday. In the meantime, volunteers wondered where else they could tackle a century of despair.

Throughout the first week of July, the search for Goodman, Schwerner, and Chaney dominated news from Mississippi. More searchers, more helicopters, more rumors. On Tuesday, a mutilated body turned up by the roadside a hundred miles north of Neshoba County. The man was about Mickey Schwerner's age, wearing blue jeans and sneakers, but fingerprints ended all speculation. A day later, a cop spotted a goateed man in a café near the Tennessee border. Mississippi newspapers plastered the news on front pages—the man looked "exactly" like Schwerner and had given the cop "dirty looks." Next, COFO headquarters heard that the three bodies, chained together, had been dumped in the Ross Barnett Reservoir off the Natchez Trace Highway. The FBI tracked down each rumor, "running down all leads on the cranks," Hoover told LBJ. And continuing to question residents, agents slowly pieced together the events of June 21.

One woman told agents what she had seen that Sunday afternoon. A blue station wagon stopped on Route 16, east of Philadelphia, opposite the Dallas Garage. Two whites and a Negro, fixing a flat. A cop and two highway patrolmen looking on. Patrolman Earl Poe confirmed the story. He and his partner had been sweating in the shade along Route 16 when the blue wagon topped the rise and "let off it." Seconds later, Deputy Cecil Price had raced by in his black-and-white '56 Chevy, red light flashing. A crackle had come over the radio—Price asking for assistance. The patrolmen followed and found the station wagon pulled over, the pudgy deputy watching the black man change the tire. Then the two "white boys" got in Poe's patrol car—the one with the goatee handed the cop the gun left in the backseat. The other patrolman rode with the "Negro boy" in the station wagon, and Deputy Price followed both cars to the jail.

What happened in jail was revealed by a man who had been in an adjacent cell. He told of Goodman, Schwerner, and Chaney being placed in segregated lockups. Schwerner had asked permission to call his wife. The jailer offered to make the call herself, but Schwerner politely declined. The man remembered Schwerner and Goodman as being calm, telling him they expected to be in jail several days. The details gave the FBI a start, but the forty hours between Sunday night and Tuesday's discovery of the smoldering station wagon remained a blank slate. And while a few locals had talked, most were still enraged by the FBI's invasion. They knew nothing. They had seen nothing. If the three were dead, several added, they "got what was coming to them." That week, a hearing on James Chaney's arrest for speeding was scheduled in the Neshoba County courthouse. Chaney did not show.

While whites talked—or refused to talk—blacks in Philadelphia opened up to the press. Mrs. Junior Cole told the *New York Times* how a white mob had gathered outside the Mt. Zion Church on the evening before it burned. The elderly woman trembled as she described emerging from a church meeting with her husband. Suddenly, a man with a gun had stepped in front of their car. Seconds later, the road was filled with white men, rifles across their chests. One shone a flashlight in Junior Cole's face, asking about the church meeting. When Cole replied that it was just a routine gathering, the white man barked, "You a damn liar. You having an N-double-A-CP meeting out here, ain't you?" Yanking the old man out of the car, the mob pummeled him to the ground, thrashing and kicking. Mrs. Cole dropped to her knees in the gravel.

"Lord, don't let them kill my husband."

"If you think prayer will do any good, you'd better pray."

As fists and a pistol butt thudded in the darkness, Mrs. Cole lifted both arms to heaven. "Father, I stretch my hands to Thee," she said. "No other help I know." The words seemed to calm the men. Leaving Junior Cole in a heap on the ground, they got into cars and pickups and drove off. A few hours later, an orange glow lit the night sky from off toward the church.

While the FBI investigated and the public feasted on rumors, 450 volunteers stifled their fears and settled into Mississippi. Bob Moses had once written to a "Friends of SNCC" chapter, explaining how that was done.

> You dig into yourself and the community to wage psychological warfare; you combat your own fears about beatings, shootings, and possible mob violence; you stymie, by your mere physical presence, the anxious fear of the Negro community . . . you organize, pound by pound, small bands of people . . . a small striking force capable of moving out when the time comes, which it must, whether we help it or not.

The time had come. The first week of July 1964 was an American Rubicon. On July 2, President Johnson would sign the Civil Rights Act, banning segregation in all public facilities. And all that holiday weekend, blacks would test the waters—ordering breakfast from white waitresses, getting haircuts from white barbers, checking into hotels where just a week before they had been welcome only as maids and kitchen help. But just offstage at this revolution, blacks and whites scattered across Mississippi won smaller victories. They signed papers on porches, learned together in Freedom Schools, played together at picnics, and shared the most integrated Fourth of July in American history.

Deepening its denial, white Mississippi continued to sneer at the invaders. "While professing to believe in 'equality,'" a *Jackson Clarion-Ledger* columnist wrote, "these self-appointed reformers evidently regard themselves as mentally and morally superior to Mississippians. What the students think of us is not very important . . . because the invaders couldn't possibly think less of us than the majority here thinks of them and their sponsors." In his home overlooking his cotton fields, Senator James Eastland echoed the denial that was becoming the common wisdom among Mississippi whites. "I find more resentment on the part of Negroes than white people to this effort in our state," the bald, bespectacled senator told reporters. But Eastland did not know the 40 percent of his constituents who had never been allowed to vote. "It's the best thing that's happened since there ever was a Mississippi," one black man said. "I just love the students like I love to eat. . . . If more come down here, I'd get out of my bed for them and sleep on a pallet in the tool shed. They're doing things we couldn't do for ourselves in years on end. . . . A lot of bad smells are getting out to the outside world that never did before. And we got out-of-state FBI in here, and federal lawsuits. It's all changing, it is sure enough changing, right this summer."

Volunteers who had been in Mississippi since the first day of summer were getting used to the place. Now the fresh arrivals struggled with each new annoyance. One woman hated the gnats that swarmed everywhere, even up her skirt. Another couldn't believe how he took a shower, dried off, and within minutes had damp armpits, a sticky shirt, and a halo of sweat. A third bristled when his host family treated him "as if I was some strange god, and I mean a dangerous one as well as a good one."

For carpenter Fred Winn, the hardest thing to get used to was midnight. Daytime kept him busy, building bookshelves, reviving rotting shacks, but each midnight he lay awake on the floor of his new home—the Ruleville Freedom School. Two weeks earlier he had been in his native San Francisco, where nights were deliciously cool. Now he lay in the muggy dampness, mulling over how one thing had led to another, leading finally to Mississippi.

Fred had learned of the summer project when SNCC's spring speaking tour came to his college in Marin County. Many students had given SNCC money, but friends were dumbfounded when Fred Winn decided to give his summer. A gregarious twenty-year-old whose Sausalito apartment was a notorious "party pad" hardly seemed a likely civil rights worker. Only a few friends knew that behind Fred's firm handshake and salty speech was a family secret. A year earlier, Fred's father, a respected San Francisco lawyer, told his family he had another child—a black child. Fred's mother threw her husband out. Siblings wanted nothing to do with the four-year-old girl, but Fred met her and was charmed. Suddenly the color line between the Winns and their black maid had blurred. And all his father's lectures about *never* using "*that* word" to describe Negroes made sense. "Now it wasn't just these 'Negroes' or 'coloreds' or whatever everyone was calling them, but people to whom I'm related," Fred recalled. "That's a consciousness changing thing."

Fred's father, worried that he and his party-loving son had nothing in common, was pleased by "Freddy's" decision to go to Mississippi. Fred's mother called the college president and threatened, if anything happened to her son, to sue for allowing SNCC on campus. The president called Fred into his office, but there was nothing an academic or a mother could do—Fred's father had signed SNCC's permission form. During the next two months the college "court jester" became insufferable, arguing on the quad about civil rights, signing his letters "We Shall Overcome." Some friends said Fred was crazy to go, others called him heroic, but he just felt righteous anger, tempered by the first cold feelers of terror. Having heard SNCC's stories, he knew what might happen to him in Mississippi. He was not sure he could take a beating without fighting back. The idea of rolling into a helpless ball while being kicked and hammered went against his every instinct. And who knew what else Mississippi had in store? Shortly before leaving for Ohio, Fred sat down to write his will. After designating who should have his car, books, and other belongings, he signed, "My spirit lives on. Wherever there is a fight of equality, whenever a person is deprived of something that is his, I will be there. The truth is behind me—We shall overcome."

Other volunteers brought white-collar expertise to Mississippi, but Fred Winn brought tools. SNCC had asked for handymen, and Fred, though a lawyer's son, had always felt an affinity for the building trades. So a few days after writing his will, he packed a toolbox, then threw in paper and crayons for Freedom Schools, his father's Bible, and a first aid kit. Boarding a Greyhound, he crossed the Sierras and rode on toward Ohio. En route, he cracked the books SNCC had recommended to volunteers—*Black Like Me*, *The Mind of the South*, *The Souls of Black Folk*. But three books could scarcely prepare him for the culture clash ahead. Naive and untested—"a young twenty-year-old"—Fred had never been to the Deep South, never slept with a woman, never thought much about black and white in America. He would spend the summer like a boy turning over rocks. On his first night in training, he watched in anger as a black man approached a white woman on a dance floor, pressing closer and closer until she shoved him away. That just wasn't how a man approached a woman in San Francisco. Yet as the week went on, Fred met SNCCs and other volunteers, "broke the ice and things got better."

When asked in workshops why he had come, Fred spoke frankly about his father's interracial affair. And on that Monday morning when Rita Schwerner told volunteers to write their congressmen, Fred wrote his, then fired off letters to the *San Francisco Chronicle* and to his mother, calling her a racist. Yet as the mood on campus turned funereal, his righteousness was tested. The disappearance had made it clear—"There were people in Mississippi who might *murder* me." His roommate, a football player from the Midwest, went home, but Fred was determined to go to Mississippi. For a laugh, he recalled his father's parting advice—"If the Klan gets a hold of you, yell 'My father is a Mason!'" A Masonic code, he was told, prevents Masons from harming each other's families. Armed with that and his tools, Fred Winn went to Mississippi, where it was midnight and he still could not sleep.

Fred found nights in Mississippi "scarier than shit." He had already faced down the food. He took one bite of pigs' feet, one of pigs' ear, no more. Okra gagged him—"It's like eating sandpaper slugs"—but he would learn to like it. Yet he could not get used to the danger. In his first letter from Ruleville, he shared news of the disappearance. "Dad, I hope you realize that I may be in that same position in a few days. Do not worry and for shit's sake don't come running down here. We have a very good investigation division of our own." His father read each letter over and over. Reminded of his own experiences as a green World War II enlistee who rose to the rank of captain, the elder Winn dutifully sent "Freddy" money, signed letters to LBJ, and worried. And each night his faraway son, after hanging screens, fixing toilets, and singing at mass meetings, made a pallet on the Freedom School floor, set his glasses beside it, and struggled to get some sleep. For protection, Fred had covered the school's windows with corrugated tin, cutting off any breeze, turning his "bedroom" into a sweatbox. A volunteer from New Jersey was stretched out nearby, breathing deeply, but Fred just lay there thinking about his fractured family back home, thinking about his tasks the next day, wondering what he had gotten himself into. The room was pitch-black, and he listened to every car that passed.

On Monday morning, June 29, Rita Schwerner and Bob Zellner were escorted into the Oval Office of the White House. Rita must have looked like a child standing before the president, more than a foot taller and more than twice her weight. LBJ stooped, shook her hand, and said he was glad to meet her. But convinced now that she was a widow—at twenty-two—Rita was brusque. "I'm sorry, Mr. President, this is not a social call," she said. "We've come to talk about three missing people in Mississippi. We've come to talk about a search that we don't think is being done seriously."

"I'm sorry you feel that way, Miss," the president replied.

The conversation was brief. Rita demanded that five thousand federal marshals be sent to Mississippi. The president said everything that could be done was being done. When LBJ abruptly turned and left, press secretary Pierre Salinger chewed out Rita, saying one did not talk to the president of the United States that way.

"We do," Rita said, and left for a press conference.

Throughout that second week, volunteers went about their business in black Mississippi. They readied Freedom Schools, opened community centers, sat on rickety front porches, shucking peas and getting to know their hosts. And white Mississippi went about its business—repelling the invasion. Perhaps due to the FBI arrests in Itta Bena, or perhaps because all America was watching, violence ebbed that week. Yet the "calm" did not calm anyone. The disappearance of three men had seeded Mississippi with omens. Each passing pickup, each hate stare, each sudden noise in the night, suggested the raw hatred lurking within striking distance. And each car of volunteers late for a scheduled return made another disappearance seem just a matter of time.

To put fear in perspective, SNCCs shared stories of nearby "tough towns" that made their own sites seem tame. In the Delta, the tough town was Drew, where the first canvassers had been chased out by a mob. Batesville volunteers were told *never* to enter Tallahatchie County, where the mangled body of Emmett Till had washed up in the muddy river. Farther south, a primitive savagery was said to lurk in the broiling farmlands of Amite County, where Herbert Lee had been gunned down, and in Pike County, where mobs had beaten SNCCs outside city hall. But even with "tough towns" still off-limits, the threats, the harassment, the attacks, just kept coming. Check-in calls to the WATS line in Jackson, dutifully typed by the volunteer manning the phone, suggested white Mississippi as a coiled snake:

June 30--Page 7

<u>Holly Springs</u>: . . . Threats of dynamiting Freedom House
    tonight. Guys driving around with guns . . .

<u>Ruleville</u>: Two reports of trucks without licenses, one
    this afternoon. Congregating on highway 8, near city
    dump, betw. Ruleville and Cleveland . . .

<u>Jackson, 10:45</u>: Two guys just passed in '64 Tempest,
    black--with gun.

<u>Holly Springs</u>: Larry, Wayne Yancy, Peter Cummings, Har-
    riet Penman, others, coming out of restaurant. They
    were passing a gas station. A guy in gas station
    with empty Coke bottle . . . cursed at Larry, shoved
    him, grabbed him by throat. Peter Cummings came

back. Guy yelled at them both. Got away from him.
"I'm going to get out a 12-gauge shotgun and shove
it up that fellow's ass. I'm going to shoot up your
office."

In Greenwood, a white and a black woman were walking when a car swerved straight toward them. They bolted out of its path. As the car passed, they noted the sign in the rear window: "You Are in Occupied Mississippi: Proceed with Caution." Listening to such stories, many lived in constant fear. "Violence hangs overhead like dead air . . . ," a Ruleville volunteer wrote. "Something is in the air, something is going to happen, somewhere, sometime, to someone." Adding to the fear was white Mississippi's bare-faced rudeness. One volunteer would never forget—"to walk along the street and have some little old lady who looks for everything like your mother give you the finger." Clarksdale volunteers watched with disbelief as the sheriff entered a courtroom and sprayed deodorant all around them. Females sometimes found the hostility sugar-coated.

"You're both purty gals," a dough-faced man said to two in Canton. "Some of the purtiest I've ever seen. But I seen you the other day up at that nigger store talking to the worst nigger slum in the county. Why, that nigger slum can't even count to ten."

"Yes, I've been talking to Negroes at the store," one woman said with a smile. The other added, "And we'd be glad to come to your home and talk to your wife and you together."

"I wouldn't let the likes of you in my house," the man replied. "Why don't you go home where you belong?"

But more often, no sugar-coating was applied. When a cop pulled over an integrated SNCC car, he eyed the lone white woman and snarled, "Which one of them coons is you fuckin'?"

Lyndon Johnson had vowed not to send troops "on my people"—if they cooperated. But would anyone in Mississippi cooperate? Despite all the violence, most whites had done their best to ignore the invasion, but throughout June's Hospitality Month and on into July, only two offered southern hospitality.

In Greenville, Hodding Carter III, editor of the *Delta Democrat-Times*, "broke bread with, drank whiskey with, and argued with about a dozen of the volunteers." Long before Freedom Summer, the Carter family's

Democrat-Times had denounced the Klan and the Citizens' Council, leading to threats, boycotts, and constant harassment. By 1964, Carter, an ex-marine who would later serve in President Jimmy Carter's State Department, was keeping guns in his car, desk drawer, pocket, and bedside table. But fear did not deter him from meeting summer volunteers and arguing politics. "I was adamantly against much of the SDS-related rhetoric and some of the tactical approaches, which I thought were deliberately designed to spark violence," he recalled. "They thought I was a young fogy, his mind clouded by knee-jerk anti-communism and simply out of it when it came to the winds of change. I was for LBJ; they thought he was a fascist, etc." Carter watched in dismay as two of his reporters dated volunteers. And he occasionally allowed volunteers to swim in his pool.

Mississippi's other island of hospitality lay seventy miles from Greenville. During that first week of July, Holmes County volunteers were hosted by a pale, red-haired woman wearing a string of pearls. Hazel Brannon Smith, the crusading editor fresh from winning the Pulitzer Prize, welcomed volunteers into the white-pillared house she called Hazelwood. Other Mississippi newspapers were blasting these "race mixing invaders," "leftist hep cat students," and "nutniks." And although most volunteers were as clean-cut as the sailors still searching the swamps, other newspapers described them as "unshaven and unwashed trash." But Smith's *Lexington Advertiser* proudly introduced "thirty college students who are interested in human and civil rights." Calling the summer project a "Peace Corps type undertaking," Smith profiled volunteers, their colleges, majors, and interests. All over town, she had heard the grumbling, the idea "that if everyone would just leave us alone we would work out all our problems." In her "Through Hazel Eyes" column, she answered back. "The truth is these young people wouldn't be here if we had not largely ignored our responsibilities to our Negro citizens."

Yet Carter and Smith stood alone. Mayors throughout Mississippi, though deciding against protesting in the nation's capital, condemned volunteers for "doing irreparable damage to the friendly relations that exist among our people." Police found any excuse to arrest them—for speeding, reckless driving, even "reckless walking." And rednecks, peckerwoods, "white trash," used every brand of terror to drive them out. The actual number of homegrown terrorists may have been only a dozen in each town, but the rest, if they disapproved of the relentless violence, said nothing.

By early July, the nerve center of Freedom Summer was run ragged. With its air-conditioning broken, the COFO office in Jackson sweltered. Sweat ran down foreheads, soaked clothes, dripped off chins. Dogs roamed freely through the clutter of old newspapers, boxes of books, and empty RC Cola bottles. A sign on one wall read, "Nobody Would Dare Bomb This Place and End This Confusion." Each day seemed to pile on the tasks—always more bail to raise, more reports, lists, and letters to type, another volunteer's hometown press to contact. Then there were visitors in need of couches to sleep on, rides to arrange, calls to raise more money. And now that everyone had settled in, the time had come to harvest democracy, shack by shack.

The Mississippi Freedom Democratic Party waited in the wings. The MFDP's bold challenge at the Democratic National Convention was still seven weeks away. To unseat Mississippi's all-white delegation, Freedom Democrats would need as many registration forms as possible for their parallel party. But in early July, both Atlantic City and late August seemed as far off as distant countries. There would be time to sign up Freedom Democrats—later. With so many eager faces suddenly swarming through project offices, SNCC's immediate goal was getting blacks down to their county courthouses in numbers no one could ignore. Freedom Days, focusing the energy of entire offices on one-day voting drives, were planned for Greenwood, Greenville, Cleveland, Holly Springs . . . To get would-be voters out, volunteers took to the streets.

Like the resurrection of so many decaying buildings, the scene was repeated all over Mississippi that week. A gravel road. A row of cabins. Men and women slumped on porches, numbed by twelve hours of cleaning, cooking, or toiling in the fields. As the western sky reddens, up the road come the "Riders," clipboards in hand, hair neatly combed, white shirts and pastel blouses spotless and starched. Some in white pairs, others racially mixed, they stride onto each porch, introduce themselves—Len and Bill, Chris and Pam—then talk about the summer project, the registration process, the dream of voting. A few blacks say "Yes, sir" or "Yes'm," but most just sit and stare. Canvassing is like conversation, volunteers are learning—something of an art. They all know how to converse, but how do you converse with someone too terrified to say "No," too tired to say much else? Fortunately, volunteers were being taught by masters.

SNCC's canvassing handbook was explicit. "Know all roads in and out of town." "If a person talks but shows obvious reluctance, don't force a long explanation on them. Come back another day to explain more." Don't overwhelm people with possibilities—focus on a single hope. A registration class. A mass meeting. A trip to the courthouse. But Mississippi native Lawrence Guyot saw canvassing in simpler terms. Canvassing was "surviving and just walking around talking to people about what they're interested in. And it didn't make any difference. If it was fishing, how do you turn that conversation into 'When are you gonna register to vote?' If it was religion, that was an easier one to turn into registering." Guyot's cardinal rule was common sense. "You don't alter the basic format that you walk into. Let's say you're riding past a picnic and people are cuttin' watermelons. You don't immediately go and say, 'Stop the watermelon cuttin', and let's talk about voter registrations.' You cut some watermelons."

As summer progressed, canvassers would see doors gently closed and doors swiftly shut. They would have men nod and swear they would "sure enough" show up for registration classes and then never appear. They would hand pamphlets to old black men, only to realize the men could not read a word. And every now and then they would be welcomed inside a sharecropper's shack. There they would try not to stare, try not to cry. Blinking back waves of heat radiating from tin roofs, they saw walls patched with yellowed newspaper, bare bulbs hanging from frayed cords, barefoot children playing on the floor—with bottle caps. Many homes had a single picture—of Jesus, John F. Kennedy, or Martin Luther King. "The whole scene," one volunteer wrote, "was from another century." One in twenty locals might open their homes. The rest stayed on porches, scratching salt-and-pepper whiskers, furrowing washboard brows.

"I just can't get my mind on all that. I just never voted and I'm too old now."

"I don't want to mess with that mess."

"I can't sign no paper."

And if a volunteer said, "Negroes have to do something to—"

"I ain't no Negro. I'm a nigger. The Boss Man, he don't say nothing but 'nigger girl' to me. I'm just a nigger. I can't sign no paper."

On to the next shack. A black snake slithers across the road. A train whistle floats by. The sinking sun serves as both time clock and barometer of their mood. If one in twenty invite them in, only one in a hundred decide that voting is worth risking a job, a home, a life. Registering to vote had always carried grave risks in Mississippi, but Freedom Summer saw those risks stalk the streets. Canvassers were often followed by a police car, inching along, shotgun on display, tires popping the gravel. One look at a cop was enough to send weary bodies scurrying inside. Volunteers loathed the police on their tail, but a cop could ward off other dangers.

Outside Batesville, Jay Shetterly and Geoff Cowan were canvassing along the Tallahatchie River as it flowed past cotton fields. Speaking to field hands with hoes propped on their shoulders, the two wondered why the men just stared. Cowan talked about voting. The men stared. Shetterly talked about the need to unite. Nervous grins. Finally, the two turned around to see a pickup, a tight-lipped white man, a shotgun on the rack behind him, a pistol on the seat.

"Did that nigger invite you in here?"

Cowan and Shetterly, both articulate Harvard students, said nothing.

"Did you know Mississippi law allows me to shoot trespassers?"

No, they did not know.

"Are you gonna get off this plantation?"

The men left without a word. The pickup roared off.

Numbers alone made the canvass worth the frustration. If a dozen teams went out for a dozen days in a dozen towns, even one out of a hundred added up to lines at courthouses. And all that first week of July, shack by shack, canvassers dragged the bottom of Mississippi and came up with just enough hope to keep them going. The lone exception to this harsh law of averages was in Panola County, where Chris Williams was the youngest canvasser in Mississippi.

During his two weeks in the state, Chris had grown confident, even brash. He had spent languid afternoons tracing lines of dirt across his skin. He had sat up nights reading the novels of Richard Wright. And most evenings he had canvassed with "a somewhat neurotic redhead" from the University of Michigan. Older volunteers were amused to hear this mere teenager, when angered by white Mississippi, spout a phrase common in his Massachusetts high school— "Goddamn motherfucker, pissed me right off!" Fellow volunteers found Chris "kind of goofy, kind of crazy—we could always depend on him to be funny."

Chris and other Batesville canvassers had an advantage in going shack to shack. In 1961, the Panola County Voters League had filed suit, charging racial bias in registration. The case dragged on for two years before a judge ruled in favor of the county, but just a month before Freedom Summer, the Fifth Circuit Court in New Orleans overturned the decision. The court issued a one-year injunction suspending the requirement that registrants— black registrants, at least—interpret the state constitution. The injunction also voided the onerous poll tax, equal to a sharecropper's daily wage, that had to be paid up for two years *before* one could vote. Suddenly, SNCC had twelve months to register as many as possible. Before the injunction, only one Panola County Negro was registered, and he had been on the books since 1892. Then, during the first week of summer, SNCC held nightly registration classes. Assistant Attorney General John Doar came from the Justice Department to check on things. Canvassers went door to door, and fifty blacks went to the courthouse. Forty-seven were registered. It was all changing, sure enough, that summer.

Chris was living with Mrs. Cornelia Robertson and her grown daughter, Pepper, in a two-room shack with no running water and bullet holes in the front screen. But both women rose early to work, so Chris made his own breakfast, showered in the sun beneath buckets of cold water, then hustled to the project office. The office had gotten off to a slow start. The man Chris called "our great leader" had spent most of his time talking to local girls. Then he was replaced by Claude Weaver, a black Harvard student with a serene face and a deft sense of humor. (Weaver also drew cartoons, circulated widely among project offices, featuring a humble black janitor who, when danger threatened, burst out of his overalls to become—ta-daa—Supersnick.)

Come early July, when Chris walked each morning past shacks and juke joints, waving, nodding to locals, he arrived at a frenetic office. Parked outside were a white Plymouth from SNCC's "Sojourner Motor Fleet," plus one volunteer's VW and another's Pontiac GTO. Inside, posters proclaimed "Freedom Now!" and "There is a street in Itta Bena called Freedom . . ." The radio blared a Memphis soul station. Aretha Franklin. Wilson Pickett. Marvin Gaye. Scurrying around the office were students from Harvard, Radcliffe, and the University of Chicago working on communications, legal affairs, and canvassing. Most days Chris studied canvassing routes or ran errands. Most evenings, after sharecroppers came home from the fields, he met them on their porches. Once a week, he went to the courthouse.

One afternoon, Chris sat in the cool, echoing corridor outside the Panola County registrar's office. A few days earlier, he had canvassed Mrs. Gladys Toliver, convincing her to take the risk. Now he sat with the old woman and three other would-be voters on a hardwood bench. As the wait dragged on,

Mrs. Toliver confided in the nice crew-cut white boy beside her. She didn't think she could pass the test. All those questions, all those laws. Chris took out a copy of the registration form and was reviewing it with her when footsteps clicked down the hall. Chris looked up to see a short, beer-bellied man with horn-rimmed glasses, a badge on his chest and a gun on his hip. Sheriff Earl Hubbard.

The sheriff began ranting. Volunteers were "agitators . . . come to Mississippi to cause trouble." Chris sat seething, stifling sarcastic replies. Finally, the sheriff told Chris to get out. A courthouse was no place for voting classes. "Did you hear me, boy? I said 'Get out.'" Muttering "Goddamn motherfucker, pissed me right off!" Chris walked down the corridor past the "Whites Only" drinking fountain and stepped outside. Scalding air slammed him in the face. Alone on the steps, his confidence wavered. SNCC lore was full of attacks in such a setting. Bob Moses beaten at the courthouse in Liberty. Several struck down in Greenwood. Any minute now. . . . Finally, his friends emerged, followed by the sheriff, still ranting. "He said they ought to send me home and let my parents teach me how to behave," Chris wrote home. "I just looked him in the eye and said nothing. He's only a stupid old man." Sheriff Hubbard gave the SNCC car a parking ticket. Back at the Mileses' house, Chris enjoyed a big meal. "I have developed a real taste for Southern cooking," he told his parents. That evening, the shotguns again came out as blacks stood guard. Some things were a long way from changing.

On Thursday, July 2, the search for Goodman, Schwerner, and Chaney spread to the Alabama border. Afternoon downpours continued to curtail the hunt. Rumors revived with word that a gas station attendant in Kosciusko had seen the three. Back in Philadelphia, agents were growing suspicious about Sheriff Lawrence Rainey. A middle-aged man with an eighth-grade education, standing six-two, weighing 240, Rainey was known as hard-drinking and "hard on the Negroes." Everyone knew the sheriff had even killed two blacks, both while he was on duty, both unarmed. Mississippi sheriffs had enormous power—each was his county's tax collector, prohibition agent, and, in some Klan-ridden counties, a proud member of the klavern. But Rainey claimed even more power. Once after pulling over a driver, he asked, "Nigger, do you know who's running this county? Lawrence A. Rainey is running this county." When the man mentioned the mayor, Rainey shot back, "Nigger, don't come talking about no mayor, 'cause I'm the sheriff in this county."

Now the sheriff was becoming a suspect. The FBI had a list of seven names, submitted by a highway patrolman from Meridian. "I have no proof," the man told agents, "but I bet you every one of these men was involved in this." Among the names were Sheriff Lawrence Rainey and Deputy Cecil Price. The FBI had already learned that Rainey had been in the pack that stormed the Mt. Zion Church meeting and beat Junior Cole unconscious. Reporters were asking Rainey about rumors that a white mob, waiting outside the jail, had abducted Goodman, Schwerner, and Chaney. He flatly denied them. On July 2, the FBI called the sheriff in for questioning.

Wearing his cowboy hat, his chaw in his cheek, his gun on his hip, the sheriff swaggered into Room 18 of the Delphia Courts Motel. With him was a county attorney, ready to rise to his defense. Rainey was shown pictures—the goateed Schwerner, the kindly Chaney, the doe-eyed Goodman. Never seen the men before, the sheriff said. Then, punctuating his answers by spitting tobacco juice, he detailed his whereabouts on the night of June 21. He had visited his wife in the hospital, then had dinner with relatives. After dropping by his office to pick up clean shirts, he had returned to relatives, watched *Candid Camera* and *Bonanza*, then made it back to Philadelphia before midnight. Stopping at the jail, he had learned about the arrest and release of the three. Then he went home. Agents listened. Agents took notes. Then one asked Rainey if he was a Klansman. He denied it, then denied that Neshoba County even had a Klan. Listening to the sheriff, the attorney found his denial strange and incredible. Hadn't a Klan recruitment flier, earlier that spring, been posted down the hall from Rainey's office for days on end? The back-and-forth continued until an agent blurted out, "Now come on sheriff and tell us what you did with those people." The sheriff said nothing and was allowed to leave. Agents began checking his story. Rainey was shocked that the FBI even called his wife in the hospital. Two days later, the attorney, still stunned by what he had heard during the interrogation, told agents that Sheriff Lawrence Rainey should be their "number one suspect."

Agents were also suspicious about Deputy Price. A high school dropout like his boss, Price hid a dull rage behind a goofy demeanor. When first approached by the FBI, he had shrugged off all accusations, then popped the trunk of his patrol car and offered the agent a swig of moonshine. Agents had since investigated Price's story about June 21—the arrest, the release, the taillights disappearing. Much of it checked out, but his whereabouts from 10:40 to 11:30 p.m. could not be confirmed. Adding to their suspicions, the

Neshoba County jailer said she normally received the car keys of suspects in jail. But Price had given her no keys for the three. Nor were keys ever mentioned. Agents also found it unusual that local cops, like the sheriff, refused to be questioned without an attorney present.

While the FBI questioned Price and Rainey, the first two Freedom Schools opened. In Clarksdale, students listened as a white woman read from James Baldwin's "Talk to Teachers": "Now if I were a teacher in this school, or any Negro school, and I was dealing with Negro children, who were in my care only a few hours of every day and would then return to their homes and to the streets . . . I would try to make them know—that those streets, those houses, those dangers, those agonies by which they are surrounded, are criminal. I would try to make each child know that these things are the result of a criminal conspiracy to destroy him."

As if such frankness were not startling enough, the teacher then encouraged students to talk. Sparked by Baldwin's fire, they opened up on Mississippi, discussing cops, a recent shooting, and why one student no longer ate watermelon because it was "nigger food." After a rousing chorus of Freedom Songs, students headed home. It was a start. That same afternoon in Holly Springs, students met under the low, leafy branches of a sweetgum tree to hear a teacher call them the "leaders of tomorrow." And that evening, tomorrow came early.

Shortly after 7:00 p.m., all network programming was interrupted. In living rooms across the nation, President Johnson urged Americans to "close the springs of racial poison." Then the president began signing the Civil Rights Act, using seventy-two different pens, handing them to congressmen and to Martin Luther King, standing behind him. The first major civil rights bill since Reconstruction had been introduced by John F. Kennedy just hours before Medgar Evers was killed. The bill had survived massive resistance, including southern senators droning through the longest filibuster in congressional history. LBJ had thrown his enormous powers of persuasion behind the bill, finally twisting enough arms to end the filibuster and win approval. Now came what the president called the "time of testing." Johnson had barely given away the last pen when a blazing cross lit the sky in central Mississippi. The town's name—Harmony.

All that holiday weekend, the testing continued. Blacks sat beside whites at lunch counters in Montgomery, Alabama, but were beaten with baseball bats in Bessemer. Blacks integrated hotels and theaters in Birmingham, but three attempting a "wade-in" at Lake Texarkana were shot. "Occupied Mississippi" braced for the worst. The Jackson Chamber of Commerce urged businesses to comply with the law, but the *Clarion-Ledger* advertised "tear gas pen guns," and Governor Paul Johnson predicted "civil strife and chaotic conditions." Across the state, whites swore "Never!," blacks tried to be hopeful, and volunteers bore witness. "People here in Clarksdale know all about that bill," one volunteer wrote home, "but tomorrow and Saturday, the 4th of July, they will still be in the cotton fields making three dollars a day. . . . They'll still be starving and afraid." SNCCs had decided against testing the law and had to talk locals out of open confrontation. A Greenwood woman kept saying, "Ah'm going swimmin' in that pool. Ah've waited a long time." Several convinced her to wait a little longer. The long holiday weekend was just beginning.

It was a Fourth like many. A million people jammed the boardwalk at Coney Island. At Yankee Stadium, Mickey Mantle hit a three-run homer to beat the Twins. The Beach Boys' "I Get Around" went to number one, and fireworks went off everywhere. Yet it was also a Fourth unlike any in memory. In Atlanta, several SNCCs, black and white, entered a rally for George Wallace. A mob descended with fists, chairs, and lead pipes until a white stranger dragged the intruders to safety. Outside Radio City Music Hall, demonstrators carried black-bordered signs in memory of Goodman, Schwerner, and Chaney. At the World's Fair in New York, SNCCs urged a boycott of the high school band from Greenwood, Mississippi. And in Greenwood, in Vicksburg, in Batesville, volunteers celebrated freedom with those for whom it remained a dream.

So far, most volunteers had met just their host families and a few neighbors. From these few, they had learned that black Mississippi was stronger than its shacks. They noticed how black women always referred to each other with the deference whites denied them—Mrs. or Miss. They learned who in "the quarters" could be trusted and who were the "Judas niggers." They met practitioners of jobs they thought had vanished—midwife, fortune teller, bootlegger—and they learned about folk remedies, superstitions, and how to survive on three dollars a day. On Sundays in church, they saw how faith and song held lives together. But the Fourth of July introduced volunteers to the local heroes.

Today, when the civil rights movement is mentioned, the same names surface—Rosa Parks and Dr. King, Rosa Parks and Dr. King. . . . The names of everyday people in Mississippi—Bob Moses' "striking force," who marched, registered, risked everything in the name of freedom—remain unknown. But volunteers were learning the names and meeting the people they would never forget. "What have I done in my life?" a graying Fred Winn asked, looking back more than forty years. "Well, I've done a little of this, a little of that. But I ate at the table of Fannie Lou Hamer, in her home and she called me by my name and we were friends." Cops called the local heroes "troublemakers" and "uppity niggers." Most were unknown outside their towns, but legends within, legends passing the potato salad that holiday afternoon.

Shortly after midday, in temperatures one volunteer guessed to be 110, people began pouring onto a farm near Hattiesburg. All afternoon, whites and blacks went on tractor-pulled hayrides, sought shade beneath moss-draped live oaks, and ate mountains of potato salad, watermelon, and catfish fried in huge kettles. Many wondered who was hosting the picnic. A rugged man in a pith helmet seemed in charge, tending the catfish, talking with everyone, but he looked white, and what white Mississippian would host a SNCC gathering? Questioning revealed that this was Vernon Dahmer. A gentle, ruddy-faced farmer white enough to "pass" yet proud of his black ancestry, Dahmer had housed the first SNCCs to work in Hattiesburg. Now he welcomed volunteers, including a group of teachers just arrived from a final training in Memphis. Everyone at the picnic had a great time until a pickup with a rifle rack passed. Dahmer and his son, on leave from the marines, went into the house and came out with rifles. The pickup passed again but drove on. The picnic continued until dusk, when volunteers scurried home before another night fell.

In Cleveland, Mississippi, the man to see—on the Fourth and throughout the summer—was still Amzie Moore. Standing over six feet tall, with a thick neck and bald head, Moore projected power and serenity. A father figure to Bob Moses, Moore now played the same role to volunteers. By early July, his home overflowed with college students sharing the spaghetti dinners he threw together while telling his own story. Moore had picked cotton into the Depression before landing a job as a janitor in a post office. During World War II, he had fought in a segregated unit in the Pacific, then returned to the Delta, hoping to buy land and get rich. But one winter day he visited a destitute woman in her shack and saw her fourteen children dressed in tatters. "I kinda figured it was a sin to think in terms of trying to get rich in view of what I'd seen," he remembered. Holding on to his post office job and opening a gas station, Moore joined the NAACP and quickly headed the local chapter. In 1961, when Bob Moses showed up at his door, he was ready. Three summers later, volunteers heading north through the Delta used Moore's home as a sanctuary. Though awed by his courage, some were shocked by his arsenal. Once, as two volunteers lay down to sleep in his living room, Moore set a loaded Luger on the night table "in case of emergency." When they said they were not likely to use the gun, he removed it. "Just as you say. Good night."

In Clarksdale, volunteers flocked to the picnic at "Doc" Henry's place. Aaron Henry had succeeded his friend Medgar Evers as black Mississippi's leading spokesman. His lengthy boycotts of Clarksdale businesses resulted in the bombing of his home and pharmacy. Arrested on a trumped-up morals charge, he had worked as a garbage collector and on a chain gang at Parchman Farm. Undaunted, Henry finally returned to his Fourth Street Drug Store, where his front window displayed the Declaration of Independence and the Emancipation Proclamation. Conservative and cautious, Henry bristled at SNCCs' overalls and T-shirts and disapproved of many SNCC tactics, but he backed Freedom Summer from the first day. On the Fourth of July, volunteers ate hot dogs and strummed guitars at "Doc's house."

Not all local heroes were men. At each holiday picnic, volunteers met strong, inspiring black women. SNCC had always welcomed women, and from its first days in Mississippi, they were marching to courthouses, rallying neighbors, singing at mass meetings that were often two-thirds female. Together, they formed an army of support, but volunteers saw some standing out from the ranks. In Greenwood, proud and defiant Laura McGhee, enraged by the shooting of her brother, had opened her small farm to SNCC in 1962. McGhee became a legend a year later when, knocked down by a cop, she yanked away his nightstick. All that summer, McGhee's son Silas would lead black Greenwood's defiance.

At the Dahmer picnic in Hattiesburg, volunteers met Victoria Gray, already a mother of three running a cosmetics business and teaching literacy when she decided to register. "When I raised my hand," Gray remembered, "I knew the rest of my life would not be the same." Within a year she was a SNCC field secretary, and within two she was running for Congress on the parallel Mississippi Freedom Democratic Party (MFDP) ticket.

But the most celebrated of all local heroes was the powerhouse who hosted her own Independence Day picnic in Ruleville. The twentieth child of share-croppers, Fannie Lou Hamer had been working in the cotton fields since the 1920s, unaware she even had the right to vote. All her life she had bristled at how Mississippi treated her. Growing up barefoot, hungry, wishing "so bad" that she was white, she had helped her mother roam the Marlowe plantation "scrapping" cotton shreds to sell. She had watched her father save to buy wagons and farm tools, only to have an envious white man poison his mules. Worn down by field work, Hamer had two stillborn children, then adopted two daughters. In 1961, she entered the hospital with "a knot on my stomach" and came out sterilized without her consent. Something had to change. She attended her first SNCC meeting in the summer of 1962. If enough blacks registered, James Forman announced, they could vote racist politicians and sheriffs out of office. When Forman asked for volunteers, Hamer's hand went up first. "Had it up as high as I could get it," she recalled. A few days later she was on a bus heading for the Sunflower County courthouse. The registration test asked her to explain de facto laws. "I knowed as much about a facto law as a horse knows about Christmas Day," she later said. She failed. When she came home, she heard the "boss man" was "raisin' Cain." Mr. Marlowe told Hamer she would have to withdraw her registration because "we're not ready for that in Mississippi." If she refused, she would have to leave the plantation where she had worked for eighteen years as a timekeeper.

"I didn't try to register for you," Hamer replied. "I tried to register for myself."

Thrown out of her shack, Hamer moved to a neighbor's where her bed-room was soon riddled by sixteen shots fired late one night. Yet she dug into herself and into the movement, becoming, as she called it, "a Snicker." James Forman said of Hamer, "She was SNCC itself." Hamer sometimes seemed a force of nature. When she threw her head back and sang, it was said you could hear her all over Sunflower County. When she spoke, she lifted audi-ences off their feet. When she moved, black Mississippi seemed to move with her. She often discounted the risks. "The only thing they could do to me was kill me and it seemed like they'd been trying to do that just a little bit at a time since I could remember." A deeply religious woman, Hamer saw the movement in biblical themes. Bob Moses' name, she often said, was no coincidence. Beatings and jail were crosses to bear. Summer volunteers were Good Samaritans, and freedom was her own Promised Land.

As Hamer had told volunteers in Ohio, she had been savagely beaten in jail in 1963, yet she refused to hate those who hated her. "The white man's afraid he'll be treated like he's been treating the Negroes, but I couldn't carry that much hate." By 1964, her signature phrase—"I'm sick and tired of being sick and tired"—was widely known among Delta blacks, and her favorite song, "This Little Light of Mine," kicked off every mass meeting she attended. Throughout Freedom Summer, her home would be a headquarters not just for volunteers but for freedom itself. Reporters looking for stories were told to go to Fannie Lou Hamer's house. Hungry volunteers always found a pot of beans cooking in her kitchen, while those who needed shade found their way beneath her pecan tree. For decades, she had seen no future beyond Ruleville's cotton fields. Yet in the spring of 1964, she waged a quixotic run for Congress and was profiled in the *Nation* and the *Washington Post*. That August, she would speak on national television. But for all her fire, it was her husband, a huge, hard-drinking stalwart she called "Pap," who best expressed how the blend of volunteers and local heroes brought the movement in Mississippi to fruition that summer. Asked by a cop how he felt having "white boys" sleep in his house, Pap Hamer replied, "I feel like a man because they treat me like a man."

At Hamer's picnic, volunteers ate "special dishes" prepared by women in Jerusalem and Sanctified Quarters. The fare included cornbread, peas in bacon and onion sauce, potato casseroles, "and more and more and more until the pies and the cakes and the ice cream came and we could not refuse." After the feast, four congressmen touring the Delta, one the father of a Ruleville volunteer, said a few words, but a local black woman said more: "These young white folks who are already free, they come here only to help us. They is proving to us that black and white can do it together, that it ain't true what we always thought, that all white folks is booger men, 'cause they sure is not."

Another week had passed in Mississippi, another week of hope and hatred. Prank calls now came to project offices asking, "Can I speak to Andy Goodman?" But for all the hostility in the air, the second week of Freedom Summer saw half the violence of the first. Not even the most naive volunteer expected the terror had ended, but might Mississippi be getting used to them? Night remained a madhouse, but could one step out during the day?

A few blocks from the Mississippi River in Greenville, Muriel Tillinghast had spent two weeks upstairs. Other volunteers had entered the office early each morning, left late each evening. Their jocularity amazed Muriel, but their confidence was not contagious. No matter how they tried to get her outside, she refused to leave. All her inherited skills, her years of protest and picketing, had been drowned in fear. Her "Sunday call," Charlie Cobb, had come back from Neshoba County with chilling tales of late-night searches for the three. Now, the affable Cobb, a poet, writer, and educator, was telling Muriel how safe Greenville was. But Muriel, sure that her skin and her natural hair made her a target, remained upstairs. Alone with her fears each night, she had them reinforced by phone threats—"Just wanted to know if you niggers are going to church this morning."

Much had happened in Greenville to soothe Muriel's concerns. Volunteers had marched around a federal building, protesting LBJ's refusal to send marshals to Mississippi. Greenville police watched but made no arrests. A Greenville jury acquitted a black man of rape charges by a white woman. No one could remember that ever happening in Mississippi. Several high school students, having led sit-ins, were in the office working, joking, easing tensions. And each morning, someone brought in the newspaper.

When Goodman, Schwerner, and Chaney disappeared, the *Delta Democrat-Times* preached tolerance. June 24, 1964: "Today would be a good day for prayer in Mississippi, a sincere prayer that the three missing civil rights workers are not dead. If our prayers are not answered, if murder has been committed, then the rest of the summer could well be pure hell." And to those who said the three "mixers" had been taught a lesson, Hodding Carter III added, "It may well be a lesson. It may be a lesson that there are people living in this state who can see three men disappear without concern simply because they felt the men were unwelcome." Upstairs, Muriel read the local news and recognized Greenville as different. But she also heard news from the rest of Mississippi and stayed inside. The office had no refrigerator, so she survived on whatever others could bring her. She lost "a lotta weight." Finally, she had "an epiphany that I couldn't register people to vote on the second floor of the office. I had to come out."

Sometime that Fourth of July weekend, Muriel edged her way down the stairs and stepped into the blinding glare, straight into the face of Mississippi. Step by step, she learned to walk beside her fears. Her first journey took her alongside the COFO building, past the dry cleaners, running her hands along the warm bricks. After a few minutes, she went back inside, but she returned to the street the next day. She visited the mom-and-pop store she had seen only from the second-story window and the juke joints farther down Nelson Street. No one drove by, shouting. No one noticed at all. By the time she began her third week in Mississippi, Muriel was herself again—shaken but ready to be the take-charge activist with the degree from Howard and the street credentials from its Non-Violent Action Group. She thought she was prepared for whatever Mississippi could throw at her. She did not know that in two weeks, Charlie Cobb would leave, putting her in charge of the Greenville project.

The week that opened with the revival of dying buildings closed with events equally unimaginable a month before. In June, it would have been easy to foresee the mob scene in Laurel when blacks tried to eat at a Burger Chef, or the brawl in Greenwood when Silas McGhee tried to integrate the Leflore Theater. But who would have predicted what occurred in Jackson on July 5? That Sunday afternoon, NAACP leaders flew to Mississippi to test the Civil Rights Act. Expecting to be arrested or beaten, they were met by police and escorted to the Heidelberg Hotel downtown. Joined by Jackson's local heroes, the black men walked into the hotel, up to the desk—and checked in. A white bellboy took their bags. They ate lunch in the Green Room. "The food was good, the service was good, and the attitude was good," said a Jackson minister whose home had been shot into just twelve days earlier. Other tests—at the Sun n' Sand Motel and the King Edward Hotel—also went off without incident. "I think we can see helpful signs that Mississippi will get in step with the nation," the minister said. The manager of the Sun n' Sand summed up the grudging attitude of much of Mississippi: "We are just going to abide by the law."

As a new week began, NAACP leaders set out to tour Mississippi and make more tests. Caught up in the same spirit, SNCC readied staffers to work in the Klan hotbed of McComb. And volunteers prepared for more canvassing and the opening of Freedom Schools across the state. Neither the NAACP, the volunteers, nor those well schooled in Mississippi violence had any notion that the holiday was over.

I'm standin' at the crossroads
And I believe I'm sinkin' down.

—Robert Johnson, "Cross Road Blues"

CHAPTER SIX

"The Scars of the System"

Moss Point, Mississippi, a small town along the Singing River near the Gulf of Mexico, had seen its share of turmoil that summer. Volunteers were in town only a few days when a meeting hall was firebombed and several were arrested. With tension rising, blacks and whites were buying guns, and one white was found carrying a grenade. Rumors of black children poisoned by candy had only been rumors, yet Moss Point remained a racial tripwire, taut, edgy, just waiting for something horrible to happen.

"Tonight the sickness struck," a Moss Point volunteer wrote home on July 6. That Monday evening, three hundred people packed into the Knights of Pythias Hall, its front door still blackened from the Molotov cocktail. Speaking to the crowd, a stocky, bespectacled man was rising to a fever pitch. Lawrence Guyot, beaten along with Fannie Lou Hamer the year before, was furious. Like Greenville, his native Gulf Coast was known for relative tolerance, yet despite steady canvassing, few had come out to register. "What will it take to make you people move?" Guyot shouted. "A rape? A shooting? A murder? What will it take?" Other speeches followed before Freedom Songs soothed tensions. Meanwhile in nearby Pascagoula, three men crammed into a small car. They barely had room for the rifle.

Back at the Knights Hall, the crowd had arrived at every meeting's final song. Glowing, ecstatic faces sang together, arms clasped, swaying like lilies in the field. The lone cop on hand, concluding the meeting was over, drove away. Then as a final "We Shall Overcome" filled the hall, the car sped past. Three sharp cracks rang out. Near the window, a black woman crumpled to the floor. A fan toppled, its whirring blades slamming into the concrete like a machine gun firing. In the chaos, one volunteer saw the fallen woman "lying on the ground clutching her stomach. She was so still and looked like a statue with a tranquil smile on her face." Several men bolted from the hall, hopped in a car, and chased the attackers into a gas station. But one white leveled the rifle, sending blacks scurrying. When police arrived, they arrested the blacks and let everyone else go. At Singing River Hospital, the woman was listed in "good" condition, but the shots sent notice that despite the hope, the singing, the new Civil Rights Act, this was still Mississippi, still the "long, hot summer," and it was just July.

June had been a blanket, but July was an oven, melting, igniting, engulfing. Timeless patterns governed July in Mississippi. The first was the relentless humidity, the sultry nights never drying the earth before the sun rose again to turn on the steam. The second pattern was the cycle of heat and rain, heat and rain. Both patterns were ingrained in locals who knew when to get chores done, when a blazing sky made a nap seem in order, when thunderheads would hover on the horizon like anvils, and when marble-sized raindrops would turn the red earth to mud, cooling the oven to a sticky 80 degrees or so. But volunteers were still learning the patterns. It was not unusual to find them alone on the street at noon. Chris Williams could not understand why no male in Mississippi wore shorts, and neither could he. Nor could volunteers swim anywhere, the rivers being muddy or snake-infested and the public pools off-limits to "invaders." Day after day the heat mounted, turning skin into hot leather and tempers into fuses. With air-conditioning in only the richest homes, relief came solely when leaden clouds unleashed their fury, releasing a collective sigh from the people and the land. And as volunteers gradually learned the patterns, Mississippi unleashed its own fury.

That week, a Confederate flag flew outside the elegant Robert E. Lee Hotel in Jackson. A sign in the door read, "Closed in Despair—Civil Rights Bill Unconstitutional." (The hotel opened a few days later as a private club.) Across town, city officials fenced off a park after whites complained about black kids running through it shouting, "I'm free!" Elsewhere in Mississippi, pools and libraries closed. Restaurant owners drove blacks off at gunpoint. Governor Paul Johnson predicted more violence "unless these people get out of the state and go back to their own problems at home." And a few hours after the Moss Point shooting, flames torched three more churches in Mississippi. The pattern was now heat and fire, heat and fire. But as this merciless climate descended, it could not smother those too innocent, too committed, to heed the mayhem all around them.

Warm, soft rains had greeted Fran O'Brien when a Greyhound bus left her on the bluffs above the Mississippi River in the Civil War siege site of Vicksburg. Being from southern California, where it never rains in summer, Fran immediately sensed Mississippi as exotic. Yet once inside COFO's Freedom House, she felt right at home among her lifelong friends—children. A black woman named Bessie, her husband killed by the Klan, her house recently bombed, was living with her six children amid the boxes and clutter. While other volunteers roamed the Freedom House that Sunday afternoon, the children flocked around the newcomer with the pale face, dark, curly hair, and sweet smile, begging Fran to do *something* with them on a rainy day. And so, fresh from an Oregon campus and two long bus rides, twenty-one-year-old Fran O'Brien began her summer. In the next seven weeks, she would meet Martin Luther King. She would have a terrifying encounter with the Klan. She would turn the red clay of Mississippi into craft projects, and although too modest to claim the role, she would represent creativity in its ceaseless battle with destruction.

Fran cared little about the politics of Freedom Summer. Instead, she saw the project as a chance to test her Christian values, and to teach. Bashful around adults, Fran came alive with children. In high school and at Pacific University in Oregon, the slim, demure woman had helped out in classrooms, doing crafts and drama with minimal materials, precisely what was planned in Freedom Schools. Learning of the summer project from her United Campus Christian Fellowship, Fran took out an application, but could not make up her mind. Finally, a scene from the film *Judgment at Nuremberg* sent her south. When a judge asked a German housekeeper what *she* had done under Hitler, Fran asked herself how she would feel if, in thirty years, someone asked what she had done during the civil rights movement and she had to say, "Nothing."

A long letter home to Whittier, California, surprised her parents. "I hope you're not *too* upset," Fran wrote. "I also hope our ceiling is still in tact." Her father, a labor attorney, felt proud. Her mother, a former social worker, tried to be supportive but kept asking, "Are you sure this is what you want to do?" Fran was sure. Her letter made it "clearly understood that this is my project." She had saved $100 and, throwing in $57.30 from her tax return, insisted on paying her own expenses. After attending a wedding, she had boarded a Greyhound for Spokane, transferred again and again, and arrived at the Ohio campus on the Sunday the three men disappeared. Throughout that grim week, Fran had tried to concentrate on workshops, yet news from Mississippi kept interrupting.

On Monday morning, when Rita Schwerner had sent volunteers to write their congressmen, Fran had found a different way to face the danger. California's was the training's largest cohort, and Fran figured no one would miss her if she took care of other business. Her niece had a birthday in July, and "it occurred to me that I might not be around." While alarm spread across campus, Fran walked into town and bought a toy teakettle, shipped it to California, then went back to the training, still determined to go to Mississippi. Vicksburg would be her site. She knew it only as a battlefield.

While rain tapped on windows of the Freedom House that Sunday, Fran sat at a broken-down piano, playing all the songs the kids knew. Other volunteers ventured into neighboring streets, but Fran spent all afternoon singing, inventing games, spinning stories. That same day in the black section of Vicksburg, three kids playing in a field found a dead body. In the coming week, a volunteer's car windshield would be shattered, Freedom School students would be struck by stones, and a nearby church would go up in flames. Fran O'Brien would only hear of each incident. She did not bother about what adults did to other adults. There were children present.

The day after Fran's arrival, volunteers spruced up the Vicksburg Community Center. All day, kids came up the long, potholed driveway to flock around the newcomers, begging to help but mostly getting in the way. Fran's classes would not start until the following Monday. In the meantime, she struggled to settle into her host home. The elderly woman who had taken her in seemed to want nothing to do with her. If Fran or her roommate took a seat in the living room, the woman moved to the kitchen. If they followed, the woman went back to the living room. "It was just the way she'd grown up," Fran remembered. "You don't sit down in the parlor with white folks; that's being uppity." Feeling as if she were chasing the woman around her own house, Fran stayed in her room as much as possible. On the evening President Johnson signed the Civil Rights Act, she was at the Freedom House. The building was crammed with volunteers and neighbors who did not have televisions. "He's signing!" someone shouted and everyone ran to the blue-lit TV, cheered, sang "We Shall Overcome" and then, for fun, "We Have Overcome."

Four days later, Fran began classes in the refurbished community center. The building still had no plumbing or electricity. Dappled light filtered through windows as Fran helped kids weave on cardboard looms. Later the class crowded close as she read stories, her serene face and California accent riveting each child. That afternoon, as a mob in Neshoba County menaced touring NAACP leaders, Fran played outdoor games with the children. After dinner, while shots rang out in Moss Point, she and other teachers planned the coming week. Just before going to bed, Fran wrote her mother.

> Please try not to worry too much. Vicksburg is the best place to work in Mississippi so far as staying out of danger is concerned. I'll admit seven weeks seems like a long time before coming home, but not nearly as long as it seemed three weeks ago when I was beginning to wonder if I'd get to Mississippi—let alone get back. . . . I'll trust God and try to keep my enthusiasm within reasonable limits. I'm very grateful to you for standing behind me in this.
>
> Good night and Love,
> Fran

By the second week of July, everyone assumed Goodman, Schwerner, and Chaney were dead—everyone, that is, except their mothers. In her Manhattan apartment, Carolyn Goodman found herself drawn to her son's room. Silent and sorrowful, she sat staring at clothes, books, folk music LPs, wondering what Andy had thought of each, fighting the thought that she would never know. One afternoon, a man called, saying he had Andy in a Brooklyn hotel and would return him for $15,000. The man grew enraged when asked to provide proof and never called again. Since the disappearance, the Goodmans had received scores of letters offering prayers, condolences, even a $500 check "which will help you discover the killer of your beautiful Andy." A ten-year-old girl had written to say she had named her cat Andrew Goodman because "I think Andrew Goodman is a heroe [*sic*] and I think something should be named after him." Of all the letters, the Goodmans were especially comforted by one from a mother in Meridian, Mississippi. Apologizing for her state, the woman asked, "Who are these fiends and where do they live who would come out of the darkness and kill?"

A thousand miles south, Fannie Lee Chaney had taken to pacing outside her home in Meridian. Each night she walked until the sky lightened, circling the house, wearing a path in the grass, humming "Rock of Ages" or some other spiritual. Each evening after work, she cleaned obsessively, mopping the kitchen floor three or four times, washing the dishes, drying them, washing them again. She refused to let twelve-year-old Ben go down the street to play ball. One evening she got a call from a young woman who told of recently giving birth to "J. E.'s" daughter. Skeptical, she had mother and child take a taxi to her house. One look at the baby, and Fannie Lee Chaney knew she was a grandmother. She took the baby in her arms, wishing she could do the same with her own son.

And still there was no trace of the men. Mississippi's raw, rugged land could not have been better suited for hiding a body. Murky rivers gave up nothing to the grappling hook. Swamps kept their secrets behind protruding trees, beneath black waters. Tangled vineroot defied anyone to tear through it. No trace. The FBI lab in New Orleans examined items from the burned station wagon—dirt and debris, keys, a charred wristwatch stopped at 12:45—but found "no evidence of human remains." The latest lead, a grave along the Chunky River south of Neshoba County, turned out to contain a dead horse. With hope disappearing, America's obsession with Mississippi was turning to other concerns—to the mounting crisis in Vietnam, to the upcoming Republican National Convention, to the topless swimsuit craze. No longer in the media spotlight, some in Mississippi again felt the impunity of "the good ol' days" when what happened in Mississippi stayed there. And the effort to stop Freedom Summer, to drive the "invaders" out, to preserve "our way of life," exploded with a vengeance.

Cops tired of arresting volunteers on any pretense and releasing them on $100 bail began upping the bail. Reckless driving—$250. Speeding—$400. Trespassing—$500. Trespassing and public profanity—$1,000. Ordinary citizens lashed out. In Hattiesburg, several black kids went to an inn whose "Whites Only" sign had been taken down. The owner's wife pulled a gun. In the Delta, a volunteer was not just told to leave the courthouse but grabbed by the neck and thrown out. In Jackson, a white man parked his pickup, got out, decked a Negro with a sucker punch, and drove off. Such incidents—more violent, more frequent, more frightening—were happening all over Mississippi. That made the silence from McComb especially terrifying.

By Tuesday, July 7, SNCC again had a "beachhead" in Mississippi's deep Deep South. During the holiday weekend, five volunteers and two SNCC staffers had crammed into a beat-up sedan and set out from Jackson. Rolling south beneath puffy blue skies, the integrated car attracted little attention along the newly opened stretch of Interstate 55. But when the interstate ended and the sedan began snaking down two-lane roads, a highway patrol car pulled behind. As if one was towing the other, the two vehicles drove on past vines and thickets that grew denser with each mile. SNCC staffers must have felt a clammy sense of dread as they passed the sign reading "Pike County." McComb (pop. 12,020) was the toughest of Mississippi's "tough towns," but because Bob Moses wanted SNCC to "share the terror" of local blacks, a Freedom House was to open on the black side of town.

With the highway patrol in its rearview mirror, the sedan drove slowly into McComb. Given what they had heard of the place, volunteers might have expected to see some redneck backwater out of *Tobacco Road*. Instead they saw well-kept drugstores and five-and-dimes, pink azaleas bursting from planters on covered sidewalks, and a billboard picture of a beauty queen beneath the words "Home of Miss Mississippi." McComb was a "railroad town." Freights rumbled through several times a day, hundreds of men worked for one railroad or another, and twice daily, the City of New Orleans stopped at the old station, taking passengers to or from Chicago. Trains were the only sign of life on a baking Sunday afternoon as SNCC veterans reacquainted themselves with the town they had fled three years earlier. There in back alleys stood the "Colored Only" entrances to restaurants. There were the city hall steps where a mob had beaten several SNCCs in 1961. And there behind them was the highway patrolman, his red light flashing.

Pulling the SNCC car over, the patrolmen took all seven men in for questioning. But to their surprise, they were not beaten, nor arrested. Released, they drove across the railroad tracks and pulled up at a small, tumbledown house in a neighborhood of small, tumbledown houses. No angry whites greeted them. No pickups circled. That evening as the new arrivals ate at a Negro café, two cops entered, walked to the back, glared at one white man, then walked out. The following day, SNCC staff, accompanied by one of the four touring congressmen, met with McComb's mayor and the Pike County sheriff. The sheriff even promised police protection for the Freedom House. SNCC sent back word to Jackson: "Morale is building." Bob Moses, however, was not fooled. On Tuesday evening, he visited the Freedom House and begged all those he had just sent there to leave. Something was going to happen, Moses said. Curtis Hayes, whose determination to work in his hometown had convinced Moses to open the house, refused to go. Others said they would depart the next morning. Moses left, and all went to sleep.

The usual incoming distress calls lit up the WATS line in Jackson that Tuesday evening, but at 1:30 a.m., the phone stopped ringing. For the next two hours, the office was eerily quiet. Then the phone rang again. A scratchy voice was on the line. From McComb. "Have just had a bombing . . . wait a minute . . ." Endless moments passed before the man said he would call back. The full report finally came on one of the new CB radios COFO was installing in offices throughout the state.

With a blast heard all over McComb, eight sticks of dynamite had blown in the front of the Freedom House. Curtis Hayes had been sleeping near the front window. The explosion knocked him across the room, knocked him unconscious. He woke up head pounding, ears ringing, arms, legs, and face laced with cuts. Crawling through the wreckage, Hayes met another staffer. "See that, motherfucker," the man said. "I told you we should get the hell outta here." A volunteer from Oregon had suffered a concussion. Others sleeping in the house were unhurt. Back in Jackson, staffers worried they had moved into McComb too soon, but another call suggested that the bomb had only strengthened spirits: "Bomb was placed between car and end of house at front of house at left, facing street. Damage on left side. Whole left side completely smashed in—can drive a car thru. Middle, all windows smashed, walls falling down from top. Shattered windows two houses across the street and next door. We are going ahead in the community. Everyone determined. Mass meeting tonight."

During the second week of July 1964, while children across America relished their freedom from classrooms, three dozen schools opened in Mississippi. Classes met in converted shacks and church basements, beneath trees and on open lawns. Teachers had few textbooks and little training. Attendance was entirely voluntary. There would be no lectures and no tests, no principals, no homework. Yet the lessons would change the lives of nearly every teacher and every student. These were the Freedom Schools.

Freedom Schools had an unusual legacy. In the fall of 1961, McComb high school student Brenda Travis was suspended for her role in a sit-in, leading one hundred fellow students to walk out in protest. When the hundred were also suspended, SNCC opened its own school, quickly dubbed "Non-Violent High." Bob Moses taught math again; other SNCCs taught history, black history, art, and literature. Non-Violent High classes continued until all the teachers were convicted of contributing to the delinquency of a minor and sentenced to six months. Ever since, parallel schooling had been a SNCC dream and, for young blacks in Mississippi, a light in the wilderness.

A decade after the *Brown* decision, Mississippi remained the last southern state whose schools were completely and defiantly segregated. Schools were just one of Mississippi's "separate but equal" institutions, but they made the biggest mockery of the phrase. Forty-two percent of Mississippi whites had finished high school; among blacks the figure was 7 percent. Statewide per-pupil expenditures for whites were four times what they were for blacks, and in some counties the ratio was fifty to one. Black teachers struggled on in dilapidated classrooms with ancient texts, no equipment, and only the most basic subjects. Yet it was their teaching that infuriated SNCC veteran Charlie Cobb. With fifty students in a class, teachers had no time for questioning or investigation, and principals hired by white school boards did not dare challenge the status quo. Freedom Schools, Cobb noted in a cowritten prospectus, would be different. The prospectus was sent that spring to all Freedom School teachers.

To those who had plowed through dry educational monographs, SNCC's "Notes on Teaching in Mississippi" must have stood out like the prose of Eudora Welty. It opened: "This is the situation. You will be teaching young people who have lived in Mississippi all their lives. That means that they have been deprived of decent education from first grade through high school. It means that they have been denied free expression and free thought. Most of all it means that they have been denied the right to question. The purpose of the Freedom Schools is to help them begin to question."

What would the students be like?

"They will be different but they will have in common the scars of the system. Some will be cynical. Some will be distrustful. All of them will have a serious lack of preparation . . . but all of them will have a knowledge far beyond their years. This knowledge is the knowledge of how to survive in a society that is out to destroy you."

And what would students demand of teachers?

"They will demand that you be honest. . . . Honesty means that you will *ask* questions as well as answer them. It means that if you don't know something you will say so." Freedom Schools, the prospectus concluded, would mount a full frontal assault on Mississippi's power structure, a structure that confined Negro education to "learning to stay in your place . . . to be satisfied—'a good nigger.'"

Planning three dozen schools for a thousand students on a budget of $2,000 took more time than most had expected. In March, SNCC meetings in Manhattan had tapped the expertise of professors and teachers. The Freedom School curriculum they devised would include (1) remedial and standard classes in reading, writing, and math; (2) a study of the movement; (3) more black history than anyone had yet taught in an American public school; (4) lessons questioning conditions in Mississippi and in northern ghettos; and (5) comparisons of the Negro and the "poor white." Teachers were also encouraged to offer the electives whites alone enjoyed in Mississippi public schools, including typing, French, Spanish, art, drama, and dance. And above all, they were urged to "be creative. Experiment. The kids will love it."

Arriving in Mississippi on June 28, teachers had spent a week arranging classrooms, shelving books, and spreading word about their schools. But with the term "Freedom School" seeming like an oxymoron, would anyone come to classes taught by strangers in the middle of summer? The answer depended less on curiosity than on terror.

Three schools were planned in Canton, half an hour north of Jackson. But a man threatened to bomb students' homes, and others broke into the new library and urinated on the books. On registration day, no one showed up at one school, just a handful at others. Then teachers went door to door and hosted their own Fourth of July picnic. Enrollment soon topped seventy-five. In Ruleville, fifty packed into the old shack that carpenter Fred Winn and others had brought back to life. Because Ruleville's public schools were still in session, morning classes were for adults, often with toddlers. While cotton baked in surrounding fields, the house swarmed with activity. Children raced in and out. Adults studied citizenship, health, and the three R's, while teachers sat on the sagging porch near the tall sunflowers, discussing *Huckleberry Finn* or the truth about Reconstruction. Following a midday break from the heat, high school students took over the school, exploring literature, African culture, art, and biology. Girls especially liked dance classes, where they taught their ungainly teachers how to flap their arms and do "the Monkey." Above the clamor, students could hear a loud clacking coming from the porch. Typing class.

In Meridian, where Rita and Mickey Schwerner had paved the way, 50 students were expected, but 120 showed up. Teachers facing classes of 30 or more struggled to draw answers from shy students. "What do we mean when we say things are bad in Mississippi?" "What do white people have that we want?" Despite the overcrowding, one Meridian teacher noticed what SNCC had said about "a knowledge far beyond their years." "If reading levels are not always the highest," he wrote home, "the philosophical understanding is almost alarming: some of the things that our 11 and 12 year olds will come out with would never be expected from someone of that age in the North."

Other schools opened that week in Greenwood and Vicksburg, Greenville and Moss Point. But the most successful schools were down south in Hattiesburg. Blacks there were still talking about "Freedom Day" the previous January, when two hundred had picketed the courthouse in the rain. Since then, more than a thousand had tried to register, some trying six, seven, eight times. Much of Hattiesburg's fervor stemmed from a single name— Clyde Kennard. The sturdy army veteran had tried to integrate Mississippi Southern College, only to be framed on a charge of stealing chicken feed. Sent to Parchman Farm, Kennard developed terminal cancer but was kept behind bars until just before his death. United in outrage, black Hattiesburg had welcomed SNCC and strengthened its NAACP. As Freedom Summer approached, plans were made for seven Freedom Schools. On registration day, 150 students were expected; 575 showed up. The first to register was an eighty-two-year-old man who had taught himself to read but needed help with the registration form. When classes opened, all seven schools were full. Directors had to promise a second session in August.

Planning and publicity had filled Freedom Schools, but could classes foster any meaningful sense of freedom? Could white college students who had first read *The Souls of Black Folk* en route to Ohio teach black history? Could they help students see "the link between a rotting shack and a rotting America"? Pamela Parker, from Bucks County, Pennsylvania, sent the answers home in a letter.

Dear Mom and Dad,

The atmosphere in class is unbelievable. It is what every teacher dreams about—real, honest enthusiasm and desire to learn anything and everything. The girls come to class of their own free will. They respond to everything that is said. They are excited about learning. They drain me of everything that I have to offer so that I go home at night completely exhausted but very happy. . . .

Not all teachers were happy, however. Many were appalled at what their students did not know. Asked the number of states in America, one boy answered, "Eighty-two" (the number of counties in Mississippi). In one Hattiesburg classroom, not a single student had heard of *Brown v. Board of Education.* "Where do roads come from?" Answer: "God." And the capital of the United States? "Ummm . . . Jackson?" Compounding the ignorance were the conditions. Walls sported just a poster or two. Students clustered on benches instead of sitting at desks, supplies were chronically short, and classrooms were so stifling that afternoon classes often met outside under trees. To surmount such obstacles, teachers applied creativity—broken windows in one school were covered by kids' watercolors—and tireless energy. Most teachers began at 7:00 a.m., planning classes that started an hour later. Teachers taught till noon, broke for lunch, ran three-hour afternoon sessions, went home for dinner, and returned for evening work with adults. Accustomed to low pay, these teachers were working for none. Their ten-dollar weekly room and board came out of their own pockets.

While most Freedom Schools hummed, a few were all but silent. In Moss Point, still reeling from the drive-by shooting, less than a dozen students showed up each day. In several towns, ministers fearful of firebombs refused to turn church halls into classrooms, and Freedom Schools had yet to open. In the destitute Delta town of Shaw, forty students had shown up the first day, ten the second. Finally, the school's director wrote Freedom School supervisor Staughton Lynd:

I think I am rapid [*sic*] losing whatever effectiveness I may have had as a coordinator, or even as a rights worker. . . . Living conditions here are so terrible, the Negroes are so completely oppressed, so completely without hope, that I want to change it all NOW. I mean this as sincerely as I can. Running a freedom school is an absurd waste of time. I don't want to sit around in a classroom; I want to go out and throw a few bombs, burn a few office buildings, not to injure people but to shake them up. . . . I really can't stand it here.

Lynd scheduled a trip to Shaw.

But despair was less common than discovery. Startled by teachers they could call by their first names, teachers who dared them to question Mississippi, kids were also amazed to learn they had a proud history. Stories of the *Amistad* slave rebellion spread smiles across black faces. Students were stunned to hear that a black man, Matthew Henson, had been one of the first to reach the North Pole. And they ate up the poetry of Langston Hughes, reading his poems aloud, begging to take his books home. Endesha Ida Mae Holland remembered reading Richard Wright's *Black Boy* in the Greenwood Freedom School. "I kept thinking, 'Well, you mean black folk can actually write *books*?' Because I'd always been told blacks had done no great things, they hadn't done anything, we had *nothing* that we could be proud of." As initial awkwardness settled into familiar rhythms of call-and-response, students and teachers shared their curiosity and their surprise at coming together across racial boundaries, across the North-South divide, and across cacophonous classrooms where young hands shot in the air and withered old hands gripped pencils, slowly writing, A . . . B . . . C . . . "Our school was by any definition a fine school," remembered Sandra Adickes, a New York English teacher who taught in Hattiesburg. "No attendance sheets, absentee postcards, truant officers, report cards—just perfect attendance."

The morning after the bomb caved in McComb's Freedom House, cops stood in the rain near the cratered driveway, studying the rubble. "Looks like termites to me," one joked. But police and everyone else in McComb knew precisely who was to blame.

The Ku Klux Klan was said to be a "secret" organization. Masked in secret handshakes, clandestine greetings, and bizarre titles from kleagle to kludd, the Klan rarely claimed responsibility for violence. Yet throughout the spring of 1964, telltale terrorism—the disappearance of five black men, the flogging of blacks in a bayou, the bombing of local heroes' homes—convinced everyone in Pike County that the Klan was rising again. In the ninety years since its vigilante violence had "redeemed" the state, the Klan had rarely been strong in Mississippi. Whites there saw little need for a Klan. Blacks knew "their place," and whites knew enough of terror to keep them in it. Only in the 1920s, when "Ku Kluxism" spread across America, did the Klan return to the Magnolia State, but courageous Delta planters had exposed its corruption, leaving the KKK dormant for decades. Then during the civil rights movement, the Klan resurged, and not just in Mississippi. By the summer of 1964, klaverns were meeting all over the South. North Carolina's Klan had seven thousand members. A "Razorback Klan" raged in Arkansas. Fiery Klan rallies sparked violence in St. Augustine, Florida, and the Klan was spreading "like wildfire" in Louisiana. Mississippi, as its legacy of lynching proved, had plenty of vigilantes—all summer, the random beatings, threats, and other mayhem were mostly perpetrated by ordinary citizens not affiliated with any klavern. But it took the Klan's deadly mix of religion, eugenics, and paranoia to turn freelance bigotry into a holy war. Several months before Freedom Summer, a new Klan offshoot began infecting the "Sovereign Realm of Mississippi."

The White Knights of the Ku Klux Klan of Mississippi had a mission as righteous as that of their ancestors. The mission was explained by *The Klan Ledger,* a pamphlet distributed that Fourth of July. "We are now in the midst of the 'long, hot summer' of agitation which was promised to the Innocent People of Mississippi by the savage blacks and their communist masters," the pamphlet began. The *Ledger* went on to denounce "the so-called 'disappearance'" of Goodman, Schwerner, and Chaney. Any fool "so simple that he cannot recognize a communist hoax which is as plain as the one they pulled on Kennedy in Dallas" was urged to read J. Edgar Hoover's treatise on communism, *Masters of Deceit.* The White Knights, the *Ledger* said, had taken no action—yet. Klansmen were "NOT involved" in the disappearance— "there was NO DISAPPEARANCE." However . . . "We are not going to sit back and permit our rights and the rights of our posterity to be negotiated away by a group composed of atheistic priests, brainwashed black savages, and mongrelized money-worshipers, meeting with some stupid or cowardly politician. Take heed, atheists and mongrels, we will not travel your path to a Leninist Hell. . . . Take your choice, SEGREGATION, TRANQUILITY AND JUSTICE OR, BI-RACISM, CHAOS AND DEATH."

Bombs and floggings were the hallmarks of the Pike County Klan, but the Neshoba klavern had other ways of making its presence known. From the day after the "so-called 'disappearance,'" the Klan was a secret shared all over Philadelphia, Mississippi. Locals speculated on which tight-lipped farmers, which hot-tempered businessmen, which brutal cops, had joined the klavern. Though Klansmen were supposed to change meeting locations and park their cars at least a block away, the same volatile white men were regularly seen entering the Steak House Café near the Neshoba County courthouse. Locals called them "the goon squad." In the wake of the Civil Rights Act, the Steak House Café became a private club with white sheets draped over windows. Other suspected Klan haunts included certain downtown barbershops, diners, and drugstores. In the white community, suspicion spread when the FBI repeatedly summoned some lean, leather-necked trucker—or his uncle—to the Delphia Courts Motel. Across the railroad tracks, blacks heard whenever a maid found white robes in her boss's closet. But Klansmen alone knew just how the Klan operated and where it would strike next.

A Klansman's weapons were as blunt as dynamite and as cheap as gasoline, but Mississippi's White Knights had four explicit tactics in their holy war. The first was publicity—mostly cross burning and leafleting. The second—"burning and dynamiting." The third tactic was flogging, and the fourth, "extermination." The Klan's Imperial Wizard was the only man who could order the fourth tactic, and no one outside the Klan knew who he was.

Sam Holloway Bowers did not fit the stereotype of a Klansman. Slim and soft-spoken, Bowers fancied himself a southern gentleman, several cuts above his followers. "The typical Mississippi redneck doesn't have sense enough to know what he is doing," Bowers said. "I have to use him for my own cause and direct his every action to fit my plan." Bowers's grandfather had served four terms in Congress, and his father, a salesman, had instilled in Bowers a fierce righteousness about all things white, southern, and Christian. After serving in the Navy during World War II, Bowers had attended the University of Southern California on the GI Bill, then returned to Mississippi to start a vending machine company in Laurel. But by the late 1950s, the southern gentleman had developed a fascination with swastikas, guns, and anything that exploded. With the cold war raging and blacks stirring throughout Mississippi, Bowers's righteousness festered into full-blown paranoia. He began warning friends that communists were training an army of blacks in Cuba. The army would soon invade the Gulf Coast. The president would then federalize the Mississippi National Guard, forcing whites to evacuate the state, leaving it defenseless against the black-communist onslaught. The Kremlin, Bowers often said, was a front for Jews trying to topple Christianity. To such a fevered mind, Freedom Summer was a clarion call.

Late in 1963, Bowers started his own klavern, and a few months later, he gathered two hundred men to form the statewide White Knights of the Ku Klux Klan. He soon drafted a Klan Konstitution calling Mississippi a "Sovereign Realm" to be protected by himself as Imperial Wizard and a two-house Klongress. From his klavern in Laurel, Bowers began relaying orders: "The purpose and function of this organization is to preserve Christian Civilization. . . . The Will and Capability of the Liberals, Comsymps, Traitors, Atheists, and Communists to resist and subvert Christian, American Principles MUST BE DESTROYED. This is our Sacred Task."

Just as no one outside the Klan knew the Imperial Wizard's identity, no one knew whether he had ordered extermination for Goodman, Schwerner, and Chaney. But Bowers's paranoia, inflaming dozens of upstart klaverns and backed by stockpiles of dynamite and gasoline, added up to a single tactic—terror. And although their primary targets were black, the Klan terrorized anyone who got in its way. Before Freedom Summer was over, crosses would burn on the lawns of two mayors, a newspaper editor, a doctor who contributed to a church rebuilding fund, a grocer who refused to fire his black workers, even a judge. The message was unmistakable and effective. And as the summer heated up, with moderate voices terrorized into silence, the Klan proceeded with its sacred task to drive off "our Satanic enemies" and ignite Mississippi.

Robert Kennedy had warned LBJ. Shortly before Freedom Summer, Kennedy had notified the president: "Some forty instances of Klan type activity or police brutality have come to the department's attention over the past four months. I have little doubt that this will increase." Come July, the president, whose father had been threatened by the Texas Klan, turned again to J. Edgar Hoover. "I think you ought to put fifty, a hundred people after this Klan . . . ," LBJ told Hoover. "You ought to have the best intelligence system—better than you've got on the Communists. . . . I don't want these Klansmen to open their mouth without your knowing what they're saying." Hoover sent more agents with instructions "to identify and interview every Klansman in the state." Then on July 9, the FBI director stunned Mississippians by announcing he was coming to Jackson. The next day.

Hoover had never been to Mississippi, and news of his arrival stirred a frenzy of speculation. "Neshoba Arrests Believed Imminent," the *Meridian Star* headlined. Arrests, however, were nowhere near. FBI agents were still finding Neshoba County a human swamp. Some residents had finally begun to talk, but not about the disappearance. Agents questioning locals were subjected to tiresome rants about Communists and Jews, Martin Luther King and Bobby Kennedy. The resistance on the street was less subtle. Agents walking through Philadelphia were shouldered off sidewalks, spat upon, hounded by threats. One even found rattlesnakes in his car. FBI veteran Joseph Sullivan, the burly, crew-cut agent heading the investigation, had found just one reliable source—the Meridian highway patrolman who had handed over the initial list of seven suspects. From late June into early July, Sullivan and his source met on sidewalks and in cafés to talk about the Klan and "whose neighbors were friendly with who." But whenever Sullivan asked about Goodman, Schwerner, and Chaney, the patrolman fell silent. As for the rest of Neshoba County, Sullivan

said it needed no Klan because its ordinary citizens were the most conspirato-
rial he had ever met. Three weeks after their arrival, many of Sullivan's men
had given up. The search was "just going through the motions," one said. But a
few held out hope: "We haven't even started leaning on suspects yet. When we
do, we're going to lean real hard. I feel like somebody will break."

On Friday morning, July 10, a bulky, bulldoggish figure strode onto the
tarmac at the Jackson airport. J. Edgar Hoover was greeted by Governor
Paul Johnson and Jackson mayor Allen Thompson. "This is truly a great
day!" the mayor said, pumping Hoover's hand. Hoover, wearing his usual
scowl, did not seem to agree. He knew next to nothing about Mississippi—he
had called the Delta town where the FBI had recently made arrests "Teeny
Weeny." Opening an office in Jackson had been Hoover's idea, but going
there in July was not. LBJ had arranged the visit. "This Mississippi thing
is awful mean," the president complained. "I'm gonna have to walk a tight-
wire there." Along with sending Hoover, Johnson had ordered the FBI to
make its presence in Jackson as public as possible, and all that week, agents
had hastily converted an abandoned bank into the bureau's first Mississippi
headquarters. Empty file cabinets were dragged in. False facades covered
bare concrete. American flags were on prominent display. But standing at a
podium in this Potemkin office, Hoover had little to announce.

He began by noting that Mississippi had the third lowest crime rate in
America. (Mississippi newspapers touted this half-truth all summer, yet
although the state's nonviolent crime rate was among the nation's lowest,
its murder rate was the highest, more than double the national norm.) When
reporters asked Hoover about Goodman, Schwerner, and Chaney, he was
blunt. "I don't close it as an absolute certainty," he said, "but I consider that
they are dead." The search, however, would go on. Another fifty agents had
arrived—solely to investigate. "We most certainly do not and will not give
protection to civil rights workers," Hoover insisted. He hinted he would visit
Neshoba County, but death threats to his motel later made him cancel his
plans. Not everyone in Mississippi thought Hoover's visit marked "truly a
great day!" Alarmed at the FBI invasion, Mississippians were joking that
the letters FBI stood for "Federal Bureau of Integration." In Jackson, a state
senator denounced the "calculated insult" of having two hundred FBI agents
in Mississippi "carrying out the wishes of Bobby Kennedy."

While Hoover spoke in Jackson that morning, the sickness struck in
the full glare of daylight. Toward noon in Hattiesburg, a middle-aged man

and his nephew tossed a tire iron into a pickup and set out to "whup" the first "white niggers" they met. They were driving near the railroad tracks when they spotted, on an embankment, three white men walking with two black teenage girls. Stopping their truck, sprinting up the grassy incline, the attackers raced past the girls, who could only watch in horror. Fists leveled one volunteer. Another, kicked and pummeled, rolled into a ball, scattering his canvassing forms. The attacker gathered the papers and shoved them in the volunteer's mouth, shouting, "Eat this shit, nigger lover!" The third victim, a rabbi from Ohio, took the full brunt of the sickness. The tire iron smashed the rabbi's temple. As he slumped to the ground, the attacker flailed away. After a minute, the men raced down the embankment and drove off. The next day, photos of Rabbi Joseph Lelyveld, his shirt more scarlet than white, circulated around the country along with his expression of "deep sorrow for Mississippi."

The weekend offered more cause for "deep sorrow." In the numbing brutality that followed, Mississippi's stark divides, separating moderate from hard-liner, redneck from socialite, assailant from onlooker, blurred in relentless revenge. And a state proud of its hospitality could no longer deny that any level of savagery now seemed possible. Canton. Browning. Laurel. Firebomb thrown at a Freedom House. Church burned. Twelve-year-old boys hit with baseball bats while cops look on. Vicksburg. Jackson. Natchez. Bomb thrown into a black café. Elderly white man beats a black woman in a coffee shop. Two more churches doused in kerosene, flames consuming the altars, the crucifixes, the wooden walls, leaving blackened cement stairs climbing from the ashes. From across Mississippi, the reports kept coming in—of assaults, bombings, and finally bodies.

On Sunday evening, July 12, a CBS reporter called the CORE office in Meridian. Had they heard the news? A fisherman downriver in Louisiana had spotted a body snagged on a log. A half body—legs only, clad in blue jeans, sneakers, bound at the ankles. No one had checked skin color, but the jeans had a leather belt with a buckle stamped M, and a gold watch and key chain in one pocket. The COFO worker shuddered. Mickey Schwerner had a similar belt, watch, and chain. And he always wore blue jeans and sneakers. Only the day before, someone had rushed in with a rumor that if the bodies were found, they would be "mutilated and scattered in different states." CORE called lawyer William Kunstler in New York. He phoned Rita Schwerner. Rita said her husband's watch was silver, not gold. He had no belt buckle with an M. But

Freedom Summer began with 250 students descending on an Ohio campus ready to spend the summer in staunchly segregated and violent Mississippi. *(Herbert Randall)*

After one week of intensive training, volunteers bid tearful good-byes and headed south. *(Ted Polumbaum/Newseum Collection)*

Eighteen-year-old Chris Williams of Amherst, Massachusetts, was the youngest volunteer. He would spend more than a year in Mississippi, dodging violence, registering voters, finally meeting the woman he would marry. *(Amherst Record)*

Civil rights legend Bob Moses, the architect of Freedom Summer, inspired volunteers with his courage and calm throughout the summer. *(Corbis)*

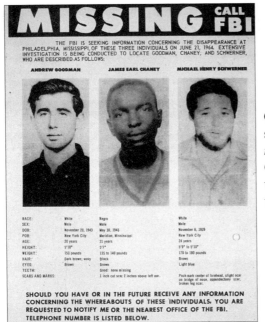

On the first day of summer, the sudden disappearance of (*left to right*) Andrew Goodman, James Chaney, and Michael Schwerner terrified volunteers and stunned the nation. *(Getty Images)*

Neshoba County sheriff Lawrence Rainey (*left*) and his deputy, Cecil Price, soon became suspects in the triple disappearance. But FBI agents searched Mississippi for weeks, finding no bodies. *(Associated Press Images)*

Warned about white Mississippi, Freedom Summer volunteers were overwhelmed by the welcome they were given in black Mississippi. *(Herbert Randall)*

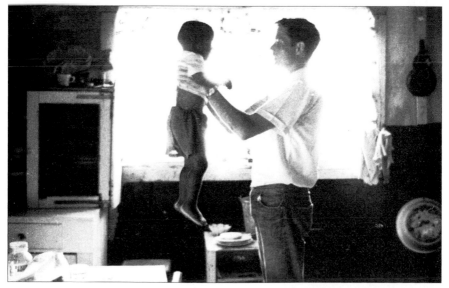

Volunteers were shocked by the poverty they saw in Mississippi but quickly adapted. Here, volunteer Mario Savio washes down in McComb. Savio, who would later lead the Free Speech Movement at Berkeley, was one of many Freedom Summer volunteers who played pivotal roles in 1960s protests. *(© 1978 Matt Herron/TakeStock)*

Violence had kept all but a handful of Mississippi blacks from voting. Throughout the summer, volunteers went door-to-door to convince locals to register. *(Herbert Randall)*

Oregon college student Fran O'Brien volunteered to teach in Mississippi, not knowing she would meet both Martin Luther King Jr. and, one night, the Ku Klux Klan. *(Whittier Daily News)*

The crown jewel of Freedom Summer, more than three dozen Freedom Schools encouraged students to question, speak out, and challenge Mississippi.
(Herbert Randall)

Working in the Mississippi Delta, California carpenter Fred Winn (*left*) grew from a "young twenty-year-old" into a savvy civil rights worker. *(San Rafael Independent-Journal)*

Numbing violence was woven into the fabric of Freedom Summer. Hundreds of volunteers were arrested and dozens were attacked. Here, Rabbi Joseph Lelyveld rests after a savage beating in Hattiesburg.
(Herbert Randall)

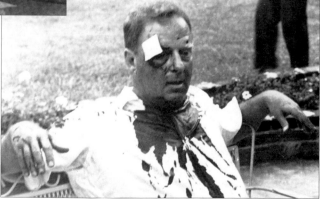

Project offices
were cluttered
beehives of
energy and
idealism.
(Herbert Randall)

Celebrities ranging from Harry
Belafonte to Shirley MacLaine
and Judy Collins came to
Mississippi to lend their names
and talents to Freedom Summer.
Here, Pete Seeger sings at a
Freedom School.
(Herbert Randall)

In midsummer,
emphasis shifted to
the Mississippi
Freedom Democratic
Party, which would
challenge the state's
all-white delegation
at the Democratic
National Convention
in Atlantic City.
(Herbert Randall)

Late in August, hundreds of protesters lined the Boardwalk in Atlantic City demanding that Freedom Democrats be seated as Mississippi's rightful delegation. Here, Martin Luther King Jr. speaks to Freedom Democrats and their supporters. *(© 1978 George Ballis/TakeStock)*

Sharecropper-turned-activist Fannie Lou Hamer electrified America by recounting how she was beaten in Mississippi. Hamer's speech and the nationwide support it drew gave Freedom Democrats hope that their challenge would succeed. *(Associated Press Images)*

In the decades since 1964, Mississippi has achieved a racial reconciliation that rivals South Africa's. Along with memorializing its martyrs, Mississippi has more black politicians than any other state.
(Bruce Watson)

By breaking down racial barriers and "cracking" Mississippi, Freedom Summer changed America. "If it hadn't been for the veterans of Freedom Summer," said Congressman John Lewis, "there would be no Barack Obama."
(Herbert Randall)

by then the FBI was already rushing to Louisiana, along with a navy frogman to search the river bottom. The following day, agents found another half body lying on a sandbar. Both corpses were black. Papers in back pockets identified the men as college students from Alcorn A & M. Abducted in May, they had been murdered, tied to the motor block of an old Jeep, and thrown in the river. "Mississippi is the only state where you can drag a river any time and find bodies you were not expecting," a volunteer wrote his parents. "Negroes disappear down here every week and are never heard about. . . . Jesus Christ, this is supposed to be America in 1964."

And when reading a son's or daughter's letter about corpses, church burnings, attacks with tire irons, what were parents supposed to think? Mississippi's "low" crime rate notwithstanding, violence there had become so common that it no longer made front pages. Friends kept asking parents how they could let their children spend summer "down there." Relatives phoned— "Did you see the horrible photo of that rabbi?" Some parents were now calling their children daily, begging them to come home. "We did not flee Hitler for my daughter to become a martyr," one mother said. But as their children soldiered on, most parents only called each other.

Ever since learning of the summer project, total strangers had been sharing worries about their dedicated, idealistic, slightly crazy kids. In late April, parents in Philadelphia (Pennsylvania) had written LBJ, asking for federal protection against the "tanks, guns, and troop carriers" stockpiled in Mississippi. A month later, Boston parents did the same. Two weeks before the disappearance, a "Parents Emergency Committee" in Manhattan telegrammed LBJ, urging action "before a tragic incident takes place." And three days after the tragic incident, two dozen parents had flown to Washington, D.C., to speak with senators, the deputy attorney general, and a White House aide.

Some parents had more clout than others. In Whittier, California, Fran O'Brien's mother could only buy a subscription to the *Vicksburg Post* and worry. In Amherst, Massachusetts, Jean Williams could merely save letters from "Xtoph" and hope for the best. In Washington, D.C., Holly Tillinghast, having taught in Mississippi, could only fear the worst. But a few parents had pipelines straight to Congress.

One morning in early July, volunteer Steve Bingham awoke in Mileston to find the Mississippi Highway Patrol looking for him. Bingham was the grandson of Hiram Bingham, discoverer of Machu Picchu and later a U.S.

senator. The Binghams were one of Connecticut's most prominent families, but now their youngest son was living with eight other volunteers in a shack on a dirt road in Mississippi, cooking on camp stoves and getting water from a hand pump in the backyard. The Binghams, though backing their son's decision to go south, were concerned. Shortly after Steve Bingham reached Mississippi, his father contacted Mississippi senator John Stennis, an old family friend. Bingham was not merely concerned about his own son—he wanted all volunteers protected. But Stennis called Governor Paul Johnson, and Steve Bingham soon found himself guarded day and night by highway patrolmen. Bingham only shed his bodyguards with the help of Bob Moses. Knowing patrolmen were as scared of the Klan as everyone else, Moses had Bingham tell the highway patrol that their protection would allow him to work in Klan-ridden Natchez. The bodyguards abandoned Bingham within an hour. Later that summer, when a New Yorker was arrested while driving Allard Lowenstein around Mississippi, cops took one look at the name on his driver's license—Franklin Delano Roosevelt III—and let him go.

But parents who could only sit and wait refused to sit and wait alone. By mid-July, parent support groups had formed across the country. Boston parents started a letter-writing campaign to the Justice Department. "Sometimes when I lie awake at night," a mother said at one meeting, "I can't get the picture of my child, either mutilated or dead, out of my mind." Long Island parents gave $2,000 to a volunteer driven out of Moss Point in June. Returning to Mississippi, he handed the money over to COFO. And in a scene as removed from Mississippi as any American setting could be, parents began meeting at a lavish poolside home in Beverly Hills.

At 8:00 p.m. on Monday, July 13, the meeting of the Parents Mississippi Emergency Committee, Los Angeles Area, was called to order. Parents in attendance were a diverse lot—a movie director, a janitor's wife, a minister, a high school teacher, the head of the biology department at the California Institute of Technology—yet their fears were one. "We didn't really know what we wanted to do when we got together," one mother said, "except protect them somehow."

On one wall in the opulent living room, a sheet of cardboard displayed the latest news from Mississippi. That morning's *Los Angeles Times* clipping—"Trussed Body Discovered in Louisiana River"—did not ease concerns, nor did a mother's story from Hattiesburg. Speaking with tight control, she described how her son, David, had been with the rabbi everyone had seen in the papers. David now had a wide strip shaved from his scalp, and seven stitches. He was saving his bloody shirt as a souvenir. Other grim-faced parents shared their children's letters—"I'm hot, I'm miserable and I can't get my clothes washed. Would you please let me stay another month?" Then the group got down to business.

One father suggested a bail fund, and within minutes, parents wrote out checks totaling $2,150. The group then heard from a Bay Area mother whose parents' group had talked to Mississippians arriving for the Republican National Convention in San Francisco. The Mississippi delegates had offered parents advice to pass on to their children—(1) leave; and (2) pray. After the Bay Area report, parents planned activities—a garden party and a picnic, a hootenanny and an art auction—with funds to go to COFO. Toward 9:30 p.m., the meeting broke up. Heading down freeways, blinking into blurred taillights, parents noted that in the firecracker towns where their crazy kids were spending the summer, it was nearly midnight.

Ten days of naked violence had taken their toll. On July 15, thirty-four Freedom Summer workers were arrested. In the Delta's "tough town" of Drew, two dozen were crammed into a stinking, twenty-by-twenty-foot cement jail, sweating, swatting mosquitoes, and singing themselves hoarse. Across Mississippi, volunteers were struggling to keep their spirits afloat. Since coming south, they had seen three men disappear, a hundred or more arrested, several churches burned, men beaten, women insulted and degraded. Some must have wondered whether coming to Mississippi had been a mistake. Others saw their faith in America turn to bitterness. "Where is the USA?" one wrote. "It is a violation of FEDERAL LAW to harass voter registration workers." Another lashed out with resentment that would soon become a signature sentiment of the 1960s. Noting the rank injustice condoned by the "decent middle-class," he shot back, "Crap on your middle class, on your decency, mister Churches man. Get out of your god-damned new rented car. Get out of your pressed, proper clothes. Get out of your unoffensive, shit-eating smile and crewcut. Come join us who are sleeping on the floor."

Midway through the third week in July, Fred Winn's father came home, took off his tie, poured a drink, and sat down to read a letter postmarked Shaw, Mississippi. Because Fred's handyman skills were needed in the bone-poor Delta town, the mustachioed carpenter had been transferred to Shaw, where he was "running my rear end off." Though his eyes had been opened by the suffering of blacks in Ruleville, Fred was still naive enough to be appalled by the deeper squalor of Shaw. There he met children with bellies swollen by hunger and visited fetid shacks tilted and sinking into the soil. Sharecroppers in Shaw had given up hope, but whites seemed determined to drive them still harder. "Dad," Fred wrote home, "the peoples' way of thinking down here is absolutely stupid and un-American."

Fred was in Shaw only a few days when he met the Bolivar County sheriff. A thin, dapper plantation owner and Citizens' Council member, Sheriff Charlie Capps considered the volunteers "dirty" and "unclean." "To me, their motives are unspeakable," the sheriff said. But Capps, neither a bully nor a Klansman, had no desire for publicity or federal marshals, and he knew a murder could bring both to his county. "What happened in Neshoba might have happened in any county in Mississippi," he remembered. To keep the peace, the sheriff deputized three dozen fellow World War II veterans. "We were a small town and we weren't used to Yankees, certainly not *that* kind," Capps said. "But I learned in the army that when you have massive firepower, there's not much gonna happen." Calling Fred Winn and other volunteers into his office, Capps advised them to go home where they belonged. Local whites, he said, hated them with a fury no sheriff could contain. Then, seeing the volunteers would not leave, the sheriff said he would do his best "to keep a lid on things." Yet as Fred's father read his son's letter, he sensed the lid boiling over.

On Saturday night, July 11, volunteers had been relaxing in Shaw's spruced-up community center, due to open that Monday. As blacks and whites talked, sang, and shared a watermelon, a local Negro boy rushed in. Stuttering, trembling, the boy said he'd just been offered $400 to blow up the building. Instantly, all lights were shut off. Everyone fled to the back office and sat in the muggy darkness. Earlier they had joked that with nothing whatsoever to do in Shaw, they were the white people's "show" that Saturday night, but no one felt like joking anymore. Volunteer Len Edwards called his father, a California congressman. Don Edwards had been in the FBI and had just returned from Mississippi. He told his son he would call the bureau and get someone out there. Fred Winn phoned the *San Francisco Chronicle*, but the night desk was not interested. As minutes inched by, Shaw, Mississippi, began to seem like some lonely outpost on the edge of civilization. From inside the shadowy, sweltering office, volunteers could hear bullfrogs bellowing, crickets pulsing. Headlights slid across dingy office walls. Seated on sticky floors or rickety chairs, volunteers wondered if Shaw might soon be the Delta's McComb, with bombs blasting in the night. Then, as stars and a sliver of a moon came out, lookouts ventured outside.

One man climbed onto the roof. Scanning the dark cotton fields in one direction, Shaw's lamplit quarters in the other, he spotted two police cars and six helmeted cops, their cigarettes glowing in the dark. The cops talked and joked while cars passed, heading for the Freedom House. From any vehicle might come a bomb, a flaming bottle, a shotgun blast. The wait continued. At 10:00 p.m., men still inside the Freedom House decided "the girls" should be evacuated. Over protest from a Radcliffe student who said women needed no special treatment, "the girls" held hands and walked to a nearby home where a plump, grizzled black man sat on the porch, a double-barreled shotgun in his lap.

Toward 11:00 p.m., lightning flashed on the western horizon. One slowly ticking hour later the storm was upon them, whipping trees, drowning conversations with thunder and finally ending the Saturday night show in Shaw. Cars and cops headed home and so did volunteers, walking in the warm and drenching night. The FBI came at 1:30 a.m.

In his posh San Francisco home, Fred Winn's father thought again of World War II as he read an angry description of "our night of terror" written by another volunteer.

I was and am furious. Here are youths who would be the glory of any nation, and they waited for a bomb to blow them out of this hostile land. . . . And this is in the land of the free. Here where millions have come seeking streets paved with gold, there have lived millions on streets drowned in mud. . . . Here in the beautiful land of the purple mountain's majesty, we sat and waited for the bombers.

I was born by the river in a little tent

And just like the river, I've been running ever since

It's been a long time coming

But I know a change is gonna come.

—Sam Cooke

"Another So-Called 'Freedom Day'"

7:00 a.m.   (2) News; Weather

                (4) Today: Hugh Downs

                (7) Ann Sothern (re-run)

7:30 a.m.   (5) Meaning of Communism

                (7) Gale Storm (re-run)

8:00 a.m.   (2) Captain Kangaroo

                (5) Sandy Becker

                (7) Courageous Cat and Minute Mouse

On Thursday, July 16, at 9:00 a.m., three black teenagers were joking on their way to summer school on Manhattan's Upper East Side. Walking through the posh neighborhood, they passed a building superintendent hosing down the sidewalk. By accident or perhaps by design, the man sprayed the teens. Some would later say he shouted, "I'm going to wash the black off of you." The teens chased the man inside and came out, laughing. Just then, an off-duty cop stepped out of a TV repair shop. Showing his badge, the cop ordered the boys to disperse. What happened next depends on whom one chooses to believe. The cop swore one teen came at him with a knife. Other onlookers said there was no knife, that the youth in question was not that kind of kid. The cop pulled his gun and fired. James Powell slumped to the pavement, dead. Within minutes, black kids were taunting police.

"Come on, shoot another nigger!"

"This is worse than Mississippi!"

The confrontation continued till noon. That Saturday night, a CORE rally in support of Goodman, Schwerner, and Chaney erupted in a protest of police brutality. And after simmering for two days, Harlem burned. Before the summer was over, urban riots would scar Rochester, Jersey City, Paterson, Philadelphia . . .

"History never turns a page," an old saying has it. "Only historians do." But if one had to find the page where the 1960s began—not the '60s on the calendar but the raucous, rebellious, world-challenging '60s—July 16, 1964, would be a good place to turn.

A Thursday. An ordinary midsummer day, a day that seemed likely to change nothing. Since the war, there had been ample talk about change in America. John F. Kennedy had promised a New Frontier, Bob Dylan had sung his anthem, but on July 16, 1964, most Americans still clung to the comforts of the 1950s. Old radio shows transferred to television still aired opposite old movies starring Ginger Rogers, Clark Gable, or Edward G. Robinson. The Beatles topped pop charts, but doo-wop and teen love songs were right behind them. The Yankees, heading for their fifth straight pennant, were still the best team in baseball. Each summer night, '57 Chevys and '59 Fords drag-raced on the outskirts of towns whose facades had changed little since the Depression. New interstate highways linked some cities, but less than half the system was finished. On that Thursday morning in midsummer, most Americans were satisfied with the status quo, hopeful that any coming changes would be incremental. And then . . .

In Greenwood, SNCC had declared July 16 "Freedom Day," but a wedding interrupted the preparations. The previous Monday, two volunteers were married in a makeshift chapel beneath the second-floor SNCC office. Bride and groom wore denim. Flowers and Freedom Day leaflets festooned the room. Because the bride was Jewish, the groom Christian, local kids had fashioned a red glitter cross and a Star of David. After the brief ceremony, Freedom Songs burst into the street. Black kids in long, twisting lines laughed and stumbled through their first *hora*. "Everybody stopped worrying for almost two hours," one volunteer remembered. Then bride, groom, and guests went back to work. Freedom Day was approaching.

On its front page, the *Greenwood Commonwealth* warned of "another so-called 'Freedom Day.'" COFO expected five hundred to march to the courthouse. Freedom Day would also bring blacks to courthouses in Greenville and Cleveland, but Greenville and Cleveland, though just across the Delta, were a world away from the "long staple cotton capital of the world."

Ever since SNCC first entered the Delta, Greenwood had been, as one marcher remembered, "our Gettysburg, our Battle of the Bulge, and our Iwo Jima all wrapped up in one." With Greenwood's very existence propped on the stoop labor of sharecroppers, the threat of a black vote put an entire cotton empire at risk. And the slightest push toward full democracy sparked violence. In the summer of 1962, a mob ransacked SNCC's office, sending staffers fleeing out the back window. Moments later, Bob Moses came in, lay down, and took a nap. The following spring, the office was hit with bullets and firebombs. One night on the flat straightaway that parted the sea of plantations, Moses and two others were driving when a white Buick pulled alongside. Its driver leveled a rifle and fired fifteen shots. Bullets lodged in Jimmie Travis's shoulder, neck, and head. As the car swerved, Moses grabbed the wheel. After a frantic rush to the hospital, Travis lived to show his scars to volunteers in Ohio.

But by Freedom Day, Greenwood's homegrown terrorism was backfiring. When SNCC first arrived, blacks had crossed the street to steer clear of "the Riders." Frightened elders warned teens that the SNCC office displayed photos of black and white men hugging. Then came the hungry winter when whites cut off sharecroppers' federal food allotments, the ugly spring of fire and bullets, and the marches attacked by dogs and cops. Each assault galvanized another victim. Each bullet brought another family into the movement. "Get up and look out the window," a high school teacher told her class, "and watch while history is being made."

By July 1964, mass meetings were drawing hundreds, singing, shouting, chanting "Freedom Now." With its summer project in full swing, SNCC had just moved its national headquarters from Atlanta to Greenwood. As Freedom Day approached, the SNCC office resembled a high school classroom when the teacher has stepped out. Kids ran in and out, dodging trunks, boxes, and adults more frenzied than usual. Two kittens, one named Freedom, the other Now, slept in corners near guitars no one had time to play. From the ringing of phones to the clacking of typewriters to the meetings around rickety tables, all energy was focused on Freedom Day. Students at the Greenwood Freedom School could talk about little else. Their school newspaper—two mimeographed pages—noted that whatever might happen on Freedom Day, "We will not let it stop us." Freedom Day signs in storefront windows urged everyone to the courthouse. "Everyone?" Stokely Carmichael shouted to mass meetings. And crowds roared back—"*Every*-one!" All through the quarters, blacks goaded each other to stand up, to come out, to register. In the SNCC office, volunteers drew lots to see who would test Mississippi's new antipicketing law. Some were relieved to be spared the honor, others excited to be chosen. "I want to go to jail," a volunteer from Berkeley said. "I'm honest. I've never been." Finally, Freedom Day arrived.

The morning of July 16 was overcast in the Delta and cooler than usual. The coffee-brown Yazoo River, flowing past cotton fields on one side, the towering cupola of the courthouse on the other, set the pace for another slothful summer day. Then toward 9:00 a.m., battered old cars began parking across the street from the courthouse. Black women in flowered dresses and men in weathered suits and fedoras shuffled toward the courthouse steps. On the sidewalk, volunteers and SNCC staffers took up picket signs. Standing in a rigid row, helmeted cops hefted their nightsticks. Across the street, a bus waited to take the arrested to jail. As picketers began their slow, steady march, a tall stick of a man with pinched eyes addressed the crowd through a bullhorn. "You are free to go and register," Police Chief Curtis Lary buzzed. "No one will interfere with you if you want to stand here to register but we will not allow any picketing." The chief gave picketers two minutes to disperse. Then the roundup began.

Cops descended, escorting some, yanking others. Several protesters went limp and were dragged along the pavement, cracked with nightsticks, shoved into the bus. At each window, black and white fingers gripped the wire mesh. The vehicle soon swayed, rocking to the clapping rhythm of a chorus:

Oh, Freedom
Oh, ohhhh, Freedom
Ohhhh, Freedom, over meee . . .

More picketers were arrested, including a pregnant woman yanked and prodded while her sister screamed. Back across the street, blacks waited in line. Inside the courthouse, three at a time patiently filled out forms and endured the "hospitality" of registrar Martha Lamb, whose rudeness was the stuff of local lore. The sun burned through the clouds as a second wave of pickets began to march. Chief Lary lifted his bullhorn. "You are free to go and register. No one will interfere . . ."

Elsewhere in the Delta, Freedom Day was less chaotic. In Greenville, several COFO cars broke down, delaying trips to the courthouse, but by noon, the line outside the registrar's office stretched to the street. Picketing proceeded without incident. Greenville cops watched but made no arrests. In Cleveland, dozens of volunteers had come from throughout the Delta. Many came from Shaw, where memories of Saturday night's bomb threat still lingered, where calls were going out to parents of prisoners still sweltering in the black-hole lockup in nearby Drew. Expecting the worst, Shaw volunteers had given nonviolence classes to locals, but the lessons proved unnecessary. At the courthouse, volunteers lined the sidewalk, chanting "Jim Crow . . . Must GO!" Across the street stood three dozen deputies with shotguns— Sheriff Charlie Capps's "massive firepower"—keeping angry whites at a safe distance. At 11:00 a.m. a crop duster veered from nearby fields to buzz the treetops, but otherwise Bolivar County's first Freedom Day was off to a peaceful start. When the courthouse closed for lunch, blacks and whites shared sandwiches beneath the trees. Three cars filled with young white men circled the integrated picnic. Volunteers asked deputies to keep them away. The cars were not seen again.

12:00 p.m.   (2) Love of Life
                  (4) Say When (color)
                  (7) Father Knows Best (re-run)
                  (9) News: John Wingate
12:15 p.m.   (9) Republican National Convention Highlights
12:30 p.m.   (2) Search for Tomorrow
                  (4) Truth or Consequences (color)
                  (5) Cartoon Playtime
                  (7) Tennessee Ernie Ford
                  (9) Joe Franklin's Memory Lane

At 12:30 p.m., Lyndon Johnson convinced his wife to take a stroll. The president was not just looking for exercise. With the Republican Convention filling the airwaves, he hoped to recapture the nation's attention. "I think it would look very spontaneous," Johnson's press secretary told him. Exiting the White House, Lyndon and Lady Bird walked with reporters and a single Secret Service agent through the gates and onto Pennsylvania Avenue. For the next half hour, the president and first lady strolled hand in hand. Tourists turned in disbelief. "You mean that's President and Mrs. Johnson? Well, how about that! Look, Bobby it's the president." Others rose from park benches to shake the president's hand. The Johnsons made a loop around the neighborhood before returning to the White House.

By July 16, 1964, another year of violence and marches across the South had widened America's racial gap. With the Civil Rights Act now law, a "white backlash" was brewing. "They're always doing something for the niggers," a Chicago man said. "When are they going to do something for the white people?" A Harris poll revealed that nearly 60 percent of whites feared that Negroes wanted to take their jobs, and a quarter thought black men wanted to take their women. Most whites *said* they supported integration, yet three of five thought social clubs and neighborhoods should be allowed to exclude blacks. California voters were piling up signatures for a ballot initiative that would soon strike down the state's Fair Housing Law. Yet racial resentment was just the tip of America's disquieting mood.

Behind the facade that still looked like the 1950s lurked fears that the times were changing much too quickly. At home, the Kennedy assassination, followed by the string of shocking murders, had shaken the illusion that America was a peaceful nation. The Supreme Court had banned school prayer, "the pill" was loosening sexual mores, and talk of bombing Vietnam, of sending thousands more "advisers," led to a growing unease. In the July 16 *New York Times*, James Reston noted "the deep feeling of regret in American life: regret over the loss of religious faith; regret over the loss of simplicity and fidelity; regret over the loss of the frontier spirit of pugnacious individuality; regret, in short, over the loss of America's innocent and idealistic youth."

A few names that would stick to the 1960s were already in the public eye. Richard Nixon was in San Francisco that day, preparing to nominate Barry Goldwater for president. Future *Easy Rider* star Jack Nicholson was making B movies like *Back Door to Hell*. Gloria Steinem was known not as a feminist but as the freelancer who went undercover to write about Playboy bunnies. Comedian Lenny Bruce was in a Manhattan courtroom, on trial for obscenity. In Flint, Michigan, the first generation of Ford Mustangs was rolling off the assembly line. But most of the upcoming 1960s lay hidden. Jimi Hendrix was backing a rhythm and blues band touring the South. Abbie Hoffman was in Worcester, Massachusetts, working for SNCC and worrying that it was too late to go to Mississippi. (The following summer, Hoffman would teach at the McComb Freedom School.) Truman Capote was at home on Long Island, waiting for two killers in Kansas to be executed so he could finish *In Cold Blood*. Neil Armstrong was one of several Apollo astronauts in training.

And on this "so-called Freedom Day," a 1939 International Harvester bus was crossing America. The bus was painted in clashing colors no one had ever seen outside a carnival. Plastered over the paint were labels—"Caution: Weird Load," "A Vote for Barry is a Vote for Fun," and, above the windshield, "Furthur." Just before entering Mississippi, these "Merry Pranksters" had been thrown off a beach at Louisiana's Lake Pontchartrain for playing loud music. Now they were heading deeper across the South. No southerner turning to stare would have been shocked to learn that the jocular men on board had taken LSD. No one outside the bus, no one south of Millbrook, New York, where Timothy Leary would soon greet the Pranksters, had any idea what LSD was.

A new Magnavox color TV with a "23-inch rectangular tube" sold for an average month's wages. Gasoline was 30 cents a gallon, but "price wars" sometimes dropped the price a nickel. A pound of steak sold for 79 cents, and a pound of chicken cost a quarter. A decent used car could be picked up for $300. The cigarettes that, despite the recent surgeon general's warning, sent smoke curling through every restaurant and meeting room sold for a quarter a pack. Yet there was no price on certain intangibles. No price on the marriages that, made in the hasty matchups that followed the war, were now held together by threads that would soon break and double the divorce rate. No price on the bonds between parent and child that, within a few years, would widen into a "generation gap." No price on the bedrock faith in America as Lincoln's "last best hope," a faith that would be shot down in Vietnam and dragged through the streets of Watts, Newark, and Detroit.

Leery of change and unaware of its coming juggernaut, most Americans had never had it so good. The median family income had risen 53 percent since 1950, inflation was at 1.2 percent, and the gross national product was at an all-time high. With more than ever to buy and more to buy it with, few adults wanted to "crap on the middle class." A poll showed that two-thirds of Americans opposed the summer project in Mississippi. "It's too much like taking the law in their own hands," a Detroit machinist said. The American press, while not as insulting as Mississippi newspapers, was scarcely sympathetic to Freedom Summer:

The denial of voting rights to most Negroes in Mississippi is shameful and indefensible but it is highly doubtful that Northern college students are the best equipped persons to remedy this wrong.

—*Chicago Tribune*

The President should now use the force of his office to attack the cause of the trouble in Mississippi. That trouble is the unjustified, uncalled for invasion of that sovereign state by a bunch of Northern students schooled in advance in causing trouble under the guise of bringing "freedom" to Mississippi Negroes.

—*Dallas Morning News*

Without condoning racist attitudes, we think it understandable that the people of Mississippi should resent such an invasion. The outsiders are said to regard themselves as some sort of heroic freedom fighters but in truth, they are asking for trouble.

—*Wall Street Journal*

Syndicated columnists toed a fine line, praising volunteers' idealism while casting doubts on the summer project itself. "It is a dreadful thing to say, but it needs saying," wrote Joseph Alsop. "The organizers who sent these young people into Mississippi must have wanted, even hoped for, martyrs." William F. Buckley asked whether Mississippi blacks were ready to vote. "Unlike the democratic absolutists," Buckley wrote, "I am perfectly capable of rejoicing at the number of people who do not exercise their technical right to vote." Lacking talk radio as a forum, Americans debated Mississippi in letters to editors. An Oklahoma woman was "outraged and disgusted that members of our U.S. Navy are used for the purpose of trying to locate three no-good rabblerousers in the South." A Louisiana woman asked, "By what stretch of the imagination does anyone consider that these kids have any right in Mississippi in the first place? The whole situation is disgusting."

Freedom Summer had opened wounds dating to the Civil War. With Mississippi as its most visible exemplar, the South suddenly seemed fair game for open insult. "Lincoln did this country a great disservice when he forced the South back into the Union," a California man wrote. "Isn't there a way to 'secede' them NOW?" Southerners rose in righteous defense. "Could you possibly bring yourselves to believe the honest opinion of one average Southerner that you are being acidly unfair to the South and its people in many of your comments?" a woman asked *Newsweek*. "I do not know any Southerners who want to kill Negroes or would condone such a thing." In the crossfire, only a few Americans praised the volunteers: "I would say that they are courageous young people who are not afraid to stand up for their convictions," a Connecticut woman argued. More common were suspicions that, in an election year, altruism was being used for politics as usual. An Indiana man found it "clear that the whole scheme is not to help the Negro people but to agitate and create unrest and strife in the hope of more votes for the liberal, left-wing Democrat leadership."

The sun had topped its long arc in the Delta sky when word of Freedom Day arrests brought volunteers and SNCC staff pouring into Greenwood. Just after lunch, a third wave of picketers hit the sidewalk. Chief Lary took up his bullhorn. Two minutes to disperse. Police arrested dozens more, dragging, manhandling, leaving some with horrors they would never forget. Volunteer Linda Wetmore will always see the agonized face of Stokely Carmichael. "I turned around just as I was getting on the bus," Wetmore remembered. "And they took a cattle prod and applied it to his penis. I can see him gritting his teeth, wanting to fight back." Seconds later, Wetmore and Carmichael were on the bus, joining the new chorus:

> *Ain't gonna let Chief Lary*
> *turn me around,*
> *turn me around,*
> *turn me around. . . .*

Revving its engine and rolling away, the bus made a left turn, another left, and pulled up behind the courthouse alongside the Yazoo River, still idling past. Overhead, thunderheads filled a blue sky.

Inside, picketers arrested for the first or the umpteenth time came face-to-face with the terror of a Mississippi police station. Arrest may have been novel for a few, but most knew the Greenwood station all too well. Here was the same graying desk sergeant, painstakingly writing their names on a yellow pad. And there were the same smirking cops, giddy at having more "nigger lovers" to torment. The station itself seemed to sneer at them. On one wall was a plaque for meritorious police service, given to "Police Dog Tiger," the German shepherd who had attacked marchers a year earlier. On another was the FBI poster of Goodman, Schwerner, and Chaney, with a mustache drawn on Goodman. Down a dark hallway were the cells where cops could beat blacks, or hand a blackjack to a white inmate to do the job. But Greenwood cops did not always unleash their rage behind bars. A week earlier, a dark-haired officer named Logan had taken out a long knife, then sharpened it while volunteers watched. "Sounds like rubbing up against nigger pussy," Logan said before poking the blade into one man's ribs. "Think it's sharp enough to cut your cock off?" Finally, Logan told another officer, "You'd better get me out of here before I do what I'd like to do." Before leaving, he aimed his revolver at a black woman and spun the chamber.

And now the time came to be marched into the cells. Another familiar face, the chubby jailer who called volunteers "nigger huggers," led them through a smelly hallway and up clammy cement stairs. Black women were thrown in one cell, white women in another. Men were segregated downstairs. Crammed into lockups, the prisoners gripped the bars, sang, and called out to each other. An hour later, when Greenwood police rounded up more picketers in a drenching downpour, the day's arrest total came to 111. But on the courthouse steps, blacks kept filing into the registrar's office.

Greenwood's Freedom Day resulted in the summer's largest number of arrests. Freedom Day in Cleveland, however, was a startling success. Forty Negroes waited in line, and more than two dozen filled out forms. Police protected blacks and whites, arresting no one. Sheriff Charlie Capps had made good on his promise to "keep a lid on things." "I am proud of the people of Bolivar County for ignoring these agitators," the sheriff announced. Similar success came in Greenville, where one hundred filled out registration forms. Staffers there even had time to schedule a baseball game that Saturday with volunteers in Greenwood.

Elsewhere in Mississippi, Freedom Day brought problems old and new. Word came to COFO headquarters that two volunteers had been arrested in Canton. Police had confiscated their truck and beaten both men with pistols. The terrified men had to be bailed out as soon as possible. A staffer headed for Canton, while calls for bail money went out to parents in Detroit and central Iowa. Then volunteer Barney Frank, a Harvard grad student and later a Massachusetts congressman, pointed out a bigger concern. The confiscated truck was loaded with registration forms for the Mississippi Freedom Democratic Party. The forms included the addresses of hundreds of blacks. Anyone finding them would have a long list of targets. COFO had to claim that truck before cops looked in the back. Making several phone calls, Frank learned that the rented truck could not be picked up without the rental agency's permission. Where was the truck now? What company had rented it? What was their number? At 3:00 p.m., COFO dispatched Frank to Canton in a frantic race to get to National Rent-a-Car and then to the auto yard before it closed.

Across the state, a more familiar fear gripped the project office in Meridian. That morning, four black staffers had ventured into rural Jasper County to investigate rumors of a murder. They had been ordered to check in by phone at 4:00 p.m. The same volunteer who had waited in vain for Mickey Schwerner's call was waiting again. The hour passed; no call came. Alarm spread through project offices across the state. At 5:00 p.m., calls went out to sheriffs. Half an hour later, COFO called Bob Moses in Vicksburg. Moses had just invited Martin Luther King to Mississippi and was busy preparing his itinerary, but he dropped everything to make his own calls. At 6:03 p.m., Meridian called the state highway patrol. No word. Moses phoned the new FBI office in Jackson. His wife, Dona, called sheriffs in Lauderdale and Jasper counties. Still no word. The sun would be down in an hour. Where were the four men?

7:00 p.m.   (2, 4, 7) Republican National Convention
            (5) Magilla Gorilla Cartoons
            (13) Columbia Seminars: Profs. Jacob C. Hurewitz and Amitai W.
                Etzioni of Columbia University discuss Israel

In Manhattan that evening, theatergoers could see Barbra Streisand in *Funny Girl* or Robert Redford in *Barefoot in the Park*. Carol Channing starred in *Hello, Dolly!* while Paul Newman drew fans to a play few had heard of. Movie lovers could see Peter Sellers in three different films, including *Dr. Strangelove* and the second *Pink Panther* movie. Ronald Reagan was featured in his final film, *The Killers*, but was playing a larger role in San Francisco. As cochair of the California Republicans for Goldwater, Reagan was welcoming GOP convention delegates to a final evening at the Cow Palace.

Eight months after the Kennedy assassination, Americans remained scarred by those split seconds that had sent the decade careening off course. Three best-selling books were about JFK, and a fourth was his *Profiles in Courage*. Ships, airports, and a new coin bore the Kennedy name. Sharecroppers' shacks in Mississippi were not the only American homes to have saintly portraits of the fallen president. Sworn to carry on Kennedy's legacy, LBJ was heavily favored to win the November election, yet all that week in San Francisco, Republicans fought for the chance to oppose him. Few could remember such a bitter convention. Candidates fired off angry letters. Pinkerton detectives guarded rival camps. Hard-line Republicans, bristling at being labeled "extremists," fought off challenges from moderates. Goldwater refused to take a concession call from "that son-of-a-bitch" Rockefeller and said LBJ's sudden support for civil rights made him "the biggest faker in the United States." Former president Eisenhower was one of many GOP stalwarts shaken by the platform's strident attacks on government. When Nelson Rockefeller denounced "extremists . . . who have nothing in common with Americanism," delegates booed, and when another speaker attacked the liberal media, delegates shook fists at broadcasting booths. In the parking lot outside, CORE protested Republicans' rejection of civil rights. One group marched behind the banner "Parents of the Mississippi Summer Project," but inside, delegates refused to back the new civil rights law that Goldwater had opposed. "The nigger issue," a Republican aide told a reporter, was sure to put Goldwater in the White House.

Toward 9:00 p.m., California time, the crisp, white-haired candidate stepped to the podium. When Goldwater declared that "extremism in the defense of liberty is no vice," applause shook the Cow Palace for nearly a minute. Back in Mississippi, Klan Imperial Wizard Sam Bowers was watching. Taken by Goldwater's signature phrase, Bowers added it to his Klan Konstitution. When Goldwater finished, red, white, and blue balloons drifted from the ceiling to the tune of "The Battle Hymn of the Republic." Goldwater would lose badly that November, but the conservative revolt he started on that so-called Freedom Day would grow throughout the decade.

Republicans in San Francisco had not yet begun to celebrate when the fear of another disappearance in Mississippi ended with a phone call. At 6:30 p.m., one of the missing in Jasper County got through to the Meridian office. He had called several times, but the phone had been busy. All four men were safe and on their way back.

In Canton, Barney Frank was at an auto yard, struggling to claim the confiscated truck and its dangerous cargo of Freedom Democrat forms. The Harvard grad student was assisted by a movie star. Richard Beymer, handsome leading man of *West Side Story* and *The Longest Day*, had taken a summer away from Hollywood to volunteer. "I was always complaining about America," Beymer remembered, "and my agent finally said, 'Look, why don't you either do something or shut up.'" So Beymer had put his career on hold to spend a summer in Mississippi. Along with canvassing in Canton, he was filming a documentary about the summer project. When he arrived at the auto yard that Thursday, Beymer found Barney Frank arguing with the owner. They would need $35 to claim the vehicle, Frank said. The two scrounged the money, and by the time an enormous orange sun silhouetted plantation shacks on the Delta, the future congressman and the movie star were driving the truck north to Greenwood. "Beymer drove because I couldn't drive a stick shift," Frank recalled. "I remember the papers were flying all over the place." No one had inspected the truck's contents. No names had been revealed. And back in Canton, the two volunteers had been released.

Freedom Day had been a harbinger of change in America. Across Mississippi, however, it was just another day. Cops harassed volunteers. Threats came into project offices. Cars and pickups roared outside. In McComb, rumor had it that whites would soon blow the Freedom House "off the map." In Natchez, a white minister was collecting funds to rebuild burned black churches. The fund already topped $1,000. And in Shaw, phone calls were still going out to parents soliciting $4,500 in bail needed for volunteers in Drew's sweatbox jail. In Greenwood, however, bail was out of the question.

Deep in the bowels of the Leflore County courthouse, 111 people were packed into dank, muggy cells. Facing a long night, the prisoners sang, talked, and refused to eat. The women had started the hunger strike after one spit out her rice and lima beans—laced with pepper. Dusk and the afternoon downpour had brought little relief from the heat. Sweat shone on faces and darkened mattresses already reeking with vomit. Did jail seem like a novelty now? In their cells, men discussed freedom and women, women and freedom, while women upstairs passed the hours pitching pennies and playing hopscotch on a grid drawn with a bar of Ivory soap. When would they hear from their lawyers? Would others join their hunger strike? When would SNCC get them *out*?

Late that evening, a tap came on the wall of the white women's cell. A small, flat panel opened, and a face appeared. A black face. Identifying himself as a "trusty," the man passed in candy bars and a note from the black women. "We are not going to eat," the note said. "Send us cigs. We don't have light." For the next hour, the women talked through the face-sized opening, talking with the trusty. His name was Patterson, and he was doing eighteen months for a crime he said he had not committed. The women gave him a dollar for cigarettes. They were thrilled to learn how many had been arrested that day. Then Patterson closed the panel and went to visit other prisoners. Toward midnight on the first day of the 1960s, the door opened for one final note. It came from the black men. "We won't eat tomorrow," it read. "We will sing loud about daybreak. Freedom."

BOOK TWO

A Bloody Peace Written in the Sky

Some things you must always be unable to bear. Some things you must never stop refusing to bear. Injustice and outrage and dishonor and shame. No matter how young you are or how old you have got. Not for kudos and not for cash: your picture in the paper nor money in the bank either. Just refuse to bear them.

—William Faulkner, *Intruder in the Dust*

I wasn't even sure, in fact, how voting was supposed to help me, but the more I heard about white people being so against it, the more I started thinking there must be something to this voting.

—Unita Blackwell, *Barefootin'*

CHAPTER SEVEN

"Walk Together, Children"

Trembling, nauseous, and terrified, the remedial reading teacher rode the bus toward McComb.

In the two weeks since he had finished classes at P.S. 624, Ira Landess had crossed a cultural divide larger than a continent. After taking a bus from Manhattan to Memphis, he was welcomed to the South by a cabdriver who, upon learning his purpose, hurled his bags to the sidewalk. With other teachers in training, Landess had hung his head to sing, "Three are missing, Lord, Kumbaya. . . ." On the Fourth of July, his group had crossed into Mississippi. Stopping for lunch in "the other Philadelphia," they stared out a café window, wondering which passing strangers might know where the missing men were. On their way out of town, they passed a billboard with a photo of John F. Kennedy splattered with black paint. Arriving that afternoon at the holiday picnic in Hattiesburg, Landess ate catfish, went on the tractor hayride, and took cover when the pickup with the gun rack passed. That night, he bolted awake, startled by strange sounds. Certain the Klan had come for him, he summoned the courage to look outside. A cow was rubbing against his shack. Later Landess met black kids who asked whether Jews like him had tails. And now here he was, riding this steamy, smoke-filled Greyhound, surrounded by blanched faces, crossing into Pike County with its kudzu-choked trees, its Klansmen in the hills, its bombs and burned-out churches.

When dynamite damaged the McComb Freedom House, SNCC had called for more volunteers to come "share the terror." Because his former Brandeis classmate, Mendy Samstein, was a SNCC staffer in McComb, Landess signed up. A few days later, terrified at what he had gotten himself into, certain he had been spotted as an "invader," a Jew, he arrived in the most dangerous town in Mississippi.

By mid-July, when nothing worse than fear had attacked him, Landess had settled in. Glad to be back in a classroom, he had shed his initial terror. But nothing made him feel more at home than the greeting he got one afternoon. He was walking through McComb's black quarters when a bent, gray-haired woman stepped out of her shack. A big smile broke out on her leathery face. She set aside her broom, waved at Landess, and shouted, "Hello, Freedom!"

As July crawled toward August, volunteers wondered—had it only been a month? The slow, sweltering afternoons, the dark, fearful nights, the roof-lifting mass meetings, the soulful dinners with host families, the Fourth of July picnics, all leading back to the shocking disappearance and rush of arrival—hadn't the summer lasted forever? Did their comfortable lives back home still exist? Bob Moses had warned of this, too. "When you're not in Mississippi, it's not real," he had told them in Ohio, "and when you're there the rest of the world isn't real."

But one eternal month had not merely warped time—it had accelerated Freedom Summer. Mississippi remained a powder keg, rife with random beatings, absurd arrests, and roaring pickups circling project offices. Several attacks per day were now being chalked onto a blackboard outside COFO headquarters in Jackson.

- *McComb:* Mount Zion Hill Baptist Church in Pike County bombed or burned to ground.
- *Philadelphia:* Columbia law student and a writer beaten with chain by two middle-aged white men in early afternoon.
- *Batesville:* 8 people detained one and one-half hours by sheriff . . . released into crowd of whites standing about. Local volunteer hit hard in jaw by white man.

Encounters with whites had become a manic game of chance. Crossing the tracks and heading downtown, one never knew what might happen. Those huddled men on the bench ahead might just glare or flash their middle fingers. The thin-lipped man in the passing car might merely pass. That trio of young toughs hanging around the gas station might settle for threats. But just as easily, the men on the bench could uncoil. Empty beer bottles could fly from that car. Those three thugs might explode. Volunteers pressed their luck every day, and most came home unscathed. But every day, luck ran out for a few.

A month of Freedom Summer had weeded out the fearful. Several volunteers had given up and gone home. The rest, hardened by Mississippi, inspired by its local heroes, dug in and focused on their jobs—teaching another class, knocking on another door, or just being there, white with black in Mississippi. By the third week of July, the tender wounds of violence were hardening into a callused defiance. The defiance showed in how volunteers joked about their lives. "The mosquitoes down here are vicious," a Hattiesburg volunteer wrote in her diary. "I'm sure they must be hired by the Klan or the White Citizens Council." From Ruleville, a man wrote home: "You will all be glad to hear that my odor is strong enough to kill a sunflower at 20 feet." And in Greenwood, a volunteer gave his parents graphic descriptions of recent mayhem, then concluded, "Ho hum. This violent life rolls on. We Shall Overcome."

The defiance also revealed itself in a new attitude toward Mississippi's "tough towns." Once avoided, places like Drew and McComb were now invaded by volunteers, filling beehive offices, meeting local heroes, daring police and locals to pounce. Even Emmett Till's watery graveyard—Tallahatchie County—would soon have its day at the courthouse. Finally, the defiance changed the way violence was described. Calls to the WATS line now spoke of "the usual police harassment," "the usual speech" from a cop, "the usual" phone calls spewing "the usual" hatred. A beating was "nothing serious. Bruises on face. And cuts."

Freedom Summer's gathering momentum spread this renewed boldness to every corner of Mississippi. COFO sued Sheriff Rainey, the Klan, and the Citizens' Council, charging that they had "engaged in widespread terroristic acts . . . to intimidate, punish and deter the Negro citizens of Mississippi." No one expected to win the suit, but at least the chaw-chewing sheriff would have to hire a lawyer and swagger into court. In Harmony, where a cross had blazed in response to the Civil Rights Act, the rhythmic rapping of hammers echoed across farms and fields. Denied a building for a Freedom School, volunteers and locals had raised enough money to build their own community center. Now, dozens were hammering away. While pickups circled, black women served fried chicken and Kool-Aid. Men in overalls sawed planks and raised skeleton walls beneath the scorching sun. One observer called the Harmony project, which included a honeymooning couple from Milwaukee, "the happiest project I have seen in Mississippi." Up in the Delta, $4,500 raised by calls to parents was claimed from Western Union at the back of Rexall Drug in Ruleville. All twenty-three prisoners, lice-infested, skin blistered by mosquito and chigger bites, were bailed out of Drew's miserable jail. Thirty miles south in the Greenwood lockup, bedraggled Freedom Day prisoners continued their hunger strike, fantasizing about ice cream, gin and tonics, and freight trains bringing carloads of chopped liver and bagels from New York.

United in spirit, volunteers also found fresh sources of support. Across the state, the spreading network of CB radios linked more SNCC cars with home bases. If James Chaney had only had such a radio. . . . Dozens of medical teams—doctors, nurses, dentists, psychiatrists—were making two-week tours of Mississippi, tending to volunteers' health, giving black children their first medical exams, then going home to share stories from the "police state" of Mississippi. More than a hundred lawyers from across America had come to prepare more lawsuits. Celebrities were arriving, too, just to lend support. One afternoon, an attractive woman with bright red hair and blue jeans dropped in on Fannie Lou Hamer. Hamer did not recognize the "little white lady." She was later surprised to hear that "a real movie star" named Shirley MacLaine was in her kitchen stirring the beans. Boston Celtics star Bill Russell was giving basketball clinics in Jackson, and within a few days, the biggest name in the civil rights movement, the Reverend Dr. Martin Luther King Jr., would tour the state. Yes, it had been only a month, and more than a month remained, but Freedom Summer rolled on.

The summer had not exhausted its surprises. In Itta Bena, the tobacco-chewing old woman whose spunk had amazed boarders way back in June was now showing off the tea set a volunteer's girlfriend sent her. You could use the little cups for tea, she told friends on Freedom Street. Or you could use them for whiskey. But a month in Mississippi had finished off the naïveté that had frightened SNCC veterans back in Ohio. Light switches on cars were now taped down, lest an opened door illuminate a nighttime target. Host families no longer found their guests "plain cute." Volunteers did not wash their hands in the water bucket; they were experts at outhouses, well pumps, and bathing in tin washtubs. They could eat whole plates of collard greens without a grimace. Their internal clocks were now set to the local time zone—Rural Southern Time. "If you want to start a meeting at 8," one wrote home, "schedule it for 7." And Fannie Lou Hamer no longer had to worry about white girls "out under the trees in the back yard playin' cards with the Negro boys!" Still, there were near-misses and constant reminders of danger.

One Saturday evening, Chris Williams was in the Mileses' backyard in Batesville. Volunteers were standing around trading jokes when the drone of insects was shattered by a rifle blast. Everyone began shouting, diving for cover, until Robert Miles, "laughing his ass off," came out to explain. Another volunteer, unfamiliar with guns, had picked up a loaded rifle. "Someone shot at you from *inside* the house," Miles said. The bullet buried itself in the field out back, near the hogs.

Fred Winn was still mired in Shaw. Since the Saturday night when they had "waited for the bombers," volunteers had settled down, but the project had not. Like the town itself, strung out along a swamp flanking its main street, Shaw's project was a backwater. With no local movement to build on, mass meetings drew just a few adults. Rumors rustling through the black community did not help. Some spoke of a white volunteer living with a black woman, even sitting, shirtless, on her porch all morning. Others talked of a tall white woman and a local black man sleeping together in the Freedom House. The California carpenter paid no attention to the rumors. Fred continued to build bookshelves, install screens, fix toilets. Writing home often, he was feeling closer than ever to the father he had barely known. And his father, feeling the same bond, had begun asking friends for donations to SNCC. (One wrote back, "I don't believe in this sort of thing and think Freddy is a big jerk for doing it.") But restless nights and disjointed days had left Fred with the nagging certainty that he would always feel like a stranger in Mississippi.

As volunteers struggled to adapt, SNCC leaders were starting to wonder. Precisely what had Freedom Summer accomplished? Freedom Schools were overenrolled, bursting with enthusiasm. A dozen community centers were offering literacy workshops, health classes, day care, sewing lessons, story hours. . . . Yet SNCC's larger purpose—voter registration—was treading water. Bob Moses had done the math. Despite all the Freedom Days, a SNCC report charted the dismal results: "Canton—Number of those who took the test—22; Number of those who passed—0. Hattiesburg: Number of those who took the test—70. Number of those who passed—5. Greenwood—Number of those who took the test—123. Number of those who passed—2." In all, of the fifteen hundred blacks who had gone to courthouses, only a handful outside Panola County had successfully registered. If any political progress was to be made in the remaining month, it had to follow the only road left open—the Freedom Party road. This time, however, the stage would not be Mississippi but all of America. On July 19, Moses sent a ten-page memorandum to all staff and canvassers regarding the "high degree of probability that we will not be prepared for the national Democratic Convention."

Since its founding in March, the Mississippi Freedom Democratic Party had survived on dreams. Fannie Lou Hamer and three other MFDP candidates had run for Congress in the June primary, yet Atlantic City remained the party's target. Now just over a month remained until the gavel at the Democratic National Convention. There, Freedom Democrats would challenge Mississippi's all-white delegation. Before a national television audience, blacks could detail Mississippi's brutal denial of democracy. And with enough support, perhaps even an outpouring of telegrams and phone calls, the MFDP could win a floor fight and be seated, sending Mississippi's "official" delegation home in disgrace. But it would take names—Moses was still hoping for 400,000—names signed up as Freedom Democrats. At midsummer, Moses had tallied just 21,431 signatures on the parallel party's roll sheet. At the present rate, just 60,000 would be enrolled when the convention began. It was not hard to imagine a challenge to the challenge— what about all the other blacks in Mississippi? They must not care about voting. Faced with failure, Moses now turned consensus into decree. There would be fewer Freedom Days, which cost too much in bail money and manpower. Instead, *everyone who is not working in Freedom Schools or Community Centers must* devote all their time to organizing for the convention challenge."

Moses lowered his sights to 200,000 signatures. Even by SNCC standards, it was a quixotic goal, but Moses, as usual, had thought things out. SNCC would flood black quarters with Freedom Registration Centers—in stores, bars, beauty parlors, barbershops, restaurants, pool halls, garages, and churches. Sound trucks would roam backstreets, blaring announcements of the campaign. Radio and newspaper ads would spread the word. "Big name" folksingers were already in Mississippi, holding concerts to promote the MFDP. More, including Pete Seeger and Peter, Paul and Mary, were said to be on their way. Then there would be "canvassing, which you all know about." And in a few days, Martin Luther King would tour Mississippi, putting his high profile behind the Freedom Democratic Party.

Moses' midcourse correction shifted Freedom Summer into high gear. Freedom School teachers began canvassing on weekends. Rollicking mass meetings were now held night after night. Sunday-morning church became obligatory as volunteers—men in shirts and ties, women in stockings and heels—waited until deacons gathered collection plates, then stood to explain the Freedom Democratic Party. They would be outside after the service to sign up everyone. Everyone! The goal of 200,000 signatures—35,000 new names per week—also sent volunteers to the far reaches of each plantation and each day.

Even in late July, morning comes early to the Mississippi Delta. Above the pancake land, the spreading sky turns salmon pink by 5:00 a.m. Here in the summer of 1964, as they had for decades at that hour, buses roam the plantations surrounding Greenwood, stopping to pick up "hands" to chop cotton. Yet for the first time ever, white hands are among the black. Standing beside shacks glowing with kerosene lamps, volunteers make their pitch to tired men in overalls, to weary women in housedresses and bandannas.

No, there's no danger in signing *this* paper.

Your name will not be listed in any newspaper.

The boss man will never know. Most whites don't even know what the MFDP is. What is it? Here's a brochure (and a flashlight)· "The Democratic National Convention is a very big meeting in August. It is a very important meeting because people in the Democratic Party choose the person they want to run for President of the United States. . . . Mississippi sends a group of people to this national meeting. This summer we are going to send a Freedom group to the national meeting."

The brochure goes on to explain democracy from the ground up. There will be precinct meetings all over the state, then county conventions, and finally a state convention in Jackson to choose delegates who will travel to Atlantic City. But as sharecroppers and canvassers board the bus, as it rumbles through the cotton fields, there is no time to go into all that. The pitch continues. With MFDP registration, there is no poll tax to pay. And no impossible tangle from the state constitution to interpret. Just fill in your name, address, and how long you've lived in Leflore County. The forms will be kept secret. No one will know. Sign here.

The pitch is as simple as the brochure, yet resistance remains.

"I got to think about it."

"I'm too old to fool with it."

"Not me. I'm the only one my children's *got*. I'm all they *have*."

Volunteers have not surrendered their summer just to take "I got to think about it" for an answer. Again and again they return to shacks, show up at church, ride the dawn buses, and wear down resistance. If it takes 35,000 new signatures each week, they will give their August as they have given their July. But the obstacles run far deeper than the fear.

No one doubts the convention in Atlantic City will be a show of party unity, nominating an incumbent president with a 70 percent approval rating. Yet the Freedom Democrat challenge threatens to splinter the Democratic Party. Lyndon Johnson has already enraged the South with his Civil Rights Act. If Democrats seat a black delegation from Mississippi and send whites home, can he win any states south of the Mason-Dixon line? Won't a convention floor fight based on race make the GOP tussles in San Francisco look like playground spats? And won't Barry Goldwater be the next president of the United States? News of the upcoming challenge is already salting old wounds, recalling 1948 when "Dixiecrats" stormed out of the Democratic convention in protest of the civil rights platform. The *Washington Post* warns of a "battle royal." The *Los Angeles Times* predicts a "potentially explosive dilemma." SNCC and the MFDP, however, are ready for a fight, a fair fight.

For the next five weeks, Freedom Democrats will carefully follow all the rules. They will sign every party form, obey every party bylaw, file every necessary paper. Armed with signatures, fired by the horror stories ready to be shared with America, backed by hundreds ready to rally on Atlantic City's Boardwalk, they feel certain. They *will* be heard. They *will* be seated. They *will* represent Mississippi. With each new signature, they are still more confident. It just takes names. Sign here.

The making of a parallel political party took more than certitude. Organization and leadership were also vital, and for these, Freedom Democrats relied on SNCC project directors. During Freedom Summer's opening weeks, a few, like Chris Williams's "great leader" in Batesville, had to be replaced. A similar breakdown occurred in Vicksburg, where white volunteers rebelled against a young black leader they nicknamed "Papa Doc," bringing Bob Moses to soothe tensions. But by late July, SNCC had replaced its weaker links, solidifying a corps of black men still in their early twenties yet coordinating manpower like five-star generals.

In Holly Springs, Ivanhoe Donaldson supervised one of Freedom Summer's most energetic projects. Donaldson had first come south in 1962, leaving Michigan State to make dozens of runs in a truck carrying supplies for ravenous Delta sharecroppers. Thin and wiry, constantly on edge, this son of a New York cop suffered from migraines that sometimes had him lying on the couch in the project office, head in his hands. Tension sometimes led Donaldson to shout at volunteers, especially women. "He has trouble relating to white women," many said. But no one questioned his dedication nor dared defy his rules. Anyone who broke a rule, Donaldson told volunteers on the first day of summer, "will have to pack his bag and get his ass out of town. We're here to work! The time for bullshitting is past!" And there would be no surrender to fear. Early that summer when a black volunteer was arrested for "blocking traffic," Donaldson ordered him back on the street. "We can't let them think that we are afraid," he said. "You know that. Go right back to the spot where you were arrested." Like many other SNCCs, Donaldson had opposed the summer project, convinced it would destroy "the one thing where the Negro can stand first." But once it began, he ran his project the same way he drove, one foot on the brake, the other on the accelerator, often topping one hundred miles per hour.

Donaldson was known and respected in Holly Springs, but the Delta's project director was known all over Mississippi and would soon be notorious across the nation. Tall and lanky, with huge eyes and a savage wit, Stokely Carmichael followed his intellect from his native Trinidad to the South Bronx, then on to Howard University. Like Bob Moses, Carmichael had majored in philosophy, and the two sometimes discussed Gödel's theorems late into the night. Like Moses, Carmichael had won a full graduate scholarship to Harvard, though he turned it down to remain on the front lines. And like Moses, Carmichael seemed to be everywhere that summer— at every meeting, every rally, every protest. Volunteers struggled to keep up with his lightning-quick references to Frantz Fanon and other philosophers of black liberation. Based in the Greenwood office, where his charisma earned him the nickname "Stokely Starmichael," Carmichael was more relaxed than his peers. He openly flirted with women, leading to speculation on how many he slept with. His constant jive kept the office as loose as his rules. Most project offices had code names on the CB network, names based on John—John Schwarz (Shaw); John August (Clarksdale), etc. But because Carmichael called everyone "Sweets," he named his CB base "Greenwood Sweets." Every week or so, when a package arrived at the office addressed to FASC, Carmichael would gather volunteers to share the latest gifts from the group he called "The Friends and Admirers of Stokely Carmichael." "Young man," he would say to a volunteer. "Tell FASC what you want and FASC will see to it." Opening the package, he would pass out toothpaste, candy, insect repellent, and other goodies mailed from "friends and admirers" volunteers could only guess at. But Carmichael was also fearless to a fault. Everyone knew how many times he had been arrested, how he was on the picket lines on Freedom Day, and in the Greenwood jail right along with them. In the coming years, when his "Black Power!" chant terrified white America, when he led an all-black SNCC, some whites would feel rejected, but Greenwood volunteers would come to his defense. Stokely had been there for them.

In contrast to Donaldson and Carmichael, Hollis Watkins was modest and unassuming, with a sweet Mississippi drawl that melted into a beautiful tenor when Freedom Songs broke out. The twelfth child of Pike County sharecroppers, Watkins had left Mississippi for California before coming home hoping to join the Freedom Rides. He arrived too late—"the Riders," including Carmichael, had been arrested in Jackson and sent to Parchman Farm. Instead of becoming a Freedom Rider, Watkins had joined Bob Moses in McComb. A SNCC staffer ever since, Watkins was known as a soulful presence, as smooth as molasses. Yet when put in charge of two dozen volunteers in Holmes County, he imposed Freedom Summer's most ironclad rules. No going out at night unless to a mass meeting. No drinking—not even a beer. No one should even visit the little country store across Highway 49 in Mileston. Who knew what redneck might show up? "I felt personally responsible for the lives of everyone who worked on my project," Watkins remembered. "These young people had come down here, and if they were serious and dedicated to the cause, they should be willing to make sacrifices." Watkins's final rule was the harshest—no dating. Period. The Holmes County project was just two days old when a female volunteer went out with a local white man. The next day, Watkins took her to Jackson and had her reassigned. Watkins's friend and peer, the equally congenial Charlie Cobb, faced the same problem in Greenville. The Mississippi river town may have been moderate, but interracial dating remained taboo. When cops arrested a black man spotted hand in hand with a white volunteer, Cobb gave the couple a choice: dating or the summer project. "They both left together," Cobb remembered. "I never saw them again."

Dedicated, brilliant, determined, such was the staff Muriel Tillinghast joined in mid-July when she became SNCC's only female project director in Mississippi. Three weeks earlier, Muriel had been afraid to leave the Greenville office. Now she was expected to run it. In turning over his command, Charlie Cobb had few reservations. "Muriel was tough, you could see that," Cobb remembered. "And I knew her reputation at Howard. She was smart, and she had experience in the sit-in movement, which doesn't tell you how she's going to be as an organizer in rural Mississippi but it's a good bet." Before leaving to tour Freedom Schools, Cobb tested Muriel in Issaquena County. The snake-shaped, bayou-infested region ran along the Mississippi River just south of Greenville. Like some remote feudal fiefdom, Issaquena was desperately poor, patrolled by the shotgun and the pickup, and as brutal as any county in Mississippi. Blacks made up more than half the population, yet none were registered to vote. In early July, two white volunteers had risked their lives to "crack" this plantation stronghold. They were instantly spotted by their pace. "We had never seen anybody walk that fast in the summer in the Mississippi Delta," sharecropper Unita Blackwell remembered.

The twentieth century came to Issaquena County the night the volunteers called a meeting at the Moon Lake Baptist Church in the county seat of Mayersville (pop. 700). Standing before rows of black faces, a pale man from Brooklyn spoke until it became clear that no one could understand a word he said. His counterpart from Virginia took over, telling locals of the movement, the summer project, their right to vote. At the back of the church, a terrified deacon sat moaning—"Oh Lord, Lord . . ." but Unita Blackwell felt "like a big drenching rain had finally come after a long dry spell." Blackwell, a sturdy, towering woman who had worked her entire life in the cotton fields, soon went with SNCC to the courthouse. She "failed" the registration test and was instantly thrown off the plantation, never to pick another boll of cotton. The movement was her new job. Two weeks later, when Muriel Tillinghast came to Issaquena County, Blackwell became her pupil, her disciple, her friend.

Seated in Blackwell's shack, surrounded by fields of waist-high cotton, Muriel found the voice of her ancestors. She began holding forth on voting rights, citizenship, and black history. "For someone so young and petite, she had a serene strength about her," Blackwell remembered. When Muriel called herself a teacher, Blackwell assumed she taught school, yet "Muriel taught things more rare and precious." Blackwell was soon gathering a dozen or more in her home or in church to hear Muriel talk about Frederick Douglass, Harriet Tubman, and W. E. B. Du Bois. Muriel read from black poetry and literature. She told them about her own family, the grandmother who had walked from Texas to D.C. and the proud generations since. "What Muriel Tillinghast really taught us was to have pride in ourselves," Blackwell remembered. Though impressed by her knowledge and spark, locals were startled by Muriel's hair. None had ever seen what would soon be called an "Afro." Some women giggled behind Muriel's back, and Blackwell constantly urged her to straighten her "nappy-headed" hair. "Okay, I'll do that sometime," Muriel would reply. Or "I've got to wash it." But Muriel let her hair grow, and within a year, Blackwell and countless other African-American women were wearing theirs the same way.

Not long after Muriel arrived in Issaquena County, calls from Greenville to Jackson reported: "Things getting pretty tight in Issaquena—whites circling certain key houses, churches." Yet Blackwell and others continued to take Muriel and her volunteers into their homes, feeding them, sheltering them, talking, learning, sharing strength. "They recognized we were in their hands," Muriel remembered. "We couldn't have lasted a single day without them." On July 20, whites fired nine shots into a car parked outside a mass meeting. Neighboring Sharkey County, where Muriel was also working, was equally feudal, equally hotheaded. When a black volunteer's car broke down there, a cop arrested the man and smashed his skull with a blackjack. "Go back to Greenville," the cop said, "and tell all the niggers in Greenville that they beat a nigger's ass in Sharkey County." But by then, locals were talking about opening a Freedom School. And more and more blacks were signing Freedom Democrat forms, singing in church, and coming out to meet Muriel and her staff. A Freedom Democratic Party precinct meeting was scheduled at the Moon Lake Baptist Church for July 26, the day after Martin Luther King's Mississippi tour would end. Unita Blackwell would be there, and so would her teacher, her friend, who now knew she could handle Mississippi.

Shortly after noon on Tuesday, July 21, Robert Kennedy phoned the White House. Another crisis in a summer of crises was pending. Martin Luther King was on a plane to Mississippi. "If he gets killed," Kennedy told LBJ, "it creates all kinds of problems. Not just being dead, but also a lot of other kind of problems." The president instantly phoned J. Edgar Hoover. Though the FBI director loathed King and was already bugging his hotel rooms, he recognized the danger. "There are threats that they're going to kill him," Hoover said. Johnson shuddered at the thought. "Talk to your man in Jackson," the president said, "and tell him that we think that it would be the better part of wisdom, in the national interest, that they work out some arrangement where somebody's in front of him and behind him when he goes over there. . . . So that we won't find another burning car. It's a hell of a lot easier to watch a situation like that before it happens than it is to call out the Navy after it happens."

King had not been to Mississippi since Medgar Evers's funeral in June 1963. There he had kept a low profile, but when the procession threatened to break into a riot, he had hustled to the airport. King's loyalists were terrified of Mississippi. "We tried to warn SNCC," Andrew Young noted. "We were all Southerners and we knew the depth of the depravity of southern racism. We knew better than to try to take on Mississippi." In the thirteen months since he had fled Jackson, King had seen his fame soar. He had shared his dream with a quarter million people on the Washington mall and was about to be nominated for the Nobel Peace Prize. He had the highest approval ratings of any Negro in America. Yet to whites in Mississippi, he was "Martin Luther Coon." Billboards along Mississippi highways showed King at the Highlander Folk School in Tennessee, the caption reading "Martin Luther King at Communist Training School." Mississippi newspapers wrote of "the unspeakable Martin Luther King," and "The Reverend Dr. Extremist Agitator Martin Luther King Junior."

King knew the risks in going to Mississippi. All that weekend before his departure, he wrestled with thoughts of dying. "I want to live a normal life," he told an aide. After pleading with King not to go, his associates enlisted one of his former professors to tell him it would be "just suicidal for you to go there." King accepted Bob Moses' invitation anyway. He did not know that SNCCs sometimes mocked him as "de Lawd." He had been warned that a "guerilla group" would try to kill him in Mississippi, but he considered SNCC's summer project "the most creative thing happening today in civil rights." And he knew the Freedom Democratic Party deserved his support. His first stop would be Greenwood.

Blacks in the volatile cotton capital could scarcely believe the news. The man whose photo graced so many walls in so many shacks was coming to be

among them. Where would Dr. King speak in Greenwood? Where would he
stay? On the day before King's arrival, homes were dusted, mopped, swept.
Women spent the afternoon in hot kitchens, pumping out fried chicken and
cornbread, pies and cakes. Preachers argued over whose church the reverend should grace. The following morning, reporters swarmed all over the
quarters. Arriving in Jackson on a flight from Atlanta, King spoke on the
shimmering tarmac, saying he had come "to demonstrate the absolute support of the Southern Christian Leadership Conference for this summer
project . . . [and] support the tremendous quest for the right to vote on the
part of the people of the state of Mississippi in the midst of bombings, murders, and many other difficult experiences." When King finished, an FBI
agent stepped up, introduced himself, and remained with him, waiting while
he met with SNCC and COFO leaders, then boarding his connecting flight.

Charcoal clouds loomed above the Delta as King, escorted by four FBI
agents, began his stroll past the shakedown hovels, along the gravel roads,
through the heart of the raw poverty and rising anger of black Greenwood.
Trailing admirers and reporters, King stopped traffic, turned heads, and
astonished those who had never heard him in person. As rain began to pelt
down, his spine-tingling baritone rolled across streets lined with pool halls
and juke joints. Standing on a bench outside the Savoy Café, he waved his
arms above the crowd. "You must not allow anybody to make you feel you
are not significant," he said. "Every Negro has worth and dignity. Mississippi has treated the Negro as if he is a thing instead of a person." King
delighted followers by stepping inside a pool hall and interrupting a game.
"Gentlemen, I will be brief," he said. While young men stood, cue sticks in
hand, King spoke about the need to "make it clear to everybody in the world
that Negroes desire to be free and to be a registered voter." Moving back
to the street, King urged people to sign Freedom Democratic Party papers,
papers volunteers handed out in his wake.

That evening, King spoke at a small church, then headed for the Elks
Hall. Waiting in the audience were Chris Williams, who had come with other
Batesville volunteers, and Greenwood's Freedom Day picketers, just released
from six days behind bars. The picketers had been sentenced to $100 fines
and thirty days in jail. Out on appeal, they broke their hunger strike with
chicken and collards, then sat waiting for "de Lawd." As the crowd swelled
in anticipation, not even the worst cynic in SNCC could deny King's appeal.
When his entourage arrived at the Elks Hall, crowds swarmed the stage.

Hundreds clapped and chanted, "We Want Free-dom! We Want Free-dom!" Stepping to the podium, King thrilled the audience that spilled out of the seats, lined the walls, peered in windows. If Negroes "mobilize the power of their souls," he said, they could "turn this nation upside down in order to turn it right side up." Goodman, Schwerner, and Chaney, King noted, had been "murdered by the silence and apathy of good people." Barry Goldwater, he added, gave aid to segregationists. And the FBI—having seen its quick work in other cases, King found it hard to believe "that these same efficient FBI men cannot locate the missing workers." King concluded with a rhythmic chant—"*Seat* the Freedom Democratic Party! *Seat* the Freedom Democratic Party!"

As King spoke, a small plane with its navigation lights off buzzed the Elks Hall. On its second pass, a white cloud of leaflets fluttered to the ground. This latest issue of *The Klansman* denounced "the Right Rev. Riot Inciter, Martin Luther King, Jr." come to "bring riot, strife, and turmoil to . . . Greenwood, Mississippi [and] to milk all available cash from the local niggers." At dawn the next day, volunteers again rode buses among field hands, finding them more willing to sign their names. That morning's *Jackson Clarion-Ledger* headline read "Small Crowd Greets King at Greenwood." At 8:23 a.m., King's flight left for Jackson.

With the movement's leading light touring Mississippi, with volunteers refusing to cower in the face of violence, those determined to derail Freedom Summer made their own midcourse correction. Rank violence and vile hatred were not enough to end the invasion. Across America, Mississippi's image had sunk so low that residents traveling to the New York World's Fair were changing their license plates to out-of-state tags. Someone had to stand up for Mississippi.

Lawrence Rainey stood up first. The Neshoba County sheriff filed a $1 million libel suit against NBC, charging that a *Huntley-Brinkley News* interview had implicated him in the disappearance. (The suit was ultimately dismissed.) Three days later, Mississippi newspapers reprinted a letter to NBC's *Today* show, whose host had criticized the state. "It is a known fact," a Hattiesburg man wrote, "that more violence has occurred in one subway in the city of New York in the last three months than in the whole state of Mississippi in the last year." Next, with riots raging in Harlem, whites gloated. "It is a sad commentary," a Mississippi congressman said on Capitol Hill, "that while mobs stalk the streets of New York . . . some 1,500 so-called civil rights workers and troublemakers are in Mississippi—a state with the nation's lowest crime rate—subjecting innocent, law abiding people to insult, national scorn and creating trouble." Mississippi newspapers, known for plastering northern crime stories on front pages, delighted in the Harlem riots. "Latest Wave of Invaders Badly Needed in New York Area Today," the *Jackson Clarion-Ledger* sneered. Batesville's weekly *Panolian,* noting the tension caused by summer volunteers, concluded, "Happily, the inclination toward violence is less in Mississippi than in New York. Otherwise there could have been a holocaust." But in Mississippi's propaganda arsenal, the strongest weapon was the oldest.

Accusations of communism in the civil rights movement dated to the *Brown* decision, handed down in the waning days of McCarthyism. Knee-jerk red-baiting did not die with McCarthy, however. It just moved south. Into the 1960s, J. Edgar Hoover fanned Cold War suspicions—"We do know that Communist influence does exist in the Negro movement and it is this influence which is vitally important." Hoover's charges, constantly invoked by southern congressmen, were woven into the fabric of the white South— anyone who worked for civil rights had to be a Communist. SNCCs had heard the red-baiting so often they could joke about it. "Hey, you don't worry about the communists," Stokely Carmichael often told the press. "Worry about SNCC. We way more dangerous, Jack." Just as the red-baiting was growing stale, Freedom Summer brought hordes of "Communists" to Mississippi. All summer, volunteers heard "the usual" taunts. Cops and sheriffs asked them whether they (1) believed in Jesus; (2) believed in God; and (3) were Communists. A Batesville volunteer was stopped on the street and asked to say something in Russian because "all communists speak Russian." But now, with Mississippi in disgrace, it was time to name names.

On July 22, as Martin Luther King toured Jackson, Senator James Eastland charged that the "mass invasion of Mississippi by demonstrators, agitators, agents of provocation, and inciters to mob violence" was a Communist conspiracy. Eastland spoke on the Senate floor for an hour, citing J. Edgar Hoover, and producing a long list of names. According to the senator, volunteer Larry Rubin had cochaired the Fair Play for Cuba Committee at Antioch College in Ohio. When arrested in Holly Springs, Eastland said, Rubin had an address book containing names of known Communists. Eastland's list of Communist "stooges and pawns" went on. A Moss Point volunteer had been thrown out of Costa Rica for distributing Communist literature. The National Lawyers Guild, notorious since the 1930s for defending Communists, was working with SNCC in Mississippi. And attorney Martin Popper, representing Andrew Goodman's family, was "a long-time Communist legal eagle." Rising to a fist-flailing righteousness, the senator charged that the summer invasion had subjected Mississippi to "a degree of vilification . . . unequaled since the black days of Reconstruction." Mississippians, he concluded, deserved "everlasting credit [for] holding their tempers so well."

Eastland's charges made headlines across Mississippi. Within days, the Sovereignty Commission began trailing Larry Rubin and his "beatnik looking crowd." The FBI did likewise, and the Mississippi legislature opened a full-scale inquiry into Communist influence in Freedom Summer. The red-baiters would find kernels of truth in Eastland's diatribe. A handful of summer volunteers, many of them "red diaper" offspring of former Communists, did sympathize with Cuba and other left-wing causes. And the National Lawyers Guild was working with SNCC, which refused to be cowed by neo-McCarthyism. "If they ain't calling you a Communist," Fannie Lou Hamer often said, "you ain't doing your job." Yet as the summer accelerated, the vast majority of volunteers were far too busy to fight the Cold War—on either side.

At the Vicksburg Community Center, Fran O'Brien had been teaching arts and crafts for three weeks when her students demanded meatier subjects One day, rummaging through the center's library, the children spotted an American history text. They brought it to the gentle, dark-haired teacher with the funny accent. They wanted to learn history too, they told Fran. Just like the big kids. With a slight smile, Fran opened the tattered book and instantly noticed the publishing date—1930. The narrative began, "The history of America really begins in England because all Americans come from England." She looked at the faces before her. She closed the book.

Three weeks in Mississippi had taught Fran far more than she had taught her students. When a girl in a school variety show recited "Four score and seven years ago," Fran had learned not to be impressed by rote memory. "Do you know what the Gettysburg Address means?" she asked. "Yes," the girl replied. "It means that all the slaves were free, and it was signed July 4, 1776." Reading to her students, Fran learned that *Little House on the Prairie* books did not mean as much to black kids in Mississippi as they did to a white girl growing up in southern California. She began searching for other stories. When Fran got nervous, she learned not to speak too quickly. After moments of blank stares, one boy finally said, "We can't understand y'all." And one morning, when a car came to take her to the Freedom House, Fran learned to check carefully before going outside. The car was not her morning ride. She and her roommate were left standing by the road when a motorcycle cop pulled up. He asked the women if they were runaways, if they were "of age." Then a second cop came and asked if they were civil rights workers. Fran's roommate sweet-talked the cops into letting them go. The education of Fran O'Brien continued.

On the evening a bomb hit Vicksburg's Melody Lounge, Fran learned not to tell her mother the whole truth about Mississippi. "You haven't a thing to worry about," she wrote home that night. "Vicksburg is a very quiet town." And with each class, Fran was learning that not all children are charming. During her afternoon chorus, two boys insisted on croaking like frogs until Fran blew up at "the little darlings." Another girl did daily "Jekyll-Hyde transformations," racing around the room, threatening other students. But Mississippi's saddest lesson taught Fran how Jim Crow crippled every black child's confidence. Thrilled by her students' creativity, she was dismayed to see so many kids throw their paintings in the wastebasket. She took them out and put them on her classroom wall.

Freedom Summer's makeshift logistics had bounced Fran around Vicksburg. In mid-July, the community center was condemned. Fran and her colleagues packed their supplies and moved two blocks to the Freedom House, where their classes had to compete with voter registration. Next, Fran had to leave her host home. The woman there had grown terrified of retaliation. Fran moved into a larger home with antique furniture and even china, all proudly tended by the black woman Fran would forever call "Mrs. Garrett." The match was ideal. Mrs. Garrett, a rotund woman with thick iron gray hair, was a retired teacher with ample advice for a beginner. Every evening, after Fran came home from a long day of classes, Mrs. Garrett sat and talked. Talked about her grandmother, who when freed, got down on her knees and hugged her children, thanking Jesus that "my babies can't be sold away." Talked about teaching in Vicksburg's black schools, with few books, few resources, just empathy and common sense. Talked about what to do with a history book decades old and whitewashed with lies—"Well, you just read the book and then you give them the right information."

The next day, Fran started teaching American history. Opening the 1930 text, she read, "The history of America really begins in England." "Now," she said, "what might be wrong with that sentence?" A hand went up.

"Well, lots of people came here who weren't from England."

Fran smiled. And what other countries might Americans have come from? Her students began touring the globe.

"France?"

"Yes."

"Italy?"

"Certainly."

"Germany?"

They moved on to Mexico and South America. Fran was impressed with their geography, but couldn't help wonder. After they tried China and India, Fran asked, "Well, what about Africa?" The classroom fell silent. Finally, a little girl raised her hand.

"Does that count?"

Fran had to blink back tears. "Yes," she said softly. "Yes, that counts."

A few days later, Fran wrote home again:

> Sometimes I feel I'm not doing much, but . . . I still feel our real hope of success is in the children. They can't avoid fear, being intelligent, nor resentment, being human. But I hope the stimulation of the Freedom School and the examples of determination set by Negro workers will save them from the apathetic "What's the use?" attitude which oppresses and binds people more than the law ever could.

On Thursday, July 23, Fran found Vicksburg's Freedom House "in a dither." All afternoon, people ran in and out, straightening, cleaning, preparing. Martin Luther King was coming. He was due around 6:00 p.m. The day before, King had shared coffee with COFO workers in Jackson, then canvassed for Freedom Democrats. That night, he had spoken at the Masonic Temple. The following morning, an FBI wiretap of King's Atlanta home picked up a death threat. But Hoover, afraid the eavesdropping would be revealed, had given a standing order not to tell King about such threats, so the FBI merely tightened its guard. On Thursday afternoon, King met with Bob Moses, James Farmer, and other leaders, discussing strategies for Atlantic City. After a press conference where he called Mississippi "the worst state in the Union," he headed for Vicksburg.

White Vicksburg paid no attention to Martin Luther King. The Miss Mississippi pageant was under way. Captivating the town with parades and parties, the pageant was in its third night—the swimsuit competition. Across town, Fran O'Brien was finishing classes as the dinner hour approached. King was scheduled to dine with volunteers, then speak at a church, but he was late, and some were beginning to wonder if he was coming at all. Toward 6:15 p.m., Fran was straightening her classroom when someone told her to hurry. The last car was leaving. She rushed down the long driveway, and there in the front seat was Martin Luther King.

At first, Fran thought it must be someone who merely looked like him, but when a friend asked whether she was just going to stand there gawking, Fran jumped in the back. All the way to dinner, other volunteers fell over themselves to tell King about their summer work. Fran sat in silence. Finally, King turned around. "And what about you, young lady?" he asked. "What do you do in the project?"

"Nothing," Fran managed to say. "I just work with the kids."

"What do you do with the kids?"

Shyness stifled Fran, but another volunteer burst in and told King what a great teacher she was, doing arts and crafts, backyard games, and now a chorus and piano and sewing lessons. . . . Fran smiled weakly. King studied her, then asked, "Do you call that 'nothing'?"

"No, sir."

Then, getting serious as only Martin Luther King could get serious, he said, "Young lady, don't you *ever* say you 'just work with the kids.' Our children are the future and you are forming it." After dinner, King spoke to a boisterous crowd, but Fran O'Brien would not remember a thing he said that was more important than what he said to her.

The following morning, back in Jackson, King taped a TV show, then headed for Philadelphia. Bob Moses had not wanted King to venture into the town where a mob had recently driven off NAACP leaders, but King insisted. No events were planned there; no locals were expecting him. FBI agents met his caravan at the Neshoba County line and cleared the road ahead. An hour later, blacks in Independence Quarters were startled to see fifteen cars rumble over the railroad tracks. Kicking up red clouds of dust, the caravan came to a halt in front of a church. King walked again through the streets and stopped at another pool hall, this time taking off his jacket, rolling up his sleeves, and playing a game of eight ball. He lost. Climbing on a bench, he addressed the crowd: "Three young men came here to help set you free. They probably lost their lives. I know what you have suffered in this state, the lynchings and the murders. But things are going to get better." Then, quoting an old spiritual, King told the group, "Walk together, children, don't you get weary." As he left the pool hall, an old woman approached and reached out a withered hand. "I just want to touch you," she said. King moved on beneath afternoon thunder and rain. He stood on the ashes of the Mt. Zion Church, sharing parishioners' sorrow but rejoicing "that there are churches relevant enough that people of ill will will be willing to burn them." He spoke that Friday evening in Meridian before returning to his hotel to sweat out his last night in Mississippi, sitting in his boxer shorts and drinking beer with friends. His plane left for Atlanta the next morning.

The night after King left Mississippi, Rita Schwerner spoke to blacks in Greenwood. "I know what fear is," she said, "but I know that you can risk much more by doing nothing. It's not unnatural to be afraid but you're cheating your children if your being afraid stops them from having something." Fear, however, had met its match in Mississippi. Another weekend of violence saw a volunteer's car burned in Mileston and another bomb thrown in McComb. In Batesville, tear gas engulfed the Mileses' home. Coughing and choking, Robert and Mona Miles grabbed their sons and, with volunteers right behind them, staggered out into the night. But with all eyes on a new prize—the Democratic National Convention—fear had become like summer thunder, startling at first but no longer sending anyone for cover.

For every bomb and beating, there was now a symbol of hope—thousands of Freedom Democrat brochures sent out across the state, hundreds of signatures gathered. Precinct meetings drew two hundred in Clarksdale, three hundred in Canton, still more in Holly Springs, where a crowd surrounded police cars and sang Freedom Songs. In the tiny hamlet of Starkville, two volunteers were dropped off alone. Confronted by the sheriff, they were soon surrounded and protected by blacks. "We've been waiting for you," several said. Nearly five hundred signed Freedom Democrat forms.

Whites in Mississippi might bloody and bruise Freedom Summer, but they could not douse its revived spirit. When Mississippi's secretary of state declared Freedom Democratic Party meetings illegal, Barney Frank fired off a mocking memo—"RE: Arguing with the Red Queen About Precinct Meetings." "We have a perfect right to hold meetings and call them precinct meetings, nominating conventions, coronations, séances, or whatever we damn well please," Frank wrote, signing the memo—Alice. And in Ruleville: "Mrs. Hamer is back. Things moving. . . ."

Even the reticent Fran O'Brien was emboldened by the collective courage. Five nights after meeting Martin Luther King, she found herself alone upstairs in the Freedom House. Everyone else had gone to Vicksburg's Freedom Democrat precinct meeting. The office was silent, dimly lit, slightly eerie. Then the phone rang. The drawl on the other end of the line asked Fran where she was from. Whittier, California. How did she like Mississippi? Oh, just fine. Then the caller casually said everyone in the Freedom House had three days to get out. Three days before the house was bombed. Fran thanked the man for calling. There was a brief silence.

"Listen," the man said. "I said I'm gonna *bomb* y'all. And there ain't gonna be no Freedom School and no freedom there or anyplace else, and no *nothin'*!"

"Yes sir," Fran replied. "I understood you the first time. Was there anything else?"

"No. . . . No, I don't believe so. But I'll call again."

"Oh, feel free," Fran said. "We'd love to hear from you. Thank you for calling. Good night."

The line fell silent. Then, "G' night."

Let a new earth rise. Let another world be born.
Let a bloody peace be written in the sky.

—Margaret Walker Alexander, "For My People"

CHAPTER EIGHT

"The Summer of Our Discontent"

Since the first headline of Freedom Summer, three faces had stared down America. Across Mississippi and the rest of the South, the faces stared out from general stores and post offices, police stations and banks, federal buildings and courthouses. Across America, the faces appeared in magazines strewn on coffee tables and beach blankets. Occasionally, the faces surfaced again in a TV news update. And as July edged toward August, the faces acquired new meanings. They meant that in rural, "redneck" Mississippi, someone had outsmarted the FBI. They meant that in the world's most modern nation, proud of its passenger jets, its Mercury astronauts, its Telstar transatlantic phone calls, men could still "disappear." And for Freedom Summer volunteers, the faces became the very meaning of summer. "How the ghosts of those three shadow all our work," a volunteer wrote. "'Did you know them?' I am constantly asked. Did I need to?"

Many—perhaps most—whites in Mississippi still considered the disappearance a hoax, but after five weeks, their indignation had turned to dismay. "I believe with all my heart they are alive somewhere," an old woman in Philadelphia said. "We may never know it, but I believe it is so nevertheless." A downtown merchant voiced a more common concern—"I just hope that if they are dead, they won't find the bodies anywhere around here." Others added red-baiting to their suspicions. "If they were murdered," a man wrote the *Jackson Clarion-Ledger,* "it is by no means the first case of such disposition by Communists of their dupes to insure their silence. However, the careful absence of clues makes it seem likely that they are quartered in Cuba or another Communist area awaiting their next task. There is no reason to believe them seriously harmed by citizens of the most law-abiding state of the union."

Aluminum skiffs no longer dredged muddy rivers, but hundreds of sailors were still scouring remote hamlets. Piling out of military buses, search parties set up day camps near Ma and Pa stores, cleared shelves of snacks and bug repellent, then set out into swamps and fields. Locals were shocked. The men didn't actually expect to find the bodies *here*? *Here* in Kemper County? *Here* in Jasper County? Sailors often answered that they expected to find the three somewhere close by, but they were just bluffing. Aside from the basics—the Sunday-afternoon arrest, the hours in jail, the late-night release, the blackened station wagon—rumors were all searchers had to go on. The most recent said the bodies had been buried in quicksand or thrown into the grinding "hog" of some backwoods sawmill.

FBI agents, having roamed ten counties beneath the Mississippi sun, joked of becoming "real rednecks." They had learned little about Goodman, Schwerner, and Chaney but they had learned all they cared to about Mississippi. Questioning reputed Klansmen, they had learned how the Neshoba klavern had grown since spring, tripling, quadrupling, its membership. They had gathered ample evidence of bootlegging—moonshine, sour-mash stills, and jugs sold on the sly—a vast web of corruption that enriched Klansmen, ranchers, and above all, Sheriff Rainey. And they had learned how routinely "everyone who had been in the county jail had had the stuffing beat out of them." Yet the FBI could not find three missing men. The latest lead came from a local white woman—"Ask Fannie Jones about her son, Wilmer."

When FBI agents tracked Wilmer Jones to Chicago's South Side, his story might have described the first night of summer. Three weeks before the disappearance, Jones had returned to Philadelphia to visit his mother. He had called a store to ask about resizing his high school ring. The next thing he knew, he was accused of asking the store's pretty clerk out on a date. Taken into custody, Jones met Sheriff Rainey. "Nigger," Rainey shouted, "did you call up that white girl and ask her for a date?" When Jones shook his head, Rainey lashed out with his meaty hand. Deputy Price got in his own licks before hacking off Jones's goatee with a pocket knife. Jones trembled until released—at midnight. Waiting outside were five men with pistols and shotguns. While Price and Rainey looked on, the men shoved Jones into a car. In the moonlight hours, they drove him all over winding roads, a pistol jabbed in his neck, shouting questions about the white woman, the "COFOs," and the NAACP. Finally, the men took Jones to "the place"—an empty well just inside a barbed-wire gate—somewhere in Neshoba County.

The FBI did not care that Wilmer Jones had finally been put on a bus and told never to show his face in Neshoba County again. They wanted to find "the place." Agents began driving Jones all over the county. Still terrified, he wore a cardboard box on his head, with holes cut for his eyes, until the heat made him groggy. The search went on for two days.

Agents were also tracing a lead from comedian Dick Gregory. In answer to his $25,000 reward, Gregory had received a three-page letter, rife with backwoods grammar: "the tipoff boys were waiting between Meridian and Philadelphia Mississippi and surrounded by a sum of five men. . . . The burial took place shortly after the mob had taken over which is a field not too far from Philadelphia, Miss., between five to eight miles off the right coming south from Philadelphia between 200 and 400 yards off the road. . . ." When Gregory turned the letter over to the FBI, agents traced it to a Mississippi native in Washington, D.C., whom they dismissed as a mental patient, "a prolific letter writer . . . a nuisance." Agents were no more impressed by Gregory's tape of a man with a Mississippi drawl naming five slayers of Goodman, Schwerner, and Chaney.

With Wilmer Jones's help, the FBI finally stumbled on "the place." Beyond the barbed-wire gate, a dozen deep wells might have hidden bodies, but they contained only water. Another dead end. Meanwhile, burly Joe Sullivan, directing the investigation, continued to meet his lone source—the Meridian highway patrolman. Though eager to talk about the Klan, the man still refused to discuss murder. As August approached, Sullivan was fed up with Mississippi and its "fair-minded, Christian people." It was time for the payoff. Three weeks earlier, meeting J. Edgar Hoover in Jackson, Sullivan said his Meridian contact might talk—for $25,000. Hoover had told his assistant to "have the money ready at FBI headquarters." By the last day of July, the money had been ready for more than a week.

All summer, the rotting shacks of Shaw, Mississippi, had seemed to drown in despair. Fred Winn had given up expecting any reaction from anyone. If paying a kid to plant a bomb did not awaken the black community, what would? Each afternoon was slower, more depressing, than the one before. Each evening the Delta sun set over burned-out ground. Shaw's planters and their hired thugs remained in tight control over hordes of blacks worn down

by work and hunger and humiliation. Then suddenly Shaw awoke. The catalyst was a single comment. "I realize it may sound foolish," Sheriff Charlie
Capps had told the *New York Times*, "but 95 percent of our blacks are happy."
An alert volunteer posted the *Times* article in the Freedom House and read
it aloud during a mass meeting. Word soon spread, and furious letters were
fired off to the newspaper:

> Only a fool would be happy in Mississippi down here chopping
> cotton for 30 cents an hour.

> If Capps thinks that we are happy why don't he try living like the
> Negroes. After he has done that, ask him if he is happy.

> I ain't going to say that we're happy because we ain't. We don't
> get justice anywhere. . . . Our boys don't want no white girls. We just
> want our justice. Half of us done worked our lives away.

Shaw's black high school was also awakening. When three volunteers
were ejected from the cafeteria, students walked out of classes. The principal
closed the school, parents joined the protest, and cops came to keep order.
But Fred would not be there to see Shaw begin to stand up. Freedom Summer was finally coming to the Delta's hub, and its project director needed a
carpenter.

In late July, Fred packed his bag, his tools, and his father's Bible that he
now carried everywhere and moved a dozen miles across the cotton fields to
the larger town of Indianola (pop. 6,714). He immediately sensed the town
as edgier, more incendiary. The main road crossing town was a drag strip for
the kind of people he wanted to avoid. Muscle cars roared down Highway
82 day and night. Unlike Sheriff Charlie Capps, Sunflower County's sheriff
was not trying to "keep a lid on things." As in Greenwood, whites were
the minority in Indianola but controlled everything and were determined to
keep it that way. Blacks were quick to remind Fred that Indianola was the
birthplace of the White Citizens' Council. All summer, white Indianola had
watched as the invaders had stirred up blacks in other Mississippi enclaves.
They had thought their town would be spared. Now, with a project office
opening and a Freedom School planned, they began marshaling a violent

resistance that would strengthen throughout the coming year, culminating in fires blazing in the night.

For the first time all summer, Fred was living in a home. He was one of three volunteers hosted by sixty-eight-year-old Irene Magruder. Short, feisty, stout as a barrel, Mrs. Magruder dipped snuff, made beautiful quilts, and survived on what Delta blacks called "mother wit." If Fred left lights on in her home, the silver-haired woman shouted, "Get the white man out of my pocket!" Along with hosting volunteers, Mrs. Magruder fed them at her White Rose Café, just down the street from a juke joint where Indianola's own B. B. King had often played. White Rose specialties included spicy hamburgers, fried baloney sandwiches, and pig's feet washed down with plenty of beer.

COFO's late-starting project thrilled black Indianola. "Where have you people been?" one kid asked. "We've been waitin' and waitin'!" The new project also gave Fred the chance to do more than handiwork. Shortly after settling in, he became the project's communications director. Late at night in the Freedom House, he fiddled with a CB radio, pulling in scratchy voices from cars and offices across the Delta from Greenville to "Greenwood Sweets." He was not on the CB long, however, before its code name—Item Base—was decoded. One afternoon, cops burst into the Freedom House, walked to the CB, wrote down its channel number, and walked out. A few late nights later, a chilling voice came on the line—"Hello, Item Base. Hello, Nigger lover!"

With his new home and new responsibilities, Fred was starting to consider staying on into fall. Though he frequently called it a "hell hole," he was coming to like Mississippi—black Mississippi, at least. Five weeks in the Delta had finally doused his fear. "To be quite frank with you all I am quite calm and un-nervous," he wrote home. "After a while you get used to the idea of being watched and hated. Also I just don't have the goddamned time to be nervous or worried. . . . I am in the midst of a revolution. This is the greatest revolution since the American Revolution." By the way, he asked his father, how was his half sister? Could a black kindergartner in San Francisco understand the movement? Had he told her how her half brother was spending the summer? Before Fred's move to Indianola, his father had hoped he might come home early. "Be very careful these last few days," he wrote to "Freddy." "I remember in World War II we dropped thousands of pamphlets—'Don't be killed on the last day of the war.'" But now the elder

Winn wondered whether his son would come home at all. Still hoping, he wrote that he was counting the days until Fred left Mississippi, "counting them like a jail sentence."

Fifty miles to the north, Chris Williams was branching out from Batesville. Panola County had become Freedom Summer's political success story. Hundreds of blacks had become registered voters. Even the high school principal had taken the leap. Names of registrants were still listed in the *Panolian*, but blacks had begun pointing to them with pride. There were simply too many new voters now for each one's house to be targeted. Yet if SNCC was to take full advantage of the federal injunction, all of Panola County had to be canvassed. In mid-July, Chris hit the road he loved so much. Each morning, the wisecracking teenager rose, donned a T-shirt and jeans, had a quick breakfast, then piled into a car already crammed with volunteers. Dust clouds trailed them through the cotton fields, past blacks in overalls, bent double, chopping, hoeing. Penetrating deeper into "the rural," Chris headed for towns as hostile as the snakes that slithered along the griddle roads. Sardis, Mississippi. Como. Crenshaw. Papers and pamphlets in hand, Chris spoke at juke joints and churches, talking up the Freedom Democrats and the upcoming convention in Atlantic City. Occasionally he ventured onto plantations but was usually run off, once by a planter who swore he "wasn't going to turn the government over to a bunch of monkeys."

In each town, Chris asked where a mass meeting might be held and if anyone wanted to host a volunteer. He managed to schedule a few meetings, but blacks anchored to plantations were terrified of offering their homes. Deacons feared their churches would be next on Mississippi's incendiary list. And if word crossed town, Chris had to do some quick talking.

On the edge of the Delta, Chris found Crenshaw a "very violent town." Its rickety storefronts and wooden sidewalks reminded him of an old Western; its stereotypical sheriff almost made him laugh. "I been deputy the past four years," the sheriff told Chris, "and I ain't never had to shoot a nigger." One Saturday toward sunset, Chris was canvassing with Pam Jones, a black volunteer from Baltimore, when a dark Chevy cut them off. Several men with bulging T-shirts piled out. Chris tried to stay calm, but the usual taunt—"Communist!"—plus the one that triggered bad childhood memories—"Nigger lover!"—brought his feistiness to the surface. What did they mean, he had "no business here"? he shouted. Americans could go where they wanted, couldn't they? Fingers were pointed, fists clenched.

Faces were jaw to jaw. But after more shouting, the men sped off, leaving Chris feeling cockier than ever.

Back in Batesville, Stokely Carmichael told Chris to expect a spike in terror. The summer project had been more successful than whites expected, Carmichael said. And the Freedom Democrat challenge was a serious threat. The Klan and Citizens' Council would surely rise to meet it. "The whole state is beginning to tighten up," Chris wrote home. "In the last week people have been shot at in the daytime on the streets of Greenwood and a mob attacked two Civil Rights workers there." August, he concluded, "will see more terrorism." At Robert Miles's home, the tear gas bomb was followed by a nearer miss. One midnight, volunteers were in the kitchen eating peanut butter and jelly sandwiches when a spark flashed outside. Bullets whizzed by the window. One volunteer crawled to the bedroom to drag the two boys to the floor. A few days later, coming to the courthouse, Chris found a dead rattlesnake nailed to the front door.

By then, Chris was living in Crenshaw, "operating a Freedom Outpost in the Delta." Frequenting black cafés, gathering locals at the Masons' hall, he was signing up Freedom Democrats "in droves." Chris had learned not to challenge whites, not even when they called him a "trashy motherfucker" and threw another volunteer to the street. Never lonely, rarely discouraged, still amazed to be in Mississippi and making history, Chris lived for the friendship of blacks who soon knew him by name, greeted him everywhere, even laughed at his jokes. One evening he saw a local black girl slug three white men and run off. It made his day.

On the last afternoon in July, the streets of Philadelphia buzzed with rumors. The talk spread at gas station pumps, in the aisles of the A & P and Piggly-Wiggly, in the post office, where three faces stared beneath the word MISSING. The FBI had grilled Sheriff Rainey! Agents offered him $30,000 to talk! They offered Deputy Price *a million bucks* and the town constable "enough money to last him the rest of his life!" As rumors multiplied, the FBI again invaded downtown. Sunglasses glinting, agents stood outside the courthouse, returning each hate stare. Something was about to happen. Or something already had.

This much was true—FBI agents spoke to Price and Rainey that Friday. The stocky sheriff later boasted of how he'd handled the Federal Bureau of Integration. Yes, he had met agents, Rainey said, but if they wanted to see

him again, they had better "come with subpoenas." Behind his bluster, however, agents knew the sheriff was scared. Fearing that COFO's suit against
him might lead to a polygraph test, the sheriff had been inquiring about
immunity from prosecution. On Friday, when agents came to his office,
Rainey listened as they laid out evidence of his bootlegging. If convicted—
when convicted—he faced fines, jail, and huge back taxes. But if he told
what he knew about the disappearance, the FBI would "take care of him"
to the tune of thirty grand. Rainey told the agents nothing. Down the hall,
agents told Deputy Price they had spent $3 million looking for the three bod-
ies and would "pay a million more just to know where they were." With that
kind of money, agents said, Price could "buy a cattle ranch in Wyoming."
The plump deputy, wearing his goofy smile, was as silent as the sheriff. But
someone talked.

In the decades since Freedom Summer, many have speculated about who
told the FBI where to find the bodies. Local suspicions ranged from a drunk
who woke up in the woods to witness a triple burial to a Dutch "seer" telling
agents the three were buried near a construction site. Many still believe the
FBI hired a New York mobster, a member of the Colombo gang known as
"The Grim Reaper." And the hit man apparently flew to Mississippi, pummeled a suspect, stuck a gun in his mouth and screamed, "What happened
to the three kids?" The apocryphal story is mistakenly connected to another
Mississippi murder; the truth is more traditional. The "someone" who talked
was money, or perhaps just the hint of money.

Thirty grand. A million. Enough to last a lifetime. The actual payoff
was said to be the lowest figure, but $30,000 in 1964 was equivalent to
more than $200,000 in 2010. "We'd have paid a lot more if we'd had to," one
agent said. "We'd have paid anything." The story of the payoff is legend in
Neshoba County, but to this day, no one is sure whether anyone received any
money. Inspector Sullivan always denied making any payoff. But he admitted that on Thursday, July 30, he took his contact—the highway patrolman
from Meridian—out to a steak dinner at the Holiday Inn. And there the FBI
finally learned where the bodies were buried. The next day, agents began
floating rumors and grilling suspects, offering them big rewards, perhaps to
stir suspicion among fellow Klansmen once the bodies were found. Someone
may have received $30,000, but the highway patrolman, who died of a heart
attack two years later, never displayed any sudden wealth. Nor could his
role in solving the mystery be revealed. Recognizing he would be killed if

identified, the FBI began calling the informant "Mr. X." On August 1, guarding his secret with rumors, agents headed for the thick woods of Neshoba County.

As the sun rose that Saturday, agents skirted downtown Philadelphia, then headed south along Route 21 toward a farm known as "The Old Jolly Place." They were looking for an enormous earthfill dam, but they found that Mississippi's tangled landscape could hide objects far larger than a human body. After an hour hacking through brush, agents phoned headquarters and had a helicopter from the Meridian Naval Air Station fly over. "We've spotted the dam," agents heard on their walkie-talkies. "It's a big one." Following directions from overhead, agents slashed through thickets, then topped a rise. Before them stood a crescent of ocher earth, twenty feet high at its midpoint and spanning a gap in the pine trees nearly twice the length of a football field. Mr. X had guaranteed the bodies were somewhere beneath it. "This is no pick and shovel job," Inspector Sullivan said. He phoned the FBI in Washington, D.C., asking permission to rent heavy equipment. He also filed for a search warrant.

Finding three bodies beneath a dam—if they could be found—would surely quicken what President Johnson had recently called "the summer of our discontent." But could anything break down the walls of white Mississippi? Persistent talk of a hoax, of media persecution, of "invaders" disrupting cordial race relations—all added up to an entire culture entrenched in denial. Even if the missing men were found, would anything change? "Maybe the best course for everybody is just to let the bodies lie and let the excitement gradually die down," a Philadelphia man said. No local jury would convict anyone, "so why should we have all this hue and cry, and a big circus trial, with everybody goddamning Mississippi?" Yet because Freedom Summer thrived on hope, at some point hope had to cross the railroad tracks.

From its early planning stages, the summer project had focused a glimmer of its idealism on Mississippi's impoverished whites. The "White Folks Project" targeted Biloxi, known for being nearly as tolerant as Greenville. In late June, eighteen volunteers had gone from Ohio to the Gulf Coast town to help poor whites "see that their enemy is not the Negro but poverty." By early July, volunteers were speaking daily with carpenters, barbers, fishermen, even the high school principal. Occasionally they met someone who would listen, but more often "there was no dialogue, just antagonism." "Why

Mississippi?" white folks asked. Why not work in your own states? The White Folks Project soon floundered. Volunteers spent days arguing about whom they should contact, what they should say. Striking out on their own, two women took jobs at a diner to "get the feel of the community" but were discovered as "COFOs" and fired. By August, six volunteers had quit, and the rest were going door-to-door, trying to convince poor whites that the Freedom Democrats were not the "nigger party." "It looks like the pilot phase of our White Community Project is pretty much over," one wrote home.

The search for tolerance continued. Could there be a few whites who, while not supporting integration, would at least listen to reason? While the White Folks Project sputtered, lone volunteers took advantage of grudging hospitality. Once it became clear that volunteers were in town for the entire summer, a few were invited into white homes. There they met polite but firm dismissal.

"You Northerners all think that every Mississippian is a bare-footed redneck."

"How can these kids presume to come into our state, not knowing our people or our customs, and tell us how to live our lives?"

"What's so hard to explain to you—to people like you—is how much we care for our niggers. You think we're heartless because we segregate our society. I tell you that the nigger prefers it that way, same as we do." Dismayed volunteers headed back to their side of town. Perhaps among the better educated . . .

On consecutive Tuesdays in late July, two volunteers visited the University of Mississippi. Nearly two years had passed since brick-throwing mobs had rioted all night to block James Meredith's enrollment, but William Faulkner's hometown had only hardened its Rebel resistance. Moderate professors continued to leave for other universities. Locals and students still blamed federal marshals for the riot that had claimed two lives and brought Oxford worldwide notoriety. And now, even if Meredith had quickly finished his degree and left the state, here were more "outsiders" coming to campus to preach integration, to stir up trouble. With city and campus police trailing them, the two volunteers met with Meredith's former adviser and the campus newspaper editor, who complained of Mississippi's tarring in the press. Invited back the next week, the two spoke to a sociology class, explaining their work, then fielding questions.

"Would you marry a Negro?"

"Is your organization Communist?"

"Why are Negroes so immoral?"

No minds were changed, but students seemed to listen. Over lunch, volunteers sat in a dining hall echoing with catcalls—"Communist! . . . Queer!" On their way out of town, a pickup chased them until they ducked down back roads. A similar exchange in Vicksburg saw volunteers meet college students in a Catholic rectory. One volunteer found the students "guilty, agonized, and profoundly frightened." A second meeting was scheduled, but no students showed up.

The summer's only prolonged cross-cultural contact took place on a series of Wednesdays. Since July 7, a group of black and white women from the Northeast had been flying to Jackson each Tuesday evening. Calling themselves "Wednesdays in Mississippi," the women were led by Dorothy Height, chair of the National Council of Negro Women, and Polly Cowan, former TV host and mother of two volunteers. Wednesday after Wednesday, the women visited Freedom Schools, talked with volunteers, and met socialites in Jackson and Meridian. As at Ole Miss, politeness and denial prevailed, this time over tea. "Wednesdays in Mississippi" women marveled at responses that seemed programmed into their hosts. No Negroes wanted to vote except for those who were Communists. Negro schools were not—ahem—a disgrace. Just look at their beautiful buildings. And Mississippi police did "a splendid job." At one meeting, however, an elderly Mississippi woman broke in. "Girls," she said, "I just have to tell you you are so wrong." While serving on a federal civil rights commission, she had heard the abuses, "and there were lots of injustices, terrible ones." Skirts were straightened, faces fell. The conversation resumed, with fewer platitudes. A few "Wednesdays in Mississippi" women, North and South, would keep in touch that fall.

Even when invited, moderation dared not speak its name in Mississippi. Visiting doctors and ministers were sometimes pulled aside by whites who, looking over their shoulders, confessed that they supported integration. Journalists met locals who admitted their state needed help, but refused to be quoted. "If you print my name next to what I'm going to tell you," one told the *Washington Post*, "I'll be ruined. I'll lose my business, my friends, I'll be run out of this state." The fear seemed exaggerated, until one heard about the Heffners.

Mississippi had few more loyal sons than Albert Heffner. Raised on a Greenwood plantation, the big, jovial man everyone called "Red" had gone to Ole Miss, where he met his wife, Malva, another native. The couple had lived in McComb for ten years. Red's downtown insurance office was always busy. He and Malva were deeply involved in church activities. Their daughter, Jan, had been Miss Mississippi, with her picture on the billboard outside McComb. When the bombings began in his town, Red had written to the Sovereignty Commission, suggesting that "responsible citizens" stand up to the Klan. "I am not an integrationist, segregationist, conservative, moderate, or liberal," he noted. "I am just an insurance man in debt up to my ears." But on July 17, Red Heffner committed what McComb's mayor would later call "a breach of etiquette." He invited two "mixers" to dinner.

He had only wanted "to let the Civil Rights workers hear the Mississippi point of view." But with bombings in McComb on the increase, and sales of guns and dynamite soaring, the jovial insurance man quickly became the target of his town's feverish fear. Just after dinner, Heffner's phone rang. The caller asked to speak to volunteer Dennis Sweeney. The conversation was brief, confirming the rumor that was inflaming the neighborhood. Then another call came. "Whose car is that in front of your house?" An hour later, when Red opened his front door, he was blinded by the headlights of ten cars parked in his yard. Volunteers slowly slipped past the blockade and made it back to the project office, but the Heffners' ordeal had just begun. First came the phone threats—"If you want to live, get out of town." "How does you wife like sleeping with niggers?" "You nigger-loving bastard. You're gonna get your teeth kicked in." Next, Red was evicted from his office. Rumors that their house would be bombed sent Malva and Jan to live at the Holiday Inn. The Heffners soon heard shocking slander—that Jan worked for the FBI, that their other daughter was in a Communist training school in New York, that Malva was a call girl. Old friends refused to speak to them. No one came to their defense. By early August, the Heffners were considering something they could not have imagined at the start of summer—leaving Mississippi. And by September, after more than three hundred phone threats, the air let out of their tires, their dog poisoned, dead on their doorstep, they were gone. They would never live in Mississippi again. Decades later, talking about their expulsion still brought them to tears.

Searching for tolerance, volunteers finally turned to the only people in Mississippi who had little to lose—alienated teenagers. On August 3, as the FBI was bringing heavy equipment to Neshoba County, Pete Seeger gave a concert in McComb. In his sweat-stained work shirt, his head thrown back, his banjo ringing, Seeger sang "Abiyoyo" and "What a Beautiful City." The outdoor concert behind the Freedom House drew dozens of black kids, along with volunteers like Ira Landess. Toward the end of the evening, the Manhattan teacher noticed two white boys standing by themselves. They were not singing—at a Pete Seeger concert?—but they did not seem dangerous. Cautiously, Landess approached. The two teens—Gary and Jack—told him they just wanted to hear Seeger. But as they talked, Landess discovered that not every white youth in Mississippi was content to live in a closed society.

One of the teens, Gary Brooks, had recently acquired a dangerous habit—asking questions. After reading *Black Like Me*, the startling best seller by a white journalist who darkened his skin to roam the South, Brooks began daring himself to cross the tracks. He told no one about his walks through the black side of McComb. He merely wondered. Why were there so few businesses, so few decent homes, such poverty? Why had students at his high school cheered when the principal announced that President Kennedy had been killed? And who were these "invaders" coming to Mississippi? When summer began, Brooks watched McComb explode. Each bomb entrenched the town's spreading siege mentality. Friends became strangers. Suspicion spread like afternoon heat. No one could be certain who might be in the Klan, what casual remark might be turned against him. Anyone who showed the slightest sympathy for "the COFOs" might be the next Red Heffner hounded out of town.

When Pete Seeger closed his concert, Gary and Jack agreed to continue their conversation with Ira Landess. Gary soon phoned the Freedom House, telling Landess he had several friends who wanted to meet him. They agreed to meet at the Holiday Inn. Some suspected a trap, but Landess trusted the teens. After reviewing security measures, he went alone to the Holiday Inn on the edge of town near Interstate 55. Taking a room, he waited. After an hour, just Gary and Jack showed up. Their friends had "chickened out." The Manhattan teacher and the Mississippi teens talked for a few hours. Throughout August, Gary and Jack would continue to drop by the Freedom House. Ira Landess welcomed them as heralds of a new Mississippi. The rest of the state would still need shock treatment.

One hundred miles per hour was not an uncommon speed in Mississippi that summer. Battered sedans and pickups flew past fields and barns, chasing SNCC cars. The chases usually ended with the lead car dodging down a back road, or the pursuers, having had their fun, peeling off. The miracle was that no one had been hurt. But until the first day of August, no one had passed on a hill.

The cars collided at the top of the rise. Head on, they slammed into each other, lifting front ends, shattering glass, crumpling chrome and steel. One car was driven by a local man, the other by a Holly Springs SNCC worker driving with Wayne Yancey, a black volunteer from Chicago. Yancey was known for his jovial attitude, his ham-handed pickup lines, and his cowboy hat. At 3:30 p.m. on August 1, the call came to the Holly Springs project office. "You folks better get down to the hospital. Two of your boys had a head-on wreck out on the highway and one of 'em is dead!" Arriving at the hospital, the COFO contingent found a hearse with one dark foot sticking out the back. The ankle was broken, dangling, and through the rear window everyone could see the face. In a monstrous flashback, it reminded some of Emmett Till in his casket. "His head went through the windshield," someone said.

High speeds were common in Mississippi that summer, but when the state wanted to slow down, nothing happened in a hurry. For the rest of the afternoon, volunteers and SNCCs argued with cops and pleaded with doctors. Hearing that the car's driver was in the hospital, a volunteer who was also a nurse rushed inside. She saw the man on a gurney, his jaw broken, his face maroon and purple. Doctors had given him a shot and an X-ray, but when the nurse-volunteer insisted he be rushed to a Memphis hospital, she was dragged outside. Cops swarming around the hearse would not let anyone touch Wayne Yancey's body. And the driver could not be taken to Memphis—he was under arrest. Hearing that the car was nearby, SNCC staffer Cleveland Sellers walked off to find it—totaled. The windshield was two spiderwebs of glass. The steering column lay in the front seat. Blood splattered the interior. When Sellers insisted on claiming the car, he was arrested. It took two more hours of arguing, but the driver was finally taken to Memphis, then flown to Chicago, where he recovered. Volunteers drove the body of Wayne Yancey to his family home in Tennessee. Back at the project office, they hung his cowboy hat on a wall. In the summer swamp of suspicion, some were certain Yancey had been murdered. Some still think so, although all evidence points to an accident. Two nights after Yancey's death, a steam shovel and a bulldozer, trucked from Jackson, arrived at the dam site in Neshoba County. Mississippi's hour of reckoning had come.

Dwarfed by the sprawling landfill, FBI agents showed up at 8:00 a.m. on August 4, armed with a search warrant valid for ten days. Agents also brought sleeping bags, tarps, and enough food to last as long as the search might take. By 8:15, they had sealed off the property, handed its owner the search warrant, and prepared the shovel that would dig to the bottom of the dam if necessary. But where along the vast landfill should they dig? Standing atop the dam, a heavy equipment operator shoved a stick in the ground fifty yards from the western end. "I'd say start digging here." But having been told the bodies were beneath the middle of the dam, an agent yanked the stick and walked fifteen paces toward the center. "We'll start here," he said. The digging began at 9:00 a.m. The death scene was framed by skinny pine trees and a cloudless sky. The temperature already neared 90.

As the steam shovel bit into the dam, agents scurried like insects, scribbling notes, taking photos, gathering dirt samples. A stinging sun soon cleared the pines, sweat-soaking white shirts and blue collars. No one beyond the site, no one in America aside from the president and top FBI officials, knew of the digging. Back at the Delphia Courts Motel, Inspector Sullivan kept in touch by walkie-talkie. The digging continued, cutting a small U atop the dam.

At 11:00 a.m. agents noticed "the faint odor of decaying material." Yet those who had fought in World War II knew that smell, and it was not faint for long. Agents halted the shovel and began digging with trowels. They found nothing, and by noon the machine was plunging deeper.

By 3:00 p.m., when the temperature topped 100, a V-shaped gash had been gouged nearly to ground level. Clouds of blue-green flies swarmed around the cut. The smell wafted to the sky, where vultures circled. One agent was writing in his logbook when another spotted the boot. A black Wellington boot sticking from the earth. Agents began digging with shovels and bare hands. In the reeking heat, one stumbled from the pit, vomiting. Others donned white masks or lit cigars, believing one stench would drown another. For the next two hours, they clawed at the Mississippi earth, uncovering legs clad in Wrangler jeans, a hand with a wedding ring, and finally a torso, shirtless, with a bullet hole under one armpit. Agents called Inspector Sullivan. "Reporting one WB. Repeat one WB." One white body. Sullivan used a more arcane code to alert his headquarters. He radioed the FBI in Washington: "We've uncapped one oil well."

At 5:07 p.m., agents unearthed Andrew Goodman. Facedown, arms outstretched, he lay under the body of Mickey Schwerner. In his left hand, Goodman held a piece of earth, gripped so tightly it could barely be pried from his fingers. Some would later wonder. Had the innocent young man believed he could fight off a lynch mob with a rock? Or, noting how the pressed clay matched the earth that covered him, some asked whether Andrew Goodman, though found with a bullet through his chest, had been buried alive. In Goodman's back pocket, agents discovered a wallet with his draft card. Word went back to Washington. Something about a second oil well. Seven minutes later, the third well was uncapped. James Chaney lay on his back, barefoot, beside the other two. "Mickey could count on Jim to walk through hell with him," the Freedom House worker had said. Now Mickey Schwerner, the man he called "Bear," and the new friend they had brought from Ohio, had reached the far side. Someone phoned the county coroner as the news began rippling across Mississippi, across America.

Like the assassination the previous fall, volunteers would forever remember where they were when they heard. Several were in a Hattiesburg church basement listening to James Forman. He had just spoken about the disappearance, calling it "the first interracial lynching in the history of Mississippi," when a man came downstairs and whispered in his ear. Forman's face went blank. He hurried upstairs, leaving volunteers to wonder. When he returned, he shared the news, then walked off. Everyone drifted out of the room.

In Meridian, many were singing along with Pete Seeger. Someone came onstage and handed him a note. Seeger lowered his eyes, then stood to his full height and told the crowd. After gasps and tears, he led the audience in a slow and haunting song.

O healing river
Send down your water
Send down your water
Upon this land
O healing river
Send down your water
And wash the blood
From off our sand.

Lyndon Johnson got the news from J. Edgar Hoover's assistant. The president's day had been consumed by the attack on two American PT boats in North Vietnam's Gulf of Tonkin. Following an earlier assault, he had promised swift retaliation, but from halfway around the world, reports of this latest attack were conflicting: "Many reported contacts and torpedoes fired appear doubtful. Freak weather effects on radar and overeager sonar men may have accounted for many reports." But moments later, the same captain confirmed the reports as "bona-fide." That afternoon, the president met with congressional leaders. By 7:00 p.m., he was with his cabinet, authorizing air strikes. At one minute past eight, the call came from Mississippi.

"Mr. Hoover wanted me to call you, sir, immediately, and tell you that the FBI has found three bodies six miles southwest of Philadelphia, Mississippi—six miles west of where the civil rights workers were last seen on the night of June 21st. . . . We have not identified them as yet as the three missing men but we have every reason to believe they are."

In a somber voice, the president asked, "When are you going to make the announcement?"

"Within ten minutes sir, if that is all right with you."

"Okay. If you can hold it about fifteen minutes, I think we ought to notify these families."

"Mr. President, the only thing I'd suggest is to not . . . do that prior to the time that they're identified."

"I think we could tell them that we don't know, but we found them and that kind of would ease it a little bit."

Robert and Carolyn Goodman had not gone out much that summer. One evening, the cast of James Baldwin's play *Blues for Mr. Charlie* had come to their apartment to offer sympathy. But August 4 was the night before Robert's birthday. A Czech mime troupe was performing at Lincoln Center. The curtain had just gone up when a man came down the aisle and signaled the couple. Robert Goodman knew instantly. Nathan and Anne Schwerner were vacationing in Vermont when their lawyer called. Anne Schwerner asked whether anyone was there to comfort Mrs. Chaney. Fannie Lee Chaney was home in Meridian. The parents would all be together soon.

By the time darkness fell across the dam site, three faces again stared at America. ABC interrupted the sitcom *McHale's Navy*. The NBC bulletin came during the high school drama *Mr. Novak*. CBS broke into a travelogue. Shortly after 8:00 p.m. Mississippi time, as floodlights lit the dam site, the county coroner arrived with Deputy Price. FBI agents watched Price for any hint of guilt. Stone-faced beneath his cowboy hat, Price helped load three black body bags into a hearse. With Sheriff Rainey vacationing in Biloxi, Price then accompanied the bodies to a medical center in Jackson, where Goodman and Schwerner, their faces worn away by time and earth, were identified by dental records. James Chaney had no such records, but being a black man buried with whites in Mississippi was enough to remove all doubt.

In the coming days, summer's discontent deepened. War now seemed certain in Vietnam, sparking a protest in Manhattan. Picketers marched outside federal buildings in Chicago, Los Angeles, San Francisco, and Washington, D.C., demanding that marshals be sent to Mississippi. After forty-four days of fearing the worst, the worst had been dug out of Mississippi clay. In their Manhattan apartment, the Goodmans spoke to the press. Surrounded by microphones, Robert Goodman droned through a prepared statement while his wife sat by his side, her face as blank as her hopes. Having recently visited the Lincoln Memorial to renew their faith in America, the Goodmans now paraphrased Lincoln—"It is for us the living to dedicate ourselves that these three shall not have died in vain." The tragedy, Robert Goodman softly said, "is not private, it is part of the public conscience of our country." In Washington, D.C., a quiet and reflective Rita Schwerner told reporters her husband was "a very gentle man . . . totally committed to the goodness in human beings." Reporters' questions were probing and personal.

"Did you love your husband?"

"Why are you so calm?"

"What did your husband die for?"

"That, I would imagine, is up to the people of the United States," Rita answered. "For me, I think three very good men were killed, men who could have made unbelievable contributions to American life." Nathan and Anne Schwerner made no public statement. James Chaney's mother said only, "My boy died a martyr for something he believed in—I believe in—and as soon as his little brother Ben gets old enough he'll take James' place as a civil rights worker."

The national press was not so restrained.

The closed society that is Mississippi is a blot on the country.

—*Hartford Courant*

The murders of Michael Henry Schwerner, Andrew Goodman, and James Earl Chaney are a horrendous example of an unthinking and inhuman reaction that might happen wherever mobs make themselves custodians or nullifiers of the law.

—*New York Times*

None of those who have died in Mississippi have died in vain. The corpses in the river, the three bodies in the levee are all damning witnesses to a way of life that is indifferent to life. . . . The discovery of the three bodies ends a long ordeal for the boys' parents. The ordeal for Mississippi has just begun.

—*Washington Post*

Back in Mississippi, those still steeped in denial anticipated a different ordeal. A few seemed repentant. "We must track down the murderers of these men and we must bring them to justice," wrote the *Vicksburg Post*. "The honor of our state is at stake." Hodding Carter's *Delta Democrat-Times* noted, "Many of us in Mississippi need to take a long hard look at ourselves. We could begin by altering the sorry record of interracial justice which we have made over the past decade." But others circled the wagons, predicting "a new hate campaign against Mississippi." A farmer in Meridian clung to the past. "It was those integration groups that got rid of them," he said. "They couldn't let them live after they disappeared for fear everyone would find out it was a hoax." Another voiced the ill many were too polite to speak of the dead: "If they had stayed home where they belonged nothing would have happened to them."

On the day the bodies were found, dozens of volunteers were arrested for passing out Freedom Democrat leaflets. That night two more churches went up in flames. But once the news spread from Neshoba County, the violence ceased. For the next four days, with Mississippi again spotlighted in shame, a tense calm prevailed. As details of the murders emerged—they had been quick, there was no evidence the men had been beaten—arguments erupted over the bodies. Distrusting Mississippi doctors, the Schwerners sent their own physician to perform autopsies. Dr. David Spain found single bullets lodged in Goodman's spine and Schwerner's left lung. Powder burns proved both had been shot point-blank. Then, examining Chaney's body, the doctor stirred a controversy that has yet to settle. Contrary to initial reports, he announced, Chaney had been horribly beaten. Shot three times, he had several broken bones, one shoulder "reduced to a pulp," his skull caved in. "In my extensive experience of twenty-five years as a pathologist and as a medical examiner," the doctor announced, "I have never witnessed bones so severely shattered, except in tremendously high speed accidents such as airplane crashes." (Chaney's beating was frequently cited as further proof of savagery. Later evidence suggested he had been run over by the bulldozer burying him, but autopsy photos revealed in 2000 showed that Chaney was severely beaten before being shot.)

When LBJ spoke at his Texas ranch, predicting "substantive results" in the Neshoba murder case, reporters flocked to Philadelphia, expecting arrests. They found the town swarming with activity. The Neshoba County Fair was just days away, and the fairgrounds, two miles south of where the bodies were found, were humming. The fair was "Mississippi's Giant House Party," drawing thousands eager to while away long, story-filled nights in wooden cabins of picture-perfect nostalgia, with creaking porches and rocking chairs. Philadelphia lived for its famous fair, and nothing, not even the stench of death, would dampen it. Reporters asking questions about bodies and burials had to settle for answers about the "giant house party." But behind closed doors, many in Philadelphia were asking the same question. After a six-week intensive search, how had the bodies suddenly turned up? Some said the dam, built in May but still holding no water, attracted suspicion. Others noted Dick Gregory's informant letter, which the FBI publicly discounted. Those still enraged by the bureau's invasion insisted agents had planted bodies beneath the dam. As talk of a payoff spread, suspicion focused on anyone displaying sudden status—a new car, a barbecue, a hunting rifle. Whoever the informant was, many said, they would "hate to be in his shoes" if his name was discovered. (The name of the informant Mr. X—agent Joseph Sullivan's chummy highway patrolman from Meridian—would not be revealed until 2005. Speculation on which Klansman revealed the burial site to Mr. X remains rampant.)

At the dam site, state troopers kept sightseers away while FBI agents sifted dirt and scoured approach roads for clues. They found none. Olen Burrage, owner of the site, denied suspicions. "I want people to know I'm sorry it happened," the burly businessman said. "I just don't know why anybody would kill them, and I don't believe in anything like that." The bodies that had lain together throughout Freedom Summer were soon separated. Rita Schwerner hoped her husband could rest in the earth with his friend, but no mortician in Mississippi would touch an integrated burial. James Chaney was to be buried on a hilltop outside Meridian. The bodies of Mickey Schwerner and Andrew Goodman were flown to New York.

The movement in Mississippi changed that weekend. SNCC's faith that "courage displaces fear [and] love transforms hate" suddenly seemed insulting. Many would continue to march, unarmed and singing, into the billy clubs, into the black buses taking them to jail. But countless members of the Student Nonviolent Coordinating Committee would no longer speak of nonviolence. Those who did would encounter disdain. "Y'all can be non-violent," one Delta man said, "but I ain't going to let them folks come up here and shoot and not have nothing to shoot back with." Black Greenwood, on edge all summer, was boiling over. Blacks were boycotting a store owned by the cop who dragged the pregnant woman on Freedom Day. Outside the store, police patrolled in full riot gear. Silas McGhee continued his campaign to integrate the Leflore Theater. Emerging into melees, pelted with bottles, Silas returned to the theater night after night. And now three bodies , , ,

On the night of August 4, blacks at a Greenwood rally raged against neighbors who still refused to join the movement, to "have some race pride!" Stokely Carmichael promised to "loudmouth everyone in this town ain't doin' right!" Then he added, "Another thing. We're not goin' to stick with this non-violence forever. We don't go shooting up *their* houses. It's not *us* who does that." Later that night at SNCC headquarters, Carmichael and others debated bringing guns back into the office. After agreeing it was about time, Carmichael left the room to call COFO headquarters "to get the mandate from Bob." No one knows what Moses said, but Carmichael returned chastened. "What I think we ought to do is work harder on freedom registration forms," he said. All that week, SNCC veteran Bob Zellner asked others, in private, if they were interested in his plan to kill Sheriff Rainey and Deputy Price. None were. Yet not even Bob Moses could keep the "nonviolent" in SNCC's name much longer.

On Friday, August 7, both James Chaney and nonviolence were laid to rest in Mississippi. Following Chaney's private burial, a memorial march through Meridian drew streams of silent mourners. At dusk, hundreds gathered inside a church lit by TV lights and filled with shouts and sobs. As a swelling chorus sang "We Shall Overcome," Fannie Lee Chaney stood in a black veil, hugging her twelve-year-old son, dressed in his Sunday suit. Deprived of his brother, his best friend, Ben Chaney wavered between sorrow and rage. On the way to the funeral, Ben had stared down a photographer, then muttered, "I'm gonna kill 'em! I'm gonna kill 'em!" Watching the casket lowered into the grave, he shouted, "I want my brother!" But now, as mournful voices filled the church, he leaned against his mother, wiped his glistening face, and sang. "We Shalllll . . ." Then realizing the finality of a funeral, that he would never see his big brother again, Ben dissolved in tears. Watching him weep, COFO chairman Dave Dennis decided to scrap the speech he had planned.

Since entering Mississippi as a Freedom Rider, Dennis had taught classes in nonviolence and helped quell the pending riot at Medgar Evers's wake. Early in 1964, Dennis had met Mickey and Rita Schwerner and suggested they work in Meridian. On June 21, he had planned to accompany Goodman, Schwerner, and Chaney into Neshoba County, but a case of bronchitis kept him home. Now he stood before mourners, overwhelmed by grief and guilt. Fannie Lee Chaney had asked him to give the eulogy—something calm, something inspiring—but Dennis suddenly saw nonviolence as "a mistake." In his high-pitched voice, he began speaking not from notes, nor from the heart, but from an entire race's resentment and wrath.

"Sorry, but I'm not here to do the traditional thing most of us do at such a gathering," the skinny, sad-eyed Dennis began. "What I want to talk about right now is the living dead that we have right among our midst, not only in the state of Mississippi but throughout the nation. Those are the people who *don't care*. . . ." As Dennis spoke, one hand trembling, the other gripping the podium, mourners rose to meet his words, calling out "Amen" and "All right!" Dennis enshrined James Chaney in the lengthening list of martyrs—Emmett Till and Medgar Evers and Herbert Lee and the countless other blacks in Mississippi whose murders had gone unpunished. Enough, his every word said. His body began to shake. His pitch rose to a fever. Enough.

"I'm sick and *tired* of going to memorials. I'm sick and *tired* of going to funerals!"

"*Yes!*"

"I've got a bitter vengeance in my heart tonight."

"*So have I!*"

"And I'm *not* going to stand here and ask anybody here not to be *angry* tonight!"

"*YES!*"

Dennis spoke of blacks fighting in World War II and coming home to Mississippi "to live as slaves." He knew that "when they find the people who killed these guys in Neshoba County" there would be a trial. Yes, and "a jury of their cousins, their aunts, and their uncles." And he knew what the verdict would be—"not guilty. Because no one saw them pull the trigger. I'm *tired* of that!"

"*Yes, God help us!*"

"*I am, too! I'm sick of it!*"

Dennis spoke for "the young kids . . . for little Ben Chaney here and the other ones like him." When some applauded, Dennis lashed out. "Don't get your frustration out by clapping your hands!" Tilting his head, biting one lip, he fought back tears, fought for words.

"This is *our* country, too!" he shouted. "We didn't *ask* to come here when they brought us over here. . . ."

"*AMEN, RIGHT!*"

"The best thing that we can do for Mr. Chaney, for Mickey Schwerner, for Andrew Goodman is stand up and DEMAND our rights!"

"*All right!*"

"Don't just look at me and the people here and go back and say that you've been to a nice service . . ."

"*Amen!*"

"If you do go back home and sit down and take it, God *damn* your souls!"

"*That's the truth!*"

"Stand up!" Dennis shouted. Then, his voice falling to a desperate whisper, he pleaded—"Don't bow *down* anymore. Hold your heads up." His eyes watering, Dennis concluded. "We want our freedom now, (*now!*) I don't want to go to another memorial. I'm *tired* of funerals." He banged his fist on the podium, then pointed to the sky. "*Tired* of it! We've got to stand up." His voice shattering, he walked off the stage.

Two days later, separate memorials were held for Goodman and Schwerner in Manhattan. Crowds of nearly two thousand attended each. Goodman's service, at the Ethical Culture Institute on the Upper West Side, was interrupted by a bomb threat, but police removed two large flowerpots and the ceremony continued. Rabbi Joseph Lelyveld, still scarred from his severe beating in Hattiesburg a month earlier, gave one of many eulogies: "The tragedy of Andy Goodman cannot be separated from the tragedy of mankind. Along with James Chaney and Michael Schwerner, he has become the eternal evocation of all the host of beautiful young men and women who are carrying forward the struggle for which they gave their lives." When the service ended, someone took the yellow rose atop the coffin and handed it to Carolyn Goodman. She came to the center aisle, turned back, and took first the arm of Fannie Lee Chaney, just flown in from Mississippi, then the arm of Anne Schwerner. Three mothers, heads bowed, dressed in black, weeping as one, walked slowly from the chapel.

So you see, fighting is an everyday thing—don't never rest.

—Winson Hudson, *Mississippi Harmony*

CHAPTER NINE
"Lay by Time"

All that weekend while three families mourned, while Mississippi seethed in denial, while America's discontent deepened, Bob Moses swathed his grief in the solace of the future. The Mississippi Summer Project had claimed four lives. Twenty black churches lay in ruin, and no one knew what further mayhem might soon scar hot and hotter nights. "Success?" Moses told the press. "I have trouble with that word. When we started we hoped no one would be killed." Yet on the same weekend that Goodman, Schwerner, and Chaney were laid to rest, more than one hundred Freedom School students gathered at a Baptist seminary in Meridian. What Moses saw there allowed his embattled soul, and Freedom Summer itself, to touch bottom and ascend again.

The students had come neither to mourn nor grieve but, in the old black tradition, to testify. Testify to the joy of their Freedom Schools, to their rights as Americans, to their hunger for learning. Beneath a banner proclaiming "Freedom Is a Struggle," the Freedom School Convention lasted three days. Moses spoke briefly—his "speech" consisted entirely of questions—but students ran the convention. Forming eight committees, they hammered out a platform demanding equal housing, slum clearance, sanctions against South Africa, and an end to the poll tax. They endorsed a revised Declaration of Independence, declaring independence "from the unjust laws of Mississippi," and cheered a student play about Medgar Evers. Throughout the convention, Moses wandered shyly from group to group, and though he rarely smiled, his contentment was unmistakable. "It was the single time in my life that I have seen Bob the happiest," an observer said. "He just ate it up. . . . He just thought this was what it was all about."

When the convention ended on August 9, students returned to their hometowns to face summer's meanest days. If July had been an oven, August was a blast furnace. Ninety-plus heat and 90 percent humidity draped a thick gauze over cotton fields and made swamps and the Piney Woods shimmer. Heat hung like a curse, making the slightest motion seem like drowning in quicksand. Although each day seemed endless, Sundays were the longest because *nothing* happened. Locals melted into the stillness, happy to hunker down for the Sabbath, but for volunteers, Sundays set internal engines grinding. With little to do but go to church, then sit and swelter, they lived the old Delta blues lament—"minutes seem like hours and hours seem like days." A turtle plodding across a road was a monumental event. A letter to or from a friend was a lifeboat. A lone figure spotted across a field seemed to flutter like a ribbon rising from a heating vent, walking, walking on without moving, like Sunday itself.

Yet unlike July, August offered surprises. Now it might not rain for a week. Dust clung to leaves and turned to slime on sweaty skin. Then in the middle of the night, rain would spatter and pound on tin roofs. And when the sun rose, Mississippi awoke to greens as glistening as the first day of creation. In mid-August, a "cold wave" dropped temperatures to a record low—63 degrees. In Vicksburg, Fran O'Brien felt comfortable for the first time all summer, but her students shivered and complained of the cold. Yet the bonfires were soon rekindled, making everything—cars, coffeepots, human hands—sizzling to the touch.

Throughout the Delta, it was "lay by time." The cotton had been cleared of weeds, and for the next several weeks, there would be no sharecroppers in the fields, just tightly packed green bolls baking until they burst into fluff. The coming cotton crop was expected to be bountiful, the boll weevils reduced by generous sprayings of DDT. Across the rest of Mississippi, "lay by time" was simply known as August—the month when only a fool or a Yankee went out in the noonday sun. Volunteers knew the daily schedule now, but still they were counting the days.

"I am tired," a man wrote home. "I want to go very much to a movie or to watch TV even. I want to be in Berkeley and do stupid things and don't look behind me in the rearview mirror. I want to look at a white man and not hate his guts, and know he doesn't hate me either." A Connecticut woman admitted she missed the luxury of Westport—"sailing and swimming and my friends"—yet wrestled with guilt at the thought. A few pleaded with parents to let them stay on into fall:

I have been here nearly two months. I know the drudgery, the dangers, and the disappointments. I know what it's like to eat meatless dinners, to be so exhausted you feel as though you will drop, to have five people show up at a meeting to which 20 should have come. Yet I also know what it's like to sing "We Shall Overcome" with 200 others till you think the roof will explode off the church. . . . I know what it's like to have a choir of little girls sing out, "Hi, Ellen," as I walk down the road and envelop me in their hugs. . . . I'm going to spend the rest of my life being a white liberal; let me have one year to see what lies below that veneer.

(At her parents' insistence, Ellen Lake went back to Radcliffe, then returned south the following summer.)

But most were ready for summer's end. Clarksdale volunteers held a "depression session," griping about how little they had accomplished. Elsewhere, a woman confessed, "If I stay here much longer, I'll become hard. That's what happens. . . . You lose patience with anyone that's not right square on your side, the liberals and the moderates and 'the good people' caught in the middle, and the Negroes who won't cooperate or are indifferent. They all become enemies." Fatigue made even gentle hosts seem more like parents than friends. "She's always in the same rut and the same statements," one woman wrote of her host. "Very wearisome."

Whether due to the heat or the ambient hatred, previous Augusts had unleashed numbing brutality—Emmett Till's murder being just one example. And this August would oblige with a weekend when Mississippi verged on anarchy. Yet just as it ripened the cotton, lay-by time brought the flowering of Freedom Summer. During these "dog days," Mississippi's first touring theater dramatized black history on makeshift stages. Folksingers strummed in "hootenannies." Two of Hollywood's biggest celebrities snuck into Greenwood. And defying one last Mississippi tradition—of taking it easy in August—volunteers mounted their final surge, knocking on doors, signing up names, helping SNCC finish frantic preparations to take Freedom Summer to the national stage.

A grim irony surrounded the name of the juke joint frequented by volunteers in Greenwood. The sign above the door read Bullin's Café, but the manager went by the name of Blood, so everyone called the place Blood's. Inside, where a red neon glow lit pool tables and pinball games, Blood's offered a safe—even air-conditioned—spot to talk over Greenwood's escalating violence. More shots fired into the SNCC office. More canvassers assaulted, cars chased, Freedom Democrat forms thrown into the street. While SNCC struggled to quell black rage—"They keep killin' our people, when are we goin' to stop them? When?"—a group of teenagers calling themselves "The Peacemakers" began pushing adults to be more militant. Silas McGhee, still trying to integrate the Leflore Theater, still getting beaten, chased, arrested, was elected Peacemaker president. Silas's entire family, feisty Laura McGhee and her sons, was now leading the outcries at raucous, bitter mass meetings. So it was with some surprise that, on the night of August 10, a different kind of Freedom Song filled the Elks Hall where Martin Luther King had appeared so triumphantly in July.

Harry Belafonte had responded to a call for help. SNCC did not have enough money to send Freedom Democrats to the convention in Atlantic City. Throughout the first week of August, the world-famous calypso singer, who had helped bankroll the Freedom Rides and the March on Washington, held $50-a-plate dinners in five East Coast cities. With the discovery of bodies making headlines, money poured in, more than Belafonte could safely wire to Mississippi. He decided to go to Greenwood himself—carrying $60,000 in cash. For security, he took a friend. "They might think twice about killing *two* big niggers," Belafonte joked to Sidney Poitier. Wary of Mississippi but wanting to help, Poitier agreed. Shortly after midnight on August 10, they sent word ahead. The singer whose "Banana Boat Song" had become a folk standard and the first black to win a Best Actor Oscar would arrive in Greenwood that same evening. Belafonte wanted to be met at the airport "by someone important," COFO heard. Preferably Bob Moses. "No press on arrival, please." Word of the visit electrified Greenwood, and by dusk, the Elks Hall was rocking.

Shortly after sunset, skimming in low over the Delta, the Piper Cub arrived right on time. So did the Klan. Three SNCC cars sat on the tarmac in the muggy darkness. From the small plane stepped the two celebrities, Belafonte's wide smile instantly recognizable, Poitier's onscreen serenity seeming on edge. James Forman met the pair, shook hands, and steered them to the middle car. The convoy pulled out and drove through the airport gate. Suddenly, headlights flashed in the distance. Belafonte, holding the satchel stuffed with cash, noted how comforting it was to see SNCC support all around them, but Forman told him the headlights belonged to Klansmen. For the next twenty minutes, the three vehicles wove through cotton fields like hunted rabbits. Klansmen repeatedly rammed the rear car, which shifted back and forth as a shield. When the Klan tried to pull alongside, the lead car fell back to block them. Poitier, who would later relive the chase while filming *In the Heat of the Night*, remembered the harrowing moments as "a ballet, though a nerve-wracking one." Only when the convoy approached the edge of black Greenwood did the Klan turn back. The three cars finally pulled up at the Elks Hall. As they approached, Poitier and Belafonte could hear rising chants of "Freedom! Freedom! Freedomfreedomfreedomfreedom!"

Jogging behind James Forman, the two stars entered the Elks Hall. The crowd exploded. A woman lowered herself from the balcony to throw her arms around Belafonte. Freedom Songs followed, including one based on Belafonte's hit:

Freee-dom! I say Free-ee-ee-dom
Freedom's comin' and it won't be long.

Belafonte later sang his own "Day-O," then, to great cheers, held up his satchel and handed it over. When Poitier stepped to the podium, his suavity failed him. "I have been a lonely man all my life," he said, choking up, "until I came to Greenwood, Mississippi. I have been lonely because I have not found love, but this room is overflowing with it." Belafonte and Poitier spent an anxious night in a house guarded by shotguns. To keep calm, they did calisthenics and told ghost stories. The next morning, they flew back to New York.

Harry Belafonte was the biggest star to grace Freedom Summer, but his was not the only famous voice. The Mississippi Caravan of Music ranged from little-known Greenwich Village acts to headliners who had just sold out the Newport Folk Festival. With the folk boom at its height, young urban whites had recently "discovered" old Mississippi bluesmen—Muddy Waters and Mississippi John Hurt had both played at Newport. Now folksingers came south to share their music. Singing in Freedom Schools, they introduced black children to English ballads and American folk songs. Singers were startled to meet kids who had never heard of Leadbelly, or even Mississippi-born "Big Bill" Broonzy. After evening performances at Freedom Houses, the musicians often sang with stragglers till well past midnight. For volunteers, the songs brought relief from long, lingering days. For singers, banjos and guitars kept terror at bay, terror that had gripped them the moment they entered Mississippi.

"Are you coming down here to sing for the niggers?" a man asked Pete Seeger when he landed in Jackson.

"I've been asked down here by some friends to sing," Seeger replied. "I hope that anyone who wants to hear me can come, Negro or white."

"Well, you just better watch your step," the man said. "If we hadn't been on the plane when I heard you talking I would have knocked the shit out of you."

To Seeger, who had cut short a world tour to lend his voice to Freedom Summer, Mississippi was just another impoverished country, but for other singers, it was a nightmare. Judy Collins planned a two-week tour but, after singing in Greenville and Clarksdale, canceled further concerts. Phil Ochs, whose song "Too Many Martyrs" eulogized Emmett Till and Medgar Evers, was convinced he would be shot onstage. At each concert, Ochs had another singer scan the audience, then sprinted offstage after his last song. Black folksinger Julius Lester felt death all around him. "Each morning I wake thinking, today I die," he wrote in his journal. Touring for two weeks, Lester slept in his car and lost fifteen pounds. Every car backfiring, every slam of a screen door, made him jump. But once back in Greenwich Village, Lester convinced other singers to head south. More came to Mississippi, although the no-shows included the Staples Singers, Tom Paxton, and Peter, Paul and Mary.

Other than polite applause, no one is sure how black kids reacted to whites strumming "Skip to My Lou" and "Hava Nagila." But none could doubt their reaction to their first live drama.

On a sultry night in early August, beneath spotlights laced with swarming insects, six actors stared out from a barren stage behind the Freedom House in McComb. Adults fanned themselves. Squirming kids fell silent. Finally a white actor spoke.

"If God had intended for the races to mix, he would have mixed them himself. He put each color in a different place."

Across the stage, a black man responded. "The American white man has a conscience, and the non-violent method appeals to that conscience."

"Negroes are demanding something that isn't so unreasonable," a white woman pleaded. "To get a cup of coffee at a lunch counter, to get a decent job."

"What they really feels on the inside never changes," answered a black woman. "Eventually they'll wind up calling you a nigger."

Throughout August, the Free Southern Theater performed in cramped Freedom Schools, on Freedom House porches, beneath starry skies from McComb to Holly Springs. Pleading, praying, strutting each small stage, actors spoke the words of Sojourner Truth, Frederick Douglass, and a host of archetypal Americans. Each performance of *In White America* reviewed subjects Freedom Schools had covered all summer—the Middle Passage to slavery, the truth about Reconstruction, the integration battle at Central High in Little Rock—but actors touched feelings teachers could never reach. For students, the drama re-created classroom history—for adults in the audience, the pain was personal.

In White America drew standing-room-only crowds, stomping, clapping, clamoring for more. As if in church, people shouted, "That's right!" and "Tell it!" In Mileston, the setting—a community center with one wall open to a bean field—brought Mississippi itself into the play. The new center was the gift of a southern California carpenter. Hearing of Freedom Summer, Abe Osheroff, veteran of the Abraham Lincoln Brigade during the Spanish Civil War, raised $10,000, then drove to Mississippi to build "a beacon of hope and love in a sea of oppression and hatred." In the Delta, *In White America* drew two dozen members of Indianola's Citizens' Council. While cops stood guard outside, actors strutted through Indianola's new Freedom School, hamming it up for whites who watched in silence. All were polite, but one later said the play convinced him the summer project was Communist inspired. Local whites also watched the play on the sagging porch of the Ruleville Freedom School, where chickens and roosters crowded the stage. But regardless of the audience, *In White America*'s final scene, juxtaposing "We, the people . . ." with the strains of "Oh, Freedom," brought crowds to their feet, and sent them out singing.

Before I'd be a slave, I'll be buried in my grave
And go home to my Lord and be free.

On Friday, August 14, *In White America* played in Greenville. Muriel Tillinghast was not in the audience. She had a Freedom Day to run. Since the first of the month, Muriel's work had taken her deeper into the shimmering plantations of Issaquena and Sharkey counties. Sleeping on the floors of shacks—one host family had sixteen children—she was learning Mississippi from the inside out. She marveled at how sharecroppers could tell whose pickup was roaring past, just by its sound. She had learned which "firecracker" whites were bluffing and which were "not playin'." Given a single contact in one "nasty little town" or another, she had scrounged up a half dozen with the courage to go to the courthouse. She now knew where to get the best meal in Mississippi—a savory stew of pork, rice, and beans served at Aaron Henry's drugstore in Clarksdale. And she had mastered black Mississippi's merciless time clock, waking at ungodly hours to talk to sharecroppers trudging to the fields, sleeping later before meeting maids crossing the tracks to clean and cook in white homes.

Responsibility for the Greenville project had restored all of Muriel's nerve, with some to spare. Her feistiness came through in her letter to a SNCC staffer.

> Dear Doug,
>
>   This letter is being brought to you by Cleve. I do hope that you and Jesse and Cleve and Guyot WILL GET TOGETHER AND WRITE A FORMAT ON WHAT THE HELL NEEDS TO BE DONE. To this date, I have not received a damn thing on what you guys are thinking/what's working and not working, etc. And I can't work in a vacuum. . . . Look, you'll have gotten mighty timid in not closing down these god-forsaking projects and not dispersing staff. Is ya' or is ya' ain't. WRITE ME—EVEN IF IT'S ONLY YOUR NAME!
>   Love,
>   Muriel

Added to her inherited bravado, the courage of local blacks gave Muriel a daring she had not known she possessed. She had learned to drive—in Mississippi. Having passed the state's written test, she even had a Mississippi driver's license. Now she was badgering others to "let me drive, let me drive!" Fortunately for her passengers, her ancient SNCC car would not go more than fifty, but once behind the wheel, Muriel bounced over rutted roads and careened alongside cotton fields. Her nemesis was the stick shift. One afternoon, she stalled the car on a slight rise, then watched in terror as a cop pulled behind her. Before she could get in gear, the car rolled backward and crunched the police car's bumper. Storming out, the cop ranted, raved, cursed, but some smooth talking got Muriel back on the road with just a warning to "get the hell out of Issaquena County." On she drove, covering fifty or more miles each day before hurrying home by sundown. Everyone had to know about Freedom Day.

Word from the first Freedom Day in another plantation fiefdom stirred the embers of Muriel's fear. On August 4 in Tallahatchie County, blacks had emerged from the courthouse to find the street filled with whites, some brandishing shotguns. The mob stood stone-faced, rigid, staring bullets at the small black contingent. Finally one man shouted, "You niggers get away from the courthouse! You don't have any business up here!" The sheriff soon came striding on the scene. Tallahatchie had just been served with an injunction resembling Panola County's, barring all voter registration tests, but the sheriff told blacks to get out of town and not come back. Every night since, cars had roared past black homes, the drivers waving guns, flashing headlights. And now, Muriel had scheduled a Freedom Day for Sharkey County, where a crop duster had recently doused canvassers with DDT, where, as one cop had boasted, "they beat a nigger's ass."

Muriel had already rescued one volunteer from Sharkey County, a fellow Howard student she remembered from her geology class. Late one afternoon, after going porch-to-porch, the man had made a frantic call from a pay phone. Hurry, he shouted. He was being chased. Men with shotguns. Men with dogs. On the line, Muriel heard the dogs baying in the background. Racing from Greenville into the plantations, she and a friend roamed back roads until they found the man hiding in a drainage ditch. Taking him back to Greenville, they let him relax for a few days, then sent him back to the plantations. As Sharkey County's Freedom Day approached, two volunteers were arrested for leafleting and held overnight in a squalid little jail. But by August 14, leaflets were spread across the county, registration classes had offered instruction, and Freedom Day was on. The morning arrived, blue and blistering. Blacks awoke, dressed, and prepared to risk their lives to vote. Everyone anticipated the worst. Stories of terror from Tallahatchie County were widely known, but as Muriel had seen all summer, "courage overcame fear."

Throughout that Friday morning and into the afternoon, blacks approached the small brick courthouse in the county seat of Rolling Fork. They shuffled up the steps, smiled meekly at the registrar, filled out papers, filed out. No one was arrested. No one was threatened or chased out of town.

Though it did not produce a single registered voter, Freedom Day in Sharkey County was an unqualified success. Merely by surmounting their terror and showing up at the courthouse, blacks raised under neo-feudalism
and steeped in the local lore of lynching had shown they would no longer
be intimidated, no longer be denied. Still, Muriel scheduled no more Freedom Days that summer. Instead, with less than a week left before Freedom
Democrats headed for Atlantic City, she turned her attention to their challenge, signing up party members, driving the back roads, rooting herself in
the Delta topsoil. One day Muriel took Shirley MacLaine to meet her friend
Unita Blackwell. The sharecropper and the movie star spent hours on a porch
overlooking the fields, drinking beer, and talking about the oppression of
women, black and white.

While Freedom Day unfolded in Sharkey County, one hundred miles south
in Hattiesburg, a Freedom School teacher helped five teenagers try to get
cards at the whites-only library. Sandra Adickes and her students quickly
learned another lesson—that in Mississippi, even librarians could be mean.
"Look, close your mouth and open your mind," the librarian snapped at
the kids. "Try to act intelligent. You don't really want to use the library."
When the students insisted, cops came and closed the library. When the
students returned the next week, the Hattiesburg Public Library was closed
indefinitely.

    That same Friday, the Neshoba County Fair drew to a close. Many left
disappointed. As expected, the storytelling and singing had lasted till
dawn. The smell of kerosene had wafted above the aroma of cotton candy
and moonshine sold by strolling vendors. But "Mississippi's Giant House
Party" had long been known for its rousing political speeches kicking off
campaigns. (Ronald Reagan would start his presidential campaign there in
1980.) In the summer of 1964, however, the stigma of speaking just two
miles from a triple grave had scared politicians away. Barry Goldwater Jr.
and George Wallace canceled appearances, leaving crowds to settle for their
own governors. Ex-governor Ross Barnett joked about summer volunteers
needing "Mr. Clean." Paul Johnson praised the "law-abiding" people of
Neshoba County and blasted Freedom Summer. "The white people of Mississippi know that the vast majority of the colored people of this state have
turned their backs on the motley crew of invaders of our state," the governor

said. "We will not permit outsiders to subvert our people and our rights."
In midweek, the Klan leafleted the fair, a small plane dropping billows of
brochures calling Goodman, Schwerner, and Chaney "Communist Revolutionaries, actively working to undermine and destroy Christian Civilization." Fairgoers were in no mood. Most simply stepped over the white trash
littering the fairgrounds. Following a Friday of harness races and Grand Ole
Opry shows, the fair closed just after midnight. By then, the lull following
the discovery of three bodies had ended. That weekend, a human firestorm
swept across Mississippi.

COFO's blackboard dutifully charted each incident, but there was no more
order to the mayhem than there was to the weather. Starting with a midnight
bomb shattering windows and gouging a gaping hole outside a supermar-
ket in McComb, the weekend spiraled into chaos. Shots echoed down the
mean streets of Jackson, the quaint streets of Canton, the embattled streets of
Greenwood. A bomb meant for the Natchez Freedom House ignited a tavern
next door. A mob in Laurel brandished baseball bats. In Greenwood, volunteers were closing the SNCC office when someone shouted, "They've shot
Silas! They've shot Silas in the head!" Peacemaker Silas McGhee, sleeping
in a car outside a restaurant, had awoken just in time to see a pistol aim, a
spark flash. When the car door was opened, Silas tumbled into the gutter.
Frantic SNCC staffers tore off their shirts to soak up the blood, plugged the
hole in Silas's jaw with their fingers, then rushed him to a hospital, where he
lay on a gurney in a hall, waiting for the "colored doctor." Though his jaw
was shattered, Silas survived after surgery. Laura McGhee, now even more
legendary after decking a cop with a right hook, kept the bullet.

Elsewhere in Mississippi, a pickup rammed a SNCC car in some little
hamlet where everyone knew everyone and everything had been peaceful
before the invaders came. Then there were arrests for no sane reason, a mind-
less beating or two, four random shootings that missed. And to cap the madness, at precisely 10:00 p.m. Saturday night, a hundred crosses blazed across
southern Mississippi and into Louisiana. Flames wafted smoke into the sky.
Six crosses burned in Jackson, one a block from the COFO office, drawing
volunteers to study this century-old symbol of hate burning in August 1964.
Before the chaos ended, two dozen cops had raided the McComb Freedom
House, ostensibly looking for liquor but rifling through papers, reading letters, enraging SNCCs, who responded by scheduling Pike County's first

Freedom Day. And it took a cop to sum up the weekend. The cop was standing on a street corner in Gulfport when a man rushed up. "I got me one," he said, rubbing his knuckles after pummeling a volunteer. Then the man asked the cop whether he was "the law." The officer replied, "We don't have any law in Mississippi."

With the Atlantic City convention looming, SNCC had become a well-oiled machine, churning out position papers, brochures, lists of delegates to be lobbied. The president of the United States, however, was not sleeping well. For weeks, LBJ had been sitting up nights brooding about the Freedom Democrats. To some, their challenge appeared quixotic, but Johnson knew that if Freedom Democrats came before the full convention, and if, moved by a summer of horror stories from Mississippi, delegates seated them and snubbed Mississippi's white power elite, the "Solid South" would be solidly incensed. On August 6, Johnson and his advisers met in the Oval Office to discuss this "ticking time bomb." A week later, they were still seeking a solution. "There's no compromise," the president said. "You can seat one or the other. You can't seat both of them because if you do, then the other one walks out." And the walkout, LBJ knew, would not be limited to Mississippi. "If we mess with the group of Negroes that were elected to nothing, that met in a hotel room . . . and throw out the governor and elected officials of the state—if we mess with them, we will lose fifteen states without even campaigning." With just a week left until the convention, United Auto Workers president Walter Reuther agreed with Johnson—if the Freedom Democrats did not drop their challenge, "We're going to lose the election. . . . We really think that Goldwater's going to be president."

With Harry Belafonte's cash, SNCC had chartered buses to leave for the Democratic Convention on August 19. As the days dwindled, canvassers accelerated their last-ditch drive. Register. Sign here. "Help make Mississippi part of the U.S.A." Because sharecroppers were no longer in the fields, Greenwood volunteers set up tables in the quarters. Whites drove past, glaring, threatening, but signatures piled up. The trick, SNCC had taught volunteers, was to link the political to the personal. Tired of trudging dirt roads? Join the Freedom Democrats, and someday your streets will be paved. Fed up with senators like John Stennis, mouthpiece of Delta planters, and James Eastland, a Delta planter himself? "If we can get enough people to register, we can throw out Senator Eastland's party at the big National Democratic

Convention in Atlantic City. . . . Yes, Mr. Jackson signed. No, no one sees these forms except us, and we take good care of them." Register. Sign here.

Freedom Schools also did their part. Teachers continued to canvass on weekends, and some even sent their older students door-to-door. The teens were appalled to meet elders who insisted they did not care about voting or "just didn't have the time." "I just stood there wondering why he kept saying 'I don't have the time,'" a student wrote, "because all he was doing was just sitting there doing nothing. . . . As I walked away, my mind kept wondering, 'Why? Why?' "

Back in class, Freedom Schools continued to surpass all expectations. A thousand students had been expected; twice that many were now enrolled. Some schools remained little more than shacks lit only by curiosity. Others met in dingy church basements or in the ample shade of chinaberry trees. Yet regardless of the setting, each school dared Mississippi to dampen its spirit. Hands flew in the air, waved, begged to be called on. Backyard games were as lively as dances. Coming back to class, teachers and students together, rare was the pale hand that did not hold a smaller, darker one. Classes relied more on enthusiasm than on textbooks. Moss Point students dramatized the Dred Scott decision. Ruleville students piled onto the floor to reenact slavery's Middle Passage. Several schools held formal debates on nonviolence, and many did role-playing, with students playing the parts of Barry Goldwater, Senator Eastland, or members of their hometown Citizens' Council. And almost every Freedom School published a newspaper. Typed by teachers onto mimeograph sheets, decorated with the students' line drawings, the *Ruleville Freedom Fighter*, the *Shaw Freedom Flame*, and the *Meridian Freedom Star* featured poetry, essays on civil rights, and news of the Freedom Democrat drive.

No matter how upbeat teachers remained, however, they could not hide one harsh truth known to all students—that when the summer ended, Mississippi would be waiting for them. To keep freedom's flame burning, students were encouraged to question Mississippi, to question their lives, to question, to question, to question.

"Why did Harriet Tubman go back into the South after she had gotten herself free in the North?"

"Why doesn't Mrs. Hamer stay in the North once she gets there?"

"Who do you think the Movement is proving right—Booker T. Washington or W. E. B. Du Bois?"

"And what comment on your own upbringing is made by the fact that you knew all about Booker T. Washington but most of you had never heard of W. E. B. Du Bois?"

One afternoon at the Harmony Freedom School, twelve-year-old Ida Ruth Griffin read her latest poem:

I am Mississippi fed
I am Mississippi bred
Nothing but a poor black boy.
I am a Mississippi slave
I shall be buried in a Mississippi grave.
Nothing but a poor, dead boy.

The class was soon tangled in debate.

"We're not black slaves!"

"We certainly are!"

"Can your father vote?"

"Can he eat where he wants to?"

At another school a boy refused to believe what his teacher said about the proud civilizations of Africa. "I think you're lying," he said, and burst into tears. The teacher also cried.

By mid-August, students were already lamenting the imminent end of Freedom School. A teacher in Canton noticed the change: "Some of them are beginning to realize, now that we're talking about the end of school and our departures, that we're not saviors and we're not staying forever and we're not leaving any miracles behind." But not all teachers were so discouraged. In Shaw, in Ruleville, in Hattiesburg, teachers knew they would be sending students back to their regular schools, fired up, demanding more. And each morning when students rushed to greet them, each evening when a gray old man read his first words, most teachers knew their summer had been worth all the sweat, the fear, the occasional chaos. "We're giving these kids a start," one said. "They'll never be the same again. This isn't something anyone can just snap off when the summer ends."

Holding hands, dancing, sharing meals, teachers and students broke racial taboos. But outside the Freedom Schools, in crowded project offices and cluttered community centers, racial harmony was proving more elusive in

August than it had been in June. As long as three men were missing, race had been just another cog in Freedom Summer. Black and white were working together, missing together, equally likely to be arrested, beaten, killed. But once Goodman, Schwerner, and Chaney were found, mourned, eulogized with "bitter vengeance," black and white were suddenly that again—black and white. And everyone on every project knew that within a few weeks, black would be staying in Mississippi, and white would be gone.

With equal alarm, blacks and whites noticed the rising tension. SNCC had integrated prior to Freedom Summer. Bob Zellner and Mendy Samstein, Sandra "Casey" Hayden and Mary King, had pioneered a small white contingent. But Freedom Summer had inundated SNCC offices with whites, and by August, their enthusiasm was wearing thin. "I saw the rug pulled out every day," Holmes County project director Hollis Watkins recalled. "Suppose we needed some paper to make fliers. Mr. Local may have been going into town and could have brought it back. But a volunteer would say, 'Oh no no, I'll run and get it.' Local people who had felt pride in operating mimeograph machines now saw *that* taken away. In meetings, very vocal volunteers automatically shut down a number of people who were struggling to come forward and talk."

Recent news from the North was driving another wedge between the races. Profiling Freedom Summer, magazines such as *Look* and the *Saturday Evening Post* focused on whites, especially white women, making blacks feel their own struggles hardly mattered. And then there were the riots. The day after Harlem erupted, staffers and volunteers sat on the lawn outside the Holly Springs Freedom School discussing the news. With few exceptions, whites deplored the riot, but blacks said it was "about time something happened to force America to wake up to racism in the North." Teacher Pamela Allen was shocked. Though she said nothing, she saw that "the project was polarized. I found it didn't matter that I never condemned the riots. I hadn't supported them. *And* I was white."

Yet nothing was eroding racial harmony more than sex. From their first day in their sites, volunteers who had never thought much about interracial sex found Mississippi obsessed with it. All summer long, white terror of "mongrelization," dating to slave days, had surfaced at every encounter. A Jackson cop asked a medical student if he had come south "to give abortions to all them white gals pregnant by nigrahs." A white woman invited to visit a project office responded, "And get raped?" SNCC recruiters had tried to

weed out whites who expressed sexual interest in blacks, and vice versa. In
Ohio, Bob Moses had warned against pursuing "My Summer Negro" or "the
white girl I made." Yet all summer blacks and whites had worked together,
gotten drunk together, faced danger together, suffusing the summer project
with a wartime sexual tension. And the fact that it was 1964, with mores
changing, birth control pills available (though not in Mississippi), and hundreds in their early twenties suddenly on their own far from the strictures of
home . . .

Many have speculated on the sexuality of that summer. One observer
claimed, "Every black SNCC worker with perhaps a few exceptions counted
it a notch on his gun to have slept with a white woman—as many as possible." But others remembered Freedom Summer as far too chaotic for sex.
"I didn't see any white women being victimized by black men," volunteer
Sally Belfrage recalled. "We were just too busy and crowded. I can't even
work out where they did it, where people went to be victimized. My greatest
problem in Greenwood was the absolute impossibility of being alone." Fred
Winn offered tacit agreement in a letter: "Now, Dad, I know the I.C.C. might
object to you sending certain things in the mail but would it be possible for
you to send a local S.F. girl?" Nonetheless, in late July, a visiting doctor had
warned volunteers of venereal disease spreading through the ranks of SNCC
and COFO. And although how much went on behind closed doors will never
be certain, many volunteers were startled by a sexual frankness unknown
back home.

Black men raised with an exacting terror—"jus' one boy touch a white
girl's hand, he be in the river in two hours"—now met white "girls" whose
gaze they did not have to avoid. And white women, suddenly the object of
obsession and desire, were confused, flattered, charmed. A strange and entic-
ing courtship dance sometimes began, driven as much by taboo as tempta-
tion. The dance accelerated when female volunteers wore makeup, earrings,
and décolletage that marked them as "easy" in a state where men did not
even wear shorts in public. Approached again and again, some surrendered
to curiosity or a need to prove they were not racist. The result, Mary King
recalled, was that some white women "fluttered like butterflies from one
tryst to another." For much of the summer, black women seemed to look
the other way. The same could not always be said of black men. "All these
black guys were dating the white volunteers," one woman remembered, "and
then one of the black girls . . . had one date one night with a white guy."

The next morning, four black SNCC men "were over at her house chewing her out."

But beyond the novelty of interracial sex, how many fell in love during Freedom Summer? "I'm sure I wasn't the only white woman to fall in love with a black man during that summer of 1964," Pamela Allen (née Parker) wrote years later. Allen went on to describe "an innocent romance" of holding hands, holding each other, then bidding good-bye to the black man just transferred to McComb. In small-town fishbowls where they dared not be seen together in public, how many other men and women, black and white, courted, touched, dared to cross one line or another, then came home changed? "There's a very good chance that a large number of white women had good friendships [with black men] that might have developed into something else in a different time," Allen recalled. "But given the times, it didn't. Still, that's much more profound than whether or not you had sex. The heart connections are the ones you remember without ambivalence."

Fran O'Brien speaks cautiously about her "heart connection" that summer. Like her, the black man she admired worked with children in the Vicksburg Freedom House. Like her, he had come from a college in the Northwest. She walked with him whenever possible, spoke quietly in quiet moments. More than once he stepped into her classroom to handle older children she could not control. He had written home, telling his parents about this woman he liked. This *white* woman. They warned him, and he told Fran about the warning. When she wrote home and mentioned the man she liked, she was afraid to reveal that he was black. Throughout the summer, Fran wanted more to happen between them. Nothing did. And nothing more was said. She never saw the man after the summer, but she never forgot him. In her memories, he remains the sweeter side of that summer, easily, fondly recalled. The savage side would prove harder to summon.

Fran had spent a rather quiet summer in Vicksburg. Despite all the threats, the flashes of violence, she had seen none of the bedlam that scarred the summer elsewhere. One afternoon, two white men barged into her classroom. Students froze. Fran hesitated. But the men just stood, glared, then walked out. By the time she deftly handled the bomb threat on the phone, Fran had become blasé about violence. She was too busy to worry. Her children loved her classes, especially chorus. One Saturday, her singers entertained the whole school with "This Little Light" and "America the Beautiful." Fran found the latter "a trifle ironic," but her students made the song their own, changing verses to honor Herbert Lee and Medgar Evers. And when children whose dreams had long been deferred came to the last verse—"O beautiful for patriot dream that sees beyond the years"—Fran realized, "we're all dreamers or we wouldn't be here."

Evening conversations with Mrs. Garrett were teaching Fran more about children than she would ever learn in college. Each evening, Mrs. Garrett, her iron hair in a bun, her stout body resting comfortably in a housedress, welcomed Fran home. Over dinner, they talked about the day in class. About simple activities that worked. About "slow learners" only starting to make progress, and others so promising or so troubled. By early August, Fran had come to cherish these talks. Other volunteers might frequent juke joints or stay at the Freedom House long after classes had ended. But every evening, Fran caught a ride home in time for dinner and discussion. Back on her Oregon campus, she had imagined doing her part in the civil rights movement. She had not expected to make a lifelong friend.

With just two weeks left, Fran was thinking more about going home than about any danger. She planned to leave on Monday, August 17. She hoped to go through New Orleans and do a little sightseeing. "I could stay longer but there doesn't seem much point," she wrote her parents. "I wish we had done more for the kids." Though complacent, Fran still recalled that morning in early July when she was confronted by cops after rushing out to her ride. She had never repeated the mistake. Each morning she waited inside with Mrs. Garrett until the SNCC car arrived. Each evening, she walked down the long driveway of the Freedom House in a group. Obeying SNCC rules, she could not imagine that Mississippi could concoct dangers impossible to foresee.

One evening, Fran and five others stood at the end of the driveway, waiting for the car to take them home. But when the car pulled up, it had seats for only five. Deferring as always, Fran let everyone else pile in. There would be room, she thought. But when she asked if she could squeeze in, the driver cut her off. They could not risk overloading the car, drawing attention, giving cops an excuse for another arrest. "Don't worry," she was told. "Someone else will be along in a minute."

Standing alone, Fran felt a shudder, but told herself not to be such a baby. Another car would be along soon. And there it was, headlights beaming down the road, slowing, slowing, stopping. Eager to get home, Fran rushed past the twin beams. Before she could draw back, she saw four men inside—in white robes and hoods. She was not imagining this. She was not dreaming. She was in Mississippi, and the quiet of her summer had ended early.

Before Fran could turn and run, one hooded man leaped out. Clamping a beefy hand over her mouth, he dragged her into the car. It roared away. She was not imagining. She was not dreaming. Rumbling over the dirt road, the four men laughed and joked. Fran could barely see their eyes through the holes in their hoods. Look what they had captured, they seemed to say. A pretty little "invader." A "little girl" who needed to be taught a lesson. Darkness had engulfed Mississippi by the time the car pulled into a vacant lot or empty field—Fran could not tell which. From that point on, terror veiled her memory. The car lurched and stopped. A deep, drawling voice barked in her ear.

"Now you just be a good little girl and do what we say. We've gotta teach you a little lesson so you'll go home to your Mama and Daddy and mind your own business after this."

Dragged out of the car, Fran tried to drop into a ball as she had been taught.

"No you don't, little lady! You bend over that hood and don't try any more funny business!"

Fran found herself shoved against the car. Somehow she recalled what Bob Moses had told female volunteers in Ohio—that their modesty was not as important as their lives. She clamped her hands over her head. Her cheek pressed against the warm hood. She inhaled the car's odor of gasoline and dust.

"That's a good little girl. Stay nice and still now, so we can whup you." All four men laughed. One said they were going to make her sorry she had ever come to Mississippi. But if she got down on her knees, he said, if she begged forgiveness, they might stop. Any time she wanted. On her knees. Fran vowed she would be thrown in the Mississippi River first. She steeled herself, clenched her teeth, felt warm air on her legs as a hand lifted her skirt. Seconds later came the searing lash of a rubber hose. Breath seized in her throat. Her eyes stung. An acrid odor emerged from nowhere. The hose lashed out again. And again, each time harder than before. Her burning legs turned red, then blue, then purple. The blows continued as the men passed the hose around, taking turns. Time slowed and stopped. The world condensed to this empty lot, in Mississippi, on a quiet summer night. More lashes fell. But there is a God, Fran knew, and so she was spared further suffering. Voices and laughter dimmed, the throbbing faded. The next thing Fran knew, she was lying in the driveway of the Freedom House. Scorching heat flushed her face and seared her body. Sitting up, she struggled for the dignity that had brought her this far. She checked herself, seeing bruises but no blood. Thinking she must have been gone for hours, she ran up the long driveway to find several people on the porch, talking and joking.

"Oh hi, Fran. I thought you'd left."

Fran started to blurt out what she could—the ride . . . no room for her . . . another due any minute . . .

"You should have come back right away," someone said. "Don't you know it's dangerous to wander around alone at night? This is Mississippi, you know. A lot of things could happen."

That was when Fran burst into tears. No words would come, not even when others gathered around.

"Her dress is all dirty."

"Did she fall down the hill?"

"There was a car circling around here about a half an hour ago—right after those other guys left. Was that it?"

With her head bowed, Fran nodded but could say no more. Her secret remained inside, a private, purple horror. Even in Mississippi, where a lot of things could happen, no one guessed what had just happened to the shy teacher with the devout love of children. Finally, the woman whose children Fran had befriended on her first day in Mississippi returned the favor. Approaching Fran, putting an arm around her, Bessie whispered, "It's okay. It's okay."

And in the care of another victim, it was okay not to say anything, not to feel anything, just to take deep breaths, to gather herself inside herself and begin the long night of suppression. Fran does not remember how she got home that evening, nor what Mrs. Garrett said about her late arrival. She remembers little of her remaining days in Mississippi. She only knows that she made a rock-firm decision not to tell anyone. She would not become an incident on a blackboard. She would not give newspapers another story. Hoping to recapture the warmth she had felt from her students, Fran kept quiet about her encounter with the Klan, quiet for twenty-five years while the terror of a quiet summer night crouched inside her. She would be leaving on August 17. She wrote home one last time, hiding her horror in vague language. She had decided not to go home through New Orleans, she told her parents. "After recent developments I don't like the idea of traveling alone through southwest Mississippi. It's always been the worst section and hasn't improved this summer." August 17. A Monday. Fran and her secret were also counting the days.

After a headline June, a lunatic July, and August's endless lay-by time, Freedom Summer had arrived at its own crossroads. On the evening of August 19, three buses stood outside the COFO office on Lynch Street in Jackson. More than a hundred people stood around them, talking, singing, their faces reflected in bus windows beside the neon red signs of the Streamline Bar. At a press conference earlier that day, Bob Moses, though troubled by the word "success," said the summer project had changed Mississippi. "The whole pattern of law enforcement of the past hundred years has been reversed," he noted. "In some areas the police are offering protection where they never did before." And Freedom Summer was not finished, Moses announced. Many volunteers were staying on to intensify voting drives in Panola and Tallahatchie counties, and to staff community centers, adult literacy programs, and mobile libraries in rural areas. But all that would only unfold after Freedom Democrats helped make Mississippi part of the U.S.A.

Since July 19, armies of canvassers had held Atlantic City aloft like some Promised Land. Now the Promised Land was just a bus ride away. Tallied in signatures alone, the Freedom Democrat drive had been disappointing. Moses had hoped for 400,000 names, then lowered his sights to 200,000, then 100,000. He had to settle for 63,000. But as delegates milled beside the buses, their hopes shone as brightly as that evening's "We Shall Overcome," belted out to the ring of a folksinger's banjo. The Freedom Democrats would be on Atlantic City's famous Boardwalk by Friday. They had followed Democratic Party rules explicitly. Papers had been filed. Affidavits and testimonies of terror were ready to be shared. After a summer of violence, could Americans deny that Mississippi was a blot on democracy? Could President Johnson, having signed the Civil Rights Act, turn them away? One by one, Freedom Democrats boarded the buses. Casey Hayden stood with a clipboard, checking off dozens of names. Arms waved out the window. Approaching the bus with his wife, Bob Moses was not as optimistic as the rest, but he was seen to smile.

At 10:00 p.m., the buses pulled out with a great cheer that broke into Freedom Songs. Instructions had been left in the COFO office—a delegate would call once the buses were safely out of Mississippi. Calculating the distance over winding roads, leaders said the call would come by 3:00 a.m. If no one checked in by 3:15, "begin action." Singing, shouting out, marveling at the Promised Land where they were bound, delegates rolled north toward the Tennessee line. The call came at 3:02 a.m. The Freedom Democrats were on their way.

If you ask what my politics are, I am a Humanitarian.

—Tennessee Williams

CHAPTER TEN

"The Stuff Democracy Is Made Of"

All 5,200 delegates descending on the faded resort of Atlantic City at the end of Freedom Summer were Democrats, and all were in a mood to celebrate. With Lyndon Johnson heavily favored to win in November, they looked forward to a political convention without politics. In lieu of debate, there would be parties, dinners, and perhaps a little hijinks. For one rollicking week, democracy would become a showcase. But for sixty-seven Mississippians stepping off buses, blinking in the morning sun, inhaling the salty air, democracy was no showcase; it was a matter of life and death.

The Freedom Democrats included two sons of slaves. Several were veterans—of World Wars I and II—and all were veterans of Mississippi. Many had bullet holes in their front doors, and one had them in his neck and shoulder. All bore the scars of Jim Crow—childhood memories of lynching, adulthoods rife with insults, lives trampled by constant intimidation. Their jobs, like their hometowns, were hardscrabble. Freedom Democrats were farmers and sharecroppers, barbers and undertakers, maids and cooks. Several were illiterate, but all had a seasoned wisdom no classroom could teach. Most were making their first trip out of Mississippi, some their first trips out of the counties where they had been born. Though more comfortable in overalls and housedresses, all had spent two nights on the bus in their Sunday clothes—suits and ties, porkpie hats, ironed skirts and blouses. Their faces were the colors of the mud from which they rose—Delta black and amber clay, brown loam and beige soil. And as proof that theirs was not a "nigger party," four Freedom Democrats were as white as the Gulf Coast sands—one was a fisherman signed up by the White Folks Project in Biloxi.

Legally, they represented no one. The Freedom Democratic Party was not a legal party in Mississippi. Many expected to be arrested, or worse, when they went home. But morally, the Freedom Democrats represented the very idea of democracy. Their presence in Atlantic City challenged the most sacred American rhetoric. Was America a nation of "liberty and justice *for all*"? Was voting a right or a privilege? Did democracy apply just to some, or did it extend from top to bottom, from mansions to shacks, from the halls of power to the broken porches of the powerless?

Their journey north had seemed eternal. Freedom Songs grew tiresome before the buses even reached the state line. Then, shortly after calling to say they were safely out of Mississippi, they were nearly ambushed in Tennessee. Spotting a Klan roadblock ahead—ten white hoods, ten men with rifles— passengers had ducked into the aisles. But a few were ready.

"They start anything, I have a gun," Hartman Turnbow said. "And my wife—she got one, too. Baby, get out your gun." Plump, moonfaced "Sweets" Turnbow reached in a paper bag and pulled out a pistol. "We gonna," her husband drawled, "we gonna kill up a few of 'em." The driver slowed, but a slim woman crept behind him, flicked a switchblade, and held it to his throat. "You better put your feet on the gas," she said. At full speed, the buses scattered the Klansmen and rolled on. Being from Mississippi, Freedom Democrats had rammed through obstacles far more relentless than the Klan.

Many had been trying to "reddish" since the murder of Emmett Till. Only a few had succeeded. The rest had taken the parallel path to democracy. Five days before Freedom Summer began, all had been shut out of county conventions choosing Mississippi's "official" Atlantic City delegation. Party leaders, alerted by the Sovereignty Commission's Informant Y of "Negroes carefully picked and trained to crash the conventions," had connived to exclude them. On June 16, blacks across Mississippi had arrived at designated halls to hear: the meeting is canceled; the meeting is over; the door is locked. "We can't open the door! They called down and told us not to open the door! There are no precinct meetings here! We don't know anything about precinct meetings!" In the few meetings they managed to "crash," blacks saw jittery whites huddling, whispering, peeking around corners. The lily-white conventions chose a lily-white delegation of sixty-eight Democrats. Blacks were left to sign affidavits detailing their exclusion, affidavits they took to Atlantic City, where they would try to force democracy's parallel paths to converge.

And so they had held their own conventions—in churches, community centers, under trees. Initially uncertain about regulations and rules of order, farmers and sharecroppers, maids and cooks had learned democracy by trial and error. Following SNCC's instructions, they elected Freedom Party chairmen, secretaries, and delegates. These went on to a rousing state convention in Jackson. There, when Freedom Songs finally ended, when the Stars and Stripes and signs with county names stopped bobbing, 2,500 delegates heard from their lawyer that the Mississippi Freedom Democratic Party stood a good chance of being seated in Atlantic City. A summer of behind-the-scenes lobbying had gathered enough support to bring their challenge to the convention floor, and enough votes there to win. They could only be stopped by Lyndon Johnson, and he would not dare, not with the whole nation watching.

Following this good news, delegates listened to keynote speaker Ella Baker, who had been tirelessly working for Freedom Democrats in Washington, D.C. Her damp face uplifted, her finger pointing at the worn faces before her, SNCC's founder praised this "assemblage of people who, yes, have come through the wilderness of tears, who, yes, have come through the beatings, the harassment, the brutalization. . . ." Turning to Goodman, Schwerner, and Chaney, whose bodies had been found two days earlier, Baker added, "Until the killing of black mothers' sons is as important as the killing of white mothers' sons, we must keep on." The convention concluded by choosing five party leaders, forty delegates, and twenty-two alternates. As the votes were announced, a volunteer from Manhattan watched from the sidelines. "This," Rita Koplowitz wrote home, "is the stuff democracy is made of."

In the thirteen days between their state convention and their departure for Atlantic City, Freedom Democrats met further obstacles. Radio stations refused to run their ads. Mississippi's attorney general denied their charter, denied them the use of the name "Democratic," and issued an injunction barring them from leaving the state. Freedom Democrats were also firebombed in Hattiesburg, arrested in Greenwood, and beaten by Klansmen near Vicksburg. By the time they stepped off their chartered buses after their long ride north, they doubted the Democratic Party could treat them worse than Mississippi had throughout their weary lives.

Stretching stiff limbs, smiling in the cool breeze, delegates sat beside piles of luggage and waited to check in to the Gem Hotel. The Gem, like its neighborhood, had seen better days. In their last mile on the bus, Freedom Democrats had been stunned into silence. They had heard stories of blacks "caged" in northern ghettoes, but now they saw them. Shirtless men walking crumbling streets. Brick row houses sadder than sharecroppers' shacks. Breezes blowing litter through Atlantic City's "Negro Northside," just a few blocks away, yet so far removed from the tacky glitz of the Boardwalk.

But all of Atlantic City had seen better days. By 1964, it was New Jersey's poorest town and a generation beyond its heyday, when summer weekends had brought millions to the shore. Carny rides still whirled, and a Ferris wheel and humpback roller coaster still rose above the clutter, but somehow they seemed smaller than before. And the crowds were smaller, much smaller. Only the Boardwalk retained its stature—six miles long and sixty feet wide, stretching from pier to pier along the white sand. Flat-roofed jitneys, like lost golf carts, still careened past sunburned tourists sampling the kitsch that clung to life. At the Steel Pier, horses and their riders still dove headlong into a pool. Nearby, a flagpole sitter sat atop her perch. Pitchmen beckoned the bored into parlors to play skee-ball or pokerino. And on Pacific Avenue, not far from the Gem Hotel, Sally Rand still did her fan dance, though at the age of sixty, she drew smaller audiences.

This year, however, the tourist season usually highlighted by the Miss America Pageant had bigger events in store. On August 30, the convention hall fronting the Boardwalk, a huge, Quonset-shaped building, would host the Beatles. And a week before the concert, the same hall was hosting the Democratic National Convention. The president would arrive that Thursday for what the press was touting as "a coronation." Posters featuring a kicking donkey welcomed Democrats to sadly neglected hotels—the Deauville, the Shelburne, the Seaside. Checking in, delegates traded Goldwater jokes and spoke of celebrities due to join them—Carol Channing, Milton Berle, and, rumor had it, Jacqueline Kennedy. On the Boardwalk, they strolled past arcades, bought ashtrays, Beatles dolls, and T-shirts proclaiming "All the Way with LBJ." Above heads bobbing in the surf, small planes towed banners for Coppertone Lotion. Amid the laughter, the squealing children, the couples arm in arm, no one paid much attention to the Freedom Democrats. No one, that is, except the president.

Depending on the poll, LBJ led Goldwater in the popular vote by 59–31, or even 67–28, percent. But with the convention not even begun, already the president's nightmare was unfolding. And Mississippi was not his only problem. Alabama delegates, asked to pledge their loyalty to the party ticket, were threatening a walkout. Incensed by the Civil Rights Act, Alabama governor

George Wallace was ranting about the Democrats' "alien philosophy," invoking the ghosts of Reconstruction and predicting a southern uprising, possibly even a third-party run in November. Wallace, Mississippi's Governor Johnson, and two other southern governors had refused LBJ's invitation to dine at the White House. And twenty-five Democratic congressmen had just urged their party to seat the Freedom Democrats. The press was predicting a floor fight, and Texas governor John Connally was telling the president where that would lead: "If you seat those black buggers the whole South will walk out!" The president sat in the White House, brooding about the spoiling of his "coronation."

As Freedom Democrats stood singing in the cramped confines of the Union Temple Baptist Church, they had little idea of the forces mounting against them. Here they were sleeping five to a room, still finishing the baloney sandwiches they had brought for their bus trip, still pinching themselves to make sure they were really here—out of Mississippi, at a *national* convention. Who could possibly regard them as a threat to the president?

That Friday afternoon, the Boardwalk beckoned, but the lobbying could not wait. Aaron "Doc" Henry, Freedom Democrat chairman, spoke to the press. Everyone knew Mississippi's official delegation would support Goldwater in November, Henry said. So the Freedom Democrats were Mississippi's only loyal Democrats. "If our case is fully heard we will be seated," Henry said. But if they were turned away, blacks across America might just "go fishing on Election Day."

While their chairman spoke, delegates focused on the Credentials Committee, which would hear their challenge the following afternoon. They reviewed work sheets listing each committee member, his hotel, and his loyalty—"definite supporter," "possible contact," "says she will support us to the end." Then they set out to plead their case. "Doc" Henry met with twenty state delegations. Unita Blackwell, Muriel Tillinghast's fast-rising pupil, focused on Wisconsin and Minnesota. "Sweets" Turnbow, still carrying her pistol in a paper bag, worked on the Oregon delegation. Whenever possible, volunteers back from Mississippi introduced Freedom Democrats to their state delegations. All that afternoon, Mississippi's unofficial delegates invaded cocktail parties and coffee klatches. They handed out booklets citing two dozen legal precedents for their challenge, and offering a primer on democracy, Mississippi style. "Who is YOUR sheriff?" the pamphlet asked. "Will he beat you and jail you if you try to exercise the basic rights guaranteed you by the Constitution of the United States?" Recounting crimes from the murder of Herbert Lee to the killing of Goodman, Schwerner, and Chaney, the handbook also included biographies of Freedom Democrats and quoted Mississippi's governor, calling the Democratic Party "a dedicated enemy of the people of Mississippi."

Meanwhile, SNCC staffers, having traded their overalls for three-piece suits, circulated among politicians and party bigwigs. From the humblest sharecropper to the equally humble Bob Moses, Freedom Democrats set their sights on two numbers—"eleven and eight." The Credentials Committee had 108 members. If 10 percent—a mere eleven people—voted to support the challenge, it would move to the convention floor. There, if just eight states requested it, a roll call would unfold on national television, a roll call most Freedom Democrats felt certain they would win. After all, every sizable state had several black delegates, and a few could even be found in delegations from Georgia, Tennessee, and North Carolina. "Eleven and eight." Throughout the afternoon and into the evening, the numbers were cited in crowded lobbies, noisy meeting rooms, and tipsy delegate dinners. Booklets were handed out, pocketed with polite smiles, sometimes even opened. "And who are we?" each booklet asked. "We are FREEDOM Democrats!"

On an overcast Saturday, shortly after noon, all sixty-seven Freedom Democrats set out on foot from the Gem Hotel. Heading into the sea breeze, they reached the Boardwalk and swept along its herringbone planks. Tourists in T-shirts turned to watch the coat-and-tie delegation. Crowds stopped to hear the stirring power of Freedom Songs. Past the Steel Pier, past movie theaters, penny arcades, and Nathan's hot dog stands, the vast blue on their left, the rest of America to their right, Freedom Democrats marched toward their rendezvous with democracy. The group reached the convention hall at 1:00 p.m., an hour early. They stood outside, some admiring the ocean, others pointing to the street sign—N. Mississippi Avenue—all waiting.

At the delegation's head stood a tall, pale man with graying blond hair, horn-rimmed glasses, and a floppy bow tie. Joseph Rauh was a consummate Washington insider. Harvard-educated, but also trained in power politics, Rauh had helped write legislation stretching from the New Deal to the Civil Rights Act. As cofounder of Americans for Democratic Action, Rauh had battled McCarthyism, defending playwrights Lillian Hellman and Arthur Miller. By the summer of 1964, he was head lawyer for both the United Auto Workers and the Mississippi Freedom Democratic Party. SNCCs were constantly amazed at the doors his name opened. "I was just talking to Joe Rauh," Stokely Carmichael might say. "What—you talked to *Joe*?" And suddenly the Freedom Democrats had another contact. At their state convention in Jackson, Rauh had promised Freedom Democrats to "move heaven and earth" to bring their challenge to the convention floor. But Rauh would have to move more than heaven and earth—he would have to move Lyndon Johnson.

Earlier that Saturday morning, an NBC cameraman shouted to Rauh, "They've screwed you, Joe!"

"My God," Rauh responded. "Already?"

Party officials had moved the Credentials Committee meeting to a room that fit only one network camera. Rauh protested to a White House aide, who phoned the Oval Office. After a half hour of calls, the president, who was controlling the convention from the contents of its souvenir book to its hourly schedule, agreed to let Freedom Democrats make their challenge in the cavernous convention hall. And at 2:00 p.m., Rauh stood on the floor beside four tall filing cabinets. Inside the cabinets were 63,000 registration forms signed on porches, in cotton fields, in barbershops and beauty parlors. On one side of Rauh sat Mississippi's all-white delegation, glaring at Mississippi's mostly black delegation on the other side. Between them was the committee—prim, nattily dressed women and men in dark suits, smoking, nodding off, or scribbling notes. All three networks carried the challenge, but it did not promise to be exciting television.

Americans stuck in front of TV on a Saturday afternoon saw a bespectacled, nasal-voiced lawyer with "only an hour to tell you a story of tragedy and terror in Mississippi." The story began with Aaron Henry denouncing Mississippi's "white power structure . . . on them is the blood and responsibility for the reign of terror." Next, the Reverend Edwin King summed up his ordeals. "I have been imprisoned. I have been beaten. I have been close to death. . . . We have shed our blood. All we ask is your help." Neither Henry nor King was especially eloquent, and many viewers may have changed the channel. But when Rauh called his third witness, all the suffering, all the oppression, all the earth-born hardships endured by generations of blacks in Mississippi limped to center stage.

Fannie Lou Hamer had not ridden a bus to Atlantic City. She and other SNCCs had flown to New York a day early to address a town hall meeting. There she had told of her beating in Winona, Mississippi, the previous summer. But her story had not gone beyond the meeting hall. On Saturday afternoon, Hamer knew she would speak to the nation. Before marching to the convention hall, she had talked with Unita Blackwell at the Gem Hotel.

"Girl, you reckon I ought to tell it?"

When Blackwell echoed encouragement, Hamer continued. "I'm going to tell it today. I'm sure going to tell it." Later she would say she felt as if she were telling it on the mountain, but as she moved to the front of the hall and placed her white handbag on the witness table, she did not seem inspired. Waiting as a microphone was fastened around her neck, Hamer looked exhausted, terrified, troubled. She began almost before she sat down.

"Mister Chairman, and to the Credentials Committee, my name is Mrs. Fannie Lou Hamer. . . ." A worried look came over her, as if tears might come, but she steeled herself. Her accent was unmistakably Deep Southern. "An' ah live at six-two-six East Lafayette Street, Ruleville, Mississippih." Her face was broad, glistening, and grim. SNCCs who had seen her lift mass meetings, volunteers who had watched her hold forth in Ohio, in church, in her kitchen, had waited all summer for this moment.

"It was the 31st of August in 1962 that eighteen of us traveled twenty-six miles to the county courthouse in Indianola to try to register to become first-class citizens. . . ."

The night before, while Freedom Democrats lobbied, Mississippi had provided additional evidence for their challenge. A church burned in Itta Bena. Several pickups surrounded a black café in Belzoni, trapping volunteers trying to register voters. A firebomb hit the project office in Tupelo. But on Saturday afternoon, Mississippi was "calm." By the time Fannie Lou Hamer began, TVs in black quarters across the state were tuned to one network or another. In Batesville, blacks hoped to glimpse delegate Robert Miles, or maybe that nice white boy, Chris Williams. In Hamer's hometown, her face on TV drew shouts.

"There's Fannie Lou!"

"Look at that!"

"Come on, kids!"

And in Philadelphia's Independence Quarters, blacks and whites in the new COFO office kept one eye on the TV and the other on the street. In the ten days since COFO had defiantly moved into Philadelphia, its office in the Evers Hotel had been a target of white rage. Rumors said a bomb would hit any day now. "We're gonna get the job done tonight," one man told a carload of whites. Calls came in every five minutes, like clockwork: "Your time is short!" "Your time is up!" More than a hundred locals met at the courthouse to discuss driving COFO out by firing "every nigger in town." Sheriff Rainey and Deputy Price often burst into the office without warning or warrants, storming through the clutter, photographing papers and people. Deputy Price took delight in racing past the Evers Hotel, his siren blaring. One morning, a car stopped across from the hotel's striped awning. The driver stepped out and leveled a double-barreled shotgun. His finger on the trigger, the man aimed, riveted, for five minutes, then drove away.

Each night, staffers stood guard on the hotel roof. The darkness pulsed with insects but was otherwise quiet. One morning the group saw a car pass on the street below. A small package hit the office door. Cautiously, they tip-toed downstairs. The *Neshoba Democrat* lay on the steps. Volunteers could joke about the "comedy of terrors," but Philadelphia's black community was panicky. "If you people leave us, they are going to kill us all," one woman said. "They gonna pile our bodies on top of one another." On August 20, Price and Rainey served an eviction notice, but COFO lawyers filed for a hearing, set for the following Thursday. A call went out for more volunteers, and several soon joined the all-night vigil atop the hotel. These were among the many who had decided that a single summer in Mississippi was not enough.

By August 22, with hundreds of volunteers about to leave, COFO's WATS line resembled a college "ride board." Was anyone headed for Boston? Denver? California? Across Mississippi, volunteers were saying sad good-byes, but eighty would not be leaving. Throughout August, they had wrestled with the thought of staying, convincing first themselves, then their distraught parents. One woman only changed her mind the night before she was to leave. After notifying advisers at Johns Hopkins, she wrote home: "I can simply no longer justify the pursuit of a Ph.D. When the folks in Flora have to struggle to comprehend the most elementary materials of history and society and man's larger life, I feel ashamed to be greedily going after 'higher learning.' . . . It would be living a kind of lie to leave here now."

Fred Winn had come up with a stock reply to explain why he had decided to remain. "I wasn't going to stay in Mississippi," he wrote his father, "until I stepped outside one day without my shoes on. Of all goddamned things I got some mud in between my toes. I haven't been able to get it out since." After moving from town to town, Fred felt right at home in Indianola. Living in stalwart Irene Magruder's house, working all hours at the project office, he was getting to know people. People like "Smith," a seven-year-old boy who came to the office, would only answer to "Smith," and just stared at him. People like the middle-aged woman who, having had childhood polio, picked cotton on her knees. In just eight weeks, the naive, slightly nerdy carpenter had become a Freedom Fighter. Fred was no longer "a young twenty." His speech was saltier, his righteousness tempered. He felt more at ease among blacks, among whites, and among women.

One of several high school seniors teaching adults at the Freedom School had caught Fred's eye. He admired the black girl's spirit as much as everything else about her. She belted out Freedom Songs, threw herself into her work, and often shared beer and fried baloney sandwiches with volunteers at Irene Magruder's White Rose Café. Each evening when someone drove the girl home, Fred rode with her in the backseat. It was not long before the more experienced high school senior made a move. Nor long before she was necking with Fred on her way home. Then one hot August night, she led him down the dark path to the empty Freedom School. Terrified on several fronts, Fred managed to lose his virginity that night. The San Francisco carpenter and the Delta high school senior made awkward love—their bodies drenched in sweat, their heads turning to glance out the window, certain the Klan would appear at any moment, equally certain they could not stop. The two coupled a few more times before friends convinced the girl to end the risky affair.

Having introduced Fred to sex, Freedom Summer had also taught him to handle Mississippi cops. When an Indianola volunteer was arrested, Fred made three quick calls and had the man bailed out within the hour. "Standard Operating Procedure," he wrote his father. And for the first time all summer, Fred could laugh at Mississippi. One day toward the end of August, he played a little joke on Indianola. A COFO lawyer, hoping to challenge the state ban on leafleting, needed evidence of a permit unjustly denied by the city. Leaflets for mass meetings were usually approved. What event was certain to be turned down? Handwritten fliers were quickly mimeographed:

COME ONE, COME ALL
To the
"FREEDOM HOP"
Indianola's First Integrated Dance
Big Mixer at the Freedom School
Let's see all you Southern Guys and Gals . . .

With leaflets in hand, Fred went before the city council. Angry council-men glared down COFO's spokesman, who could not say a word. Finally a councilman barked, "What's this all about?" Fred stood and, with-out cracking a smile, explained that an integrated dance "would be good for the community, would get everybody together." Faces reddened. Men muttered—"asking for trouble, just asking for trouble." A calmer official called an executive session, where the permit was refused. Indianola never held its integrated Freedom Hop, but the law on leafleting was eventually overturned.

On the afternoon Fannie Lou Hamer spoke in Atlantic City, Fred and several others crowded around Mrs. Magruder's black-and-white TV. Like many volunteers, Fred had heard Hamer tell her story. "We all knew that if she told it on national TV, it would really hit the fan." She was due to speak . . . due to speak . . . She was speaking—on TV!—telling America about being ordered to withdraw her registration, of telling her boss, "I didn't try to reg-ister for you. I tried to register for myself." Hamer's voice was strengthening now. "I had to leave that same night." She sat, arms bulging from her flow-ered dress, hands folded. At committee tables, members leaned forward, all eyes focused on her.

On the tenth of September 1962, *six*-teen bullets was fired into the home of Mr. and Mrs. Robert Tucker—for me. That same night two girls were *shot*—in Ruleville, Mississippi. Also, Mr. Joe McDonald's house was shot in. And June the ninth, 1963, I had attended a voter registration workshop; was returning back to Mississippi. Ten of us was traveling by the Continental Trailway bus. When we got to Win-ona, Mississippi . . .

Suddenly the networks cut in: "We will return to this scene in Atlantic City but now we switch to the White House."

Suddenly, on all three networks, the president was preempting the share-cropper. "On this day nine months ago," LBJ began, "at very nearly this same hour in the afternoon, the duties of this office were thrust upon me by a terrible moment in our nation's history." Johnson, knowing he had to talk for ten or more minutes to forestall Fannie Lou Hamer, went on to discuss— nothing. He told reporters he had not chosen a running mate. He explained, in painstaking detail, his criteria. By the time he finished, so had Hamer. Testimony continued. Rita Schwerner told of Governor Paul Johnson slamming the door in her face. CORE's James Farmer and the NAACP's Roy Wilkins backed the challenge. Martin Luther King said any political party should be proud to seat the Freedom Democrats, "for it is in these saints in ordinary walks of life that the true spirit of democracy finds its most proud and abiding expression." Mississippi then had its hour. A state senator denied any discrimination and denounced Freedom Democrats as "power-hungry soreheads," their "rump group" rife with Communists and as secretive as the Klan. Rauh's rebuttal offered the Credentials Committee a choice—to "vote for the power structure of Mississippi that is responsible for the death of those three boys, or . . . vote for the people for whom those three boys gave their lives." Committee members stood and applauded. The meeting was over. But had it "moved heaven and earth"? Or even America?

As Lyndon Johnson had planned, his impromptu press conference had taken Fannie Lou Hamer off the air. But not even the president could silence her. That evening, all three networks, before audiences much larger than the afternoon's, replayed her speech in full. Now Americans saw the stout woman, her head shaking, her voice rippling with emotion.

> . . . I was carried to the county jail and put in the booking room. They left some of the people in the booking room and began to place us in cells. I was placed in a cell with a young woman called Miss Ivesta Simpson. After I was placed in the cell I began to hear sounds of licks and screams. I could hear the sounds of licks and *horrible* screams. And I could hear somebody say, "Can you say, 'Yes, sir,' nigger?"

Now the same booming voice that had filled so many cramped churches in Mississippi filled living rooms across America.

> . . . And he said, "We're going to make you wish you was dead." I was carried out of that cell into another cell where they had two Negro prisoners. The state highway patrolmen ordered the first Negro to take the blackjack. The first Negro prisoner ordered me, by orders from the state highway patrolman, for me to lay down on a bunk bed on my face. And I laid on my face, the first Negro began to beat me . . .

Some parents, shocked, must have switched channels, but others saw Hamer reach deep within herself.

> . . . And I was beat by the first Negro until he was exhausted. I was holding my hands behind me at that time on my left side, because I suffered from polio when I was six years old. After the first Negro had beat until he was exhausted, the state highway patrolman ordered the second Negro to take the blackjack. The second Negro began to beat . . .

The tears came, welling up but not softening her speech. Now she rose to righteous indignation and leveled her accusation at the entire nation:

> All of this is on account of we want to register, to become first-class citizens. And if the Freedom Democratic Party is not seated— NOW—*I question America. Is this America?* The land of the free and the home of the brave? Where we have to sleep with our telephones off of the hooks because our lives be threatened daily. Because we want to live as *decent* human beings, in America?

If she had not been brimming with rage, Fannie Lou Hamer might have repeated her signature phrase. "Is this America?" "Is this America where . . .?" "Is this America?" But with her voice wavering, she said a simple "Thank you," stood, took her handbag, and walked off the mountaintop.

Within minutes, telegrams flooded the White House. More than four hundred were received that evening, all but one demanding the Freedom Democrats be seated. NOW. Suddenly it seemed the Freedom Democrats were everywhere in Atlantic City—their challenge dominating all discussion, their supporters keyholing delegates, phoning from motel rooms, lobbying into the night. By Sunday morning, Joseph Rauh could count higher than "eleven and eight." Seventeen Credentials Committee members supported the challenge, and ten state delegations were ready to call for a floor vote. Even Bob Moses was optimistic. Standing in shirt and tie before a crowd on the Boardwalk, he announced, "I don't think that if this issue gets to the floor of this convention that they can possibly turn them down." Reporters interviewed sharecroppers and maids. Two thousand supporters massed on the Boardwalk that afternoon. When Oregon congressman Wayne Morse told the crowd that his delegation had voted 20–0 to take the challenge to the floor, cheers erupted. Above the sounds of seagulls, of barkers selling frying pans and radios blaring Beatles hits, Fannie Lou Hamer belted out "This Little Light of Mine."

The Credentials Committee met again that Sunday afternoon, promising a decision by 6:00 p.m. They had three options. All Freedom Democrats might be seated in lieu of the white delegation. None might be seated— they were not a legal party, after all. Or both delegations, if willing to sign loyalty oaths to support LBJ, could be seated, each delegate given half a vote. As a Freedom Democrat handout noted, this 50/50 solution had settled several previous convention disputes, including one in 1944 when Congressman Lyndon Johnson had led a pro-FDR challenge to a conservative Texas delegation.

But warned that the entire South would walk out, President Lyndon Johnson wanted no such solution. His plan was to seat Freedom Democrats as "honored guests," with no voting privileges. Freedom Democrats were dead set against such a "back of the bus" treatment. After voting down the 50/50 split, the Credentials Committee was deadlocked. Then an Oregon congressman offered a fourth plan. Two Freedom Democrats could be seated "at large." Joseph Rauh's heart sank "because he was on our side, and here our side was reducing its demand to two before the fight had started." No vote was taken on the two-seat compromise. A subcommittee, chaired by Minnesota attorney general Walter Mondale, continued the discussion into the evening. At 8:45 p.m., a bomb threat was phoned to the SNCC/CORE office. Sometime that evening, a call to the White House told the president that the Freedom Democrats definitely had enough support for a floor vote. "Tell Rauh if he plans to play with us in this administration," the president said, "he better not let that get out on the floor."

Born and raised in Mississippi, the Freedom Democrats had few illusions about democracy. They knew how far power would go to protect its pecking order. Though still testing democracy's breadth, they knew all too well its depths. Moderation, ethics, principles—these were for stable times, when blacks in Mississippi "knew their place." But they were not in Mississippi anymore. They had bused a thousand miles to put its horrors behind them. Here at a higher level of power, nearly every Freedom Democrat thought that this time, democracy might live up to its name. The lessons would come quickly.

That weekend, FBI agents broke into the SNCC/CORE office on Atlantic Avenue, a block from the convention hall. The agents had just come from tapping Martin Luther King's hotel phone. It took them just a few minutes to wiretap phones used by Freedom Democrats. The surveillance had been ordered by the president himself. J. Edgar Hoover considered wiretapping one's own party convention "way out of line" but still sent twenty-seven agents and his special assistant. Information from the wiretaps, fed hourly to the Oval Office, paid off immediately. By Sunday night, Lyndon Johnson knew which delegates Freedom Democrats were lobbying and which governors Martin Luther King was pushing to lead a floor fight. And thanks to a list Bob Moses had reluctantly given a black congressman, LBJ knew which Credentials Committee members backed the challenge. Now the pressure tightened. Calls went out across America. Judgeships and appointments, loans and promotions still in the making would suddenly vanish if the men and women on that list did not turn their backs on Freedom Democrats. Joseph Rauh kept counting, but to his dismay, he found he had just eleven supporters. Then ten. Then eight.

On Monday, the day the convention was to begin, FBI agents went undercover as NBC reporters. Black informers infiltrated the SNCC/CORE office, and more wiretaps bugged the motel rooms of farmers and sharecroppers, barbers and undertakers, maids and cooks. SNCC was unaware of the surveillance. Other power plays would be more transparent.

Chris Williams was neither a delegate nor an official Freedom Democrat, but he had come to Atlantic City to help in any way he could. He had spent the weekend chauffeuring Freedom Democrats, and singing in boisterous meetings at the Union Temple Baptist Church. Though relieved to be out of the blast furnace, he did not even have time to jump in the ocean. There was always another delegate to drive, another meeting to attend. Chris felt frustrated by his limited role, but on Monday morning his restless energy found a focal point.

When dawn broke on August 24, 150 people, some in overalls, some in suits, sat on the Boardwalk outside the convention hall. Most were silent. Many held signs:

SUPPORT THE FREEDOM DEMOCRATS
1964, NOT 1864
STOP HYPOCRISY, START DEMOCRACY

Above the seated crowd, three picket signs bore sketches of Goodman, Schwerner, and Chaney. Holding the sign with the picture of his beloved brother stood little Ben Chaney. And alongside the crowd, as if in a museum, Mississippi democracy was on display. A 1950s sedan, gutted and blackened, sat on the trailer that had trucked it from Mississippi to represent the burned Ford wagon. Photos showed sharecroppers' destitution. The charred bell from the Mt. Zion Church lay in the bed of a pickup labeled "Mississippi Terror Truck." The Boardwalk sit-in continued all that Monday, growing to include hundreds of people. Vacationers strolled past, turning their heads. A few stopped to talk. "Don't you understand?" one couple was told. "You must try. People have died behind the Mississippi Freedom Democratic Party and the least we can do is support them here." Most walked on, but a few brought food to the vigil—apples, hot dogs, or saltwater taffy.

While the protest continued, LBJ's fears mounted. "Alabama's done gone," he told a friend, "and they tell me that Louisiana and Arkansas are going with them. And I'm afraid it's going to spread to eight or ten." With the Credentials Committee promising a decision before Monday evening's opening gavel, attention shifted to the Pageant Hotel. Located opposite the convention hall, with a towering Miss America crown atop its white facade, the Pageant had become "Atlantic City's White House." White House aides and the president's teenage daughter were spotted in its lobby. Calls from the Oval Office poured into the switchboard. And the likely vice presidential candidate, Minnesota senator Hubert Humphrey, rushed in and out of the elevator. The balding, ebullient Humphrey had a job more weighty than any he might assume as vice president. LBJ had ordered him to handle the Freedom Democrats. The prize dangled before him was the vice presidency. "You better talk to Hubert Humphrey," Johnson told a friend, "because I'm telling you he's got no future in this party at all if this big war comes off here and the South all walks out and we all get in a helluva mess."

At 1:40 p.m. on Monday, Humphrey convened a meeting in his suite at the Pageant. To back his plea that Freedom Democrats accept the two-seat compromise, Humphrey had invited several members of the Credentials Committee and a handful of moderate black leaders—Martin Luther King and his assistant, Andrew Young, plus CORE's James Farmer, and Aaron Henry. But Henry brought two friends, uninvited—Bob Moses and Fannie Lou Hamer. The scene was a study in black and white—black and white faces, black ties and white shirts, black resentment and white rationalization.

Arguing from one corner of the suite to the other, the leaders kept at it for three hours. When the compromise came up, Moses softly stated that it was time "for Negroes to speak for Negroes, for Negroes to represent Negroes." Freedom Democrats, he said, "can accept no less than equal votes at the convention." Hubert Humphrey fought back. If whites could not also represent Negroes, he said, "Then democracy is not real." He then reminded everyone in the room of his stellar record on civil rights. (In 1948, Humphrey had spearheaded the most liberal civil rights platform in American history, proclaiming, "The time has arrived in America for the Democratic party to get out of the shadow of states' rights and walk forthrightly into the bright sunshine of human rights." Humphrey later single-handedly integrated the dining room of the U.S. Senate by inviting a black aide to lunch and refusing to leave.) Humphrey concluded by noting that his vice presidential nomination hinged on the compromise.

In one corner of the suite, Fannie Lou Hamer listened in silence. Before coming to Atlantic City, Hamer had heard about Humphrey's civil rights record and had looked forward to meeting him. Now she struggled to see the heart of a good Samaritan behind the smile of a politician. "Senator Humphrey," she said, "I've been praying about you and you're a good man, and you know what's right. The trouble is you're afraid to do what you know is right. You just want this job. . . . But Mr. Humphrey, if you take this job, you won't be worth anything. Mr. Humphrey, I'm going to pray for you again." Hamer had tears in her eyes. Some said Humphrey also cried. The meeting broke up after another hour. That afternoon, the Credentials Committee postponed its decision until Tuesday. Joseph Rauh, talking to reporters, hid his sinking sense of betrayal. "We can win on the floor and we'll take it all the way," he said. The convention began that night with rows of empty seats wrapped in ribbons labeled "Mississippi." Walter Mondale's subcommittee argued until dawn.

By Tuesday morning, Lyndon Johnson had descended into despair. An aide had called to relay Humphrey's report from Monday's meeting. He had walked "into the lion's den," Humphrey said. He had "listened patiently . . . argued fervently . . . used all the heartstrings that I had, and I made no headway." Watching the convention's opening night, Johnson had heard the most widely watched newsmen in America, Chet Huntley and David Brinkley, warn of a floor fight or even a full southern walkout. Telegrams to the White House were now complaining "that the Negroes have taken over the country."

Feeling caught in a racial crossfire, losing control of *his* convention, Johnson began to contemplate his most drastic option—quitting. He had steamrolled the Civil Rights Act into law, only to watch urban ghettos erupt. He had defied southern segregationists, only to see this ragtag band from Mississippi poised to tear his party apart. "The Freedom Party," Johnson told a friend, "has control of the convention." Their challenge was just "an excuse to say I turned on the Negro." Convinced that his old nemesis, Robert Kennedy, had masterminded the whole affair to embarrass him, Johnson denounced the challenge as "Bobby's trap." As his mood darkened, Johnson felt he had no choice. He would finish his term and go home to Texas.

Toward noon, the president summoned his press secretary. He had ordered a helicopter to stand by, he said, ready to take him to Atlantic City. There he would read the speech he had just drafted: "The times require leadership about which there is no doubt and a voice that men of all parties, sections, and color can follow. I have learned after trying very hard that I am not that voice or that leader."

LBJ's press secretary tried to remain calm. "This would throw the nation in quite an uproar, sir," George Reedy replied.

For the next few hours, the president wavered between his conscience and his worst fears. He acknowledged the Freedom Democrats' moral case. "These people went in and begged to go to the conventions," he said. "They've got half the population and they won't let 'em [vote]. They lock 'em out . . . But we're going to ignore that. We're going to say [to Mississippi], 'Hell yes, you did it. You're wrong. You violated the '57 [civil rights] law and you violated the '60 law, and you violated the '64 law, but we're going to seat you—every damn one of you. You lily-white babies, we're going to salute you.'" Georgia senator Richard Russell told his old friend to "take a tranquilizer and get a couple of hours' sleep." But John Connally called to again predict "a wholesale walkout from the South" if the Freedom Democrats were seated. And Georgia's governor was complaining, "It looks like we're turning the Democratic party over to the nigras . . . it's gonna cut our throats from ear to ear." LBJ, though his threat may have been a ploy, continued to insist he would step down. "By God, I'm gonna go up there and quit. Fuck 'em all!" Only his wife could talk him out of it.

After watching her husband brood in a dark room, Lady Bird Johnson wrote him a note. "Beloved," she began. "You are as brave a man as Harry Truman—or FDR—or Lincoln. . . . To step out now would be wrong for your country, and I see nothing but a lonely wasteland for your future. . . . I love you always, Bird."

All that Tuesday, the Freedom Democrat vigil continued on the Boardwalk. Beneath a forest of picket signs, hundreds sat in silence outside the convention hall. Backs ached and hours crawled at a Mississippi Delta pace. To rally spirits, Dick Gregory and Harlem congressman Adam Clayton Powell spoke to the crowd. When protesters got word of the proposed two-seat compromise, they passed it on in whispers. No one could be certain what was afoot, but volunteers manning the phones at the Gem Hotel already suspected the worst.

"Is the Credentials Committee meeting tonight?"

"They adjourned because we had enough support, and they have to figure out how to screw us."

Shortly before 2:00 p.m., Joseph Rauh was told to call his boss, UAW president Walter Reuther. At LBJ's urging, Reuther had taken a red-eye flight to Atlantic City, arriving to convince Humphrey that the two-seat compromise was the only possible solution. On the phone, Reuther now said the same to Rauh. Two seats, at large, given to a party with no legal standing was "a tremendous victory," Reuther said. Rauh balked. He had been expressly told that Freedom Democrats would never accept the two seats, yet now he said they might. He needed to talk to Aaron Henry. Reuther applied pressure, Detroit style—Rauh would march straight to the Credentials Committee and accept the compromise, or he would no longer work for the United Auto Workers. Feeling decidedly screwed, Rauh headed for the committee room, hoping to filibuster until he could talk to his other bosses. But Freedom Democratic leaders were busy.

By 3:00 p.m., the challenge was unraveling on both sides of North Mississippi Avenue. In an upstairs room at the convention hall, Rauh faced the Credentials Committee, arguing desperately for a recess, struggling to be heard above cries of "Vote! Vote!" Across the street, Hubert Humphrey had called another meeting at the Pageant. This time, there would be no tears, no conciliation, no scenes in black and white. There would be only flaring tempers, pressure politics, and trickery. From the meeting's first moments, blacks sensed the tightening pincers. When Martin Luther King balked at the compromise, Walter Reuther reminded him that the UAW had bankrolled King's campaign in Birmingham. "Your funding is on the line," Reuther

said. King came around quickly. When the Reverend Edwin King, recommended with Aaron Henry as a delegate at large, said he would give his seat
to Fannie Lou Hamer, Humphrey refused. "The President has said he will
not let that illiterate woman speak on the floor of the Democratic convention." And toward 3:30 p.m., when a TV was wheeled in, announcing that
the Mississippi challenge had been resolved, that the Credentials Committee
had just approved the compromise, Bob Moses lost the composure that had
made him a legend.

Three years ago that week, Moses had been beaten with a knife handle
outside the courthouse in Liberty, Mississippi. A friend had taken Moses'
T-shirt and "wrung out the blood." A week later, Moses took more blacks to
the courthouse. As he had labored on in McComb, in Greenwood, in Jackson,
the brutality of an entire state had not destroyed Moses' faith that American
democracy could work, even in Mississippi. SNCC had stockpiled reams of
affidavits chronicling every assault. SNCC and Moses had sued county registrars and the federal government. Moses, his coworkers, and his summer
disciples had visited thousands of shacks, preaching democracy. In its name,
blood had been shed all summer. Three men murdered and buried beneath
a dam. Torsos washing up in the river. Churches reduced to ashes. Heading to Atlantic City, Moses had not allowed himself to be swept up in the
euphoria. But after Hamer's speech, after all the Boardwalk rallies, he had
shed his caution. The Democratic Party would not refuse Freedom Democrats, he said, "if they really understand what's at stake." Now America had
slapped Bob Moses in the face. Now he saw what he had perhaps suspected
all along—that naked coercion, arm twisting, and sneaky backroom deals
were also "the stuff democracy is made of."

Certain that Hubert Humphrey had called Freedom Democrats to his
suite to keep them from arguing their case where it mattered, Moses shouted,
"You cheated!" Then he stood, strode out of the crowded suite, and slammed
the door.

The echo was the sound of SNCC slamming the door on the American political process. Moses soon declared he would never again trust politics. Other SNCCs agreed. James Forman: "Atlantic City was a powerful
lesson. . . . No longer was there any hope, among those who still had it,
that the federal government would change the situation in the Deep South."
Ella Baker: "The kids tried the established methods, and they tried at the
expense of their lives. . . . But they were not willing to wait and they had paid

a high price. So they began to look for other answers." Freedom Democrats described their own dismay.

"Stokely," Hartman Turnbow asked. "So this is what y'all calls democracy?"

"No, Mr. Turnbow," Carmichael replied. "It's politics—as usual."

"Well now, sure t'ain't the same thing, now is it?"

"No, suh, it sure ain't."

At 4:00 p.m., when demonstrators seated on the Boardwalk learned that the two-seat compromise had been approved, they stood in silence. A call had just gone back to SNCC headquarters in Greenwood, Freedom Democrats asking for the latest violent incidents so "they can use the info in pleading their case." But suddenly it became clear that no evidence—not four filing cabinets filled with names, not stacks of affidavits, not the most heart-searing testimony—would do any good. As they stood in the breeze off the ocean, so far removed from cotton fields and Piney Woods, volunteers and SNCC staffers felt the same gut-wrenching fury they had known each day in Mississippi. Tourists passed. Waves crashed on the beach. Seagulls circled overhead. It was August 25. A week remained before college classes absorbed volunteers, but the summer that had begun in innocence on an Ohio campus, burst onto front pages, then trudged on through fear and Freedom Songs, finally bringing all its idealism before a national audience, was over.

That evening on the convention floor, the compromise was explained and adopted in less than a minute. With tears in his eyes, Joseph Rauh, fresh from a meeting where Freedom Democrats formally voted down the compromise, marched to the podium to turn in two badges labeled "at large." But the compromise included more than two seats. It also promised that future conventions would never again seat all-white delegations. (They never did.) And it required Mississippi's official delegation to swear allegiance to the Democratic ticket. Mississippi delegates were outraged. Their state had been "cowhided and horsewhipped," subjected to "cheap, degrading insults." How dare they be required to prove themselves loyal Democrats! On orders phoned in by Governor Johnson, delegates began packing. Since Reconstruction, the governor declared, Mississippi had owed a great debt to the Democratic Party. Now, "that debt is paid in full." And he had "no intention of ever working for President Johnson at any time." The convention continued with four loyal Mississippi delegates seated—alone in rows of empty chairs. They soon had company.

Tuesday night's program was proceeding with the usual speeches when

reporters noted a commotion. NBC's John Chancellor shouted that the Freedom Democrats were marching into the convention hall. Racing to catch up,
Chancellor followed the flow, past New Jersey state troopers and onto the
floor. As some Freedom Democrats entered, others left, carrying floor badges
borrowed from sympathizers, badges they handed to delegates outside. One
volunteer, feeling "like Mata Hari and the French Resistance and the Under-
ground Railroad all rolled into one," made several trips. Inside, first ten,
then twenty or more Freedom Democrats took the seats denied them. All sat
proudly, as if their mere presence proved their first-class citizenship. Back in
the White House, LBJ ordered the Freedom Democrats removed, but an aide
sensed the outcry if cops were seen struggling with blacks on the convention
floor. One delegate was taken out, but the rest stayed. "All we want," Fannie
Lou Hamer told a reporter, "is a chance to be a part of America."

The following morning, Freedom Democrats gathered again to reconsider
two seats at large. The previous evening, the Union Temple Baptist Church
had overflowed with bitterness. Moderate black leaders had told the delegation that two seats amounted to victory, that more progress would come.
But SNCC leaders vehemently disagreed. "We've shed too much blood,"
John Lewis said. "We've come much too far to back down now." Fannie Lou
Hamer "told it" better. "We didn't come all this way for no two seats," she
said. "All of us is tired." But on Wednesday morning, with the compromise
now formally adopted by the convention, moderates made one last plea for
unity. LBJ needed their full support. A Goldwater presidency would be disas-
trous for civil rights. "You have made your point," Roy Wilkins told Hamer,
"but you don't know anything and should go home to Mississippi." Talk
spiraled into argument and argument into resentment. Freedom Democrats
found themselves split by class. Aaron Henry and the few other white-collar
delegates supported the compromise; Fannie Lou Hamer and the rest stood
firm. Martin Luther King wavered. "Being a Negro leader, I want you to take
this," he admitted, "but if I were a Mississippi Negro, I would vote against
it." Then Bob Moses rose. For much of the meeting, he had stared at the
floor, seeming to be somewhere else, as if beyond politics now. Moving to
the podium, reminding one onlooker of "Socrates or Aristotle," he summed
up the exhausting week in a single sentence. "We're not here to bring politics
into our morality," he said, "but to bring morality into our politics."

Moses made no recommendation on the compromise. That was for Mississippi's unofficial delegation to decide. Toward noon, delegates were left

alone to vote. At stake was all their name now implied, all Freedom Summer stood for. As Democrats, they should back their party and its compromise. But as *Freedom* Democrats, they had a certain principle to uphold. When one eighty-year-old sharecropper spoke for the compromise, Hamer and others cried out. "When they got through talking and hoopin' and hollerin' and tellin' me what a shame it was for me to do that," Henry Sias said, "I changed my mind right there." Finally, the vote was taken. SNCCs filed back into the room to learn how well they had taught their lessons. The sharecroppers and maids, barbers and cooks, seasoned by their introduction to democracy, had again rejected the compromise.

On Wednesday night, all chairs marked "Mississippi" were removed from the convention floor, but several Freedom Democrats were allowed to stand. And throughout Thursday night's long tribute to JFK, Bob Moses and others stood in a silent circle, holding hands. No one inside the convention hall seemed to care. The Mississippi challenge now seemed as dated as the huge photos of FDR and Harry Truman looming above the platform. That night, an ebullient Lyndon Johnson came to Atlantic City to accept his party's nomination. He and Hubert Humphrey linked hands in triumph. Fireworks blazed above the Boardwalk, some even forming a portrait of LBJ. With all the noise, Fannie Lou Hamer needed a microphone to be heard as she stood before exhausted Freedom Democrats and their supporters, belting out one last chorus of "Go Tell It on the Mountain." As always, Hamer's eyes looked skyward, numbed by fatigue but swept up in song and spirit.

The following morning, sixty-seven Freedom Democrats filed onto buses. Perhaps a few took final glances at the pale blue above the shoreline, at the ghetto surrounding their hotel, at the Ferris wheel spinning slowly in the distance. Then the buses pulled out. Across America, the compromise was being hailed in the press—"a significant moral and political victory" (*Los Angeles Times*); "a triumph of Moral force" (*New York Times*); "nothing short of heroic" (*Washington Post*). But Freedom Democrats did not feel victorious. They were headed back to Mississippi, where sharecroppers would soon return to the fields and volunteers would be gone, taking with them the nation's attention. "You don't know how they goin' to do us!" a black man in Greenwood said. "It's goin' to be hell when you leave!" The Freedom Democrats continued their long, sad return, west across Pennsylvania and Ohio, then south through Kentucky and Tennessee, heading home.

The last departing volunteers also went home that weekend. The summer of solidarity, of songs sung with hands clasped, heads swaying, ended with young men and women, battered and exhausted, slipping one by one out of the state. Most left unnoticed, but one was spotted on a bus out of Clarksdale. A woman seated beside her noticed her midwestern accent and asked if she had been part of the summer project. When the volunteer nodded, the Mississippi native turned somber. "I just want you to know," the woman said, "that some of us have really done our best, and we've educated the people who have worked for us and have lived with us, and we care about them." Then the bus crossed the Mississippi line.

Sometime during that final week of Freedom Summer, a Sovereignty Commission investigator went to Batesville to check out voter registration in Panola County. Parking behind the courthouse, the man spotted several black women beside a young white man. All were discussing how to register.

Stepping inside the courthouse, the investigator found his way to the registrar's office and asked how the voting drive was progressing.

"Fine," the registrar answered.

And how many Negroes had been registered that summer?

"Something over seven hundred."

The investigator was shocked. "My country man!" he said. "What has happened that could justify that many Negroes qualifying in the last sixty days to vote in this county?"

"Well, you know, I'm under an injunction."

"Yes, I'm aware of that but I still can't see how that many could qualify in so short a period of time."

The registrar wearily explained. It seemed some clerks had taken the federal injunction very seriously. They were actually *helping* Negroes fill out forms. Pointing out mistakes. Allowing them to be corrected. The investigator tried to contain his anger. This was not what the injunction intended, he said. But the registrar insisted—he did not want to be subpoenaed again. Another trip to federal court might bring an even harsher ruling.

Shaking his head, the investigator walked down the hall. In the district attorney's office, he heard worse news. The COFO drive had "snowballed," the DA said. It had gone "completely out of control." Negroes were coming in from all over the county. Nothing seemed to stop them. They just kept filling out forms, dozens each week, all passing without a test, all approved as voters. This was bound to spread to the whole Delta. Tallahatchie was already under an injunction, and more would surely come. What could be done? The investigator said he would take up the matter with the state attorney general. He would be back on Friday. On his way out, he saw more blacks coming, walking up the steps, out of the heat, into the coolness of the courthouse.

However beautiful the golden leaves may be, they will have to decay and become manure for the future of civilization. But it is only the seed persons that really count. And it is those you should look for.

—Victoria Gray Adams

CHAPTER ELEVEN

"Give unto Them Beauty for Ashes"

For the rest of the twentieth century, Mississippi struggled to put the past in its proper place. The lessons were bitter, and some refused to learn them. In the years following Freedom Summer, rancor and hatred reigned. Torn between nonviolence and a surging militance, blacks split into factions, arguing about everything, even funding for child care. Marches continued, and cops continued roughing up marchers. The Klan rallied in public, plotted in private, and made a last-ditch stand for its ludicrous lost cause of white supremacy. But with time, the state haunted by the Civil War surrendered to the inevitable future. Old customs died out with old people, and new generations found neither the energy nor the hatred needed to prop up Jim Crow. The past, in defiance of William Faulkner's cautionary adage, came to be past. Like some cantankerous grandfather, Mississippi's cruel legacy of war and Reconstruction, segregation and lynching, night riding and shotgun justice, was relegated from the kitchen table to the back porch. There it no longer required constant vigilance, let alone violence.

Even as Mississippi shed timeworn ways, life remained hard. Air-conditioning tamed the savage summers, while industry drew thousands from the land. New highways—asphalt and electronic—linked remote hamlets, bringing fresh faces and ideas, yet Mississippi remained America's poorest state. Touring the Delta in 1967, Robert Kennedy visited sharecroppers' shacks, reached out to touch starving children, and came away stunned. "My God," he said, "I did not know this kind of thing existed. How can a country like this allow it?" More machines picked cotton and more field hands fled, leaving the land dotted by empty shacks. Hurricane Camille splintered the

Gulf Coast. The river rose and fell, but the price of cotton never returned to what it had been. And through it all, decade by decade, a halting progress accumulated until by the new century, Mississippi had achieved a racial reconciliation few states or countries can match. But the first steps came on a minefield.

By mid-September 1964, another "lay-by time" was over. August's gauze lifted, leaving a stark and flaxen beauty across the land. Crisp air smelled of smoldering leaves. Even the swamps seemed magical, tinged in gold and green. Black schools in the Delta closed, sending students and their parents back into the fields. To whites, the field hands in their cloth caps and overalls seemed as perennial as the goldenrod blooming beside the roads. So it had been for more than a century, but it would not be so for long.

Autumn soothed the scars of summer, yet ten weeks of tension had frayed nerves to a nub. Many volunteers had thought they were used to the stress, but when they returned home, they discovered that they would never return home. Not for the rest of their lives.

Among SNCC staff, bitterness over Atlantic City mixed with relief. "The longest nightmare I have ever had," as Cleveland Sellers called Freedom Summer, was over. Some eighty volunteers were staying on, but with the rest gone, SNCCs could go back to helping locals shine their own lights. Or could they? "At the end of summer, I knew I had been right in opposing the project," Hollis Watkins remembered. "Trying to reactivate and get people motivated was much, much harder." And along with enervating blacks, Freedom Summer left white Mississippi filled with shock, shame, and outrage.

In September, six more churches went up in flames. Another black body was pulled from a river. South of Jackson, the Klan went on a rampage, bombing the mayor's home in Natchez and the Vicksburg Freedom House where Fran O'Brien had taught. And in McComb?

On September 9, McComb COFO director Jesse Harris wrote the Justice Department: "If the present increase in violence is not halted, it is almost certain that within the coming weeks there will be a civil rights worker killed in Pike County." No protection was offered. Whenever COFO called the FBI to complain about police harassment, they were told that McComb cops "are very fine people and you shouldn't criticize them." Free to strike at will, the Klan terrorized the city. Bombs hit another church and a preacher's home. Thugs beat volunteers in broad daylight. Pickups circled the Freedom House nightly, while police set up roadblocks, arresting dozens of blacks on charges of "criminal syndicalism." And there were more bombs, midnight explosions splintering homes, spreading terror, steeling the black community.

While McComb approached a state of siege, Americans inspired by Freedom Summer shone their own lights on Mississippi. Volunteers' parents continued to meet, raise funds, and send them south. Pharmaceutical companies shipped vitamins and first aid kits. Public schools across America adopted Freedom Schools, sending books and supplies. And with nearly three dozen churches destroyed, congregations responded to a "Committee of Concern." Formed by Mississippi clergy, black and white, the committee's campaign collected $10,000 in its first week, enough to begin building. The title of the committee's campaign, "Beauty for Ashes," came from the biblical book of Isaiah: "The Lord hath anointed me to preach good tidings unto the meek . . . to give unto them beauty for ashes. . . ." By Christmas, college students were giving up their vacations to build churches in Mississippi.

But Freedom Summer's wounds could not be confined to Mississippi. Back at her Oregon college, Fran O'Brien was restless and angry. The once demure teacher now argued with old friends who seemed to have become bigots. No one understood what Fran had been through, but no one failed to notice her testiness. "I didn't realize yet that it was because *I* was a different person, so my whole senior year was confusing," she remembered. Fran talked about the children of Mississippi but told no one about being beaten by Klansmen. She did not even tell herself. And so the horror festered, leaving her alone, aloof, and strangest of all, dreaming of returning to Mississippi the following summer. A similar estrangement could be found at colleges around the country.

In Chicago, Len Edwards, the congressman's son, was back at law school. One evening at a bar, friends were talking about the Cubs, about "girls," about the Johnson-Goldwater race, when someone asked, "Well, what was happening down there in Mississippi?" Edwards managed to get out two sentences, "and I started crying, I just burst out crying." In North Hanover, Massachusetts, Linda Wetmore found "everything was awful." Wetmore's arrest during Greenwood's Freedom Day had been on the front page of the *Boston Globe*. Back home she found herself notorious. At church, someone asked her, "You're telling me you'd want to live next door to a nigger?" Her boyfriend came over to say, "I could never kiss anybody who'd kiss a black man." Wetmore had not kissed any black men, but she replied, "Then I guess we can't go out anymore."

Studying returned volunteers, psychiatrist Robert Coles saw signs of "battle fatigue . . . exhaustion, weariness, despair, frustration and rage." Many volunteers wanted to talk about Mississippi, but how could they describe a sharecropper's shack? A Mississippi jail? Madhouse summer nights of pickups and shotguns and flaming crosses? Some spoke to service clubs, but many more refused to talk to anyone. First in hometowns, then back on campus, their white world seemed so isolated, so pointless. Summer had immersed them in a movement, swarming with people, anointed in spirit, struggling for others. And now they were asked to resume their studies, to go to parties, to focus on careers. There was simply no way to explain this to friends, to parents. One mother lamented, "Our very normal, bright young child has changed."

Many spent long hours in their rooms. Guilt over leaving Mississippi blacks—"the best people I ever met"—overwhelmed them. When they went out, they found themselves dodging whites and drawn to any passing black face. Politics was a distant drone from an America whose talk of equality seemed laughable. "I went from being a liberal Peace Corps–type Democrat to a raging, maniacal lefty," one volunteer recalled. Decades later, sociologist Doug McAdam, surveying some 250 volunteers, found that Freedom Summer had moved two-thirds leftward and crippled respect for authority. In just ten weeks, 42 percent lowered their estimation of the president, 40 percent lost esteem for Congress, half for the Justice Department, and nearly three-quarters for the FBI. In the fall of 1964, this sea change spearheaded a generational challenge to America, a challenge that began on a single campus.

On October 1, a crowd at the University of California at Berkeley surrounded a police car holding a student arrested for handing out CORE leaflets. For the next thirty-two hours, the car sat trapped by swarms of students, many singing Freedom Songs, while one after another jumped on its roof and spoke about free speech. The most eloquent speaker, the one who would speak throughout that fall about the connections between Mississippi and Berkeley, had just returned from McComb. Before the summer, Mario Savio had impressed a SNCC interviewer as "not a very creative guy . . . [who] did not play much of a leadership role." But back at Berkeley, Savio was on fire with summer memories. He remembered staying up late in Ohio talking about Goodman, Schwerner, and Chaney. He recalled being chased by angry whites in Jackson, hearing the bombs in McComb, talking in sharecropper shacks. "Can I now forget Mississippi?" he wondered. "In other words, was that my summer job?"

With Savio leading the protests, Berkeley's Free Speech Movement kept students protesting through December, culminating in a sit-in that closed the administration building. Inspired by Berkeley's call for free speech, student protests soon broke out across America—against the war, the draft, the patriarchy. And in the forefront of each were veterans of Freedom Summer: who had seen democracy denied, who had watched "the law" subjugate an entire people, and who had come home angry and disillusioned. For the rest of the 1960s, Mississippi would remain their benchmark of injustice, the place where one generation's American dream went to die. Time and again, 1960s spokesmen—not just Mario Savio but Tom Hayden, Abbie Hoffman, William Kunstler, and others—would refer to Mississippi as the school where they had learned to question America. And as protests became increasingly shrill, bewildered parents would ask why their children seemed so cynical about their country. The answer was easy. The children had been to Mississippi.

As volunteers struggled to cope with an unbearably white America, several SNCCs decided they had to leave Mississippi, if only for a few weeks. Racial tensions were rising. Staffers were working without paychecks. SNCC's Sojourner Fleet cars, after a summer of racing volunteers and staffers around Mississippi, were now lost, wrecked, scattered around the country. A year earlier, SNCC leaders would have faced down these problems, but Freedom Summer had left them even more exhausted than the volunteers.

On his visit to Greenwood in August, Harry Belafonte had seen the emotional toll. Handing over $60,000, the singer made a deal. SNCC could have another $10,000 if leaders agreed to an all-expenses-paid trip—to Africa. On September 11, Belafonte and eleven SNCCs, including Bob and Dona Moses, Fannie Lou Hamer, John Lewis, and James Forman, flew from New York to the new nation of Guinea. Shortly after they arrived in the palm-shaded, whitewashed capital of Conakry, President Sékou Touré summoned them to his palace. When the invitation came, Fannie Lou Hamer was taking a bath. "I'm definitely not ready to meet no president," she said. But an hour later, she stood in an opulent palace, in awe. Here was a Delta sharecropper, her recent speech cut off by LBJ, now being kissed on both cheeks by another president, enveloped in his white robe, praised in his flowing French.

For ten days, the frazzled Mississippi veterans soaked up the rarefied air of a nation where blacks ran everything. The trip, Hamer later said, was "the proudest moment of my life. I saw black men flying the airplanes, driving buses, sitting behind the big desks in the bank and just doing everything that I was used to seeing white people do." Hamer was particularly taken by African women—"so graceful and so poised. I thought about my mother and my grandmother." From Guinea, two SNCCs went on to Kenya where they met Malcolm X, but the rest returned home to sort through the residue of Freedom Summer.

SNCC's "beloved community" was coming apart. Once a handful of the bravest and boldest, SNCC suddenly had four hundred staffers, 20 percent of them white. Bob Moses saw racial resentment "welling out like poison." Too many blacks called whites smug, superior, condescending. Too many whites saw blacks as slow or lazy. With the majority of holdovers being white women, sexual tension flared. "The Negro girls feel neglected because the white girls get the attention." Black women on her project, one white woman wrote, "just seemed to hate me." SNCC was also nagged by the future. Should it become a structured CORE-like organization? Or should it remain a freewheeling movement whose members "do what the spirit say do"? What should SNCC's position be on urban riots? On Vietnam? On Third World movements? And did anyone have the energy to plan for the summer of '65?

On November 5, 160 SNCC staffers gathered at a church in the seaside town of Waveland, Mississippi. James Forman opened the conference by calling SNCC "a band of brothers." "We must decide if the circle will be unbroken," he concluded. "If we remain a band of brothers, a circle of trust, we shall overcome!" But few Freedom Songs followed. Slumped in folding chairs, black and white seemed more at odds than ever. Hands went to hips, brows furrowed, and irritation punctuated every weary sigh, every roll of the eyes. SNCCs had often boasted of being "many minds, one heart," but now, even hearts were at odds. Disputes broke out over the smallest details. One morning, SNCCs squared off with baseball bats and pool cues. The issue? Cafeteria meal tickets. SNCC, Forman noted, was suffering from "too many people high on freedom, just going off and doing what they want."

In bungalows overlooking the Gulf of Mexico, the rancor continued after hours. Class remained a rut, race a chasm in the road ahead. And there was a new obstacle—gender. One of many position papers presented was "Women in the Movement." The paper outlined how men in SNCC excluded women from top decision making, relegated them to typing and stenography, and treated even female staffers as mere "girls." Just as "the average white person doesn't realize that he assumes he is superior," the authors wrote, "so too the average SNCC worker finds it difficult to discuss the woman problem because of the assumption of male superiority . . . This is no more a man's world than it is a white world."

As the authors had expected, the paper "hardly caused a ripple." Yet "Women in the Movement," written by SNCC veterans Casey Hayden and Mary King, would ripple far beyond the Mississippi beach town. Revised and expanded, the SNCC paper became a founding doctrine of the burgeoning women's movement. When later read at a Students for a Democratic Society meeting, it would lead women to walk out and form their own caucus. Circulated among friends, the King-Hayden manifesto would lead to women's consciousness-raising circles, many led by Freedom Summer veterans.

Yet in Waveland, the conference continued as if nothing had happened. After a few days, several members, disgusted by the "brutally aggressive hostility," walked out. Others kept bickering. Returning to their projects, staffers found more disarray. Rumors of an impending "coup" swept through SNCC. Volunteers sat at typewriters banging out long lists of gripes. Whites lashed out at "bullshitting Negroes." Blacks refused to "take orders from white folks!" Project directors saw workers wandering in and out of offices. One wrote, "Typical day: Rise at noon, eat, get the mail, drive around, eat, play cards, watch TV and spend the rest of the evening and night drinking at the local café." Muriel Tillinghast, who had moved to Jackson to run the COFO office, saw SNCC "morphing into a different kind of organization, but we didn't know where we were going. Many original SNCCs didn't embrace the change. They thought we would never be the same and that was true."

Within six months, Bob Moses would resign from SNCC and leave Mississippi. Within a year, many SNCCs would no longer be on speaking terms. Within two years, new SNCC chairman Stokely Carmichael, arrested again in Greenwood, would lead a crowd in a hypnotic chant: "Black—Power! Black—Power!" Fannie Lou Hamer was one of many baffled by the new militancy. Addressing a SNCC dinner, Hamer lamented that her old peers had become "cold." Beyond cold, many were carrying guns, even to meetings. It was not long before SNCCs gathering in upstate New York would argue till 2:00 a.m., and then, against Carmichael's wishes, narrowly vote to expel all whites. When Hamer's words were invoked against such segregation, one member noted, "Mrs. Hamer is no longer relevant."

With Moses and other gentle militants gone, SNCC surrendered to rage and resentment. Focus shifted to urban ghettos where the enemy was not the local sheriff but police raids and FBI surveillance, where arrests were not for leafleting but for inciting riots. Endorsing Third World movements, including the Palestine Liberation Organization, SNCC lost much of its white liberal funding. "Black Power," recognized by Martin Luther King as "an unfortunate choice of words," made SNCC a lighting rod for white backlash, while "Stokely Starmichael" made SNCC as much talk as action. Too much of the talk, Julius Lester remembered, featured "a growing litany of hatred." And the only thing anyone in SNCC agreed upon was that Freedom Summer had both cracked Mississippi and shattered the circle of trust.

While SNCC unraveled, the FBI finally cracked the Klan in Mississippi. The first fissure opened two weeks after Freedom Summer, when a Klansman broke his vow of silence. Wallace Miller had joined the Klan less to fight integration than to fit in. "I got the feeling that anyone who wasn't a Klansman wasn't anything," he told the FBI. But the chubby cop, best known for his barbecue skills, had not counted on covering up murder. Meeting agents in a restaurant, Miller told of a Klan gathering in May where "one of the boys" announced, "We've got to get Goatee." He told how the extermination order on Mickey Schwerner had soon come from the Klan's Imperial Wizard. He revealed that the Mt. Zion Church had been burned to lure "Goatee" into Neshoba County, and he gave the first inside account of what really happened on the night of June 21.

Precisely as Deputy Cecil Price had said, Goodman, Schwerner, and Chaney had been released at 10:30 p.m. But Price had not watched their taillights disappear—he had led the chase. Overtaken by three cars, the station wagon had finally pulled over on Route 19. The three were taken up a dirt road, murdered in cold blood, buried beneath the dam. Two Klansmen were supposed to take the station wagon to Alabama and burn it, but for some reason did not. Officer Miller also gave the FBI the name of the man who shot Goodman and Schwerner. But when asked for more, he refused. He had told all he dared. It might not be enough to convict anyone, but could it lead to an indictment?

The FBI hoped Mississippi might press murder charges, but Governor Paul Johnson refused, even when more evidence was gathered. The state attorney general saw no point in a Neshoba County trial, where the judge and several jurors would probably be Klansmen. And Johnson balked, lest his constituents think "[Martin Luther] King was calling the shots." So on the first day of autumn, Judge O. H. Barnett, cousin of former Mississippi governor Ross Barnett, convened a federal grand jury in Biloxi. "Now is the time for the government to put up or shut up," the judge announced. Because murder is not a federal crime unless committed on federal property, the grand jury could only weigh indictments for civil rights violations. With denial still rampant in Mississippi, any indictment would be a landmark. But when the grand jury subpoenaed FBI agents, J. Edgar Hoover, unwilling to scare off future informers, refused to let his men testify. The grand jury, complaining that "our investigation has been curtailed, and in fact stymied" by the FBI, failed to issue indictments in the Neshoba killings. The case dragged on. The FBI went looking for more informants, men who could, as J. Edgar Hoover boasted, "put the fear of God into the Ku Klux Klan."

James Jordan was a balding, middle-aged construction worker known to agents as a "floater," a "hustler." Jordan had moved to Gulfport to get a job, but the FBI tracked him there in mid-October. He soon learned that agents knew all about his role in the killings. A fellow Klansman had told them. Jordan said nothing at first, but five subsequent interrogations got tougher. "I'm going to see your ass in jail," an agent told Jordan. Offered $3,500 and federal protection, Jordan finally told all he knew. And the FBI, after spending more than $800,000, after interviewing a thousand locals and nearly five hundred Klansmen, finally learned the darkest details from the first night of Freedom Summer.

The sun was setting but the June evening was holding hot and humid when word went out from the Neshoba County jail—"Goatee" was in custody. Klansman Edgar Ray Killen hurried to the Longhorn Drive-in on the edge of Meridian to gather a lynch mob. "Killen said they had three civil rights workers in jail in Philadelphia and that they needed 'their asses tore up,'" Jordan told the FBI. The job had to be done in a hurry because the men, held on a minor charge, would soon be released. One man hurried to a pay phone. Others hopped in a car to gather Klansmen who did not have phones. Killen, a short, scrawny man known as "The Preacher" because he occasionally spoke from local pulpits, said they would need gloves. At a Klansman's grocery store, the men got six pairs, brown cotton. A Klansman's trailer park became the rendezvous point. The men would meet there, then head for the jail. Everyone should bring guns.

It was not every day a klavern carried out an extermination order, and as volunteers settled in for their first night in Mississippi, more than a dozen Klansmen converged on the silent streets of Philadelphia. The killers were a random lot—the preacher, assorted truck drivers and contractors, Neshoba County's former sheriff, cops young and old—but all shared their Imperial Wizard's fanatical resolve to get "Goatee" and repel "the nigger-communist invasion of Mississippi."

At 9:00 p.m., three cars and a pickup parked outside the courthouse. One man entered the jail and returned with the news: "Goatee," some other white man, and a nigger were still behind bars. Killen led his crew to a dark street within sight of the jail, then had the group drop him at a funeral home as an alibi. The men came back downtown and waited until a fat old cop came up. The three were gone, he said, headed south on Route 19. Three cars set out in pursuit. They were soon joined by Deputy Cecil Price in his patrol car, chasing the fleeing station wagon over roller-coaster hills, faster and faster. All the cars were roaring at a hundred miles per hour when James Chaney finally decided to pull over. No one ever found out why.

Price ordered the men out of their car and into his. Strobe-lit by his red light, Goodman, Schwerner, and Chaney piled into the backseat. Blinding headlights from behind told them that this time they would not get off with a speeding ticket. One Klansman drove the station wagon, following Price and other cars back toward Philadelphia.

Roads in Neshoba County do not merge; they cut away from the highway, plunging into forest and thickets. Price abruptly turned onto a narrow slash of gravel known as Rock Cut Road. Passing two houses, the cars headed through cut clay banks surrounded by woods. Jordan waited on the highway, then drove up Rock Cut Road. Approaching, he heard muffled voices. Engines stopped. Car doors slammed. Then came "a volley of shots."

The bodies were tossed into the station wagon. "Everyone follow me," one man said. "We'll go the back way." The convoy of cars drove to the dam where the men got out and stood in the warm night, smoking, talking.

"Someone go and get the operator," one finally said. Twenty minutes later, the murder party heard the grinding of a bulldozer. "They will be under twenty feet of dirt before it is all over," one man said. Someone asked about the station wagon, and when the bulldozer fell silent, several men went to a garage on Route 19, where the owner of the dam site filled a glass jar with enough gasoline to burn it. After swearing each other to silence, the men went home. Mississippi had been redeemed again. "Goatee" and his friends would never be found. Everyone would soon forget them.

Seeking evidence, FBI agents had not asked James Jordan the questions a parent or a wife might have. When had Goodman, Schwerner, and Chaney realized they were in the hands of killers? As the chase accelerated, had Goodman remembered what he had told a friend—"I'm scared, but I'm going"? Did Schwerner recall the threats—"That Jewboy is dead!" Did Chaney remember his mother asking, "Ain't you afraid?" What had the three said to each other as they rode in the back of the police car? What had they thought when they felt the car lurch off the highway and onto the gravel?

A few weeks after James Jordan signed his confession, another informant filled in final details. Auto parts salesman Horace Doyle Barnette remembered Preacher Killen saying, "We have a place to bury them, and a man to run the dozer to cover them up." He described Cecil Price clubbing James Chaney with his blackjack, and sketched a grisly murder scene complete with final words. James Jordan, it seemed, had not heard shots in the distance. He had ridden "shotgun" with Deputy Price while the three sat in the back. The car had skidded to a stop along Rock Cut Road. Racing up and opening the rear door, Wayne Roberts, a man so volatile he had been dishonorably discharged from the marines, had yanked Schwerner out and spun him around.

"Are you that nigger lover?" Roberts shouted.

"Sir," Schwerner replied, "I know just how you feel."

Roberts, his left hand gripping Schwerner's shoulder, put a bullet through his chest. Schwerner fell facedown in the ditch. Seconds later, Roberts yanked out Goodman and, without a word, killed him with a single shot. Just then, Jordan got out of the car, saying, "Save one for me!" Jordan dragged out James Chaney, who scrambled to get away. Three shots gunned Chaney down. "You didn't leave me anything but a nigger," Jordan said, "but at least I killed me a nigger." Back in Philadelphia, the killers met with Sheriff Rainey.

"I'll kill anyone who talks," Rainey told them, "even if it's my own brother."

On December 4, 1964, Christmas decorations adorned the streets of Philadelphia when, beneath gloomy skies, sixty FBI agents fanned out across Neshoba County with arrest warrants. The accused, including truck drivers, farmers, cops, and the owner of the burial site, were taken from cafés, farmhouses, and trailers. Sheriff Rainey and Deputy Price, their boots caked in red clay, returned from a raid on a moonshine still to find agents waiting at the courthouse. Rainey asked to see the warrant. Both men handed over guns and badges. Like others arrested that morning, both carried startling amounts of cash—Price, $403; Rainey, more than $1,100. By afternoon, nineteen men sat in the Meridian courthouse, talking amiably. In front sat Sheriff Rainey, legs crossed, enormous chaw in his cheek, dipping tobacco from a pouch labeled "RED MAN." Someone cracked a joke. Price smiled, Rainey guffawed and a *Life* photographer snapped a famous photo that came to symbolize the southern redneck—smirking at the charge of murder, or even a "civil rights violation." Six days later, Rainey's arrogance was rewarded.

At a preliminary hearing on December 10, Meridian's federal commissioner, a schoolmarmish woman, ruled the latest Klan confession "hearsay"— and dismissed all charges. Shaking hands, slapping each other on the back, all nineteen men went free. "Ol' Rainey could be elected governor now," a man outside the courthouse said. The Justice Department filed new charges on New Year's Day.

Throughout 1965, Mississippi was torn between law and custom, past and present. In Neshoba County, Sheriff Rainey and his plump deputy were more popular than ever. Cecil Price was talking about running for sheriff when his boss's term expired. Locals doubted the two lawmen or anyone else would ever be convicted. Elsewhere, Klansmen met in open rallies drawing hundreds. Crosses still blazed at night. COFO's office in Laurel was burned to the ground, and its offices elsewhere had electricity cut off, windows shot out. Yet shame was finally bringing moderates out of hiding.

Years later, writer Willie Morris remembered "a feeling that we hit the bottom of the barrel with these three murders in 1964." Following Freedom Summer, investment in Mississippi plummeted. Tourism on the Gulf Coast was cut in half. "I favor dropping an atom bomb on the state of Mississippi," an Ohio man wrote *Time* after the Neshoba indictments were dismissed.

"I am ashamed that such a savage state exists in the country." America's disgust was summed up by Phil Ochs's ballad, written after his week in Mississippi and debuted to stomps and cheers in a Greenwich Village nightclub.

> Here's to the state of Mississippi,
> For underneath her borders, the devil draws no lines,
> If you drag her muddy rivers, nameless bodies you will find.
> The fat trees of the forest have hid a thousand crimes,
> And the calendar is lying when it reads the present time.
> Oh, here's to the land you've torn out the heart of,
> Mississippi, find yourself another country to be a part of.

Faced with economic reprisals and nationwide scorn, a critical mass in Mississippi realized they had no choice but to topple what one Jackson lawyer called "that wall of Never."

After more than a dozen bombings, McComb had finally fought back against the Klan. In November 1964, sensing that the life of their community was at stake, embattled citizens pooled $5,000 in rewards for information about bombings. Business and civic leaders formed Citizens for Progress, calling for "equal treatment under the law for all citizens regardless of race, creed, position, or wealth." And on November 18, FBI agents and highway patrolmen watched as a black man was served a bowl of gumbo in a restaurant on Main Street. "The waitress smiled and said, 'Thank you,'" noted C. C. Bryant, who had welcomed Bob Moses in 1961. "She even asked us to come back." A few hours later, blacks desegregated McComb's Holiday Inn, Woolworth's, Palace Theater, bus station, and Continental Motel.

In the year following Freedom Summer, similar harbingers of an edgy change surfaced across the state. Forced by federal lawsuits, schools in Jackson, Biloxi, Clarksdale, and Leake County desegregated first-grade classes. In response, all-white private schools, known as "seg academies," began to spring up wherever integration seemed near. Many had long waiting lists. Two blacks enrolled at Ole Miss, but no one rioted. Early in 1965, the Mississippi Economic Council called for full compliance with the Civil Rights Act, and Governor Paul Johnson praised the position. But good intentions mouthed in Jackson had never meant much in the Piney Woods or the Delta. Full democracy would come to Mississippi only by federal law, or the threat of intervention. As another long hot summer loomed, as Congress inched closer to passing LBJ's Voting Rights Act, Governor Johnson urged the state legislature to concede the inevitable by removing barriers to black registration. During the debate, cops arrested more than a thousand marchers, herding them into pens at the state fairgrounds. But in the end, the legislature complied. The Jim Crow relics—poll taxes and literacy tests—were finally put to rest. And to everyone's surprise, voters approved the change in a statewide referendum.

In July 1965, four summers after Bob Moses came to Liberty, Mississippi, the town had its first Freedom Day. SNCC staff had organized for months in preparation, and by 9:00 a.m., the line to register stretched from the courthouse—where Moses had been beaten—all the way to the sidewalk. The sheriff approached. "Okay, who's first?" he asked. A shriveled farmer stepped forth and said softly, "Me." Twenty-two people filled out forms that day in Liberty. All twenty-two passed the test. Within a month, two hundred more were registered, including the widow and oldest son of Herbert Lee.

The following month, a further challenge to Mississippi's old order came to a head on Capitol Hill. Shut out of the 1964 election, when Mississippi gave Barry Goldwater 87 percent of its vote, Freedom Democrats had quickly filed a formal challenge in Congress. Mississippi's all-white congressional delegation was not duly elected, the challenge claimed, because blacks had been systematically disenfranchised. When the challenge was introduced on the floor of the House, 149 congressmen supported it, not enough to win but enough to shake the assurance of Mississippi. Congress then gave Freedom Democrats time to gather affidavits proving voter discrimination. William Kunstler put out a nationwide call for lawyers and more than a hundred came to Jackson. Depositions describing voter fraud, beatings, and shootings were taken throughout Mississippi. Rita Schwerner returned to roam the state getting affidavits notarized. Federal hearings in Jackson stunned commissioners who listened as blacks told of terror inflicted on them just for registering to vote.

By the end of summer, Kunstler's team had assembled more than ten thousand pages of testimony. As he prepared to submit his evidence, Kunstler saw "a lawyer's dream case. Almost everyone in the United States conceded that Negroes could not vote in Mississippi." On September 17, 1965, the challenge was finally heard before a congressional gallery packed with Freedom Democrats. Nearly five hundred had come to Washington, D.C., to hold a silent, all-night vigil outside the Capitol. On the morning of the debate, Freedom Songs broke out. Then dozens of sharecroppers and maids, barbers and cooks filed into the House chamber where three MFDP candidates, Fannie Lou Hamer, Victoria Gray, and Annie Devine, were seated below them, the first black women ever allowed on the House floor. But when the challenge was finally heard, southern congressmen argued that if Mississippi's delegation was unseated, "every congressman from the Potomac to El Paso can expect the same." After two hours of debate the vote was finally taken. One hundred and forty-three congressmen supported the challenge, 228 opposed it. Speaking to the crowd gathered outside the Capitol, Fannie Lou Hamer broke into tears. "I'm not crying for myself," she said. "I'm crying for America."

> **Yes, Mississippi *was,* but Mississippi *is,* and we are proud of what we have become.**
>
> —Myrlie Evers Williams

Epilogue

On a sunny October morning in 1967, Sheriff Lawrence Rainey and Deputy Cecil Price waved to crowds of supporters as they strode toward the granite courthouse in Meridian. Wearing suits and fedoras instead of cowboy hats and police uniforms, both men looked more like salesmen than "the law." Rainey still had a chaw in his cheek but horn-rimmed glasses made him seem less the caricature of a southern sheriff. Price, who had lost his recent run to succeed Rainey, smiled softly at rows of clicking cameras. Both men, along with the sixteen others about to be tried with them, seemed in high spirits, confident that no jury of their peers would convict them. In the thirty-three months it had taken to bring the Neshoba murder case to trial, Price and Rainey had toured the South. Appearing before cheering Klansmen, the two lawmen had become symbols of the dying Civil War revanchism the Klan was still dragging through the dirt. Now, as they reached the courthouse door, a cheer went up across the street. A Confederate flag had been hoisted.

The ensuing years had seen violence in Mississippi wax and wane. Yet whenever white rage exploded, it strengthened the Mississippi movement and hastened the future. One dark night in January 1966, the gentle Hattiesburg farmer Vernon Dahmer, whom volunteers remembered for his Fourth of July picnic during Freedom Summer, was brutally murdered. When Klansmen threw flaming jugs of gasoline into Dahmer's home, Hattiesburg's local hero stood in the blaze, firing back at his assailants, allowing his wife and children to escape. Consumed by fire and bullets, Dahmer died the next day. Yet as a signal of how things were changing, Mississippi style, Governor Johnson denounced "these vicious and morally bankrupt criminals," and within months, the FBI charged fifteen men with Dahmer's murder. Among the accused was the soft-spoken businessman who had issued the order to get "Goatee," Klan Imperial Wizard Sam Bowers.

The following June, James Meredith returned to Mississippi vowing to march from Memphis to Jackson to encourage voter registration. Meredith was just inside the Mississippi border on his one-man "March Against Fear" when he was ambushed by shotgun. His wounds were superficial but the outrage drew civil rights leaders from across the country. Martin Luther King, Stokely Carmichael, and others came to Mississippi to continue Meredith's march, steering it through the heart of the Delta, drawing thousands who walked, sang, and registered.

In October 1966, after the U.S. Supreme Court unanimously reinstated the Neshoba murder case, the defense came up with another twist. The grand jury, it seemed, had been all white. Again the case was postponed until a new grand jury could hand down more indictments. This time the list included the Klan's gentlemanly, homicidal Imperial Wizard. By then, Mississippi was deeply divided on the case that had brought it national shame. The state still refused to press murder charges, yet many hoped justice would come in federal court. Just as many, however, continued to see the defendants as heroes standing up for the sovereignty of their embattled state. Even as the FBI sent more undercover agents to infiltrate the Klan, Sheriff Rainey and Deputy Price attended fund-raising dinners among hundreds eager to back a desperate defense of Jim Crow. By the time their trial on "civil rights violations" finally began, after three years of preparation, appeals, and dismissals, it was remarkably short.

Inside the courtroom, Judge Harold Cox, the notorious racist who had ranted against "niggers on a voting drive," sat before a huge mural depicting Mississippi history, including slaves picking cotton. Cox was silent as prosecutor John Doar led informants through the same stories they had told the FBI—of Klansmen armed with the "elimination" order, of "Preacher" Killen convening the lynch mob, of cars chasing "Goatee," pulling the three over, taking them to Rock Cut Road. But the judge soon served notice of how things were changing. Early in the trial, a defense attorney questioned a black minister. Hadn't Michael Schwerner advocated "the burning of draft cards"? Wasn't he an atheist? Hadn't he tried to "to get young Negro males to sign statements that they would rape one white woman a week during the hot summer of 1964 here in Mississippi"? Judge Cox had heard enough.

"Who is the author of that question?" he snapped. Preacher Killen, who had suggested it to lawyers, meekly raised his hand.

"I'm not going to allow a farce to be made of this trial," Cox said. The accused donned straight faces, yet continued to joke and smirk during recesses. All were stunned, however, when the Imperial Wizard's most trusted aide stepped into the witness box to testify for the prosecution.

Delmar Dennis, a tall, stalwart Methodist minister, had joined the Klan because it was "a white, Christian, militant organization dedicated to states' rights, segregation, and the preservation of the white civilization." At his swearing in, Preacher Killen had warned Dennis, "You ain't joined no Boy Scout group," but murder did not set well with the minister's conscience. In October 1964, Dennis had given the FBI enough inside information to fill forty pages. Now, he sat with fists clenched, quoting Klansman after Klansman. Imperial Wizard Sam Bowers on the killings: "It was the first time that Christians had planned and carried out the execution of Jews." Preacher Killen: "He said . . . people would need to be beaten and occasionally there would have to be elimination."

"What did he mean by elimination?"

"He meant killing a person."

Eight lawyers rose to defend the accused and, by proxy, Mississippi. Delmar Dennis was "a Judas witness" who "instead of thirty pieces of silver . . . got $15,000!" The FBI's tactics had resembled the Soviet system, "neighbors informing on neighbors." More than a hundred witnesses swore to seeing the defendants late that Father's Day evening. Preacher Killen had been at a funeral home. Triggerman Wayne Roberts was with his aunt, playing canasta. The accused were "salt of the earth kind of people . . . as innocent and pure as the driven snow." Imperial Wizard Sam Bowers was "in church every time the doors are open." But Goodman, Schwerner, and Chaney were "low-class riffraff. . . . Mississippians rightfully resent some hairy beatnik from another state visiting our state with hate and defying our people." As for the murders, "It may well be that these young men were sacrificed by their own kind for publicity or other reasons."

Summing up, John Doar sought to defuse lingering resentment of "the invasion": "The federal government is not invading Philadelphia or Neshoba County, Mississippi. . . . These defendants are tried for a crime under federal law in a Mississippi city, before a Mississippi federal judge, in a Mississippi courtroom." But the defense tapped resentments as old as Confederate

culture. "The strong arm of the federal government" had come to Mississippi to prove "that there is a group of people here in Mississippi so filled
with that hate that they conspire together . . . to do away and murder outsiders." Would the tired old bitterness still work? Even if the charge was a "civil
rights violation," could a Mississippi jury convict "good ol' boys" of killing
two "outsiders" and a "nigger"?

While the jury deliberated, the defendants yucked it up in the hallway.
Only Sam Bowers seemed concerned, smoking and brooding on his own.
When the jury deadlocked, the judge ordered them back into deliberation.
Finally, a verdict was reached. When read to the court, it left Klansmen vis-
ibly shaken. Seven men—Bowers, Roberts, Price, and four others—were
found guilty. Seven more, including Sheriff Rainey, were acquitted. A hung
jury was declared for four, including Edgar Ray Killen. Claiming she "could
never convict a preacher," a Meridian secretary had been the lone juror
defending the organizer of the lynch mob. For the next two months, jurors'
homes were guarded. Many received death threats. Crosses blazed in their
hometowns. But in late December 1967, Judge Cox sentenced Wayne Roberts and Sam Bowers to ten years, the rest to three to six. "They killed one
nigger, one Jew, and a white man," the judge declared. "I gave them all what
I thought they deserved."

Outside the courtroom, an onlooker called the verdict "the best thing
that's ever happened to justice in Mississippi." In Manhattan, Carolyn Goodman hailed the "landmark decision." Nathan Schwerner hoped Mississippi
would soon bring murder charges. Fannie Lee Chaney remarked, "They did
better than I thought they would." After two years of appeals, the convicted
went to federal prison in 1970. The case marked the first time since Reconstruction that any white had been convicted of civil rights violations in Mississippi, yet the state still had a generation to travel down the long arc of
justice.

Shortly after his Civil Rights Act passed during Freedom Summer, Lyndon Johnson had summoned Nicholas Katzenbach to the Oval Office. "I want
you to write me the goddamn best, toughest voting rights act that you can
devise," the president said. Throughout spring and summer of 1965, Congress debated the act. Several congressmen invoked the names Goodman,
Schwerner, and Chaney, urging passage "to insure that they did not die in
vain." Signed into law that August, the Voting Rights Act abolished literacy
tests, authorized federal supervision of elections in seven southern states,

and required those states to get federal approval for any changes in voting laws. By the end of 1965, 60 percent of Mississippi's blacks were registered voters. Getting their leaders into office, however, was another matter.

Jim Crow was always based on privilege and power as much as hatred. Mississippi could not hold back the tide of law, but it could enact a new round of legislative voodoo. Responding to the Voting Rights Act, the state legislature passed a dozen bills curbing black political power. City and county elections suddenly became "at-large," allowing white votes to dilute black votes. School superintendents became appointees. Getting on the ballot became tougher, requiring ten times as many signatures. And the Delta's "black belt," a single congressional district for as long as anyone could remember, was carved into three bloated districts aptly resembling pigs at a trough.

In 1967, 108 blacks ran for office in Mississippi. Just twenty-two were elected, most to low-level county positions. A lone black entered the all-white legislature. For the next few years, the Mississippi Freedom Democratic Party challenged every new voting law, and in 1969, theirs and similar challenges reached the Supreme Court. By a 7–2 margin, the court invalidated all efforts to dilute black votes. The Voting Rights Act, Chief Justice Earl Warren wrote, should have "the broadest possible scope." But as with the *Brown* ruling, compliance would take a decade or more. In 1972, two-thirds of all blacks in Mississippi could vote, yet just 2.7 percent of state officials were black.

Throughout the 1970s, while Mississippi's politicians patched their leaky "wall of Never," ordinary people changed the state. Not by fiat and no longer at a shotgun standoff, white and black slowly came together. Most found that, in hailing from that unique place called Mississippi, they had something in common. "After Freedom Summer," said Batesville publisher John Howell, a teenager in 1964, "we met black people who, when we got over our grudge at them for having the audacity to want to do things like vote and go to decent schools, were, almost without exception, such sweet and forgiving people." Bigotry did not disappear, but each act of kindness, each common concern helped southern hospitality melt age-old hostilities. No one can pinpoint a date or time, but at some point "boy" no longer referred to a black man. Titles of respect were bestowed on white *and* black. And sidewalks, though no wider than before, had room for black and white, sometimes side by side.

When Panola County pioneer Robert Miles ran for county supervisor, he lost a run-off but was stunned when a white man handed him fifty dollars to help take blacks to the polls. "I never dreamed I'd live to see such a day," Miles said. Medgar Evers's brother was elected mayor of Fayette, Mississippi, the state's first black mayor since Reconstruction. "Hands that picked cotton can now pick the mayor," Charles Evers said. A few years into his term, Evers got the backing of a former Klan leader. "I count Mayor Evers as a friend now and I have a lot of respect for the man," E. L. McDaniel said. "We realized it's not blacks against whites, but the little folks against the big shots." Ten years after the Ole Miss riots, students elected a black football player as "Colonel Rebel," the university's top sports honor. Another first came in 1977 when Unita Blackwell, Muriel Tillinghast's pupil, became Mississippi's first black female mayor. Blackwell remained mayor until 1997, eventually winning a MacArthur genius grant and addressing the 1984 Democratic National Convention.

As school busing battles tore apart Boston and other cities, Mississippi schools did their own dance around integration. "Seg academies" continued to flourish, but whites who could not gain admission and those unafraid of "mixing" sat beside blacks in public schools. Cafeterias remained self-segregated, but in locker rooms, in hallways, at pep rallies, black and white talked, sometimes fought, and discovered they could get along. Lyndon Johnson had predicted as much during Freedom Summer. "I can't make people integrate but maybe we can make them feel guilty if they don't," he had told an aide. "And once that happens, and they find out the jaws of hell don't open, and fire and brimstone doesn't flood down on them, then maybe they'll see just how they have been taken advantage of."

Late in 1979, the Mississippi legislature finally obeyed the U.S. Supreme Court. The Delta again became one congressional district. Hundreds of blacks were elected as mayors, city councilmen, and state legislators. In 1986, Mike Espy became Mississippi's first black congressman since Reconstruction, and the following year, a black woman was crowned Miss Mississippi. Throughout the 1990s, black political power steadily grew, giving Mississippi more black elected officials than any other state. At the time of this writing, 28 percent of the legislature is black, and the list of cities run by black mayors reads like a tour of Freedom Summer: McComb, Jackson, Hattiesburg, Itta Bena, Greenville, Greenwood, Holly Springs, Ruleville, Drew. . . . In 2009, even Philadelphia, Mississippi, elected a black mayor. Today, the Mississippi Delta still holds America's deepest pockets of poverty. Black income there remains just over half that of local whites, and in Greenwood or Greenville, as in towns throughout Mississippi, railroad tracks still demarcate stark differences in housing, education, and living standards. Yet in any town from Biloxi north to the Tennessee border, one can enter a café and see whites and blacks talking in ways one rarely sees farther north. And no one taken into custody has to fear the sheriff, his deputies, or the terror the night used to bring. But is Mississippi's racial progress more than skin-deep?

"The Promised Land is still far off," Hodding Carter III observed. "Black folks are still on the outside, looking in when it comes to jobs, equal education, housing, etc. But here, sadly enough, that does not much distinguish Mississippi from the rest of the country. What did distinguish us—racism red of fang and claw, in the saddle and riding hard—no longer prevails. What is in the hearts of individuals is one thing; how they now find they must operate in public is another. We are talking about fundamental change, which has left the state still far from the mountaintop, but it has been climbing for some time. It may go sideways from time to time, but it isn't going back."

Poet Margaret Walker Alexander agreed: "I believe that despite the terrible racist image Mississippi has had in the past, despite her historic reputation for political demagoguery, despite racial violence and especially lynching, despite all the statistics about being on the bottom, Mississippi, and especially urban Mississippi, offers a better life for most black people than any other state in which I have lived or visited."

In just a generation, Mississippi had progressed so far that its children were shocked by stories from the recent past. In 1984, when a former activist told kids about having to duck down in integrated cars, the kids gasped. "Not in Mississippi!" some said. But as Mississippi shed its past, would anyone dare to dredge up the horrors of Freedom Summer?

After the savage season, volunteers had gone separate ways—careening through the 1960s, then settling into the rest of their lives. Tenth and twentieth anniversaries of Freedom Summer passed but no one had the energy to mend a broken circle of trust. In 1989, however, feelers went out, and dozens of volunteers came to the first full reunion. Meeting in Philadelphia, they visited the rebuilt Mt. Zion Church and heard Mississippi's attorney general formally apologize to the families of Goodman, Schwerner, and Chaney. It was a short reunion, but the healing had begun. Five years later, nearly four hundred volunteers descended on Mississippi and no one spoke of an invasion.

At the airport in Jackson, a banner read "Welcome Homecoming 1964–1994." On this thirtieth anniversary, most veterans were returning to Mississippi for the first time. After comparing lives, sharing photos of children and grandchildren, crossing hands for tearful renditions of Freedom Songs, volunteers boarded buses. Back at their old sites, few could believe this was, in fact, Mississippi. The sight of black cops startled them. Holly Springs' black mayor gave volunteers the key to the city. Freedom School teachers met former students, learning of their college degrees and political offices. Beneath the surface, however, bigotry still seethed. Visiting James Chaney's grave, volunteers found it vandalized. Ben Chaney, a civil rights activist, told them, "There has not been meaningful change in Mississippi." Many agreed; others took their doubts deep into communities where they had once lived. The poverty was still painful, but reunions with white-haired hosts soothed spirits. Yet even though Mississippi had recently convicted Medgar Evers's assassin, many "ghosts of Mississippi" remained.

It took Fran O'Brien twenty-five years to exorcise the demons of that single summer night. In June 1965, still repressing the Klan beating, finding memories of Mississippi "rosier and rosier," she had returned to Vicksburg. She found her old Community Center in rubble and her project running on a shoestring. Fran hoped to teach former students, but she had "stepped into a hornet's nest." The statewide power struggle over child care sent her from COFO to Head Start and back again. After four weeks, she went home to southern California. That fall, she entered grad school and, in 1967, began teaching in California's central valley.

During her first spring in the classroom, Martin Luther King was killed. Overhearing kids say, "It's a good thing they got that Communist," Fran decided to speak to them. "I told them that Martin Luther King was not a Communist and I knew because I had met him." She spoke about the civil rights movement as a veteran. She spoke as she would continue to speak to children all her life. But decades would pass before she could speak about *all* of what happened that summer.

As the terror buried itself deeper, any talk of civil rights gave Fran nightmares. When she watched slaves flogged during the TV miniseries *Roots*, she woke up screaming. But in 1989, after attending the first Freedom Summer reunion, she sat down to write and the horror came pouring out. "It had been a rather quiet summer in Vicksburg . . ." Writing about the beating allowed Fran to face down fear and humiliation, but after a lifetime of empathy, she could not bring herself to blame the Klan. "One might as well hold a skunk morally accountable for spraying or a rattlesnake for striking," she wrote. Fran's "Journey into Light" was later published in an anthology of writings about Freedom Summer.

Though she worked her entire life with children, Fran never married—"I never really had the time"—nor had children of her own. Before retiring, she taught for thirty-four years, usually in classrooms for physically or mentally handicapped kids. In her students' struggle for acceptance, she found parallels to the civil rights movement. Over the years, she nurtured a devout Christian faith that she cannot imagine living without. This quiet, gentle woman lives alone in a small house on a hillside near Bakersfield, California. None of her neighbors suspects she was once part of the summer that changed even their own attitudes about race and freedom.

In his final nine months in Indianola, Fred Winn faced an explosive violence that escalated all winter and into the spring. Arrested five times, hounded by his draft board, targeted by local whites, Fred somehow survived, but relentless pressure led to drastic moves. In February 1965, suddenly classified 1-A and in no mood to fight for the country whose racism he was confronting, he took a female coworker to Greenville and married her. The wedding was a joke, with the "flowers" just grass yanked from outside the church, and a cold kiss. "Yes, I know it sounds a bit wild," he wrote his father. "It was the only thing I could do to get out." The marriage would be annulled later that year, but the wedding—and Fred's arrest record—kept the draft at arm's length. Nothing, however, could tamp down Indianola's surging violence.

In March 1965, a Molotov cocktail burned the Freedom School to the ground. Several who had been living in the school crammed into Irene Magruder's house, forcing Fred to sleep in her living room. All continued working on a new voting drive. Come April, the drive became a rush when Sunflower County was slapped with a federal injunction and three hundred blacks were registered. Many stood outside the courthouse, hugging and crying. "I was so glad I wanted to holler 'Freedom,'" one old woman said. The payback came swiftly.

On May 1, Fred fell asleep on Irene Magruder's couch. At 2:30 a.m., a woman came out of the kitchen screaming "Fire!" In the rush of smoke and panic, Fred grabbed a fire extinguisher but it was like a squirt gun against the flames. He helped Mrs. Magruder stagger from her burning home, then remembered what he had left inside. Racing into the blazing building, he grabbed the project's account books and his father's Bible. By the time he reached the lawn again, the house was engulfed. Firemen stood by, watching. Word soon came from down the street. "They got Giles!" Giles Penny Saver, a store frequented by volunteers, was also burning. Fred grabbed a bicycle and rode to find Oscar Giles spraying the flames with a hose. From off in the distance, he saw another orange glow, and another. Fred rode to visit each fire, then returned to the Freedom House to alert Fannie Lou Hamer.

With his host home and school in ashes, Fred could no longer joke about Mississippi mud between his toes. Relations in the SNCC office were also smoldering, and Fred had thrown his own match by falling for another black girl. Janell was seventeen years old but told Fred she was eighteen. A few days after the fires, the bespectacled, mustachioed carpenter and his girlfriend began talking about leaving. They could get an apartment in San Francisco. They could get jobs, go to school, walk down the street holding hands, and no one would care. "Janell and I are coming home," Fred wrote his father. "Yes, I know we had planned to stay until July, but I am tired. You might recall what battle fatigue was like during the war." A week later, the couple took a bus to Memphis and a train to San Francisco.

Fred and Janell hoped to continue working for civil rights, but when they volunteered at a San Francisco agency, five black men listened to Fred's tales from Freedom Summer, then said, "We don't need you." Fred was devastated. A fixture in Indianola's black community, he now found himself an invader in his own city, isolated by rising black separatism. It was not long before blacks on his street would talk to Janell but not to him. Sensing the drift, he found work as a longshoreman. Janell got a job with the Economic Opportunity Commission. They moved to the Haight-Ashbury district but, separated by background and skin color, Janell "fell in with another crowd." Feeling rejected not just by a woman but by the race he had befriended, Fred was crushed. "The fact that I went into dope and became a hippie doesn't surprise me," he remembered.

After studying education at San Francisco State, Fred found teaching jobs scarce, so he "took some time to fuck off." He followed the culture and cannabis trail, bumming around Europe and Morocco, Colombia and Ecuador. When he finally returned to San Francisco, he took up the trade he had practiced in Mississippi—plumbing. He dropped "Fred" and began using his middle name, "Bright." After serving his apprenticeship, Bright Winn set up his own business and has been a highly articulate plumber ever since. Twice married and twice divorced, a father of two, he still speaks regularly with the half sister whose birth split his family and sent him to Mississippi. His work during Freedom Summer cemented his relationship with the father he had barely known before 1964. And more than forty years after signing his letters "We Shall Overcome," Bright Winn remains devoted to civil rights. "Someone asked me if I'm still active in the movement," he remembered. "I said, 'I hire people of color. I raised my children with certain strong beliefs about integration. I live the movement.'"

Muriel Tillinghast left Mississippi in 1965 but stayed with SNCC, working in Atlanta. In the fall of 1967, she returned to Howard University, doing grad studies in Mexican and Chinese history, but after Mississippi, she found Howard "too containing." She moved on to Manhattan, working for SNCC and in various social programs. For years, she organized in Appalachia, eventually serving there as a presidential appointee under Jimmy Carter. Returning to Manhattan, she continued to apply the lessons of Mississippi throughout her life. "I was born with a fighting nature," she says. "Even when I try not to be a fighter, the fight comes out. But I try to be earnest and honest. I've worked in prisons, Head Start, for immigrants, health rights— pretty much of everything." In 1996, Muriel turned to politics, running as Ralph Nader's vice-presidential candidate for the Green Party in New York. In 2004, she tapped her religious roots, becoming the manager of the Bethlehem Lutheran Church in Brooklyn. She currently lives in Brooklyn with two cats, a dog, and a turtle. Raising two daughters, she has spoken of Mississippi whenever possible. "It was like going to war," she remembered. "A lot of veterans will tell you they don't discuss war stories. But sometimes you have to—to let your children know, 'That's why we don't do this in this family.' Because of the way things were in Mississippi."

During Chris Williams's final months in Mississippi, the luck that got him through the summer ran out. In November, while canvassing a Panola County plantation, he was surrounded by raging whites threatening to throw him in the Tallahatchie River. The men settled for having Chris arrested. After two days in jail, he went right back to work. Throughout that fall and winter, Chris drove muddy backroads, spoke in churches, called registration meetings, and helped organize a co-op that earned farmers higher prices for okra. And in his spare time, he fell in love.

Two years older than Chris, Penny Patch had left Swarthmore College to work in Georgia, the first white female SNCC in the Deep South. She had come to Mississippi in January 1964 to run COFO's book drive. In September, she moved to Batesville, where she began working on the farm co-op and discussing birth control with black women eager to avoid having child after child after child. Chris was not immediately smitten by the petite, short-haired brunette. He and Penny spent the fall in mutual avoidance, but by December, they noticed each other noticing each other and by the new year, they were inseparable. Walking together to host homes, returning together in the morning, they were soon known to locals as "Chrisnpenny." It wasn't long before they were talking about leaving Mississippi . . . someday . . . together. But neither felt like going home—to Massachusetts or New Jersey. Where would they go? And when? Mississippi answered the latter question for them.

One day in March, Chris and Penny sat in a car outside the courthouse in Batesville. The town's first sit-in had whites in an uproar. Pickups circled the town square, their drivers waving guns, ax handles, and baseball bats. Suddenly several people spotted the clean-cut white couple. As they rushed the car, Penny frantically locked the doors. A snarling, screaming mob began rocking the old Pontiac. This was no college stunt, Chris realized. These people wanted to flip the car and drag them out. He gunned the engine but the car was trapped between pickups. The rocking continued, lifting the hood higher and higher. Finally, the pickup in front pulled away and Chris hit the accelerator.

A few days later, Chris was sitting downtown when four men bolted from a pickup. He barely had time to roll into a ball before they began kicking him. Robert Miles decked one man with a haymaker punch, sending the attackers fleeing, leaving Chris with a three-inch gash in his forehead. The next evening, Chris and Penny were in Miles's living room, watching TV, breathing again. Suddenly the front window shattered. Chris shoved Penny to the floor as buckshot lodged in the wall. Chris was soon taking his turn on the Mileses' all-night vigil, holding a rifle.

The mob, the beating, the shooting, left Chris more shaken than hurt, but Mississippi was no longer an "adventure." "I felt I'd given it a good shot," he remembered. "I had been involved in lot of different parts of it, I'd met extraordinary people, and maybe this was as far as it went." Late that summer, Chris and Penny got a ride in a VW bus taking them out of Mississippi, but they did not head north. This was a different America, seemingly a different decade, and they wanted to be at the heart of it. By the fall of 1965, they were living in Berkeley. Penny, feeling "ragged and lost," certain her years in the civil rights movement had come to nothing, took classes while Chris worked as a carpenter. He later studied agriculture at UC Davis and worked with César Chávez and the United Farmworkers of America. But before he could finish a degree, he and Penny heard the sixties' next call.

In the spring of 1967, the couple moved "back to the land." In Vermont's Northeast Kingdom, where they had purchased one hundred acres, Chris, Penny, and other civil rights veterans built a house, planted gardens, and lived far removed from the America they had given up on. But white-out winters made close quarters seem even closer. Although Chris and Penny married and had a son, the commitments that had brought them together in Mississippi could not keep them together. They split up in 1970, setting Chris adrift again. To Jamaica. To Manhattan. To the edge of despair. Wherever he went, he kept designing, building, and in 1974, he began studying architecture at the Pratt Institute in Brooklyn.

Married again and with two kids, Chris spent the 1980s as an architect in Manhattan. Then in 1989, he became director of architectural services at Williams College in western Massachusetts. Twenty-five years after hitchhiking south, he had come home. And there he remains. Every now and then, as he looks toward retirement, Chris finds himself checking on the Internet for houses in Panola County. He wonders what it would be like to live there—"Mississippi without fear"—if only for a few years. Mississippi is a part of him in ways he could never have expected when he left high school to spend a summer there. "Other people went to Vietnam and that impacted their lives," he said, "but Mississippi was the thing in my life that has resonated down through the years. I'm very clear that the person who got the most out of it was me. I feel grateful every day to have been part of it."

Individual cameos vary, but taken as a group, Freedom Summer volunteers appear, as they did on arrival in Ohio, as a group portrait of American idealism. Almost without exception, the lives they led after their Mississippi summer have been as principled as the season itself. Whether they steered the sixties or were steered by them, a majority remained involved in social causes. Freedom School teachers continued to teach—many in college. Dozens of volunteers, having seen Jim Crow justice, became attorneys fighting for the poor. Others became full-time activists, running nonprofit agencies. And several became writers, including feminist Susan Brownmiller, *Mother*

Jones cofounder Adam Hochschild, memoirist Sally Belfrage, and *Village Voice* reporter Paul Cowan and his brother Geoff.

As with any group, there were fringes, some dangerous. Dennis Sweeney, having suffered a concussion and frequent arrests in McComb, descended into paranoid schizophrenia. Voices in his head caused Sweeney to gouge dental crowns from his teeth. But the voices did not cease. On a March day in 1980, Sweeney took a gun and entered the Manhattan office of Allard Lowenstein, the "Pied Piper" who had brought Sweeney and other volunteers to the 1963 Freedom Election. Sweeney emptied his gun, killing his former mentor. Found not guilty for reasons of insanity, Sweeney was confined to a mental hospital. Twenty years after the murder, psychiatrists, noting his recovery, released him from all care.

During the Reagan era, sociologist Doug McAdam found ex-volunteers increasingly restless. Many remained searchers, moving from job to job or relationship to relationship, looking for what one called "the ultimate Mississippi." McAdam also found volunteers, when compared to a national average, more likely to be loners, unmarried or divorced. Just a handful, having seen the stuff democracy is made of, had entered politics. Harold Ickes, son of a member of FDR's Brain Trust, went from Freedom Summer to law school and then into Democratic Party politics. Ickes later became President Bill Clinton's deputy chief of staff and ran Hillary Clinton's campaigns for Senate and the presidency. Barney Frank has been a Massachusetts congressman since 1980. Of Freedom Summer, he spoke for many volunteers: "I am prouder of being there than of anything else in my life." .

No less than those they recruited, the leaders of Freedom Summer were transformed by its hope and violence. A few months after the summer ended, Bob Moses began a painful withdrawal from Mississippi. Late in 1964, disdaining what James Forman called the "almost Jesus like aura that he and his name had acquired," Moses changed his surname to Parris, his mother's maiden name. The following spring, he and Dona moved to Birmingham, Alabama, where they worked with young black students. Soon Moses was in Washington, D.C., speaking out against the Vietnam War. In the fall of 1965, he briefly returned to Africa, where, appalled by American propaganda about the progress of blacks back home, he cut off all contact with whites. Drawn back to Mississippi, he lived again with Amzie Moore in the Delta, but Moore found his protégé bitter and withdrawn.

Although he had filed as a conscientious objector and proven his pacifism daily, Moses got his draft notice in 1966. With his marriage crumbling, his hopes shattered, Moses fled to Montreal, where he worked as a janitor, a night watchman, an airline cook. He also married a former SNCC field secretary. In 1968, Bob and Janet Moses moved to Tanzania, where they taught in a rural school and raised four children. They stayed eight years, returning only when President Jimmy Carter offered amnesty to draft evaders. Moses went back to Harvard to finish the doctorate he had been forced to abandon. Then one day, he visited his daughter's algebra class. Concerned that inner-city students were falling behind in math, he began devising ways to involve them in his favorite subject. With help from a MacArthur genius grant, Moses' lessons grew into the Algebra Project.

Moses has since turned the Algebra Project into a continuation of his life's work. He crafted a clever curriculum using subway trips to model number lines, and lemonade recipes to teach ratios. By 1990, he was traveling all over America, even back to Mississippi to work with teachers and organize parents too often dismissive of math. "Like working with sharecroppers demanding the right to vote, we're trying to get students demanding quality public education in algebra," he says. After several years of commuting from Massachusetts to Mississippi, Moses is currently an Eminent Scholar at Florida International University in Miami. In his seventies now, bearded and white-haired, Moses still speaks at math and civil rights conferences around the country. He remains an unforgettable presence to all who have known him. No living American has risked more or done more to make America a full democracy.

Wherever he speaks, Moses mentions Fannie Lou Hamer as an icon of empowerment, but the woman everyone called Mrs. Hamer did not share in the gains she helped Mississippi blacks achieve. Though she kept running for office and speaking out—even addressing the 1968 Democratic Convention—Hamer was soon marginalized by younger activists. She also suffered personal losses and failing health. In 1967, her daughter was injured in a car crash and, denied treatment in the Delta, died en route to a Memphis hospital. Still grieving, Hamer threw herself into child development programs and was quickly embroiled in their acrimonious politics. She worked on Martin Luther King's Poor People's Campaign and later started her own pig farm to help sharecroppers. But the blackjack beating she had taken in Winona, Mississippi, compounded by a lifetime of poor nutrition and stress, took its toll. Gradually confined to her home, she gave away her last few dollars and died in 1977, penniless. By then, however, she was more spirit than flesh. Her funeral drew a thousand people, including dignitaries from President Jimmy Carter's administration. Mourners sang "This Little Light of Mine." The Mississippi legislature, still overwhelmingly white, passed a unanimous resolution commending her. Today, anyone entering Ruleville sees the ornate sign reading "Home of Fannie Lou Hamer," but her grave-stone best sums up her strength. Beneath the sadly shortened lifespan—1917–1977—is her motto: "I'm sick and tired of being sick and tired."

Long after Freedom Summer had changed Mississippi, the rest of America refused to notice. Movies and TV rehashed stale stereotypes—the fat sheriff, bloodhounds and chain gangs, the rope and the shotgun. So when the Holly-wood film *Mississippi Burning* came out in 1988, dramatizing the Freedom Summer murders and investigation, it managed to offend everyone. Former volunteers and SNCCs were outraged to see FBI agents portrayed as heroes rather than the bystanders they had been before LBJ ordered them into the swamps. Blacks appeared powerless. And whites complained that the film showed them at their worst. When would America move beyond its stereo-types of Mississippi? Such a day would come only when Mississippi erased the darkest blot on its name.

On the twentieth anniversary of the Neshoba killings, Philadelphia's mayor observed, "To me, it was sort of like a plane crash. It was just a part of history that happened near Philadelphia, and there's nothing we could do to erase it." There was something Philadelphia could do, however, yet the wheels of justice refused to turn. The final redemption began only in 1998, when word leaked of what the Klan's Imperial Wizard, finally convicted of the Vernon Dahmer murder after four mistrials, had said about his most famous "elimination." "I was quite delighted to be convicted and have the main instigator of the entire affair walk out of the courtroom a free man," Sam Bowers said. The "main instigator" was "Preacher" Killen, and hearing of Bowers's boast, the families of Goodman, Schwerner, and Chaney called for the case to be reopened. Early in 1999, Mississippi's attorney general began investigating.

The investigation dragged on for five years. *Jackson Clarion-Ledger* reporter Jerry Mitchell dug up new witnesses who had heard Killen discuss the murders. Lawyers plowed through the FBI's 44,000-page file and the 1967 trial transcript. Meanwhile, key witnesses were dying. Cecil Price, said to be cooperating with the prosecution, fell from a cherry picker. Lawrence Rainey, who after his 1967 acquittal never worked in law enforcement again, died of throat cancer. Two others among the accused also passed away, leaving just eight still living. The most visible was "The Preacher." Fortunately for investigators, he had a big mouth.

"Had I done it," Killen said of the Neshoba murders, "I wouldn't have any regrets." Others reported hearing "The Preacher" preach the righteousness of the Klan's most notorious killing. "I'm not going to say they were wrong," Killen said in 2004. "I believe in self-defense." That September, the Philadelphia Coalition, an interracial group formed to lobby for further prosecutions, invited Carolyn Goodman and brothers of Michael Schwerner and James Chaney to meet with townspeople. In an emotional encounter, clergymen, high school students, and businessmen told of growing up under the stigma of 1964 and urged Mississippi's new attorney general to file murder charges. The following January, police arrested Killen in his home.

On June 12, 2005, Philadelphia, Mississippi, awoke to find dozens of cable news trucks surrounding its courthouse. Townspeople were divided on the impending trial. "It was what I'd been wanting and what I'd been praying here for years," said Deborah Ray Posey, a member of the Philadelphia Coalition. But another resident complained, "The media has profited for four decades by smearing Neshoba County and Mississippi. I ask, 'When is enough enough?'" Despite misgivings, the trial spread word that Mississippi had long since ceased to be a closed society. Civil rights historical markers were—and still are—occasionally vandalized, and some older whites spoke of Freedom Summer as that time when "Communists invaded the state of Mississippi," yet reporters noted blacks and whites joking together, working together, sometimes even marrying. When the trial began, Philadelphia was again on front pages across America and Europe, but the little town no longer had anything to hide.

Just after 9:00 a.m., Edgar Ray Killen approached the courtroom in his wheelchair. Bald, bespectacled, disabled by a recent logging accident, he breathed through an oxygen tube. Before the trial reached its second day, he was hospitalized for shortness of breath, yet he remained "as strong for segregation as I ever was." Simmering in his own bile, the bitter old man showed no emotion as he was wheeled to the defense table. In the gallery behind him sat Rita Schwerner Bender, Carolyn Goodman, and Ben and Fannie Lee Chaney. Forty-one years they had waited.

Mickey Schwerner's widow had remarried, raised a family, and begun practicing law in Seattle, specializing in Restorative Justice, the movement uniting victims with their assailants to foster personal reconciliation. Andrew Goodman's ninety-year-old mother still lived in the Upper West Side apartment decorated with photos of her lost son. After earning a doctorate in psychology, Carolyn Goodman had developed programs for families in psychiatric crisis. One day, she had opened the door of her apartment to find a man, speaking in a southern accent, asking forgiveness for his role in her son's murder. "If you want my forgiveness," she said, "work in your community and help other people. That way lies forgiveness." The man left in silence.

Beside Goodman sat "J. E.'s" kid brother. Ben Chaney had grown into a tireless civil rights advocate, but only after surrendering to rage over his brother's murder. Constantly threatened in Mississippi, the Chaneys had moved to New York in 1965, settling in with the help of the Goodmans and Schwerners. Ben seemed to be doing well at a private school, but shortly before his eighteenth birthday, he and friends headed south with a plot. Chaney was not even present at a Florida shootout that killed four whites, but he was sentenced to life in prison. After serving thirteen years, he was paroled with the help of former attorney general Ramsey Clark, who hired him as a law clerk. Chaney has held the same job ever since, doing civil rights work on the side. As head of the James Earl Chaney Foundation, Ben led the Freedom Summer 2004 Ride for Justice, a bus tour visiting civil rights sites, registering voters, and lobbying Mississippi to prosecute his brother's killers. Fannie Lee Chaney worked as a maid in a nursing home before retiring. Learning of the impending trial, the eighty-two-year-old woman said only, "Mighty long time." Now the time had arrived.

The past permeated the courtroom. One of Killen's attorneys had defended Sheriff Rainey in 1967. The judge had first met Killen as a boy presiding over his parents' funerals. Yet the present also held its ground. Many in the audience had not yet been born by 1964. The district attorney, a Philadelphia first-grader that year, just vaguely recalled the commotion. He had hoped to bring charges against all living members of the Neshoba klavern, but the grand jury had indicted only Killen. Now, as a jury of nine whites and three blacks looked on, he called the first witness—Rita.

While reporters typed on laptops, the freckled woman with close-cropped gray hair told of coming to Mississippi with her husband in 1964. Rita remembered bidding good-bye to Mickey in Ohio and never seeing him again. She remained composed until she recalled first hearing that the blue station wagon had been found, gutted and burned. That was when "it really hit me for the first time that they were dead." Fannie Lou Hamer had been with her. "She just wrapped her arms around me and the two of us had our faces together and our tears were mingling with each other and we cried." Some in the gallery wept. Later, a tearful Carolyn Goodman read the court her son's postcard from Meridian—"This is a wonderful town, and the weather is fine. I wish you were here. . . ."

In between the grieving women, most evidence came from the dead— testimony read from witnesses long deceased. From the 1967 trial transcript, jurors heard of Killen telling his klavern about the "elimination" order, Killen gathering Klansmen, Killen siccing the men on their prey. Living witnesses added more details. A former Meridian cop recalled Killen telling him all about the murders. A convict in a prison jumpsuit recalled his grandfather asking Killen "if he had anything to do with those boys being killed, and he said 'yes,' and he was proud of it." After three days, Fannie Lee Chaney, walking with a cane to the witness box, concluded the prosecution's case. She remembered making breakfast that Sunday for the trio. Young Ben had cried as his brother prepared to leave. Her oldest son had promised his brother to take him out when he came back, but "J. E. never come back."

Defense attorneys called on the alibi Killen had used in 1967. He had been at a funeral home that night, mourning for "old Uncle Alex Rich." But Rich's family claimed he was not related to Killen, and another witness said Killen had merely entered the funeral home and looked around. "I thought it was unusual because he wasn't that close to the family." Summing up, the defense called the trial "nothing but stirring a pot of hate for profit." But Mississippi's attorney general compared the Klan to terrorists in Iraq, then urged the jury, "Do your duty. Honor Mississippi. Honor Neshoba County."

Jurors deliberated for an afternoon before telling the judge they were deadlocked. The judge ordered them to resume deliberation the next day— June 21. At 11:30 a.m., they filed back into the courtroom. Killen sat in a dark sport coat, his head shaking slightly as the verdict was read. On each of three counts, the jury found him guilty of manslaughter. Families hugged and fought back tears. Speaking for his mother, Ben Chaney said, "She believes the life of her son has value." Rita Schwerner Bender was disgusted that the charge had been reduced to manslaughter but thanked the people of Neshoba County for bringing about this "day of great importance." Killen was sentenced to sixty years. Released on bail pending appeal and his own complaints of poor health, he was soon seen driving around Neshoba County, flaunting his freedom. In August, an angry judge ordered him back to jail, where he remains.

Each June 21, as they have every Freedom Summer anniversary since 1965, dozens come to Neshoba County to remember. Setting out in a caravan, they visit James Chaney's grave, now braced upright to deter vandals. Then, driving along Route 19, recently renamed Chaney, Goodman, and Schwerner Memorial Highway, they turn onto Rock Cut Road and enter its eerie, haunted woods. At the exact site of the three murders, they set stones on the sacred ground. And they ask "Why only Killen?" Five men convicted of civil rights violations in 1967 are still living. In 1969 a federal appeals court found these men complicit "in a calculated, cold-blooded and merciless plot to murder the three men," so why not try them for murder? Further prosecution, however, remains elusive. In 2008, the federal Emmett Till Unsolved Civil Rights Crime Act was passed to fund investigations into such "cold cases." Yet Jerry Mitchell thinks more than money will be needed. The *Clarion-Ledger* reporter sees enough evidence for another "Mississippi Burning" trial, but wonders whether the state has the will. "Other cold cases are not very viable," Mitchell said. "This one, on the other hand, you've got 40,000 pages of documents, living witnesses, trial transcripts—the real basis of a case. It should be investigated again, and I don't know why it hasn't been."

The legacy of Freedom Summer remains embattled. Was it a catalyst for change or an unnecessary provocation that instilled new venom in a dying culture? Interviewed in the mid-1980s, Citizens' Council president William Simmons remained defiant. "That was the time of the hippies just coming in," he said, missing the date by three years. "Many had on hippie uniforms and conducted themselves in hippie ways. . . . The arrogance that they showed in wanting to reform a whole state in the way they thought it should be created resentment." SNCC staffer Charlie Cobb concedes that the summer "changed Mississippi forever," but believes the changes were inevitable. "You were going to get these federal laws—the Civil Rights Bill in '64, and the Voting Rights Act in '65. And eventually you were going to get some slowing of the violence." Given the loss of momentum among locals, Cobb concluded, "It would have been better to go the other way."

But many others cannot praise Freedom Summer highly enough. Aaron Henry called it "the greatest sociological experiment the nation has ever pulled off." The summer changed Mississippi and "the minds of blacks . . . [who] began to look upon themselves as somebody." Fannie Lou Hamer all but sanctified the "Christ-like" volunteers. "They, were the best friends we ever met," she said. " . . . We had wondered if there was anybody human enough to see us as human beings instead of animals." And Georgia congressman John Lewis, interviewed during the 2008 presidential campaign, saw a longer legacy. "Freedom Summer injected a new spirit into the very vein of life in Mississippi and the country," the former SNCC chair said. "It literally brought the country to Mississippi. People were able to see the horror and evil of blatant racial discrimination. If it hadn't been for the veterans of Freedom Summer, there would be no Barack Obama."

Tuesday, January 20, 2009, was clear and chilly in Mississippi. Light snow fell in Oxford. Even the Gulf Coast awoke to freezing temperatures. For most of the morning, Mississippians went about their business. In small diners near courthouse squares, waitresses served biscuits and gravy, eggs and grits. Light trucks rolled off the assembly line at the Nissan factory outside Canton. Cars zipped along Interstate 55—north toward Memphis, south toward the Louisiana line. But then toward 11:00 a.m., time seemed to stop as Mississippi bore witness to Freedom Summer's final fruit.

Barack Obama handily won Mississippi's Democratic primary, but come November, he did not win the state that has voted Republican in all but one election (Jimmy Carter's) since 1964. Yet throughout the 2008 campaign, Mississippi's reconciliation was on display. The *Jackson Clarion-Ledger* and other papers endorsed Obama. On election day, a white plantation owner in Panola County, though not an Obama supporter, loaded black workers in his pickup and drove them to the polls. Voter turnout hit record highs, and, as in the rest of America, voting for a black presidential candidate brought tears and celebration. But when the votes were tallied, some had a hard time getting used to the idea of a black family in the White House.

The day after the election, racial tension flared at a high school in Columbus, Mississippi. A heated argument over Obama scared some teens into texting their parents, who came to take them home. Elsewhere in Mississippi, some whites grew tired of hearing about the "first black president." "Why can't it be that he's the next president?" one woman asked. "If he can get America back to where it should be, it doesn't matter what color he is." And near Jackson, a school bus driver ordered two boys to stop talking about Obama. They refused. "This is history, woman," one said to the driver, who threw both kids off the bus. District officials promised to discipline the driver. By Inauguration Day, however, Mississippi seemed more amazed than concerned by the change. "I voted for Obama," said seventy-eight-year-old James "Little Man" Presley, still working the cotton fields in Panola County. "There's a heap of pride in voting for a black man."

As the new president put his hand on the Lincoln Bible, Mississippi held its breath. In classrooms that had excluded their ancestors, in courthouses where registration had been a cruel farce, in cafés they had dared not even enter, blacks watched alongside whites. And when President Obama finished his oath, cheers erupted. In Hattiesburg, Vernon Dahmer's widow wept. "Oh, if he'd just been able to see it, Lord," Ellie Dahmer said. "I hope he can see this day." At a Greenville café where Obama had stopped during his primary campaign, the elderly owner beamed. "It's the most wonderful day of my life," Demetrius Buck said. And in Ruleville, Fannie Lou Hamer's searching question from 1964 seemed to echo down through the decades. Was this *finally* America?

Amid many celebrations in the nation's capital, one group had an especially poignant reunion. Two dozen SNCC veterans gathered in Washington, D.C., to share stories of old times, old battles. Yet the vast majority of Freedom Summer volunteers were nowhere near the limelight on Inauguration Day. Bob Moses spoke on the cable program *Democracy Now*, recapping the 1964 Freedom Democrat challenge "where the stage was set that allowed this to happen." But the mainstream media remained fixated on Rosa Parks and Martin Luther King. Meanwhile in New Bedford, Massachusetts, and Mendocino, California; in Englewood, New Jersey, and Lewistown, Montana; in Omaha and Memphis, Indianapolis and Atlanta, some seven hundred Americans no one had ever heard of watched as the living embodiment of the hope that sent them to Mississippi stepped to the podium.

My fellow citizens:

I stand here today humbled by the task before us, grateful for the trust you have bestowed, mindful of the sacrifices borne by our ancestors. . . .

An hour before the inauguration, Chris Williams addressed his colleagues at Williams College. Few had any idea that the gregarious architect had once been a civil rights worker. Chris recapped his tenure as a teenager in Mississippi, told of how three men had been murdered on his first day there, how he had gone to Atlantic City, how America had changed since. Then he went to watch.

. . . They saw America as bigger than the sum of our individual ambitions; greater than all the differences of birth or wealth or faction . . .

For Fran O'Brien, Inauguration Day was "the closest thing to a perfect day one can reasonably expect in this world." Not having a TV, she listened to the ceremony on the radio, alone in her home. After it was over, she went to a diner and watched clips on TV. She did not plan to tell anyone about Freedom Summer, but a black waitress noticed the white-haired woman's tears. So Fran told Ebony about teaching in Vicksburg, befriending Mrs. Garrett, enjoying the children. She spoke of fear and hope, but not of horror. The waitress asked many questions and Fran answered patiently. She then went to an art museum, but many of the paintings were blurred.

. . . What the cynics fail to understand is that the ground has shifted beneath them—that the stale political arguments that have consumed us for so long no longer apply . . .

Bright Winn took time out from his plumbing business to watch in his San Francisco home. He looked in vain for his son in the crowd on the Mall, then got a call from him, with cheering in the background. Muriel Tillinghast, though having worked tirelessly for Obama, declined to celebrate in Washington, D.C. Wary of crowds in her native city, she watched the inauguration alone with her cats and turtle in her church in Brooklyn.

. . . and why a man whose father less than sixty years ago might not have been served at a local restaurant can now stand before you to take a most sacred oath. So let us mark this day with remembrance, of who we are and how far we have traveled. . . .

During the speech, many who had been in Mississippi thought about the martyrs—not just Goodman, Schwerner, and Chaney, but Herbert Lee and Emmett Till and Medgar Evers and more than a dozen others killed in Mississippi in the name of civil rights. And later that afternoon, some Freedom Summer veterans called each other for the first time in a decade. "It took forty-five years," one said, "but we helped make this day." Looking back, they took measure of the summer so long ago. They had not been heroes— that honorific was still reserved for the locals. Nor were they crusaders— many had gone before them. The volunteers had merely gone to Mississippi when few others dared to go. As witnesses, as spotlights, they had lent their youthful energy to the struggles of the downtrodden and neglected. Living in shacks, singing in mass meetings, surviving sticky summer nights and inching afternoons, they had endured Mississippi's hardships. Yet the men and women of Freedom Summer had done more than endure. Echoing William Faulkner's famous dictum, they had prevailed. They had transcended the hatred, spread the hope, lifted and revived the trampled dream of democracy. Forty-five years after Freedom Summer, their own personal past, filtered through the historic inauguration of a black president, added up to a "freedom high" that lasted for days. And then time went back to work, marching on into an America most dared not imagine they would live to see.

"At the end of it all, I guess what really caught me by surprise is that my fellow citizens voted for Obama in such large numbers, giving him a resounding victory," Chris Williams said. "I didn't think we had reached that place yet. How can we not be optimistic?"

Acknowledgments

Because Freedom Summer involved more than one thousand people, each with stories to tell, I am indebted to those who shared their stories, either with me or in letters, journals, diaries, and other first-person sources. Of the fifty-two people I interviewed, some were telling their stories for the first time, and I thank them for their bravery and candor. Many more, including Bob Moses, Hollis Watkins, and other SNCC veterans, graciously took time out from their ongoing activism to share, once again, oft-told stories of that singular summer.

Four names in particular stand out from my list. To Chris Williams, Muriel Tillinghast, Fran O'Brien, and Fred Bright Winn, I offer my deepest thanks. Each put up with two long interviews followed by innumerable nit-picking questions that surfaced from out of nowhere on their e-mail queues. And each responded with more thought and detail than I had any right to expect. Along with my admiration for their courage in going to Mississippi, each has my thanks for looking back over so many years to dredge up memories both joyous and painful.

To my mother's best friend, dedicated teacher Georgie Cooper, I owe heartfelt thanks for getting me started with a detailed reading list from her native Mississippi. Sadly, Georgie passed away before I could show her all she had taught me. I will never forget her enthusiasm, her accent, or her passion for life and literature.

Thanks also to Jan Hillegas, a Freedom Summer volunteer who has lived in Mississippi since 1964. Jan opened her sizable archive of COFO documents, notably the complete WATS line reports that gave me access to hourly events throughout the summer. Jan's work to preserve COFO records continues, including the revival of the long-abandoned COFO headquarters on Lynch Street, which will soon open as an educational center.

Though I have never met her, I offer special thanks to Elizabeth Martinez, who began compiling volunteers' letters moments after Freedom Summer ended. Her book, *Letters from Mississippi,* was of invaluable help. It is also the most moving compilation of historical letters I have seen on any subject. Thanks also to ex-volunteer Jim Kates, whose Zephyr Press rereleased *Letters from Mississippi*, and who offered advice early in my research.

Thanks to my patient and wise editor at Viking, Wendy Wolf, for allowing me to give my own touch to another American story. And to my agent, Jeff Kleinman, for his continued help in negotiating the Manuscript Jungle. Two friends and former civil rights activists—Bob Winston and Sue Thrasher—provided encouragement along the way. Bob also offered kind comments on the initial draft. And as always, I owe more than I can express to my wife, Julie, and our two children, for allowing me to head south three times in a single year, and for trying the grits I brought back.

Finally, to the people of Mississippi who spoke freely with me during my visits there, I owe more than gratitude. Freedom Summer was not their beloved state's finest hour, but Mississippians continue to treat it with remarkable frankness. Their honesty and hospitality made each trip to Mississippi a genuine pleasure. In particular, thanks to Dr. Stacy White for sharing stories of her great-aunt, Irene Magruder, for giving me a tour of Freedom Summer sites in Indianola, and for inviting me back for the Sunflower County Civil Rights Reunion. Thanks to Robert Miles Jr. for inviting me into the Batesville home of his courageous father, and to Neil White for insights and hospitality over coffee in Oxford. Former sheriff Charles W. Capps Jr., retired after a long career in the state legislature, demonstrated true Mississippi hospitality when he agreed to be interviewed on an hour's notice about a time he would probably rather forget. And thanks to Gary Brooks, who came all the way from New Orleans to show me around his hometown of McComb. These memories, and not the scars of the Jim Crow system, are the Mississippi I know, convincing me that more Americans should go to the Magnolia State. It's a wonderful place, to which I hope to return again and again.

Notes

Book One

1 *"Niggers down here don't need to vote":* Eric Burner, *And Gently He Shall Lead Them: Robert Parris Moses and Civil Rights in Mississippi* (New York: New York University Press, 1994), p. 118.

2 *"I'm not going to talk to you":* Charles Payne, *I've Got the Light of Freedom: The Organizing Tradition and the Mississippi Freedom Struggle* (Berkeley and Los Angeles: University of California Press, 1995), p. 122.

2 *"I'm not playing with you this morning!":* Taylor Branch, *Parting the Waters: America in the King Years, 1954–1963* (New York: Simon and Schuster, 1988), p. 511

Prologue

6 *"Paul Stood Tall Last Fall".* New York Times, July 5, 1964.

6 *"Niggers, Alligators, Apes, Coons, and Possums":* "Mississippi: Battle of the Kennedys," *Newsweek*, August 19, 1963, p. 24.

6 *"white folks' business":* John Dittmer, *Local People: The Struggle for Civil Rights in Mississippi* (Urbana: University of Illinois Press, 1994), p. 205.

7 *"goddamned NAACP Communist trouble makers":* Ivanhoe Donaldson, "Southern Diaries," in *Mississippi Freedom Summer*, ed. John F. McClymer (Belmont, Calif.: Wadsworth/Thomson Learning, 2004), p. 90.

7 *"not only have a right but a duty":* Jackson Clarion-Ledger, June 12, 2005.

7 *"too beautiful to burn":* Port Gibson Heritage Trust Web site, http://www .portgibsonheritagetrust.org/port_gibson.

8 *"the War for Southern Independence":* Dittmer, *Local People*, p. 112.

8 *"It's a rotten, miserable life"* and *"We don't hate niggers":* "How Whites Feel About a Painful America," *Newsweek*, October 21, 1963, pp. 44–51.

9 *"Negroes are oversexed,"* and *"I don't like to touch them":* Ibid., p. 50.

9 *"There is no state with a record":* Henry Hampton, dir., "Mississippi—Is This America?" episode 5 of *Eyes on the Prize: America's Civil Rights Movement* (Boston: Blackside, 1987).

9 *"During the past ten years":* Walker Percy, *Signposts in a Strange Land* (New York: Farrar, Straus and Giroux, 1991), p. 42.

9 *"Everybody knows about Mississippi, goddamn":* "Mississippi Goddam," *The Nina Simone Web,* http://boscarol.com/nina/html/where/mississipigoddamn.html.

10 *"Foreign Mail":* "Mississippi Airlift," *Newsweek,* March 11, 1963, p. 30.

10 *"as common as a snake":* Roy Torkington Papers, Civil Rights Collection, McCain Library and Archives, University of Southern Mississippi (hereafter, USM).

10 *"the long staple cotton capital of the world":* Dittmer, *Local People,* p. 129.

10 *"America's Most Beautiful Street":* Cardcow.com, Vintage Postcards and Collectibles, http://www.cardcow.com/48738/grand-boulevard-greenwood-us-state-town-views-mississippi-greenwood/.

10 *"neckid, buck-barefoot, and starvin'":* Student Nonviolent Coordinating Committee Papers, Harvard University (hereafter, SNCC Papers), reel 40.

11 *"makes it clear that the Negroes of Mississippi":* Dittmer, *Local People,* p. 206.

11 *"Before the Negro people get the right to vote":* "Mississippi: Allen's Army," *Newsweek,* February 24, 1964, p. 30.

11 *"invasion," "invaders," and "dastardly scheme":* Richard Woodley, "A Recollection of Michael Schwerner," *Reporter,* July 16, 1964, p. 23.

12 *"We are going to see that law and order is maintained":* Marilyn Mulford and Connie Field, dirs., *Freedom on My Mind* (Berkeley, Calif.: Clarity Film Productions, 1994).

12 *"This is it":* "Mississippi: Allen's Army."

12 *"We give them everything":* Seth Cagin and Philip Dray, *We Are Not Afraid: The Story of Goodman, Schwerner, and Chaney, and the Civil Rights Campaign for Mississippi* (New York: Nation Books, 2006), p. 193.

12 *"our way of life":* Council of Federated Organizations (COFO), WATS line report (hereafter, WATS line), August 12, 1964, COFO documents, Hillegas Collection, Jackson, Miss.

12 *"nigger-communist invasion of Mississippi":* Howard Ball, *Murder in Mississippi: United States v. Price and the Struggle for Civil Rights* (Lawrence: University Press of Kansas, 2004), p. 55.

12 *"dedicated agents of Satan": Famous Trials:* U.S. vs. Cecil Price et al. *("Mississippi Burning Trial")* Web site, http://www.law.umkc.edu/faculty/projects/ftrials/price&bowers/Klan.html.

12 *"Get your Bible out and PRAY!":* Cagin and Dray, *We Are Not Afraid,* p. 265.

13 *"Nobody never come out into the country":* Howell Raines, *My Soul Is Rested: Movement Days in the Deep South Remembered* (New York: Penguin, 1977), p. 233.

13 *"Mississippi changed everything":* Gloria Clark, personal interview, October 3, 2007.

CHAPTER ONE: **"There Is a Moral Wave Building"**

16 *"At Oxford, my mental picture of Mississippi"*: Elizabeth Martinez, ed., *Letters from Mississippi* (Brookline, Mass.: Zephyr Press, 2006), p. 186.

17 *"I may be killed and you may be killed"*: *New York Times*, June 17, 1964.

17 *"They—the white folk"*: John Lewis, *Walking with the Wind: A Memoir of the Movement* (New York: Simon & Schuster, 1998), p. 249.

17 *"They take you to jail"*: *New York Times*, June 21, 1964.

18 *"A great change is at hand"*: John F. Kennedy, "Radio and Television Report to the American People on Civil Rights," June 11, 1963, http://www.jfklibrary.org/Historical+Resources/Archives/Reference+Desk/Speeches/JFK/003POF03CivilRights06111963.htm.

18 *"cannon fodder for the Movement"*: Bob Cohen, "Sorrow Songs, Faith Songs, Freedom Songs: The Mississippi Caravan of Music in the Summer of 1964," in *Freedom Is a Constant Struggle: An Anthology of the Mississippi Civil Rights Movement,* ed. Susie Erenrich (Montgomery, Ala.: Black Belt Press, 1999), p. 178.

18 *"honor the memory"* and *"carry out the legacy"*: Doug McAdam, *Freedom Summer* (New York: Oxford University Press, 1988), p. 48.

18 *"Through nonviolence, courage displaces fear"*: Ibid., p. 30.

18 *"possess a learning attitude"*: SNCC Papers, reel 39.

18 *"John Brown complex"*: John Fischer, "A Small Band of Practical Heroes," *Harper's*, October 1963, p. 28.

18 *"A student who seems determined"*: SNCC Papers, reel 39.

19 *"an unmistakable middle-class stamp"*: *New York Times*, June 17, 1964, p. 18.

19 *"I don't see how I have any right"*: *New York Times*, July 11, 1964, p. 22.

19 *"You've deserted us for the niggers"*: Alice Lake, "Last Summer in Mississippi," *Redbook*, November 1964; reprinted in Library of America, *Reporting Civil Rights: American Journalism, 1963–1973* (New York: Library of America, 2003), p. 234.

19 *"Absolutely mesmerized"*: McAdam, *Freedom Summer*, p. 56.

19 *"Surely, no challenge looms larger"*: Ibid., p. 46.

20 *"You didn't run into many situations"*: Chris Williams, personal interview, October 9, 2007.

20 *"to actually do something worthwhile"*: Ibid.

20 *"The Birmingham church bombing had occurred"*: Williams, interview, November 23, 2007.

20 *"do-nothings"*: *Greenfield Recorder-Gazette*, June 26, 1964.

21 *"like I was the nation's most wanted criminal"*: Chris Williams, journal, Summer 1964, p. 7.

21 *"That government which governs best"*: Ibid.

21 *"a homosexual," "a car full of hoods"*: Ibid.

21 *"and the whole Mississippi adventure began":* Williams, interview, October 9, 2007.

21 *"I realized Mississippi was more educational":* Ibid.

22 *"the hairy stories":* Williams, journal, pp. 8–9.

22 *"When you go down those cold stairs":* Cagin and Dray, *We Are Not Afraid*, p. 22.

23 *"That man beat me till he give out":* Ibid., pp. 24–25.

23 *"It just scared the crap out of us":* Williams, journal, pp. 8–9.

23 *"I turned down a chance to work":* Martinez, *Letters from Mississippi*, p. 11.

23 *"I just ran until I was really tired":* Williams, journal, p. 9.

23 *"We don't know what it is to be a Negro":* Martinez, *Letters from Mississippi*, p. 5.

24 *"They would argue with a signpost":* Cheryl Lynn Greenburg, ed., *A Circle of Trust: Remembering SNCC* (New Brunswick, N.J.: Rutgers University Press, 1998), p. 143.

24 *"beautiful community," and "a circle of trust":* Ibid.

24 *"cracking Mississippi," "beachheads," and "behind enemy lines":* James Atwater, "If We Can Crack Mississippi . . . ," *Saturday Evening Post*, July 25, 1964, p. 16; Calvin Trillin, "Letter from Jackson," *New Yorker,* August 29, 1964, p. 105; Dittmer, *Local People*, p. 198.

24 *"To be with them, walking a picket line":* Howard Zinn, *SNCC: The New Abolitionists* (Boston: Beacon Press, 1964), pp. 1–2.

24 *"because I met those SNCC people":* Sara Evans, *Personal Politics* (New York: Vintage, 1980), p. 70.

24 *"group-centered leadership":* Daniel Perlstein, "Teaching Freedom: SNCC and the Creation of the Mississippi Freedom Schools," *History of Education Quarterly* 30, no. 3 (Fall 1990): 298.

25 *"He is more or less the Jesus":* Martinez, *Letters from Mississippi*, p. 19.

25 *"the Masters' degree from Harvard":* Atwater, "If We Can Crack," p. 16.

26 *"Before, the Negro in the South had always looked":* Burner, *And Gently He Shall Lead Them*, p. 17.

26 *"words are more powerful than munitions":* Albert Camus, "Neither Victims nor Executioners," in *The Power of Nonviolence: Writings by Advocates of Peace*, ed. Howard Zinn (Boston: Beacon Press, 2002), p. 73.

26 *"We were immensely suspicious of him":* Payne, *I've Got the Light*, p. 105.

27 *"uncover what is covered":* Raines, *My Soul Is Rested*, p. 235.

27 *"a tree beside the water":* Burner, *And Gently He Shall Lead Them*, p. 28.

27 *"There's something coming":* Ibid., p. 41.

27 *"rural, impoverished, brutal":* Robert P. Moses and Charles E. Cobb Jr., *Radical Equations: Math Literacy and Civil Rights* (Boston: Beacon Press, 2001), p. 24.

28 *"You the nigger that came down from New York":* Ibid., p. 48.

28 *"Boy, are you sure you know":* Burner, *And Gently He Shall Lead Them*, p. 49.

28 *"Dr. King and some other big people":* Hollis Watkins, personal interview, June 14, 2008.

29 *"No administration in this country":* *New York Times*, June 21, 1964; Cagin and Dray, *We Are Not Afraid*, p. 30.

29 *"It's not working":* Tracy Sugarman, *Stranger at the Gates: A Summer in Mississippi* (New York: Hill and Wang, 1966), p. 8.

29 *"No one should go* anywhere *alone":* SNCC Papers, reel 39.

29 *"We have talked about interracial dating":* "The Invaders," *Newsweek*, June 29, 1964, p. 25.

30 *"You should be ashamed!":* Dittmer, *Local People*, p. 243.

30 *"The flash point":* Mulford and Field, *Freedom on My Mind*.

30 *"Ask Jimmie over there what he thinks":* "Mississippi—Summer of 1964: Troubled State, Troubled Time," *Newsweek*, July 13, 1964, p. 20.

31 *"The crisis is past, I think":* William Hodes Papers, State Historical Society of Wisconsin (hereafter, SHSW).

31 *"When you turn the other cheek":* Nicholas Von Hoffman, *Mississippi Notebook* (New York: David White, 1964), p. 31.

31 *"You must understand that nonviolence":* Sugarman, *Stranger at the Gates*, p. 28.

31 *"Your legs, your thighs":* Cagin and Dray, *We Are Not Afraid*, p. 33.

31 *"I got me a twen'y foot pit out bay-ack":* Muriel Tillinghast, personal interview, November 28, 2007.

32 *"morally rotten outcasts of the White race":* SNCC Papers, reel 38.

32 *"We were renegades":* Tillinghast, interview, November 28, 2007.

32 *"NAG's local Mississippi":* Stokely Carmichael, *Ready for Revolution: The Life and Struggles of Stokely Carmichael (Kwame Ture)*, with Ekwueme Michael Thelwell (New York: Scribner, 2003), pp. 337–48.

32 *"I did not come out of a family":* Tillinghast, interview, November 28, 2007.

32 *"no bigger than a match stick":* Ibid.

33 *"a distant well of human woe":* Ibid.

33 *"He would tell me about":* Ibid.

33 *"At NAG meetings, I was informed":* Ibid.

34 *"a sponge":* Ibid.

34 *"brought us to the stark reality":* Tillinghast, interview, October 31, 2007.

34 *"It was* esprit de corps*":* Ibid.

34 *"As we depart for that troubled state":* Dittmer, *Local People*, p. 239.

34 *"Part of it is the American dream":* Atwater, "If We Can Crack," p. 18.

34 *"The injustices to the Negro in Mississippi":* *Los Angeles Times,* June 20, 1964.

35 *"a long, hot summer,"* and *"racial explosion":* "Mississippi Girds for Its Summer of Discontent," *U.S. News & World Report*, June 15, 1964, p. 46.

35 *"guerilla war"*: Joseph Alsop, "The Gathering Storm," *Hartford Courant*, June 17, 1964.

35 *"The guy from* Life *was a real jerk"*: Williams, journal, pp. 10–11.

35 *"Look magazine is searching"*: Martinez, *Letters from Mississippi*, p. 22.

35 *"Now get this in your heads"*: Cagin and Dray, *We Are Not Afraid*, p. 31.

36 *"real heroes": New York Times*, June 20, 1964.

36 *"What are you going to do"*: Len Holt, *The Summer That Didn't End* (New York: William Morrow, 1965), p. 50.

36 *"We can protect the Vietnamese"*: *National Observer*, n.d., Hillegas Collection.

36 *"We don't do that"*: Carmichael, *Ready for Revolution*, p. 370.

36 *"Dear People at home"*: Martinez, *Letters from Mississippi*, p. 10.

37 *"Before You Leave Oxford": New York Times*, June 21, 1964.

37 *"We hit the Mississippi state line"*: Tillinghast, interview, November 28, 2007.

CHAPTER TWO: **"Not Even Past"**

38 *"more or less bunk"*: Justin Kaplan, ed., *Familiar Quotations,* 16th ed. (Boston: Little, Brown, 1992), p. 499n.

38 *"The past is never dead"*: William Faulkner, *Requiem for a Nun* (New York: Penguin Books, 1953), p. 81.

39 *"Mississippians don't know"*: Geoffrey C. Ward, Ric Burns, and Ken Burns, *The Civil War: An Illustrated History* (New York: Alfred A. Knopf, 1990), p. 212.

39 *"Meridian, with its depots"*: Shelby Foote, *The Civil War: A Narrative— Fredericksburg to Meridian* (New York: Random House, 1963), p. 926.

39 *"Chimneyville"*: John Ray Skates, *Mississippi: A Bicentennial History* (New York: W. W. Norton, 1979), p. 108.

40 *"Things was hurt"*: Eric Foner, *A Short History of Reconstruction, 1863– 1877* (New York: Harper & Row, 1990), p. 86.

41 *"The whole public are tired out"*: William C. Harris, *The Day of the Carpetbagger: Republican Reconstruction in Mississippi* (Baton Rouge: Louisiana State University Press, 1979), p. 668.

41 *"Democrats Standing Manfully by Their Guns!"*: *Atlanta Constitution*, November 3, 1875.

41 *"A revolution has taken place"*: Foner, *Short History*, pp. 235–36.

42 *"we could study the earth through the floor"*: Aaron Henry, *Aaron Henry: The Fire Ever Burning*, with Constance Curry (Jackson: University of Mississippi Press, 2000), p. 91.

42 *"Naught's a naught"*: Richard Wright, *Uncle Tom's Children* (New York: HarperCollins, 1993), p. 157.

42 *"jus' as different here from other places"*: Sally Belfrage, *Freedom Summer* (New York: Viking, 1965), p. 46.

42 *"the necessity of it":* C. Vann Woodward, *The Strange Career of Jim Crow,* 3d ed. (New York: Oxford University Press, 1974), p. 73.

42 *"one of the most grotesque bodies":* Claude G. Bowers, *The Tragic Era: The Revolution after Lincoln* (Boston: Houghton-Mifflin, 1929), pp. 414, 448.

42 *"Rape is the foul daughter":* Ibid., p. 308.

42 *"was organized for the protection":* Ibid., p. 309.

43 *"The South needs to believe":* Gunnar Myrdal, *An American Dilemma: The Negro Problem and Modern Democracy* (New York: Harper & Row, 1962), p. 448.

43 *"The problem of the twentieth century":* W. E. B. DuBois, *The Souls of Black Folk* (New York: Vintage, 1990), p. 16.

43 *"What are the three largest cities in Mississippi?":* John Beecher, "McComb, Mississippi: May 1965," *Ramparts,* May 1965; reprinted in Library of America, *Reporting Civil Rights,* p. 398.

43 *"worse than slavery":* David M. Oshinsky, *"Worse Than Slavery": Parchman Farm and the Ordeal of Jim Crow Justice* (New York: Simon and Schuster, 1997), flyleaf epigram.

44 *"Never was there happier dependence":* David W. Blight, *Beyond the Battlefield: Race, Memory, and the American Civil War* (Amherst: University of Massachusetts Press, 2002), p. 260.

44 *"the loveliest and purest of God's creatures":* Hodding Carter III, *The South Strikes Back* (Garden City, N.Y.: Doubleday, 1959), p. 30.

44 *"reckless eyeballing":* Kim Lacy Rogers, *Life and Death in the Delta: African American Narratives of Violence, Resilience, and Social Change* (New York: Palgrave Macmillan, 2006), p. 37.

44 *"Nigger, Don't Let the Sun":* Adam Gussow, *Seems Like Murder Here: Southern Violence and the Blues Tradition* (Chicago: University of Chicago Press, 2002), p. 70.

44 *"making such criticism so dangerous":* W. J. Cash, *The Mind of the South* (New York: Random House, 1941), p. 93.

45 *"When civil rights came along":* Jason Sokol, *There Goes My Everything: White Southerners in the Age of Civil Rights, 1945–1975* (New York: Alfred A. Knopf, 2006), p. 63.

45 *"The Negro is a lazy":* Curtis Wilkie, *Dixie: A Personal Odyssey Through Events That Shaped the Modern South* (New York: Simon & Schuster, 2003), p. 57.

45 *"I am calling upon every red-blooded American":* Skates, *Mississippi,* p. 155.

45 *"Segregation will never end in my lifetime":* Carter, *South Strikes Back,* p. 13.

46 *"shocked and stunned":* Neil R. McMillen, *The Citizens' Council: Organized Resistance to the Second Reconstruction, 1954–1964* (Urbana: University of Illinois Press, 1971), p. 15.

46 *"We are about to embark":* Dittmer, *Local People,* p. 37.

46 *"to separate them from others":* Diane Ravitch, ed., *The American Reader: Words That Moved a Nation* (New York: Harper Perennial, 1991), p. 306.

46 *"The Citizens' Council is the South's answer":* Carter, *South Strikes Back*, p. 43.

46 *"the uptown Klan":* Hodding Carter quoted in James W. Silver, *Mississippi: The Closed Society*, rev. ed. (New York: Harcourt, Brace & World, 1966), p. 36.

46 *"Why Separate Schools Should be Maintained":* McMillen, *Citizens' Council*, p. 242.

47 *"right thinking":* Carter, *South Strikes Back*, p. 34.

47 *"God was the original segregationist":* *New York Times*, November 7, 1987.

47 *"dat Brown mess":* Endesha Ida Mae Holland, *From the Mississippi Delta: A Memoir* (New York: Simon & Schuster, 1997), p. 65.

47 *"And then there were the redneck boys":* Willie Morris, *North Toward Home* (Boston: Houghton Mifflin, 1967), pp. 21–22.

48 *"odd accident":* Dittmer, *Local People*, pp. 53–54.

48 *"the world see what they did to my boy":* Juan Williams, *Eyes on the Prize: America's Civil Rights Years, 1954–1965* (New York: Penguin, 2002), p. 44.

48 *"Good morning, niggers"* and *"every last Anglo Saxon one of you":* Paul Hendrickson, *Sons of Mississippi: A Story of Race and Its Legacy* (New York: Alfred A. Knopf, 2003), pp. 9–10.

48 *"If we in America":* Dittmer, *Local People*, 57.

48 *"There's open season on Negroes now":* Ibid., p. 58.

48 *"From that point on":* Raines, *My Soul Is Rested*, p. 235.

48 *"It was the so-called dumb people":* Youth of the Rural Organizing and Cultural Center, *Minds Stayed on Freedom: The Civil Rights Struggle in the Rural South, an Oral History* (Boulder, Colo.: Westview Press, 1991), p. 59.

49 *"that damn few white men":* Winson Hudson and Constance Curry, *Mississippi Harmony: Memoirs of a Freedom Fighter* (New York: Palgrave Macmillan, 2002), p. 37.

49 *"invalid, unconstitutional, and not of lawful effect":* Dittmer, *Local People*, pp. 59–60.

49 *"working hand-in-glove with Communist sympathizers":* Sokol, *There Goes My Everything*, p. 88.

50 *"Sorry, Cable Trouble":* Dittmer, *Local People*, pp. 65–66.

50 *"The following program":* Belfrage, *Freedom Summer*, 109.

50 *"Negro cow-girl":* Dan Classen, *Watching Jim Crow: The Struggles over Mississippi TV, 1955–1969* (Durham, N.C.: Duke University Press, 2004), pp. 101–3.

50 *"a veiled argument for racial intermarriage":* Mark Harris, *Pictures at a Revolution: Five Movies and the Birth of the New Hollywood* (New York: Penguin Press, 2008), p. 57.

51 *"intellectual straight-jacketing":* *New York Times*, June 18, 1964.

51 *"who will lynch you from a low tree":* Belfrage, *Freedom Summer*, p. 56.

51 *"private Gestapo":* Lynne Olson, *Freedom's Daughters: The Unsung Heroines of the Civil Rights Movement from 1830 to 1970* (New York: Scribner, 2001), p. 327.

51 *"Today we live in fear":* Silver, *Mississippi*, p. 39.

51 *"assdom":* John Howard Griffin, *Black Like Me,* 2nd ed. (Boston: Houghton Mifflin, 1961), p. 82.

51 *"Join the Glorious Citizens Clan":* McMillen, *Citizens' Council*, p. 257.

51 *"goons" and "Hateists":* Ira B. Harkey Jr., *The Smell of Burning Crosses: An Autobiography of a Mississippi Newspaperman* (Jacksonville, Fla.: Delphi Press, 1967), p. 126.

52 *"We hate violence":* Silver, *Mississippi*, p. 46.

52 *"The project is concerned with construction":* COFO letter to Mississippi sheriffs, May 21, 1964, Hillegas Collection.

52 *"communists, sex perverts":* Yasuhiro Katagiri, *The Mississippi State Sovereignty Commission: Civil Rights and States' Rights* (Jackson: University Press of Mississippi, 2001), p. 159.

52 *"It will be a long hot summer":* Mississippi State Sovereignty Commission Files, Mississippi Department of Archives and History, Jackson, Miss. (hereafter, MDAH) SCR ID# 9-31-1-43-1-1-1.

52 *"The white girls have been going around":* James L. Dickerson, *Dixie's Dirty Secret* (Armonk, N.Y.: M. E. Sharpe, 1998), p. 91.

53 *"where black and white will walk together":* MDAH SCR ID# 9-32-0-1-2-1-1.

53 *"carpetbagger" and "scalawag":* Carter, *South Strikes Back*, pp. 143, 191.

53 *"I know we've had a hundred years":* Von Hoffman, *Mississippi Notebook*, p. 3.

53 *"In my life span":* Jackson *Clarion-Ledger*, June 16, 1964.

53 *thirty thousand "invaders":* Los Angeles Times, June 18, 1964.

53 *Negro gangs were "forming to rape white women":* Tupelo Journal, June 19, 1964.

54 *"This is just a taste":* Chicago Tribune, June 9, 1964.

54 *"Don't do no violence":* Atwater, "If We Can Crack," p. 18.

54 *"Guidelines for Self-protection and Preservation":* Hodding Carter, *So the Heffners Left McComb* (Garden City, N.Y.: Doubleday, 1965), pp. 69–71.

54 *"This summer, within a very few days":* Don Whitehead, *Attack on Terror: The FBI Against the Ku Klux Klan in Mississippi* (New York: Funk & Wagnalls, 1970), pp. 6–8.

54 *"I hear that this summer":* Suzanne Marrs, *Eudora Welty: A Biography* (Orlando, Fla.: Harcourt, 2005), p. 309.

54 *"increased activity in weapon shipments":* Simon Wendt, *The Spirit and the Shotgun: Armed Resistance and the Struggle for Civil Rights* (Gainesville: University Press of Florida, 2007), p. 116.

CHAPTER THREE: **Freedom Street**

56 *"unpleasant, to say the least":* Chris Williams, correspondence, June 21, 1964.

56 *"Impeach Earl Warren":* Frederick M. Wirt, *Politics of Southern Equality: Law and Social Change in a Mississippi County* (Chicago: Aldine, 1970), p. 136.

57 *"so big they could stand flatfooted":* Karl Fleming, *Son of the Rough South: An Uncivil Memoir* (New York: Public Affairs, 2005, p. 361).

57 *"We're gonna give you a hard time":* Williams, correspondence, June 21, 1964.

58 *"that you did not come down":* New York Times, June 21, 1964, p. 64.

58 *"Their demeanor, how they treated us":* Mulford and Field, *Freedom on My Mind.*

58 *"He thinks out his moves carefully":* Williams, correspondence, June 21, 1964.

58 *"something I had to live with":* Robert Miles memorial service, program.

59 *"on account of your father":* Congressional Record 111, pt. 10 (June 22, 1965): H 13929.

59 *"I don't see why they don't let us swim":* Williams, correspondence, June 30, 1964.

59 *"Y'all gonna hear":* Williams, personal interview, February 1, 2008.

60 *"Have you seen my girls yet?":* Martinez, *Letters from Mississippi*, p. 51.

60 *"skinny" or "pretty":* Ibid.

60 *"We're mighty glad" and "It's a right fine Christian thing":* Sugarman, *Stranger at the Gates*, p. 53.

60 *"There they is!":* Ibid., p. 50.

60 *"I've waited eighty years":* Martinez, *Letters from Mississippi*, p. 51.

61 *"There are people here":* Ibid., p. 61.

61 *"I could kick down":* Ibid., p. 64.

61 *"the most appalling example":* McAdam, *Freedom Summer*, p. 87.

61 *"a fiery and fast moving old woman":* Martinez, *Letters from Mississippi*, pp. 47–48.

62 *"I was really surprised":* Mulford and Field, *Freedom on My Mind.*

62 *"Greetings from Batesville, Miss.":* Williams, correspondence, June 21, 1964.

63 *"some good old southern bourbon":* Ibid.

63 *"Had Moses not wanted it to happen":* Raines, *My Soul Is Rested*, p. 287.

63 *"either an act of madness":* Carmichael, *Ready for Revolution*, p. 350.

63 *"We had worked so hard":* Watkins, interview, June 16, 2008.

63 *"This was Bob Moses talking":* Carmichael, *Ready for Revolution*, p. 350.

63 *"taken over the Jackson office":* Dittmer, *Local People*, p. 208.

63 *"a bunch of Yalies":* Ibid., p. 209.

63 *"If we're trying to break down":* Zinn, *SNCC*, p. 188.

63 *"We don't have much to gain":* Nicolaus Mills, *Like a Holy Crusade: Mississippi 1964—The Turning of the Civil Rights Movement in America* (New York: Knopf, 1992), p. 58.

64 *"get rid of the whites":* Burner, *And Gently He Shall Lead Them*, p. 129.

64 *"all black":* Raines, *My Soul Is Rested*, p. 287.

64 *"a question of rational people":* Burner, *And Gently He Shall Lead Them*, p. 129.

64 *"How large a force":* Dittmer, *Local People*, p. 208.

64 *"Too difficult," "huge influx" and "sociological research":* SNCC Papers, reel 38.

64 *"You killed my husband!":* Branch, *Parting the Waters*, p. 510.

64 *"when you're dead":* Council of Federated Organizations (COFO), *Mississippi Black Paper: Fifty-seven Negro and White Citizens' Testimony of Police Brutality* (New York: Random House, 1965), p. 37.

65 *"For me, it was as if everything":* Moses and Cobb, *Radical Equations*, p. 76.

65 *"other than to dedicate":* Bob Moses, personal interview, December 10, 2008.

65 *"The staff had been deadlocked":* Moses and Cobb, *Radical Equations*, p. 76.

65 *"Notes on Teaching," "Techniques for Field Work," and "The General Condition":* SNCC Papers, reels 39, 40, 64.

67 *"Niggers , , , Beatnicks":* SNCC Papers, reel 38.

67 *"Would you please give":* SNCC Papers, reel 64.

67 *"for the good work":* Ibid.

67 *"Robert Moses, 708 Avenue N":* Fischer, "Small Band," p. 26.

67 *"I'm sorry it isn't more":* SNCC Papers, reel 64.

68 *"hooking people up":* Constance Curry, Joan C. Browning, Dorothy Dawson Burlage, Penny Patch, Theresa Del Pozzo, Sue Thrasher, Elaine DeLott Baker, Emmie Schrader Adams, and Casey Hayden, *Deep in Our Hearts: Nine White Women in the Freedom Movement* (Athens: University of Georgia Press, 2000), p. 346.

68 *"The mass media are":* SNCC Papers, reel 38.

68 *"for we think it is important":* Ibid.

68 *"a clear and present danger":* Ibid., reel 40.

69 *"I can say there will be a hot summer":* Congressional Record 111, pt. 10 (June 22, 1965): H 14002.

69 *"They don't arrest white people in Mississippi":* Ibid., H 14003.

69 *"I was":* Ibid., H 14008.

69 *"incidents of brutality and terror":* SNCC Papers, reel 38.

69 *"nearly incredible that those people":* Dittmer, *Local People*, p. 239.

69 *"Sojourner Motor Fleet":* Lewis, *Walking with the Wind*, p. 259.

69 *"We're sitting this one out":* Ibid., p. 249.

70 *"danger to local Negroes":* SNCC Papers, reel 38.

70 *"more convinced than ever":* Mary King, *Freedom Song: A Personal Story of the 1960s Civil Rights Movement* (New York: Quill/William Morrow & Co., 1987), pp. 226, 312.

70 *"lead people into the fire":* Ibid., p. 313.

70 *"No one can be rational about death":* SNCC Papers, reel 38.

70 *"is so deeply ingrained":* King, *Freedom Song*, p. 318.

70 *"When whites come into a project":* SNCC Papers, reel 38.

71 *"to take the revolution one step further":* Ibid.

71 *"We have a responsibility":* King, *Freedom Song*, p. 319.

72 *"It was so quick":* Tillinghast, interview, November 28, 2007.

73 *"I was petrified":* Ibid.

73 *"rather get arrested in Greenville":* Sugarman, *Stranger at the Gates*, p. 167.

73 *"Many Mississippi towns were predatory":* Tillinghast, interview, November 28, 2007.

74 *"Mississippi has a black and inky night":* Ibid.

75 *"said they knew nothing at all about the case":* SNCC Papers, reel 39.

76 *"Keep me informed of what happens":* Ibid.

CHAPTER FOUR: **"The Decisive Battlefield for America"**

77 *"handle the niggers and the outsiders":* William Bradford Huie, *Three Lives for Mississippi* (New York: WCC Books, 1964, 1965), p. 132.

77 *"one of the wettest dry counties":* Florence Mars, *Witness in Philadelphia* (Baton Rouge: Louisiana State University Press, 1977), p. 18.

78 *"folks yah met on the street":* Huie, *Three Lives*, p. 130.

78 *"We don't bother no white folks":* Ibid., p. 140.

78 *"reddish to vote":* Raines, *My Soul Is Rested*, p. 260.

78 *"You don't know me":* William M. Kunstler, *My Life as a Radical Lawyer,* with Sheila Isenberg (New York: Birch Lane Press, 1994), p. 140.

79 *"for investigation":* Cagin and Dray, *We Are Not Afraid*, p. 18.

79 *"lay low":* Williams, journal.

79 *"Mississippi is closed, locked":* Belfrage, *Freedom Summer*, p. 10.

79 *"There is an analogy":* Ibid., p. 11.

79 *"Yesterday morning, three of our people":* Ibid.

80 *"You are not responsible":* Taylor Branch, *Pillar of Fire: America in the King Years, 1963–65* (New York: Simon & Schuster, 1998), p. 363.

80 *"that Communist Jew Nigger lover":* Cagin and Dray, *We Are Not Afraid*, p. 274.

80 *"full of life and ideas":* Huie, *Three Lives*, pp. 46, 54.

80 *"More than any white person":* Ibid., p. 114.

81 *"I am now so thoroughly identified":* Cagin and Dray, *We Are Not Afraid*, p. 259.

81 *"I would feel guilty"*: *New York Times*, June 25, 1964, p. 18.

81 *"Mississippi's best hope"*: Cagin and Dray, *We Are Not Afraid*, p. 261.

81 *"We're actually pretty lucky here"*: Woodley, "Recollection of Michael Schwerner," p. 23.

81 *"I just want you to know"*: "Interview with Civil Rights Activist Rita Bender," in *Microsoft Encarta Premium 2007* (Redmond, Wash.: Microsoft, 2006).

82 *"You must be that Communist-Jew"*: Cagin and Dray, *We Are Not Afraid*, p. 274.

82 *"That Jewboy is dead!"*: Ball, *Murder in Mississippi*, p. 32.

82 *"a marked man"*: Huie, *Three Lives*, p. 81.

82 *"I belong right here in Mississippi"*: Ibid., p. 117.

82 *"Mickey could count on Jim"*: Ibid., p. 95.

82 *"Mama," he said, "I believe I done found"*: "Mississippi—'Everybody's Scared,'" *Newsweek*, July 6, 1964, p. 15.

83 *"a born activist"*: Carolyn Goodman, "Andrew Goodman—1943–1964," in Erenrich, *Freedom Is a Constant Struggle*, p. 321.

83 *"Because this is the most important thing"*: *New York Times*, June 25, 1964.

83 *"I want to go off to war" and "a great idea"*: Carolyn Goodman, "My Son Didn't Die in Vain!" with Bernard Asbell, *Good Housekeeping*, May 1965, p. 158.

83 *"We couldn't turn our backs"*: *New York Times*, June 25, 1964.

83 *"I'm scared"*: Carolyn Goodman Papers, SHSW.

84 *"Don't worry," he told them*: Mills, *Like a Holy Crusade*, p. 103.

84 *Dear Mom and Dad:* Federal Bureau of Investigation, Mississippi Burning Case, File 44-25706 (hereafter, MIBURN), part 3, p. 53.

84 *"issuing dictatorial orders"*: Association of Tenth Amendment Conservatives brochure, MDAH SCR ID# 2-61-1-95-2-1-1.

85 *"What're you doing here?"*: COFO, *Mississippi Black Paper*, pp. 67–68.

85 *"sons of bitches"*: Branch, *Pillar of Fire*, p. 143.

85 *"niggers on a voter drive"*: Zinn, *SNCC*, p. 204.

85 *"arrest any Mississippi law enforcement officer"*: http://sunsite.berkeley .edu/meiklejohn/meik-8_2/meik-8_2-4.html.

85 *"cooling off period"*: Payne, *I've Got the Light*, p. 108.

86 *"a true Marxist-Leninist"*: Nick Kotz, *Judgment Days: Lyndon Baines Johnson, Martin Luther King Jr., and the Laws That Changed America* (Boston: Houghton Mifflin, 2005), p. 103.

86 *"We do not wet nurse"*: Ball, *Murder in Mississippi*, p. 57.

86 *"Which side is the federal government on?"*: Zinn, *SNCC*, p. 215.

86 *"There is a street in Itta Bena"*: Martinez, *Letters from Mississippi*, p. 192.

86 *"Good evening. Three young civil rights workers"*: Walter Cronkite, "History Lessons: Mississippi 1964—Civil Rights and Unrest," June 16, 2005, http://www.npr.org/templates/player/mediaPlayer.html?action=1&t=1&isli st=false&id=4706688&m=4706689.

87 *"the other Philadelphia"*: *New York Times*, June 29, 1964.

88 *"fair-minded, Christian people":* Ibid.

89 *"They're sending them in by buses":* Michael R. Beschloss, ed., *Taking Charge: The Johnson White House Tapes, 1963–1964* (New York: Simon & Schuster, 1997), p. 313.

89 *"I asked Hoover two weeks ago":* Ibid., pp. 425–26.

89 *"I'm afraid that if I start":* Ibid., p. 431.

89 *"I think they got picked up":* Ibid., pp. 431–32.

90 *"I don't believe there's three missing":* Ibid., p. 434.

90 *"Are they all right?":* Goodman, "My Son Didn't Die," p. 164.

90 *"changed from a public figure":* Ibid.

91 *"Burned Car Clue": Washington Post,* June 24, 1964.

91 *"Dulles Will Direct Rights Trio Hunt": Los Angeles Times,* June 24, 1964.

91 *"Wreckage Raises New Fears": New York Times,* June 24, 1964.

91 *"They had no business down here":* Mars, *Witness in Philadelphia,* pp. 87–88.

91 *"Farmer, don't go over there":* James Farmer, *Lay Bare the Heart: An Autobiography of the Civil Rights Movement* (New York: New American Library, 1985), p. 273.

92 *"Where do you think you're goin'?":* Cagin and Dray, *We Are Not Afraid,* p. 343.

92 *"hid somewhere trying to get": New York Times,* June 23, 1964.

92 *"destroy evidence":* Lewis, *Walking with the Wind,* p. 257.

92 *"If there has been a crime":* Ibid.

92 *"We don't want anything to happen":* Farmer, *Lay Bare the Heart,* p. 276.

93 *"It's a shame that national concern":* Lewis, *Walking with the Wind,* p. 258.

93 *"I imagine they're in that lake":* Beschloss, *Taking Charge,* p. 440.

93 *"We are basically a law abiding nation": New York Times,* June 24, 1964.

93 *"We need the FBI before the fact":* Belfrage, *Freedom Summer,* p. 15.

94 *"knowed for mean":* Carmichael, *Ready for Revolution,* p. 377.

94 *"praying for sunrise":* Ibid.

94 *"those same peckerwoods":* Ibid., p. 378.

94 *"Ain't no telling":* Cleveland Sellers and Robert Terrell, *The River of No Return: The Autobiography of a Black Militant and the Life and Death of SNCC* (New York: William Morrow, 1973), p. 88.

94 *"So and so said":* Charles Cobb Jr., personal interview, July 16, 2008.

95 *"would have an irretrievable effect":* "Mississippi—Summer of 1964: Troubled State, Troubled Time," *Newsweek,* July 13, 1964, p. 20.

95 *"a local matter for local law enforcement": New York Times,* June 25, 1964, p. 20.

95 *"a thousand of these youngsters":* Kotz, *Judgment Days,* p. 171.

95 *"the chiefs of police":* Ibid.

95 *"this breathtakingly admirable group": Washington Post,* June 25, 1964.

95 *"a second Reconstruction": New York Times,* June 26, 1964.

95 *"firm, positive statement" and "will be on the hands":* Tupelo Journal, June 25, 1964; and *Washington Post,* June 25, 1964.

95 *"I'm not going to send troops":* Randall B. Woods, *LBJ: Architect of American Ambition* (New York: Free Press, 2006), p. 479.

96 *"We throw two or three":* "The Limpid Shambles of Violence," *Life*, July 3, 1964, p. 35.

96 *"Why don't you just float":* Huie, *Three Lives*, p. 39.

96 *"You know damn well our law":* Mars, *Witness in Philadelphia*, p. 98.

96 *"The idea of these people":* Ibid.

96 *"if it was boiled down to gravy":* Huie, *Three Lives*, p. 195.

96 *"Bloody Neshoba":* Ball, *Murder in Mississippi*, p. 64.

96 *"I believe them jokers":* Mulford and Field, *Freedom on My Mind*.

96 *"to all parents everywhere":* New York Times, June 26, 1964.

97 *"a Negro, a friend":* Cagin and Dray, *We Are Not Afraid*, p. 366.

97 *"I'm just hoping":* New York Times, June 25, 1964.

97 *"For God's sake":* Cagin and Dray, *We Are Not Afraid*, p. 366.

97 *"We're now looking for bodies":* New York Times, June 25, 1964.

97 *"I am going to find my husband":* Marco Williams, dir., *Ten Days That Unexpectedly Changed America—Freedom Summer* (New York: History Channel, 2006).

97 *"that scores of federal marshals":* Cagin and Dray, *We Are Not Afraid*, p. 354.

97 *"I'm sure Wallace is much more important":* Huie, *Three Lives*, p. 203.

97 *"Governor Wallace and I":* Robert Zellner, "Notes on Meeting Gov. Johnson," June 25, 1964, COFO documents, Hillegas Collection.

97 *"that you and Governor Wallace here":* Robert Zellner, *The Wrong Side of Murder Creek: A White Southerner in the Freedom Movement*, with Constance Curry (Montgomery, Ala.: NewSouth Books, 2008), p. 250.

98 *"I don't want your sympathy!":* Los Angeles Times, June 26, 1964.

98 *"What in the goddamn hell":* Cagin and Dray, *We Are Not Afraid*, p. 360.

98 *"Well, at least he still has a wife":* Ibid.

98 *"as near to approximating a police state":* Silver, *Mississippi*, p. 151.

99 *"A wave of untrained":* SNCC Papers, reel 38.

99 *"This is for the three in Philadelphia":* Chicago Tribune, June 27, 1964.

99 *"swarm[ing] upon our land":* Jackson Clarion-Ledger, July 7, 1964.

99 *"Where, oh where":* Turner Catledge, "My Life and 'The Times,'" in *Mississippi Writers—Reflections of Childhood and Youth*, vol. 2, *Non-fiction*, ed. Dorothy Abbott (Jackson: University Press of Mississippi, 1986), p. 85.

99 *"Be frank with you, Sitton":* Gene Roberts and Hank Klibanoff, *The Race Beat: The Press, the Civil Rights Struggle, and the Awakening of a Nation* (New York: Random House, 2007), p. 360.

99 *"Beware, good Negro citizens":* Mississippi Summer Project, running summary of incidents, transcript, USM (hereafter, COFO incidents).

99 *"Want us to do to you": New York Times*, June 27, 1964.

100 *"You dig it?":* Hodes Papers, SHSW.

100 *"like a funeral parlor":* Martinez, *Letters from Mississippi*, p. 33.

100 *"near psychosis," or just "character disorders":* Robert Coles, *Farewell to the South* (Boston: Little, Brown, 1972), pp. 246–47.

100 *"Suddenly hundreds of young Americans":* Ibid., p. 269.

100 *"You know what we're all doing":* McAdam, *Freedom Summer*, p. 71.

100 *Dear Mom and Dad:* Martinez, *Letters from Mississippi*, p. 26.

101 *Dear Folks:* Ibid., p. 27.

101 *"The kids are dead":* Belfrage, *Freedom Summer*, pp. 25–27.

101 *"In our country we have some real evil":* Ibid.

102 *"I would have gone anywhere":* Mulford and Field, *Freedom on My Mind*.

102 *"If someone in Nazi Germany":* Paul Cowan, *The Making of an Un-American: A Dialogue with Experience* (New York: Viking, 1970), p. 29.

102 *"You're killing your mother!":* Heather Tobis Booth, personal interview, October 8, 2007.

103 *"Be strong and of good courage": New York Times*, June 29, 1964.

103 *"racial holocaust": New York Times*, June 28, 1964.

104 *"I don't know what all the fuss is about":* Belfrage, *Freedom Summer*, p. 29.

CHAPTER FIVE: **"It Is Sure Enough Changing"**

106 *"History," "Reference," "Language," "Crud":* Sugarman, *Stranger at the Gates*, p. 108.

106 *the Ruleville Freedom School was ready for classes:* Ibid., pp. 107–12.

106 *looked "exactly" like Schwerner: Jackson Clarion-Ledger*, July 1, 1964.

106 *"dirty looks": Meridian Star*, June 30, 1964.

106 *"running down all leads on the cranks":* Beschloss, *Taking Charge*, p. 438.

107 *"let off it":* MIBURN 3-96.

107 *"Negro boy":* MIBURN 3-93.

107 *"got what was coming to them":* MIBURN, 8-75.

107 *"You a damn liar": New York Times*, June 28, 1964.

108 *"You dig into yourself":* Moses and Cobb, *Radical Equations*, p. 59.

108 *"While professing to believe in 'equality' ": Jackson Clarion-Ledger*, June 23, 1964.

108 *"I find more resentment": Christian Science Monitor*, June 30, 1964.

108 *"It's the best thing that's happened":* John Hersey, "A Life for a Vote," *Saturday Evening Post,* September 26, 1964; reprinted in Library of America, *Reporting Civil Rights*, p. 223.

109 *"as if I was some strange god":* Coles, *Farewell to the South,* pp. 250–51.

109 *"Now it wasn't just these 'Negroes' ":* Fred Bright Winn, personal interview, November 13, 2007.

109 *"We Shall Overcome":* Fred Bright Winn, correspondence, June 15, 1964.

110 *"My spirit lives on":* Ibid.

110 *"a young twenty-year-old":* Winn, interview, November 13, 2007.

110 *"broke the ice":* Ibid.

110 *"There were people in Mississippi":* Ibid.

110 *"If the Klan gets a hold of you":* Ibid.

111 *"scarier than shit":* Ibid.

111 *"It's like eating sandpaper slugs":* Ibid.

111 *"Dad, I hope you realize":* Winn, correspondence, June 1964.

111 *"I'm sorry, Mr. President":* Greenburg, *Circle of Trust*, p. 191.

112 *"June 30—Page 7 Holly Springs":* WATS Line, June 30, 1964.

113 *"You Are in Occupied Mississippi":* Belfrage, *Freedom Summer*, p. 52.

113 *"Violence hangs overhead like dead air":* Martinez, *Letters from Mississippi*, p. 168.

113 *"to walk along the street":* Rims Barber, Oral History, USM.

113 *"You're both purty gals":* Lake, "Last Summer in Mississippi," p. 243; and Ellen Lake Papers, SHSW.

113 *"Which one of them coons":* Wesley C. Hogan, *Many Minds, One Heart: SNCC's Dream for a New America* (Chapel Hill: University of North Carolina Press, 2007), p. 164.

113 *"broke bread with":* Hodding Carter III, e-mail interview, September 26, 2008.

114 *"I was adamantly against":* Ibid.

114 *"race mixing invaders":* Greenwood Commonwealth, June 30, 1964.

114 *"leftist hep cat students":* Jackson Clarion-Ledger, June 29, 1964.

114 *"nutniks":* Carthage Carthaginian, July 2, 1964.

114 *"unshaven and unwashed trash":* David R. Davies, ed., *The Press and Race: Mississippi Journalists Confront the Movement* (Jackson: University of Mississippi Press, 2001), p. 45; and Katagiri, *Mississippi State Sovereignty Commission*, p. 163.

114 *"thirty college students":* Lexington Advertiser, July 2, 1964.

114 *"doing irreparable damage":* Jackson Clarion-Ledger, July 1, 1964.

114 *"reckless walking":* Martinez, *Letters from Mississippi*, p. 147.

115 *"Nobody Would Dare Bomb":* New York Times Sunday Magazine, July 5, 1964, p. 6.

116 *"Know all roads":* SNCC Papers, reel 40.

116 *"surviving and just walking around":* Raines, *My Soul Is Rested*, pp. 239–40.

116 *"The whole scene":* Martinez, *Letters from Mississippi*, p. 55.

116 *"I just can't get my mind on all that":* "Mississippi—Summer of 1964: Troubled State, Troubled Time," *Newsweek*, July 13, 1964, p. 18.

116 *"I don't want to mess with that mess":* Belfrage, *Freedom Summer*, p. 50.

116 *"I can't sign no paper":* Martinez, *Letters from Mississippi*, p. 69.

117 *"Did that nigger invite you in here?":* Jay Shetterly and Geoff Cowan, personal interview, January 15, 2008; and "Mississippi—Summer of 1964," 19.

117 *"a somewhat neurotic redhead":* Williams, journal.

117 *"Goddamn motherfucker, pissed me right off!":* Claire O'Connor, personal interview, January 5, 2008.

117 *"kind of goofy":* Ibid.

118 *"our great leader":* Williams, journal.

119 *"agitators . . . come to Mississippi":* Ibid.

119 *"He said they ought to send me home":* Williams, correspondence.

119 *"I have developed a real taste":* Ibid.

119 *"hard on the Negroes":* Mars, *Witness in Philadelphia*, p. 76.

119 *"Nigger, do you know":* Cagin and Dray, *We Are Not Afraid*, p. 255.

120 *"I have no proof":* Ibid., p. 340.

120 *"Now come on sheriff":* MDAH SCR ID# 1-8-0-18-2-1-1.

120 *"number one suspect":* Jackson Clarion-Ledger, December 3, 2007, p. 4A.

121 *"Now if I were a teacher":* James Baldwin, "A Talk to Teachers," in *Critical Issues in Education,* ed. Eugene F. Provenzo (Thousand Oaks, Calif.: Sage, 2006), p. 203.

121 *"nigger food":* SNCC Papers, reel 39.

121 *"leaders of tomorrow": New York Times,* July 3, 1964.

121 *"close the springs of racial poison": Los Angeles Times*, July 5, 1964.

121 *"time of testing":* Beschloss, *Taking Charge*, p. 450.

122 *"tear gas pen guns": Jackson Clarion-Ledger*, July 2, 1964, SNCC Papers, reel 39.

122 *"civil strife and chaotic conditions": New York Times*, June 22, 1964.

122 *"People here in Clarksdale":* Martinez, *Letters from Mississippi*, p. 70.

122 *"Ah'm going swimmin' ":* Ibid., pp. 71–72.

122 *"Judas niggers":* Huie, *Three Lives*, p. 69.

123 *"What have I done in my life?":* Winn, interview, November 13, 2007.

123 *"troublemakers" and "uppity niggers":* Holland, *From the Mississippi Delta*, p. 203.

123 *"I kinda figured":* Raines, *My Soul Is Rested*, p. 234.

124 *"in case of emergency":* Sugarman, *Stranger at the Gates*, p. 75.

124 *"When I raised my hand":* Sandra E. Adickes, *Legacy of a Freedom School* (New York: Palgrave Macmillan, 2005), p. 15.

125 *"scrapping" cotton shreds: New York Times*, August 24, 1964.

125 *"a knot on my stomach":* Kay Mills, *This Little Light of Mine: The Life of Fannie Lou Hamer* (New York: Penguin Books, 1993), p. 21.

125 *"Had it up as high":* Fannie Lou Hamer, "To Praise Our Bridges," in Abbott, *Mississippi Writers*, p. 324.

125 *"I knowed as much about a facto law":* Mills, *This Little Light*, p. 37.

125 *"boss man" was "raisin' Cain":* Charles Marsh, *God's Long Summer: Stories of Faith and Civil Rights* (Princeton, N.J.: Princeton University Press, 1997), p. 15.

125 *"we're not ready for that in Mississippi" and "I didn't try to register for you":* Raines, *My Soul Is Rested*, p. 251.

125 *"a Snicker":* Unita Blackwell, *Barefootin': Life Lessons from the Road to Freedom*, with JoAnne Prichard Moore (New York: Crown, 2006), p. 83.

125 *"She was SNCC itself":* James Forman, *The Making of Black Revolutionaries* (Washington, D.C.: Open Hand, 1985), p. 385.

125 *"The only thing they could do":* Hamer, "To Praise Our Bridges," p. 324.

126 *"The white man's afraid":* Silver, *Mississippi*, pp. 341–42.

126 *"I feel like a man":* Sugarman, *Stranger at the Gates*, p. 116.

126 *"and more and more and more":* Martinez, *Letters from Mississippi*, p. 72.

126 *"These young white folks":* Ibid.

126 *"Can I speak to Andy Goodman?":* Belfrage, *Freedom Summer*, p. 64.

127 *"Just wanted to know":* WATS Line, July 5, 1964.

127 *"Today would be a good day for prayer":* Delta Democrat-Times, June 24, 1964.

127 *"It may well be a lesson":* Ibid.

127 *"a lotta weight":* Tillinghast, interview, November 28, 2007.

127 *"an epiphany":* Ibid.

128 *"The food was good":* New York Times, July 6, 1964.

128 *"We are just going to abide":* Ibid.

CHAPTER SIX: **"The Scars of the System"**

129 *"Tonight the sickness struck":* Martinez, *Letters from Mississippi*, p. 137.

129 *"What will it take":* Ibid., p. 138.

129 *"lying on the ground":* Ibid., p. 137.

130 *"Closed in Despair":* "Civil Rights: And the Walls Came Tumbling Down," *Time*, July 17, 1974, p. 25.

130 *"I'm free!":* Los Angeles Times, July 16, 1964.

130 *"unless these people get out":* New York Times, July 5, 1964.

131 *she had to say, "Nothing":* Fran O'Brien, personal interview, November 12, 2007.

131 *"I hope you're not too upset":* Fran O'Brien, correspondence, May 27, 1964.

131 *"Are you sure":* Ibid.

131 *"clearly understood":* O'Brien, correspondence, May 27, 1964.

132 *"it occurred to me":* O'Brien, interview, November 12, 2007.

132 *"It was just the way she'd grown up":* Ibid.

132 *"He's signing!":* Ibid.

133 *"Please try not to worry":* O'Brien, correspondence, July 6, 1964.

133 *"which will help you discover":* Goodman Papers, SHSW.

133 *"I think Andrew Goodman is a heroe":* Ibid.

133 *"Who are these fiends":* Goodman, "My Son Didn't Die," p. 158.

134 *"no evidence of human remains":* MIBURN 6-78.

135 *"share the terror":* New York Times, July 6, 1964.

135 *"Morale is building":* WATS Line, July 7, 1964.

136 *"See that"*: Curtis (Hayes) Muhammad, personal interview, August 29, 2008.

136 *"Bomb was placed"*: WATS Line, July 8, 1964.

136 *"Non-Violent High"*: Dittmer, *Local People*, p. 113.

137 *"This is the situation"*: Charlie Cobb, "Organizing Freedom Schools," in Erenrich, *Freedom Is a Constant Struggle*, p. 136.

138 *"be creative"*: "A Note to the Teacher, undated," Michael J. Miller Civil Rights Collection, Historical Manuscripts and Photographs, USM.

138 *do "The Monkey"*: Adickes, *Legacy of a Freedom School*, p. 112.

139 *"What do white people have"*: Martinez, *Letters from Mississippi*, p. 111.

139 *"If reading levels"*: Ibid., p. 113.

139 *"the link between a rotting shack"*: SNCC Papers, reel 39.

139 *Dear Mom and Dad*: Martinez, *Letters from Mississippi*, p. 108.

140 *"Eighty-two"*: Ibid., p. 106.

140 *"Where do roads come from?"*: Branch, *Pillar of Fire,* p. 393.

140 *"Ummm . . . Jackson?"*: Martinez, *Letters from Mississippi*, p. 106.

140 *"I think I am rapid"*: Ibid., p. 119.

141 *"I kept thinking"*: Mulford and Field, *Freedom on My Mind.*

141 *"Our school was by any definition"*: Adickes, *Legacy of a Freedom School*, p. 4.

141 *"Looks like termites to me"*: Von Hoffman, *Mississippi Notebook*, p. 35.

141 *"Razorback Klan" and "like wildfire"*: *Los Angeles Times*, July 5, 1964.

142 *"Sovereign Realm of Mississippi"*: Cagin and Dray, *We Are Not Afraid*, p. 246.

142 *"We are now in the midst"*: Belfrage, *Freedom Summer*, pp. 104–5.

142 *"the goon squad"*: Mars, *Witness in Philadelphia*, p. 101.

143 *"burning and dynamiting"*: Huie, *Three Lives*, pp. 105–6.

143 *"extermination"*: Dittmer, *Local People*, p. 217.

143 *"The typical Mississippi redneck"*: Wyn Craig Wade, *The Fiery Cross: The Ku Klux Klan in America* (New York: Oxford University Press USA, 1998), p. 334.

143 *"Sovereign Realm"*: Cagin and Dray, *We Are Not Afraid,* p. 246.

143 *"The purpose and function"*: Mars, *Witness in Philadelphia,* p. xvii.

144 *"our Satanic enemies"*: Belfrage, *Freedom Summer*, p. 104.

144 *"Some forty instances"*: Dittmer, *Local People*, p. 238.

144 *"I think you ought to put fifty"*: Beschloss, *Taking Charge*, p. 450.

144 *"to identify and interview"*: Whitehead, *Attack on Terror*, p. 91.

144 *"Neshoba Arrests Believed Imminent"*: *Meridian Star*, July 10, 1964.

144 *"whose neighbors were friendly with who"*: *Jackson Clarion-Ledger,* June 12, 2005.

145 *"just going through the motions"*: *New York Times*, July 11, 1964.

145 *"We haven't even started leaning"*: "Mississippi—Summer of 1964: Troubled State, Troubled Time," *Newsweek,* July 13, 1964, p. 20.

145 *"This is truly a great day!"* Branch, *Pillar of Fire,* p. 398.

145 *"Teeny Weeny"*: Ibid., p. 393.

145 *"This Mississippi thing":* Beschloss, *Taking Charge*, p. 444.

145 *"I don't close it":* Whitehead, *Attack on Terror*, p. 96.

145 *"We most certainly do not":* New York Times, July 11, 1964.

145 *"calculated insult":* Los Angeles Times, July 11, 1964.

146 *"whup" the first "white niggers":* Martinez, *Letters from Mississippi*, pp. 140–42.

146 *"Eat this shit":* WATS Line, July 10, 1964.

146 *"deep sorrow for Mississippi":* Los Angeles Times, July 12, 1964.

146 *"mutilated and scattered":* WATS Line, July 12, 1964.

147 *"Mississippi is the only state":* McAdam, *Freedom Summer*, p. 97.

147 *"We did not flee Hitler":* New York Times, July 11, 1964.

147 *"tanks, guns, and troop carriers":* SNCC Papers, reel 39.

147 *"before a tragic incident":* Hodes Papers, SHSW.

148 *"Sometimes when I lie awake":* Boston Globe, July 4, 1964.

148 *"except protect them somehow":* Los Angeles Times, July 19, 1964.

148 *"Trussed Body Discovered":* Los Angeles Times, July 13, 1964.

149 *"I'm hot, I'm miserable":* Los Angeles Times, July 19, 1964.

149 *"Where is the USA?":* Martinez, *Letters from Mississippi*, p. 165.

149 *"decent middle-class":* Ibid., p. 288–89.

149 *"running my rear end off":* Winn, correspondence, mid-July 1964.

150 *"Dad," Fred wrote home:* Winn, correspondence, July 14, 1964.

150 *"dirty" and "unclean":* New York Times, July 17, 1964.

150 *"What happened in Neshoba":* Charlie Capps Jr., personal interview, September 11, 2008.

150 *"We were a small town":* Ibid.

150 *"to keep a lid on things":* Fred Bright Winn, e-mail, May 26, 2008.

151 *"I was and am furious":* Winn, correspondence, July 14, 1964.

INTERLUDE: **"Another So-Called 'Freedom Day'"**

152 *"I'm going to wash the black off of you":* New York Times, July 17, 1964.

152 *"Come on, shoot another nigger!":* "Worse Than Mississippi?" *Time*, July 24, 1964.

153 *"Everybody stopped worrying":* Belfrage, *Freedom Summer*, p. 103.

153 *"another so-called 'Freedom Day'":* Greenwood Commonwealth, July 15, 1964.

154 *"our Gettysburg":* Holland, *From the Mississippi Delta*, p. 243.

154 *"Get up and look out the window":* Ibid., p. 218.

154 *"We will not let it stop us":* SNCC Papers, reel 39.

154 *"Everyone?":* Belfrage, *Freedom Summer*, p. 136.

155 *"I want to go to jail":* Ibid.

155 *"You are free to go and register":* Greenwood Commonwealth, July 17, 1964.

156 *"Jim Crow . . . Must GO!":* Sugarman, *Stranger at the Gates*, p. 160.

156 *"I think it would look very spontaneous":* Rick Perlstein, *Before the Storm: Barry Goldwater and the Unmaking of the American Consensus* (New York: Hill and Wang, 2001), p. 385.

157 *"You mean that's President and Mrs. Johnson?":* New York Times, July 17, 1964.

157 *"They're always doing something":* New York Times, August 3, 1964.

157 *"the deep feeling of regret":* New York Times, July 16, 1964.

157 *Back Door to Hell:* Internet Movie Data Base, http://www.imdb.com/title/tt0057864/.

158 *"Caution: Weird Load":* Tom Wolfe, *The Electric Kool-Aid Acid Test* (New York: Bantam, 1968), p. 63.

158 *"A Vote for Barry":* Kevin Kerrane and Ben Yagoda, *The Art of the Fact: A Historical Anthology of Literary Journalism* (New York: Simon and Schuster, 1998), p. 176.

158 *"Furthur":* Wolfe, *Electric Kool-Aid Acid Test*, p. 63.

158 *"It's too much like":* Louis Harris, "The Backlash Issue," *Newsweek,* July 13, 1964, p. 24.

159 *"The denial of voting rights":* Chicago Tribune, June 25, 1964.

159 *"The President should now use":* Huie, *Three Lives*, p. 150.

159 *"Without condoning racist attitudes":* Wall Street Journal, June 30, 1964.

159 *"It is a dreadful thing to say":* Washington Post, June 29, 1964.

159 *"Unlike the democratic absolutists":* Boston Globe, July 4, 1964.

159 *"outraged and disgusted":* Letters, *Newsweek*, July 17, 1964.

159 *"By what stretch of the imagination":* New York Times, July 10, 1964.

159 *"Lincoln did this country":* Letters, *Life*, July 24, 1964.

160 *"Could you possibly bring yourselves":* Letters, *Newsweek*, July 27, 1964, p. 2.

160 *"I would say":* Hartford Courant, July 7, 1964.

160 *"clear that the whole scheme":* Greenwood Commonwealth, July 17, 1964.

160 *"I turned around":* Linda Wetmore, personal interview, March 27, 2008.

161 *"Sounds like rubbing":* Belfrage, *Freedom Summer*, p. 126.

161 *"nigger huggers":* Ibid., p. 139.

161 *"I am proud":* Delta Democrat-Times, July 17, 1964.

163 *"that son-of-a-bitch":* New York Times, July 16, 1964.

163 *"extremists . . . who have nothing in common":* Christian Science Monitor, July 17, 1964.

163 *"The nigger issue":* Perlstein, *Before the Storm*, p. 374.

164 *"I was always complaining":* Richard Beymer, personal interview, July 6, 2008.

164 *"Beymer drove":* Congressman Barney Frank, personal interview, June 18, 2008.

164 *"off the map":* WATS Line, July 16, 1964.

165 *"We are not going to eat":* Belfrage, *Freedom Summer*, p. 144.

165 *"We won't eat tomorrow":* Ibid., p. 145.

Book Two

CHAPTER SEVEN: **"Walk Together, Children"**

169 *"Three are missing, Lord":* Ira Landess, personal interview, November 28, 2007.

170 *"Hello, Freedom!":* Ibid.

170 *"When you're not in Mississippi":* Martinez, *Letters from Mississippi*, p. 18.

170 McComb: *Mount Zion Hill Baptist Church:* COFO Incidents.

171 *"The mosquitoes down here":* Jinny Glass Diary, USM.

171 *"You will all be glad to hear":* Len Edwards, correspondence, August 5, 1964.

171 *"Ho hum. This violent life rolls on":* Hodes Papers, SHSW.

171 *"nothing serious":* WATS line, July 20, 1964.

171 *"engaged in widespread terroristic acts":* COFO v. Rainey, et al., Meikeljohn Civil Liberties Institute Archives, Bancroft Library, University of California, Berkeley, http://sunsite.berkeley.edu/meiklejohn/meik-10_1/meik-10_1-6.html #580.7.

172 *"the happiest project":* Dittmer, *Local People*, p. 257.

172 *"a real movie star":* Carmichael, *Ready for Revolution*, p. 399.

172 *"plain cute":* Hudson and Curry, *Mississippi Harmony*, p. 82.

173 *"If you want to start a meeting":* James Kates Papers, SHSW.

173 *"out under the trees":* Sugarman, *Stranger at the Gates*, p. 114.

173 *"laughing his ass off"* and *"Someone shot at you":* Williams, interview, November 24, 2007.

173 *"I don't believe in this sort of thing":* Fred R. Winn, correspondence, July 29, 1964.

173 *"Canton—Number of those":* SNCC Papers, Reel 38.

174 *"high degree of probability":* SNCC Papers, reel 40.

174 *"everyone who is not working":* Ibid.

174 *"canvassing, which you all know about":* Ibid.

175 *"The Democratic National Convention is a very big meeting":* Mississippi Freedom Democratic Party brochure, Chris Williams private papers.

176 *"I got to think about it":* Belfrage, *Freedom Summer*, p. 187.

176 *"battle royal":* Washington Post, July 23, 1964.

176 *"potentially explosive dilemma":* Los Angeles Times, July 26, 1964.

176 *"Papa Doc":* Dittmer, *Local People*, p. 262.

177 *"He has trouble relating to white women":* Chude Pamela Allen, "Watching the Iris," in Erenrich, *Freedom Is a Constant Struggle*, p. 418.

177 *"will have to pack his bag":* Sellers and Terrell, *River of No Return*, p. 96.

177 *"We can't let them think":* Ibid., p. 98.

177 *"the one thing where the Negro":* Barbara Ransby, *Ella Baker and the Black Freedom Movement: A Radical Democratic Vision* (Chapel Hill: University of North Carolina Press, 2003), p. 314.

178 *"Young man":* Martinez, *Letters from Mississippi*, p. 207.

178 *"I felt personally responsible"*: Watkins, interview, June 16, 2008.

179 *"They both left together"*: Charlie Cobb, personal interview, July 16, 2008.

179 *"Muriel was tough"*: Ibid.

179 *"We had never seen anybody"*: Blackwell, *Barefootin'*, p. 70.

179 *"Oh Lord, Lord"*: Ibid., p. 78.

179 *"For someone so young"*: Ibid., p. 79.

180 *"Muriel taught things"*: Ibid., p. 80.

180 *"What Muriel Tillinghast really taught"*: Ibid.

180 *"Okay, I'll do that"*: Ibid., p. 81.

180 *"Things getting pretty tight"*: WATS Line, July 13, 1964.

180 *"They recognized we were"*: Tillinghast, interview, December 16, 2008.

180 *"Go back to Greenville"*: COFO, *Mississippi Black Paper*, pp. 88–89.

180 *"If he gets killed"*: Beschloss, *Taking Charge*, p. 460.

181 *"There are threats"*: Ibid., p. 461.

181 *"Talk to your man in Jackson"*: Ibid.

181 *"We tried to warn SNCC"*: Payne, *I've Got the Light*, p. 103.

181 *"Martin Luther Coon"*: Hampton, "Mississippi—Is This America?"

181 *"Martin Luther King at Communist"*: Blackwell, *Barefootin'*, p. 68.

181 *"the unspeakable Martin Luther King"*: Davies, *Press and Race*, p. 41.

181 *"I want to live a normal life"*: Kotz, *Judgment Days*, p. 176.

181 *"just suicidal"*: Ibid., p. 177.

181 *"the most creative thing"*: King, *Freedom Song*, pp. 307–8.

182 *"to demonstrate the absolute support"*: Branch, *Pillar of Fire,* p. 410.

182 *"You must not allow anybody"*: New York Times, July 22, 1964.

182 *"Gentlemen, I will be brief"*: Ibid.

183 *"mobilize the power"*: Washington Post, July 23, 1964.

183 *"murdered by the silence"*: Ibid.

183 *"that these same efficient FBI men"*: Delta Democrat-Times, July 22, 1964.

183 *"Seat the Freedom Democratic Party!"* Forman, *Making of Black Revolutionaries,* p. 384.

183 *"the Right Rev. Riot Inciter"*: Belfrage, *Freedom Summer*, p. 164.

183 *"Small Crowd Greets King"*: Jackson Clarion-Ledger, July 22, 1964.

183 *"It is a known fact"*: Hattiesburg American, July 21, 1964.

183 *"It is a sad commentary"*: Shirley Tucker, *Mississippi from Within* (New York: Arco, 1965), p. 130.

184 *"Latest Wave of Invaders"*: Jackson Clarion-Ledger, July 22, 1964.

184 *"Happily, the inclination toward violence"*: Panolian, July 30, 1964.

184 *"We do know that Communist influence"*: New York Times, April 22, 1964.

184 *"Hey, you don't worry"*: Carmichael, *Ready for Revolution*, p. 304.

184 *"all communists speak Russian"*: Panolian, July 4, 1964.

184 *"mass invasion of Mississippi"*: Congressional Record 110 (July 22, 1964): S 16036–37.

184 *"stooges and pawns"*: Jackson Clarion-Ledger, July 23, 1964.

185 *"a long-time Communist legal eagle"*: *Congressional Record* 110 (July 22, 1964): S 16040.

185 *"beatnik looking crowd"*: MDAH SCR ID# 2-20-2-2-2-1-1.

185 *"If they ain't calling you a Communist"*: Blackwell, *Barefootin'*, p. 118.

185 *"The history of America"*: O'Brien, interview, November 12, 2007.

185 *"Do you know what the Gettysburg Address means?"*: O'Brien, correspondence, July 18, 1964.

186 *"We can't understand y'all"*: Ibid.

186 *"You haven't a thing to worry about"*: O'Brien, correspondence, July 10, 1964.

186 *"the little darlings"*: Ibid., July 13, 1964.

186 *"Jekyll-Hyde transformations"*: Ibid., July 28, 1964.

186 *"my babies can't be sold away"*: O'Brien, interview, November 12, 2007.

186 *"Well, you just read the book"*: Ibid.

187 *"Now," she said*: Ibid.

187 *"Sometimes I feel I'm not doing much"*: O'Brien, correspondence, July 18, 1964.

187 *"the worst state in the Union"*: *Los Angeles Times*, July 24, 1964, p. 21.

188 *"And what about you, young lady?"*: O'Brien, interview, November 12, 2007.

189 *"Three young men came here"*: *New York Times*, July 25, 1964.

189 *"I just want to touch you"*: Ibid.

189 *"that there are churches"*: Ibid.

189 *"I know what fear is"*: Belfrage, *Freedom Summer*, p. 169.

189 *"We've been waiting for you"*: SNCC Papers, reel 39.

189 *"RE: Arguing with the Red Queen"*: Ibid.

190 *"Mrs. Hamer is back"*: WATS Line, July 20, 1964.

190 *"Listen," the man said*: O'Brien, correspondence, July 28, 1964.

Chapter 8. "The Summer of Our Discontent"

191 *"How the ghosts of those three"*: Martinez, *Letters from Mississippi*, p. 216.

191 *"I believe with all my heart"*: Mars, *Witness in Philadelphia*, p. 105.

191 *"I just hope"*: Ibid.

191 *"If they were murdered"*: Jackson *Clarion-Ledger*, August 4, 1964.

192 the grinding *"hog"*: Tucker, *Mississippi from Within*, p. 43.

192 *"real rednecks"*: *Delta Democrat-Times*, August 6, 1964.

192 *"everyone who had been"*: Cagin and Dray, *We Are Not Afraid*, p. 374.

192 *"Nigger," Rainey shouted*: Whitehead, *Attack on Terror*, p. 114.

193 *"the tipoff boys were waiting"*: *Meridian Star*, August 6, 1964.

193 *"a prolific letter writer"*: *New York Times*, August 7, 1964.

193 *"have the money ready"*: Cartha "Deke" DeLoach, *Hoover's FBI: The Inside Story by Hoover's Trusted Lieutenant* (Washington, D.C.: Regnery, 1995), p. 185.

194 *"I realize it may sound foolish"*: *New York Times*, August 9, 1964.

194 *"Only a fool would be happy":* Ibid.

195 *"mother wit":* Blackwell, *Barefootin'*, p. 19.

195 *"Get the white man out":* Dr. Stacy White, e-mail correspondence, May 20, 2008.

195 *"Where have you people been?":* Sugarman, *Stranger at the Gates*, p. 173.

195 *"Hello, Item Base":* Winn, interview, November 13, 2007.

195 *"To be quite frank with you":* Winn, correspondence, n.d.

195 *"Be very careful":* Winn, correspondence, August 18, 1964.

196 *"counting them like a jail sentence":* Winn, correspondence, August 13, 1964.

196 *"wasn't going to turn the government over":* Williams, correspondence, July 13, 1964.

196 *"very violent town":* Ibid.

196 *"I been deputy":* Ibid.

196 *"Communist!" and "Nigger lover!":* Ibid., July 28, 1964.

197 *"The whole state is beginning to tighten up":* Ibid.

197 *"operating a Freedom Outpost":* Ibid.

197 *"in droves":* Ibid.

197 *"trashy motherfucker":* Ibid., July 20, 1964.

197 *"enough money to last him":* Branch, *Pillar of Fire,* p. 430.

198 *"come with subpoenas":* Meridian Star*, August 3, 1964.

198 *"take care of him":* MDAH SCR ID# 2-112-1-49-1-1-1.

198 *"pay a million more":* Ibid.

198 *"buy a cattle ranch":* Ibid.

198 Dutch *"seer": Meridian Star,* August 9, 1964.

198 *"What happened to the three kids?":* Ball, *Murder in Mississippi*, p. 75.

198 *"We'd have paid a lot more":* Kenneth O'Reilly, *"Racial Matters": The FBI's Secret File on Black America, 1960–1972* (New York: Free Press, 1989), p. 174.

199 *"We've spotted the dam":* Whitehead, *Attack on Terror*, p. 128.

199 *"This is no pick and shovel job":* Ibid., p. 129.

199 *"the summer of our discontent": New York Times*, July 29, 1964.

199 *"Maybe the best course":* Huie, *Three Lives*, p. 214.

199 *"see that their enemy":* COFO brochure, White Folks Project Collection, USM.

199 *"there was no dialogue":* Ed Hamlett Papers, White Folks Project Collection, USM.

199 *"Why Mississippi?":* Ibid.

200 *"get the feel":* William and Kathleen Henderson Papers, SHSW.

200 *"It looks like the pilot phase":* Martinez, *Letters from Mississippi*, p. 181.

200 *"You Northerners all think":* Ibid., p. 186.

200 *"How can these kids presume":* Sugarman, *Stranger at the Gates*, pp. 138–39.

200 *"What's so hard to explain":* Ibid., p. 145.

200 *"Would you marry a Negro?":* Martinez, *Letters from Mississippi*, p. 179.

201 *"Communist! . . . Queer!":* Ibid.

201 *"guilty, agonized":* Adam Hochschild, *Finding the Trapdoor: Essay, Portraits, Travels* (Syracuse, N.Y.: Syracuse University Press, 1997), p. 147.

201 *"a splendid job":* Virginia Center for Digital History, "Wednesdays in Mississippi: Civil Rights as Women's Work," The Effects: Southern Women, p. 20, http://www.vcdh.virginia.edu/WIMS/.

201 *"Girls," she said:* Ibid.

201 *"If you print my name":* Washington Post, August 16, 1964.

202 *"I am not an integrationist":* MDAH SCR ID# 99-38-0-493-2-1-1.

202 *"a breach of etiquette":* Carter, *So the Heffners Left McComb,* p. 125.

202 *"to let the Civil Rights workers":* Ibid., p. 80.

202 *"Whose car is that":* Ibid., p. 49.

202 *"If you want to live":* Ibid., p. 79.

203 *"chickened out":* Ira Landess, personal interview, November 28, 2007.

204 *"You folks better get down":* Sellers and Terrell, *River of No Return*, p. 103.

204 *"His head went through the windshield":* Ibid., p. 104.

205 *"I'd say start digging here":* Whitehead, *Attack on Terror*, p. 133.

205 *"We'll start here":* Cagin and Dray, *We Are Not Afraid*, p. 397.

205 *"the faint odor":* Ibid., p. 398.

205 *"Reporting one WB":* Whitehead, *Attack on Terror*, p. 134.

205 *"We've uncapped one oil well":* Ibid.

206 *"Mickey could count on Jim":* Huie, *Three Lives*, p. 95.

206 *"the first interracial lynching":* Umoja Kwanguvu Papers, USM.

206 *"O healing river":* David King Dunaway, *How Can I Keep from Singing* (New York: McGraw Hill, 1981), p. 235.

207 *"Many reported contacts":* Branch, *Pillar of Fire,* p. 434.

207 *"Mr. Hoover wanted me to call you":* Beschloss, *Taking Charge*, pp. 501–2.

208 *"It is for us the living":* New York Times, August 6, 1964.

208 *"Did you love your husband?":* Washington Post, August 6, 1964.

208 *"My boy died a martyr":* McComb Enterprise-Journal, August 6, 1964.

208 *"The closed society that is Mississippi":* Hartford Courant, August 6, 1964.

209 *"The murders of Michael Henry Schwerner":* New York Times, August 6, 1964.

209 *"None of those who have died":* Washington Post, August 6, 1964.

209 *"We must track down the murderers":* Vicksburg Post, August 6, 1964.

209 *"Many of us in Mississippi":* Delta Democrat-Times, August 9, 1964.

209 *"a new hate campaign":* Meridian Star, August 6, 1964.

209 *"It was those integration groups":* Delta Democrat-Times, August 6, 1964.

209 *"If they had stayed home":* Hattiesburg American, August 5, 1964, cited in Tucker, *Mississippi from Within*, p. 136.

210 *"reduced to a pulp":* Cagin and Dray, *We Are Not Afraid*, p. 407.

210 *"In my extensive experience":* Ibid.

210 *"substantive results":* New York Times, August 9, 1964.

210 *"hate to be in his shoes":* MDAH SCR ID# 2-112-1-49-1-1-1.

210 *"I want people to know":* New York Times, August 6, 1964.

211 *"Y'all can be non-violent":* Blackwell, *Barefootin'*, p. 98.

211 *"have some race pride":* Belfrage, *Freedom Summer*, p. 182.

211 *"loudmouth everyone":* Ibid., pp. 182–83.

211 *"to get the mandate from Bob":* Ibid., p. 183.

212 *"I'm gonna kill 'em!":* Hank Klibanoff, "Moment of Reckoning," *Smithsonian*, December 2008, p. 12.

212 *"I want my brother!":* Cagin and Dray, *We Are Not Afraid*, p. 409.

212 *"a mistake":* Wendt, *Spirit and the Shotgun*, p. 118.

212 *"Sorry, but I'm not here to do":* Bradley G. Bond, *Mississippi: A Documentary History* (Jackson: University of Mississippi Press, 2003), pp. 254–59.

214 *"The tragedy of Andy Goodman":* New York Times, August 10, 1964.

CHAPTER NINE: **"Lay by Time"**

215 *"Success?" Moses told the press:* Newsweek, August 24, 1964, p. 30.

215 *"from the unjust laws of Mississippi":* SNCC Papers, reel 39.

215 *"It was the single time in my life":* Dittmer, *Local People*, p. 260.

216 *"lay by time":* Blackwell, *Barefootin'*, p. 17.

216 *"I am tired":* Martinez, *Letters from Mississippi*, p. 225.

216 *"sailing and swimming":* Ibid., p. 221.

217 *"I have been here nearly two months":* Ellen Lake Papers, USM.

217 *"depression session":* Wilkie, *Dixie*, p. 144.

217 *"If I stay here much longer":* Coles, *Farewell to the South*, pp. 252–53.

217 *"She's always in the same rut":* Margaret Hazelton Papers, USM.

218 *"They keep killin' our people":* Belfrage, *Freedom Summer*, p. 225.

218 *"They might think twice":* Branch, *Pillar of Fire*, p. 450.

218 *"by someone important":* WATS Line, August 10, 1964.

219 *"a ballet":* Sidney Poitier, *Life Beyond Measure: Letters to My Great-Granddaughter* (New York: HarperCollins, 2008), p. 174.

219 *"I have been a lonely man":* Adam Goudsouzian, *Sidney Poitier: Man, Actor, Icon* (Chapel Hill: University of North Carolina Press, 2004), p. 224.

220 *"Are you coming down here":* Dunaway, *How Can I Keep*, p. 234.

220 *"Each morning I wake":* Julius Lester, *All Is Well* (New York: William Morrow, 1976), p. 112.

220 *"If God had intended":* Martin Duberman, *In White America* (London: Faber and Faber, 1964), p. 4.

221 *"That's right!":* Elizabeth Martinez, "Theater of the Meaningful," *Nation*, October 19, 1964, p. 255.

221 *"a beacon of hope and love":* "Dream in a Bean Field," *Nation*, December 28, 1964, p. 514.

222 *"nasty little town":* Tillinghast, interview, December 16, 2008.

222 *"Dear Doug":* SNCC Papers, reel 40.

222 *"let me drive":* Tillinghast, interview, December 16, 2008.

223 *"get the hell out of Issaquena County":* Ibid.

223 *"You niggers get away":* United States Commission on Civil Rights, *Hearings Before the United States Commission on Civil Rights*, vol. 1, *Voting: Hearings Held in Jackson, Miss. February 16–20, 1965* (Washington, D.C.: U.S. Government Printing Office, 1965), p. 132.

223 *"courage overcame fear":* Tillinghast, interview, November 28, 2007.

224 *"Look, close your mouth":* "Freedom Summer Journal of Sandra Adickes," USM, http://anna.lib.usm.edu/~spcol/crda/adickes/ad001.htm.

224 *"Mr. Clean":* Huie, *Three Lives*, p. 226.

224 *"The white people of Mississippi":* Ibid.

225 *"Communist Revolutionaries":* Mars, *Witness in Philadelphia*, p. 108.

225 *"They've shot Silas!":* Belfrage, *Freedom Summer*, p. 222.

225 *"colored doctor":* Zellner, *The Wrong Side*, p. 261.

226 *"I got me one":* WATS Line, August 17, 1964.

226 *"ticking time bomb":* Kotz, *Judgment Days*, p. 190.

226 *"There's no compromise":* Beschloss, *Taking Charge*, p. 515.

226 *"If we mess with the group":* Ibid., p. 516.

226 *"We're going to lose the election":* Dittmer, *Local People*, p. 291.

226 *"Help make Mississippi":* Herbert Randall and Bob Tusa, *Faces of Freedom Summer* (Tuscaloosa: University of Alabama Press, 2001), n.p.

226 *"If we can get enough people":* Charles Miller Papers, SHSW.

227 *"I just stood there":* SNCC Papers, reel 67.

227 *"Why did Harriet Tubman":* Liz Fusco, "Deeper Than Politics," *Liberation* 9 (November 1964): 18.

228 *"I am Mississippi fed":* Martinez, *Letters from Mississippi*, p. 279.

228 *"We're not black slaves!":* Washington Post, July 20, 1964.

228 *"I think you're lying":* Adickes, *Legacy of a Freedom School*, p. 68.

228 *"Some of them are beginning to realize":* Ibid., p. 264.

228 *"We're giving these kids a start":* Washington Post, July 20, 1964.

229 *"I saw the rug pulled out":* Watkins, interview, June 16, 2008.

229 *"about time something happened":* Chude Pamela Allen, "Watching the Iris," in Erenrich, pp. 419–420.

229 *"the project was polarized":* Ibid.

229 *"to give abortions":* Carmichael, *Ready for Revolution*, p. 389.

229 *"And get raped?":* Martinez, *Letters from Mississippi*, p. 185.

230 *"My Summer Negro":* Rothschild, *Case of Black and White*, p. 56.

230 *"Every black SNCC worker":* Evans, *Personal Politics*, p. 80.

230 *"I didn't see any white women":* Dittmer, *Local People*, p. 263.

230 *"Now, Dad":* Winn, correspondence, mid-July 1964.

230 *"jus' one boy touch":* Belfrage, *Freedom Summer*, p. 45.

230 *"fluttered like butterflies":* King, *Freedom Song*, p. 44.

230 *"All these black guys":* McAdam, *Freedom Summer*, p. 106.

231 *"I'm sure I wasn't the only white woman":* Chude Pamela Allen, "Thank You," in Erenrich, *Freedom Is a Constant Struggle*, p. 502.

231 *"There's a very good chance":* Chude Pamela Allen, personal interview, November 12, 2007.

232 *"we're all dreamers":* O'Brien, correspondence, July 28, 1964.

232 *"I could stay longer":* Ibid.

232 *"Don't worry," she was told:* Fran O'Brien, "Journey into Light," in Erenrich, *Freedom Is a Constant Struggle*, p. 285.

233 *"Now you just be a good little girl":* Ibid., p. 286.

233 *"No you don't, little lady!"* Ibid.

233 *"That's a good little girl":* Ibid.

234 *"Oh hi, Fran":* Ibid.

234 *"It's okay":* Ibid., p. 287.

235 *"After recent developments":* O'Brien, correspondence, August 4, 1964.

235 *"The whole pattern":* "The Evangelists," *Newsweek*, August 24, 1964, p. 30.

236 *"begin action":* WATS line, August 19, 1964.

CHAPTER TEN: **"The Stuff Democracy Is Made Of"**

238 *"They start anything":* Blackwell, *Barefootin'*, p. 108.

238 *"You better put your feet on the gas":* Ibid.

238 *"Negroes carefully picked":* MDAH SCR ID # 9-32-0-6-2-1-1.

238 *"We can't open the door!"* Mississippi Freedom Democratic Party Papers (hereafter MFDP Papers), SHSW.

239 *"assemblage of people":* Mulford and Field, *Freedom on My Mind*.

239 *"Until the killing of black mothers' sons":* Cagin and Dray, *We Are Not Afraid*, p. 391.

239 *"the stuff democracy is made of":* Martinez, *Letters from Mississippi*, pp. 250–51.

240 *"coronation":* New York Times, August 25, 1964.

241 *"alien philosophy":* New York Times, August 22, 1964.

241 *"If you seat those black buggers":* Dittmer, *Local People*, p. 290.

241 *"If our case is fully heard":* SNCC Papers, Reel 41.

241 *"go fishing on Election Day":* Washington Post, August 22, 1964.

241 *"definite supporter":* MFDP Papers, SHSW.

241 *"Who is YOUR sheriff?":* Ibid.

242 *"eleven and eight":* Lewis, *Walking with the Wind*, p. 279.

242 *"And who are we?":* MFDP Papers, SHSW.

243 *"I was just talking to Joe Rauh":* Carmichael, *Ready for Revolution*, p. 403.

243 *"move heaven and earth":* Los Angeles Times, August 7, 1964.

243 *"They've screwed you, Joe!":* Branch, *Pillar of Fire*, p. 457.

243 *"only an hour":* Cagin and Dray, *We Are Not Afraid*, p. 389.

243 *"white power structure"*: *Washington Post*, August 23, 1964.

243 *"I have been imprisoned"*: Ibid.; and Cagin and Dray, *We Are Not Afraid*, p. 415.

244 *"Girl, you reckon I ought to tell it?"*: Blackwell, *Barefootin'*, p. 111.

244 *"Mister Chairman"*: Fannie Lou Hamer, testimony before the Democratic National Convention, American Radio Works Web site, http://americanradio works.publicradio.org/features/sayitplain/flhamer.html.

244 *"There's Fannie Lou!"*: Len Edwards, personal interview, October 29, 2008.

244 *"We're gonna get the job done tonight"*: WATS Line, August 20, 1964.

245 *"Your time is short!"*: Ibid.

245 *"every nigger in town"*: Whitehead, *Attack on Terror*, p. 163.

245 *"comedy of terrors"*: Cagin and Dray, *We Are Not Afraid*, p. 383.

245 *"If you people leave us"*: WATS Line, August 20, 1964.

245 *"I can simply no longer justify"*: Martinez, *Letters from Mississippi*, p. 265.

245 *"I wasn't going to stay"*: Winn, correspondence, September 1, 1964.

246 *"Standard Operating Procedure"*: Ibid., August 14, 1964.

246 *"COME ONE, COME ALL"*: Jerry Tecklin Papers, SHSW.

247 *"What's this all about?"*: Winn, interview, November 13, 2007.

247 *"We all knew"*: Ibid.

247 *"I didn't try to register for you"*: Hamer, testimony.

247 *"On the tenth of September 1962"*: Ibid.

247 *"We will return to this scene"*: Hampton, "Mississippi—Is This America?"

247 *"On this day nine months ago"*: Branch, *Pillar of Fire*, p. 460.

248 *"for it is in these saints"*: Ibid.

248 *"power-hungry soreheads," their "rump group"*: Murray Kempton, "Conscience of a Convention," *New Republic*, September 5, 1964, p. 6.

248 *"vote for the power structure"*: Erenrich, *Freedom Is a Constant Struggle*, p. 312.

248 *"I was carried to the county jail"*: Hamer, testimony.

248 *"And he said, 'We're going to make you wish' "*: Ibid.

249 *"And I was beat by the first Negro"*: Ibid.

249 *"All of this is on account of"*: Ibid.

249 *"I don't think that if this issue"*: Mulford and Field, *Freedom on My Mind*.

250 *"honored guests"*: Kotz, *Judgment Days*, p. 201.

250 *"back of the bus"*: *Los Angeles Times*, August 24, 1964.

250 *"because he was on our side"*: Dittmer, *Local People*, p. 289.

250 *"Tell Rauh if he plans"*: Kotz, *Judgment Days*, p. 208.

251 *"way out of line"*: Branch, *Pillar of Fire*, p. 461.

251 *"SUPPORT THE FREEDOM DEMOCRATS"*: *Christian Science Monitor*, August 26, 1964.

251 *"1964, NOT 1864" and "STOP HYPOCRISY, START DEMOCRACY"*: *Los Angeles Times*, August 26, 1964.

252 *"Mississippi Terror Truck"*: Mulford and Field, *Freedom on My Mind.*

252 *"Don't you understand?"*: *Los Angeles Times*, August 26, 1964.

252 *"Alabama's done gone"*: Beschloss, *Taking Charge*, p. 523.

252 *"Atlantic City's White House"*: *Washington Post*, August 25, 1964.

252 *"You better talk to Hubert Humphrey"*: Kotz, *Judgment Days*, p. 200.

253 *"for Negroes to speak for Negroes"*: Ibid., p. 211.

253 *"Then democracy is not real"*: Kotz, *Judgment Days*, p. 211.

253 *"The time has arrived"*: Joshua Zeitz, "Democratic Debacle," *American Heritage*, June/July 2004, online edition.

253 *"Senator Humphrey," she began:* Chana Kai Lee, *For Freedom's Sake: The Life of Fannie Lou Hamer* (Urbana: University of Illinois Press, 1999), p. 93; and Olson, *Freedom's Daughters*, p. 320.

253 *"We can win on the floor"*: *New York Times*, August 25, p. 23.

253 *"listened patiently . . . argued fervently"*: Kotz, *Judgment Days*, p. 211.

253 *"that the Negroes have taken over"*: Beschloss, *Taking Charge*, p. 527.

254 *"The Freedom Party," Johnson told a friend:* Kotz, *Judgment Days*, p. 213.

254 *"an excuse to say I turned"*: Beschloss, *Taking Charge*, p. 525.

254 *"Bobby's trap"*: Ibid., p. 525.

254 *"The times require leadership"*: Branch, *Pillar of Fire,* p. 468n.

254 *"This would throw the nation"*: Ibid., p. 468.

254 *"These people went in and begged"*: Ibid., p. 471.

254 *"But we're going to ignore that"*: Robert David Johnson, *All the Way with LBJ: The 1964 Presidential Election* (New York: Cambridge University Press, 2009), p. 186.

254 *"take a tranquilizer"*: Kotz, *Judgment Days*, pp. 212–13.

254 *"a wholesale walkout"*: Branch, *Pillar of Fire*, p. 471.

254 *"It looks like we're turning the Democratic party"*: Ibid.

255 *"By God, I'm going to go up there"*: Branch, *Pillar of Fire,* p. 473.

254 *"Beloved," she began:* Lady Bird Johnson, *A White House Diary* (New York: Holt, Rinehart, and Winston, 1970), p. 192.

255 *"Is the Credentials Committee meeting"*: Belfrage, *Freedom Summer*, p. 239.

255 *"a tremendous victory"*: Kotz, *Judgment Days*, p. 215.

255 *"Your funding is on the line"*: Ibid.

256 *"The President has said"*: Ibid., p. 216.

256 *"wrung out the blood"*: Jack Newfield, *A Prophetic Minority* (New York: New American Library, 1966), p. 76.

256 *"if they really understand"*: Mulford and Field, *Freedom on My Mind.*

256 *"You cheated!"*: Kotz, *Judgment Days*, p. 216.

256 *"Atlantic City was a powerful lesson"*: Forman, *Making of Black Revolutionaries*, pp. 395–96.

256 *"The kids tried the established methods"*: Olson, *Freedom's Daughters*, p. 325.

257 *"Stokely," Hartman Turnbow asked:* Carmichael, *Ready for Revolution*, p. 408.

257 *"they can use the info":* WATS Line, August 25, 1964.

257 *"cowhided and horsewhipped":* New York Times, August 27, 1964.

257 *"cheap, degrading insults":* Jackson Clarion-Ledger, August 27, 1964.

257 *"that debt is paid in full":* Chicago Tribune, August 26, 1964.

258 *"like Mata Hari and the French Resistance":* Martinez, *Letters from Mississippi*, p. 256.

258 *"All we want":* Mulford and Field, *Freedom on My Mind*.

258 *"We've shed too much blood":* Lewis, *Walking with the Wind*, p. 281.

258 *"We didn't come all this way":* Blackwell, *Barefootin'*, p. 115.

258 *"You have made your point":* Kotz, *Judgment Days*, p. 221.

258 *"Being a Negro leader":* Ibid.

258 *"Socrates or Aristotle":* Burner, *And Gently He Shall Lead Them*, p. 187.

258 *"We're not here to bring politics into our morality":* Ibid.

259 *"When they got through talking":* Dittmer, *Local People*, p. 301.

259 *"a significant moral and political victory":* Los Angeles Times, August 27, 1964.

259 *"a triumph of Moral force":* New York Times, August 27, 1964.

259 *"nothing short of heroic":* Washington Post, August 26, 1964.

259 *"You don't know how they goin' to do us!":* Belfrage, *Freedom Summer*, p. 197.

260 *"I just want you to know":* Zoya Zeman, Oral History Collection, USM.

260 *"Fine," the registrar answered:* MDAH SCR ID# 2-61-1-101-5-1-1.

261 *"snowballed" and "completely out of control":* Ibid

CHAPTER ELEVEN: **"Give unto Them Beauty for Ashes"**

262 *"My God," he said:* Anthony Walton, *Mississippi: An American Journey* (New York: Alfred A. Knopf, 1996), p. 254.

263 *"The longest nightmare":* Sellers and Terrell, *River of No Return*, p. 94.

263 *"At the end of summer":* Watkins, interview, June 16, 2008.

263 *"If the present increase in violence":* SNCC Papers, reel 38.

263 *"are very fine people":* Mendy Samstein Papers, SHSW.

264 *"I didn't realize yet":* O'Brien, interview, November 12, 2007.

264 *"Well, what was happening":* McAdam, *Freedom Summer*, p. 134.

264 *"everything was awful":* Linda Wetmore, personal interview, March 27, 2008.

264 *"You're telling me":* Ibid.

264 *"I could never kiss anybody" and "Then I guess":* Ibid.

265 *"battle fatigue":* Lewis, *Walking with the Wind*, p. 273.

265 *"Our very normal":* McAdam, *Freedom Summer*, p. 136.

265 *"the best people I ever met":* Martinez, *Letters from Mississippi*, p. 259.

265 *"I went from being a liberal"*: McAdam, *Freedom Summer*, p. 127.

265 *"not a very creative guy"*: Ibid., p. 165.

266 *"Can I now forget Mississippi?"*: "The Reminiscences of Mario Savio," Oral History Research Office Collection, Columbia University, p. 40.

266 *"I'm definitely not ready"*: Mills, *This Little Light*, p. 135.

267 *"the proudest moment of my life"*: Abbott, *Mississippi Writers*, p. 329.

267 *"welling out like poison"*: Ibid.

267 *"The Negro girls feel neglected"*: Olson, *Freedom's Daughters*, p. 309.

267 *"just seemed to hate me"*: McAdam, *Freedom Summer*, p. 124.

267 *"do what the spirit say do"*: Lewis, *Walking with the Wind*, p. 294.

267 *"We must decide"*: Clayborne Carson, *In Struggle: SNCC and the Black Awakening of the 1960s* (Cambridge, Mass.: Harvard University Press, 1981), p. 146.

267 *"too many people high on freedom"*: Casey Hayden, in Curry et al., *Deep in Our Hearts*, p. 364.

268 *"the average white person doesn't realize"*: Casey Hayden and Mary King, "Women in the Movement," Student Nonviolent Coordinating Committee position paper, The Sixties Project Web site, http://www2.iath.virginia.edu/sixties/HTML_docs/Resources/Primary/Manifestos/SNCC_women.html.

268 *"hardly caused a ripple"*: Hayden, in Curry et al., *Deep in Our Hearts*, p. 365.

268 *"brutally aggressive hostility"*: King, *Freedom Song*, p. 450.

268 *impending "coup"*: Lewis, *Walking with the Wind*, p. 300.

268 *"bullshitting Negroes"*: Adickes, *Legacy of a Freedom School*, p. 135.

268 *"take orders from white folks!"*: Ibid.

268 *"Typical day"*: Samuel Walker Papers, SHSW.

268 *"morphing into a different kind"*: Tillinghast, interview, December 16, 2008.

269 *"cold"*: Andrew Kopkind, "The Future of 'Black Power': A Movement in Search of a Program," *New Republic*, January 7, 1967, p. 17.

269 *"Mrs. Hamer is no longer relevant"*: Payne, *I've Got the Light*, pp. 365, 372.

269 *"an unfortunate choice of words"*: Carson, *In Struggle*, p. 210.

269 *"a growing litany"*: Ibid., p. 238.

269 *"I got the feeling"*: Whitehead, *Attack on Terror*, p. 161.

269 *"We've got to get Goatee"*: Ibid.

270 *"King was calling the shots"*: Branch, *Pillar of Fire*, p. 535.

270 *"Now is the time"*: Whitehead, *Attack on Terror*, p. 172.

270 *"our investigation has been curtailed"*: Mars, *Witness in Philadelphia*, p. 130.

270 *"put the fear of God"*: Branch, *Pillar of Fire*, p. 535.

270 *a "floater," a "hustler"*: Cagin and Dray, *We Are Not Afraid*, p. 432.

270 *"I'm going to see your ass in jail"*: Branch, *Pillar of Fire*, p. 498.

270 *"Killen said they had three civil rights":* MIBURN, 4-81.

271 *"the nigger-communist invasion":* Ball, *Murder in Mississippi,* p. 55.

271 *"a volley of shots":* MIBURN, 4-77.

271 *"Everyone follow me":* MIBURN, 4-75, and *Jackson Clarion-Ledger,* December 2, 1967, p. 1A.

272 *"They will be under twenty feet of dirt":* MIBURN, 4-73.

272 *"Someone go and get the operator":* Ibid., 4-74.

272 *"We have a place to bury them":* Ibid., 4-46, and Erenrich, *Freedom Is a Constant Struggle,* p. 348.

272 *"Are you that nigger lover?" and "Sir, I know just how you feel":* MIBURN, 4-47.

272 *"Save one for me!" and "You didn't leave me anything but":* Ibid., 4-45–48.

273 *"I'll kill anyone who talks":* Ibid., 4-50; *Jackson Clarion-Ledger,* July 12, 2005.

273 *"Ol' Rainey could be elected":* Los Angeles Times, December 11, 1964.

273 *"a feeling that we hit":* Jack Bales, ed., *Conversations with Willie Morris* (Jackson: University Press of Mississippi, 2000), p. 103.

273 *"I favor dropping an atom bomb":* Letters, *Time,* December 25, 1964, p. 10.

274 *"Here's to the state of Mississippi":* Phil Ochs, "Here's to the State of Mississippi," *I Ain't Marching Anymore,* Elektra Records, 1965.

274 *"that wall of Never":* Trillin, "Letter from Jackson," p. 85.

274 *"equal treatment under the law":* McComb Enterprise-Journal, November 17, 1964.

274 *"The waitress smiled":* Paul Good, "A Bowl of Gumbo for Curtis Bryant," *Reporter,* December 31, 1964, p. 19.

275 *"Okay, who's first?":* Newfield, *Prophetic Minority,* p. 95.

275 *"a lawyer's dream case":* Kunstler, in Curry et al., *Deep in My Heart,* p. 345.

276 *"every Congressman from the Potomac":* Ibid., p. 349.

276 *"I'm not crying for myself":* New York Times, September 18, 1965.

Epilogue

277 *"these vicious and morally bankrupt criminals":* Ibid., p. 237.

278 *"niggers on a voting drive":* Zinn, *SNCC,* p. 204.

278 *"the burning of draft cards":* Testimony of Charles Johnson, *U.S. v. Price et al.* ("Mississippi Burning" trial), http://www.law.umkc.edu/faculty/projects/ftrials/price&bowers/Johnson.html.

278 *"to get young Negro males":* Whitehead, *Attack on Terror,* p. 237.

279 *"Who is the author":* Los Angeles Times, October 9, 1967, p. 7.

279 *"I'm not going to allow":* Cagin and Dray, *We Are Not Afraid,* p. 446.

279 *"a white, Christian, militant organization":* Whitehead, *Attack on Terror,* p. 187.

279 *"You ain't joined no Boy Scout group":* Washington Post, October 10, 1967.

279 *"It was the first time":* Testimony of Delmar Dennis, *Famous Trials* Web site, http://www.law.umkc.edu/faculty/projects/ftrials/price&bowers/Dennis .html.

279 *"What did he mean by elimination?"* Ibid.

279 *"a Judas witness":* Los Angeles Times, October 19, 1967; Ball, *Murder in Mississippi,* p. 127.

279 *"salt of the earth kind of people":* Ibid., pp. 128, 130.

279 *"in church every time":* Ibid., p. 128.

279 *"low-class riffraff":* Whitehead, *Attack on Terror,* p. 280.

279 *"It may well be:* Ibid.

279 *"The federal government is not invading":* John Doar, Summary for the Prosecution, on *Famous Trials* Web site, http://www.law.umkc.edu/faculty/ projects/ftrials/price&bowers/doarclose.htm.

280 *"The strong arm":* H. C. Watkins, Summary for the Defense, on *Famous Trials* Web site, http://www.law.umkc.edu/faculty/projects/ftrials/price&bowers/ watkinsclos.html.

280 *"could never convict a preacher":* Ball, *Murder in Mississippi,* p. 133.

280 *"They killed one nigger":* O'Reilly, *"Racial Matters,"* pp. 175–76.

280 *"the best thing that's ever happened":* Washington Post, October 21, 1967.

280 *"landmark decision":* New York Times, October 21, 1967.

280 *"They did better than I thought":* Ibid.

280 *"I want you to write me":* Woods, *LBJ,* p. 480.

280 *"to insure that they did not die in vain":* Congressional Record 111, pt. 10 (June 22, 1965): S 13931.

281 *"the broadest possible scope":* Chandler Davidson and Bernard Grofman, eds., *Quiet Revolution in the South: The Impact of the Voting Rights Act, 1965–1990* (Princeton, N.J.: Princeton University Press, 1994), p. 138.

281 *"After Freedom Summer, we met black people":* John Howell, personal interview, March 11, 2008.

282 *"I never dreamed I'd live to see":* Wirt, *Politics of Southern Equality,* p. 160.

282 *"Hands that picked cotton":* Cambridge Encyclopedia, vol. 1, s.v. "Charles (James) Evers," http://encyclopedia.stateuniversity.com/pages/185/-James-Charles-Evers.html.

282 *"I count Mayor Evers as a friend":* Skates, *Mississippi,* pp. 168–69.

282 *"Seg academies":* Wilkie, *Dixie,* p. 35.

282 *"I can't make people integrate":* Woods, *LBJ,* pp. 479–80.

283 *"The Promised Land is still far off":* Hodding Carter III, e-mail interview, September 26, 2008.

283 *"I believe that despite the terrible racist image":* Margaret Walker, "Mississippi and the Nation in the 1980s," in Abbott, *Mississippi Writers,* p. 612.

283 *"Not in Mississippi!":* Erenrich, *Freedom Is a Constant Struggle,* p. 409.

284 *"There has not been meaningful change":* Adickes, *Legacy of a Freedom School,* p. 163.

284 *"rosier and rosier":* O'Brien, interview, November 12, 2007.

284 *"stepped into a hornet's nest":* Ibid.

284 *"It's a good thing they got that Communist":* Ibid.

284 *"It had been a rather quiet summer":* O'Brien, "Journey into Light," p. 285.

285 *"One might as well hold a skunk":* Ibid., p. 288.

285 *"I never really had the time":* Fran O'Brien, e-mail correspondence, October 17, 2008.

285 *"Yes, I know it sounds a bit wild":* Winn, correspondence, no date.

285 *"I was so glad":* Winn, correspondence, September 15, 1964.

286 *"They got Giles!":* Winn, interview, November 13, 2007.

286 *"Janell and I are coming home":* Winn, correspondence, no date.

286 *"We don't need you":* Winn, interview, November 13, 2007.

286 *"fell in with another crowd":* Ibid.

286 *"The fact that I":* Ibid.

286 *"took some time to fuck off":* Ibid.

287 *"Someone asked me":* Ibid.

287 *"too containing":* Tillinghast, interview, December 16, 2008.

287 *"I was born with a fighting nature":* Ibid.

287 *"It was like going to war":* Ibid.

288 *"Chrisnpenny":* Chris Williams, e-mail correspondence, October 17, 2008.

288 *"I felt I'd given it a good shot":* Ibid.

289 *"ragged and lost":* Penny Patch, in Curry et al., *Deep in Our Hearts,* p. 165.

289 *"Mississippi without fear":* Williams, interview, September 21, 2008.

289 *"Other people went to Vietnam":* Ibid.

290 *"the ultimate Mississippi":* McAdam, *Freedom Summer,* p. 229.

290 *"I am prouder of being there":* Adickes, *Legacy of a Freedom School,* p. 159.

290 *"almost Jesus like aura":* Burner, *And Gently He Shall Lead Them,* p. 200.

291 *"Like working with sharecroppers":* Bob Moses, personal interview, December 10, 2008.

292 *"To me, it was sort of like a plane crash":* Cagin and Dray, *We Are Not Afraid,* p. 454.

292 *"I was quite delighted":* Ibid., p. xv.

293 *"Had I done it":* Chicago Tribune, November 13, 1978.

293 *"I'm not going to say they were wrong":* New York Times, January 7, 2005.

293 *"It was what I'd been wanting":* New York Times, June 12, 2005.

293 *"The media has profited":* Ibid.

293 *"Communists invaded":* Jackson Clarion-Ledger, June 18, 2005.

293 *"as strong for segregation":* Jackson Clarion-Ledger, June 12, 2005.

294 *"If you want my forgiveness":* New York Times, August 21, 2007.

294 *"Mighty long time":* New York Times, January 7, 1905.

295 *"it really hit me":* Williams, dir., *Ten Days.*

295 *"She just wrapped her arms":* Ibid.

295 *"if he had anything to do with those boys":* New York Times, June 18, 2005.

295 *"J. E. never come back":* Jackson *Clarion-Ledger*, June 19, 2005.

295 *"I thought it was unusual":* Jackson *Clarion-Ledger*, June 20, 2005.

295 *"nothing but stirring":* Ibid.

295 *"Do your duty":* Ibid.

295 *"She believes the life of her son":* New York Times, June 22, 2005.

296 *"day of great importance":* Jackson *Clarion-Ledger*, June 22, 2005.

296 *"in a calculated":* Arkansas Delta Truth and Justice Center, "Neshoba Murders Case—A Chronology," Civil Rights Movement Veterans Web site, http://www.crmvet.org.

296 *"Other cold cases":* Jerry Mitchell, personal interview, October 9, 2008.

296 *"That was the time of the hippies":* Hampton, "Mississippi—Is This America?"

296 *"changed Mississippi forever":* Charlie Cobb, Oral History Collection, USM.

297 *"the greatest sociological experiment":* Burner, *And Gently He Shall Lead Them*, p. 166.

297 *"Christ-like":* Marsh, *God's Long Summer*, p. 45.

297 *"They were the best friends we ever met":* Ibid.

297 *"Freedom Summer injected a new spirit":* John Lewis, personal interview, September 12, 2008.

297 *"Why can't it be":* Jackson *Clarion-Ledger*, November 6, 2008, p. 1.

298 *"This is history, woman":* "Students Asked Not to Say Obama's Name," WAPT, Channel 16, Jackson, Miss., http://www.wapt.com/video/17928161/index.html.

298 *"I voted for Obama":* Wayne Drash, "Crossing the Railroad Tracks amid a New Time in History," CNN, January 16, 2009, http://www.cnn.com/2009/US/01/12/crossing.railroad.tracks/.

298 *"Oh, if he'd just been able":* Jackson *Clarion-Ledger*, January 21, 2009.

298 *"It's the most wonderful day":* Delta *Democrat-Times,* January 21, 2009.

298 *"where the stage was set":* "Pulitzer Prize-Winning Writer Alice Walker and Civil Rights Leader Bob Moses Reflect on an Obama Presidency and the Struggle for African Americans to Vote," *Democracy Now!* January 20, 2009, http://www.democracynow.org/2009/1/20/pulitzer_prize_winning_writer_alice_walker.

298 *"My fellow citizens":* New York Times, January 21, 2009.

299 *"They saw America as bigger":* Ibid.

299 *"the closest thing to a perfect day":* Fran O'Brien, e-mail correspondence, January 21, 2009.

299 *"What the cynics fail to understand":* New York Times, January 21, 2009.

299 *"and why a man whose father":* Ibid.

299 *"It took forty-five years":* Linda Wetmore Halpern, e-mail correspondence, January 21, 2009.

300 *"At the end of it all":* Williams, e-mail correspondence, January 21, 2009.

Bibliography

Archives

Barber, Rims. Oral History Collection. McCain Library and Archives, University of Southern Mississippi.

Cobb, Charles. Oral History Collection. McCain Library and Archives, University of Southern Mississippi.

Dahl, Kathleen. Papers. McCain Library and Archives, University of Southern Mississippi.

Federal Bureau of Investigation. Mississippi Burning Case, File 44-25706.

Glass, Jinny. Papers. McCain Library and Archives, University of Southern Mississippi.

Goodman, Carolyn. Papers. State Historical Society of Wisconsin.

Guyot, Lawrence. Oral History Collection. McCain Library and Archives, University of Southern Mississippi.

Hamer, Fannie Lou. Papers. State Historical Society of Wisconsin.

Hamlett, Ed. Papers. White Folks Project Collection, McCain Library and Archives, University of Southern Mississippi.

Hazelton, Margaret. Papers. McCain Library and Archives, University of Southern Mississippi.

Henderson, William and Kathleen. Papers. State Historical Society of Wisconsin.

Hillegas Collection. Private collection of Jan Hillegas, Jackson, MS.

Hodes, William. Papers. State Historical Society of Wisconsin.

Hudson, Winson. Oral History Collection. McCain Library and Archives, University of Southern Mississippi.

Hunn, Eugene. Papers. State Historical Society of Wisconsin.

Johnson, Paul B. Papers. McCain Library and Archives, University of Southern Mississippi.

Kates, James. Papers. State Historical Society of Wisconsin.

Kwanguvu, Umoja. Papers. McCain Library and Archives, University of Southern Mississippi.

Lake, Ellen. Papers. McCain Library and Archives, University of Southern Mississippi.
———. Papers. State Historical Society of Wisconsin.

Miller, Charles. Papers. State Historical Society of Wisconsin.

Mississippi Freedom Democratic Party. Papers. State Historical Society of Wisconsin.

North Mississippi Oral History and Archives Project. McCain Library and Archives, University of Southern Mississippi.

Orris, Peter. Oral History Collection. McCain Library and Archives, University of Southern Mississippi.

Owen, David. Papers. McCain Library and Archives, University of Southern Mississippi.

Samstein, Mendy. Papers. State Historical Society of Wisconsin.

Savio, Mario. "The Reminiscences of Mario Savio." Oral History Research Office Collection, Columbia University.

Student Nonviolent Coordinating Committee. Papers. Harvard University.

Tecklin, Jerry. Papers. State Historical Society of Wisconsin.

Torkington, Roy. Papers. Civil Rights Collection, McCain Library and Archives, University of Southern Mississippi.

Vogel, Lisa. Papers. State Historical Society of Wisconsin.

Walker, Samuel. Papers. State Historical Society of Wisconsin.

Zeman, Zoya. Oral History Collection. McCain Library and Archives, University of Southern Mississippi.

Magazines and Journals

Atwater, James. "If We Can Crack Mississippi . . ." *Saturday Evening Post*, July 25, 1964, pp. 15–19.

Beecher, John. "All You Have to Do Is Lie." *New Republic*, October 24, 1964, pp. 9–10.

"Civil Rights: And the Walls Came Tumbling Down." *Time*, July 17, 1974, pp. 25–26.

Coles, Robert. "Social Struggle and Weariness." *Psychiatry* 27, no. 4 (November 1964): 305–15.

Cowan, Geoff, and Paul Cowan. "And Three Letters Home from Mississippi." *Esquire*, September 1964, pp. 104–5, 190.

"Crusade in Mississippi." *Ebony*, September 1964, pp. 24–29.

DeMuth, Jerry. "Summer in Mississippi: Freedom Moves In to Stay." *Nation*, September 14, 1964, pp. 104, 108–10.

"Do Not Despair." *Time*, November 27, 1964, p. 35.

"Dream in a Bean Field." *Nation*, December 28, 1964, p. 514.

"The Evangelists." *Newsweek*, August 24, 1964, pp. 30–31.

Fischer, John. "A Small Band of Practical Heroes." *Harper's*, October 1963.

Fusco, Liz. "Deeper Than Politics." *Liberation* 9 (November 1964): 17–19.

Good, Paul. "A Bowl of Gumbo for Curtis Bryant." *Reporter*, December 31, 1964, pp. 19–22.

Goodman, Carolyn. "My Son Didn't Die in Vain!" With Bernard Asbell. *Good Housekeeping*, May 1965, pp. 98, 158–64.

Harris, Louis. "The Backlash Issue." *Newsweek*, July 13, 1964, pp. 24–27.

"How Whites Feel About a Painful America." *Newsweek*, October 21, 1963, pp. 44–51.

"The Invaders." *Newsweek*, June 29, 1964, pp. 25–26.

Jencks, Christopher. "Mississippi: When Law Collides with Custom." *New Republic*, July 25, 1964, pp. 15–19.

Kempton, Murray. "Conscience of a Convention." *New Republic*, September 5, 1964, pp. 5–7.

Klibanoff, Hank. "Moment of Reckoning." *Smithsonian*, December 2008, pp. 12–14.

Kopkind, Andrew. "The Future of 'Black Power': A Movement in Search of a Program." *New Republic*, January 7, 1967, pp. 16–18.

"The Limpid Shambles of Violence." *Life*, July 3, 1964, pp. 32–35.

Lynd, Staughton. "The Freedom Schools: Concept and Organization." *Freedomways*, Second Quarter 1965, pp. 303–9.

McMillen, Neil R. "Black Enfranchisement in Mississippi: Federal Enforcement and Black Protest in the 1960s." *Journal of Southern History*, August 1977, pp. 351–72.

Mannes, Marya. "The G.O.P. and the Gap." *Reporter*, August 13, 1964, pp. 28–30.

Martinez, Elizabeth. "Theater of the Meaningful." *Nation*, October 19, 1964, pp. 254–56.

"Mississippi Airlift." *Newsweek*. March 11, 1963, pp. 30–32.

"Mississippi: Allen's Army." *Newsweek*, February 24, 1964, p. 30.

"Mississippi: Battle of the Kennedys." *Newsweek*, August 19, 1963, p. 24.

"Mississippi—'Everybody's Scared.'" *Newsweek*, July 6, 1964, pp. 15–16.

"Mississippi: Storm Signals." *U.S. News & World Report*, July 6, 1964, p. 37.

"Mississippi—Summer of 1964: Troubled State, Troubled Time." *Newsweek*, July 13, 1964, pp. 18–20.

Morton, Eric. "Tremor in the Iceberg." *Freedomways*, Second Quarter 1965, pp. 321–22.

"Out of the Ashes." *Newsweek*, October 12, 1964, p. 72.

Perlstein, Daniel. "Teaching Freedom: SNCC and the Creation of the Mississippi Freedom Schools." *History of Education Quarterly* 30, no. 3 (Fall 1990): 297–324.

Pouissant, Alvin F., M.D. "The Stresses of the White Female Worker in the Civil Rights Movement in the South." *American Journal of Psychiatry* 123, no. 4 (October 1966): 401–7.

Ross, Lillian. "Meeting." *New Yorker*, April 11, 1964, p. 33.

"The Terrible Silence of the Decent." *Life*, July 10, 1964, p. 4.

Trillin, Calvin. "Letter from Jackson." *New Yorker*, August 29, 1964, pp. 80–105.

———. "State Secrets." *New Yorker*, May 29, 1995, pp. 54–64.

Watson, Bruce. "A Freedom Summer Activist Becomes a Math Revolutionary." *Smithsonian*, February 1996, pp. 115–25.

Wechsler, James A. "The FBI's Failure in the South." *Progressive*, December 1963, pp. 20–23.

Woodley, Richard. "A Recollection of Michael Schwerner." *Reporter*, July 16, 1964, pp. 23–24.

———. "It Will Be a Hot Summer in Mississippi." *Reporter*, May 21, 1964, pp. 21–24.

"Worse Than Mississippi?" *Time*, July 24, 1964, pp. 29–30.

Zeitz, Joshua. "Democratic Debacle." *American Heritage*, June/July 2004, http://www.americanheritage.com/articles/magazine/ah/2004/3/2004_3_59.shtml.

Books

Abbott, Dorothy, ed. *Mississippi Writers: Reflections of Childhood and Youth*. Vol. 2, *Nonfiction*; vol. 3, *Poetry*. Jackson: University Press of Mississippi, 1986.

Adickes, Sandra E. *Legacy of a Freedom School*. New York: Palgrave Macmillan, 2005.

Bales, Jack, ed. *Conversations with Willie Morris*. Jackson: University Press of Mississippi, 2000.

Ball, Howard. *Murder in Mississippi: United States v. Price and the Struggle for Civil Rights*. Lawrence: University of Kansas Press, 2004.

Belfrage, Sally. *Freedom Summer*. New York: Viking, 1965.

Beschloss, Michael R., ed. *Taking Charge: The Johnson White House Tapes, 1963–1964*. New York: Simon & Schuster, 1997.

Blackwell, Unita. *Barefootin': Life Lessons from the Road to Freedom*. With JoAnne Prichard Moore. New York: Crown, 2006.

Blight, David W. *Beyond the Battlefield: Race, Memory, and the American Civil War*. Amherst: University of Massachusetts Press, 2002.

Bond, Bradley G. *Mississippi: A Documentary History*. Jackson: University of Mississippi Press, 2003.

Bowers, Claude G. *The Tragic Era: The Revolution After Lincoln*. Boston: Houghton Mifflin, 1929.

Branch, Taylor. *Parting the Waters: America in the King Years, 1954–63*. New York: Simon & Schuster, 1988.

———, *Pillar of Fire: America in the King Years, 1963–65*. New York: Simon & Schuster, 1998.

Brownmiller, Susan. *In Our Time: Memoir of a Revolution*. New York: Dial Press, 1999.

Burner, Eric R. *And Gently He Shall Lead Them: Robert Parris Moses and Civil Rights in Mississippi*. New York: New York University Press, 1994.

Cagin, Seth, and Philip Dray. *We Are Not Afraid: The Story of Goodman, Schwerner, and Chaney, and the Civil Rights Campaign for Mississippi*. New York: Nation Books, 2006.

Carmichael, Stokely, and Ekwueme Michael Thelwell. *Ready for Revolution: The Life and Struggles of Stokely Carmichael (Kwame Ture)*. New York: Scribners, 2003.

Carson, Clayborne. *In Struggle: SNCC and the Black Awakening of the 1960s*. Cambridge, Mass.: Harvard University Press, 1981.

Carter, Hodding III. *The South Strikes Back*. Garden City, N.Y.: Doubleday & Co., 1959.

———. *So the Heffners Left McComb*. Garden City, N.Y.: Doubleday, 1965.

Cash, W. J. *The Mind of the South*. New York: Random House, 1941.

Chalmers, David. *Backfire: How the Ku Klux Klan Helped the Civil Rights Movement*. Lanham, Md.: Rowman & Littlefield, 2003.

Classen, Dan. *Watching Jim Crow: The Struggles over Mississippi TV, 1955–1969*. Durham, N.C.: Duke University Press, 2004.

Coles, Robert. *Farewell to the South*. Boston: Little, Brown, 1972.

Council of Federated Organizations (COFO). *Mississippi Black Paper*. New York: Random House, 1965.

Cowan, Paul. *The Making of an Un-American: A Dialogue with Experience*. New York: Viking, 1970.

Cummings, Richard. *The Pied Piper: Allard K. Lowenstein and the Liberal Dream*. New York: Grove Press, 1985.

Curry, Constance, Joan C. Browning, Dorothy Dawson Burlage, Penny Patch, Theresa Del Pozzo, Sue Thrasher, Elaine DeLott Baker, Emmie Schrader Adams, and

Casey Hayden. *Deep in Our Hearts: Nine White Women in the Freedom Movement.* Athens: University of Georgia Press, 2000.

Davidson, Chandler, and Bernard Grofman, eds. *Quiet Revolution in the South: The Impact of the Voting Rights Act, 1965–1990.* Princeton, N.J.: Princeton University Press, 1994.

Davies, David R., ed. *The Press and Race: Mississippi Journalists Confront the Movement.* Jackson: University of Mississippi Press, 2001.

DeLoach, Cartha "Deke." *Hoover's FBI: The Inside Story by Hoover's Trusted Lieutenant.* Washington, D.C.: Regnery, 1995.

Dent, Thomas C., Richard Schechner, and Gilbert Moses. *The Free Southern Theater by the Free Southern Theater.* Indianapolis: Bobbs-Merrill, 1969.

Dickerson, James L. *Dixie's Dirty Secret.* Armonk, N.Y.: M. E. Sharpe, 1998.

Dittmer, John. *Local People: The Struggle for Civil Rights in Mississippi.* Urbana: University of Illinois Press, 1994.

Duberman, Martin. *In White America.* London: Faber and Faber, 1964.

Du Bois, W. E. B. *The Souls of Black Folk.* New York: Vintage, 1990.

Dunaway, David King. *How Can I Keep from Singing.* New York: McGraw-Hill, 1981.

Eliot, Marc. *Death of a Rebel, Starring Phil Ochs and a Small Circle of Friends.* New York: Anchor Books, 1979.

Erenrich, Susie. *Freedom Is a Constant Struggle: An Anthology of the Mississippi Civil Rights Movement.* Montgomery, Ala.: Black Belt Press, 1999.

Evans, Sara. *Personal Politics.* New York: Vintage, 1980.

Farmer, James. *Lay Bare the Heart: An Autobiography of the Civil Rights Movement.* New York: New American Library, 1985.

Fleming, Karl. *Son of the Rough South: An Uncivil Memoir.* New York: Public Affairs, 2005.

Foner, Eric. *A Short History of Reconstruction, 1863–1877.* New York: Harper & Row, 1990.

Foote, Shelby. *The Civil War: A Narrative—Fredericksburg to Meridian.* New York: Random House, 1963.

Forman, James. *The Making of Black Revolutionaries.* Washington, D.C.: Open Hand, 1985.

Goudsouzian, Adam. *Sidney Poitier: Man, Actor, Icon.* Chapel Hill: University of North Carolina Press, 2004.

Greenberg, Cheryl Lynn, ed. *A Circle of Trust: Remembering SNCC.* New Brunswick, N.J.: Rutgers University Press, 1998.

Griffin, John Howard. *Black Like Me,* 2d ed. Boston: Houghton Mifflin, 1961.

Gussow, Adam. *Seems Like Murder Here: Southern Violence and the Blues Tradition.* Chicago: University of Chicago Press, 2002.

Hack, Richard. *Puppetmaster: The Secret Life of J. Edgar Hoover.* Beverly Hills, Calif.: New Millennium Press, 2004.

Harkey, Ira B. Jr. *The Smell of Burning Crosses: An Autobiography of a Mississippi Newspaperman.* Jacksonville, Fla.: Delphi Press, 1967.

Harris, Mark. *Pictures at a Revolution: Five Movies and the Birth of the New Hollywood.* New York: Penguin Press, 2008.

Harris, William C. *The Day of the Carpetbagger: Republican Reconstruction in Mississippi.* Baton Rouge: Louisiana State University Press, 1979.

Hearings Before the United States Commission on Civil Rights, Jackson, MS, February 16–20, 1965, U.S. Government Printing Office, Washington, D.C., 1965.

Henry, Aaron. *Aaron Henry: The Fire Ever Burning.* With Constance Curry. Jackson: University of Mississippi Press, 2000.

Hochschild, Adam. *Finding the Trapdoor: Essays, Portraits, Travels.* Syracuse, N.Y.: Syracuse University Press, 1997.

Hogan, Wesley C. *Many Minds, One Heart: SNCC's Dream for a New America.* Chapel Hill: University of North Carolina Press, 2007.

Holland, Endesha Ida Mae. *From the Mississippi Delta: A Memoir.* New York: Simon & Schuster, 1997.

Holt, Len. *The Summer That Didn't End.* New York: William Morrow, 1965.

Howe, Florence. *Myths of Co-education: Selected Essays, 1964–1983.* Bloomington: Indiana University Press, 1984.

Hudson, Winson, and Constance Curry. *Mississippi Harmony: Memoirs of a Freedom Fighter.* New York: Palgrave Macmillan, 2002.

Johnson, Lady Bird. *A White House Diary.* New York: Holt, Rinehart, and Winston, 1970.

Johnson, Robert David. *All the Way with LBJ: The 1964 Presidential Election.* New York: Cambridge University Press, 2009.

Katagiri, Yasuhiro. *The Mississippi State Sovereignty Commission: Civil Rights and States' Rights.* Jackson: University Press of Mississippi, 2001.

King, Mary. *Freedom Song: A Personal Story of the 1960s Civil Rights Movement.* New York: Quill/William Morrow, 1987.

Kotz, Nick. *Judgment Days: Lyndon Baines Johnson, Martin Luther King Jr., and the Laws That Changed America.* Boston: Houghton Mifflin, 2005.

Kunstler, William M. *Deep in My Heart.* New York: William Morrow, 1966.

———. *My Life as a Radical Lawyer.* With Sheila Isenberg. New York: Birch Lane Press, 1994.

Lasky, Victor. *It Didn't Start with Watergate.* New York: Dial Press, 1977.

Lee, Chana Kai. *For Freedom's Sake: The Life of Fannie Lou Hamer.* Urbana: University of Illinois Press, 1999.

Lemann, Nicholas. *Redemption: The Last Battle of the Civil War.* New York: Farrar, Straus and Giroux, 2005.

Lester, Julius. *All Is Well.* New York: William Morrow, 1976.

Lewis, John. *Walking with the Wind: A Memoir of the Movement.* New York: Simon & Schuster, 1998.

Library of America. *Reporting Civil Rights: American Journalism, 1963–1973.* New York: Library of America, 2003.

McAdam, Doug. *Freedom Summer.* New York: Oxford University Press, 1988.

McCord, William. *Mississippi: The Long Hot Summer.* New York: W. W. Norton, 1965.

McIlhany, William H. II. *Klandestine: The Untold Story of Delmar Dennis and His Role in the FBI's War Against the Ku Klux Klan.* New Rochelle, N.Y.: Arlington House, 1975.

McMillen, Neil. *The Citizens' Council: Organized Resistance to the Second Reconstruction, 1954–1964.* Urbana: University of Illinois Press, 1971.

Marrs, Suzanne. *Eudora Welty: A Biography.* Orlando, Fla.: Harcourt, 2005.

Mars, Florence. *Witness in Philadelphia.* Baton Rouge: Louisiana State University Press, 1977.

Marsh, Charles. *God's Long Summer: Stories of Faith and Civil Rights.* Princeton, N.J.: Princeton University Press, 1997.

Martinez, Elizabeth, ed. *Letters from Mississippi.* Brookline, Mass.: Zephyr Press, 2007.

Mills, Kay. *This Little Light of Mine: The Life of Fannie Lou Hamer.* New York: Penguin Books, 1993.

Mills, Nicolaus. *Like a Holy Crusade: Mississippi 1964—The Turning of the Civil Rights Movement in America.* New York: Alfred A. Knopf, 1992.

Morris, Willie. *My Mississippi.* Jackson: University of Mississippi Press, 2000.

———. *North Toward Home.* Boston: Houghton Mifflin, 1967.

Moses, Robert P., and Charles E. Cobb Jr. *Radical Equations: Math Literacy and Civil Rights.* Boston: Beacon Press, 2001.

Myrdal, Gunnar. *An American Dilemma: The Negro Problem and Modern Democracy.* New York: Harper & Row, 1962.

Newfield, Jack. *A Prophetic Minority.* New York: New American Library, 1966.

Novick, Peter. *That Noble Dream: The "Objectivity Question" and the American Historical Profession.* Cambridge, England: Cambridge University Press, 1988.

Olson, Lynne. *Freedom's Daughters: The Unsung Heroines of the Civil Rights Movement from 1830 to 1970.* New York: Scribners, 2001.

O'Reilly, Kenneth. *"Racial Matters": The FBI's Secret File on Black America, 1960–1972.* New York: Free Press, 1989.

Oshinsky, David M. *"Worse Than Slavery": Parchman Farm and the Ordeal of Jim Crow Justice.* New York: Simon & Schuster, 1997.

Parker, Frank R. *Black Votes Count: Political Empowerment in Mississippi After 1965.* Chapel Hill: University of North Carolina Press, 1990.

Payne, Charles. *I've Got the Light of Freedom: The Organizing Tradition and the Mississippi Freedom Struggle.* Berkeley and Los Angeles: University of California Press, 1995.

Percy, William Alexander. *Lanterns on the Levee: Recollections of a Planter's Son.* New York: Alfred A. Knopf, 1941.

Perlstein, Rick. *Before the Storm: Barry Goldwater and the Unmaking of the American Consensus.* New York: Hill and Wang, 2001.

Poitier, Sidney. *Life Beyond Measure: Letters to My Great-Granddaughter.* New York: HarperCollins, 2008.

Provenzo, Eugene F., ed. *Critical Issues in Education.* Thousand Oaks, Calif.: Sage, 2006.

Raines, Howell. *My Soul Is Rested: Movement Days in the Deep South Remembered.* New York: Penguin, 1977.

Randall, Herbert, and Bob Tusa. *Faces of Freedom Summer.* Tuscaloosa: University of Alabama Press, 2001.

Ransby, Barbara. *Ella Baker and the Black Freedom Movement: A Radical Democratic Vision.* Chapel Hill: University of North Carolina Press, 2003.

Ravitch, Diane, ed. *The American Reader: Words That Moved a Nation.* New York: Harper Perennial, 1991.

Roberts, Gene, and Hank Klibanoff. *The Race Beat: The Press, the Civil Rights Struggle, and the Awakening of a Nation.* New York: Random House, 2007.

Rogers, Kim Lacy. *Life and Death in the Delta: African American Narratives of Violence, Resilience, and Social Change.* New York: Palgrave Macmillan, 2006.

Rothschild, Mary Aickin. *A Case of Black and White: Northern Volunteers and the Southern Freedom Summers, 1964–1965.* Westport, Conn.: Greenwood Press, 1982.

Schumacher, Michael. *There But for Fortune: The Life of Phil Ochs.* New York: Hyperion, 1996.

Sellers, Cleveland, and Robert Terrell. *The River of No Return: The Autobiography of a Black Militant and the Life and Death of SNCC.* New York: William Morrow, 1973.

Silver, James W. *Mississippi: The Closed Society.* Rev. ed. New York: Harcourt, Brace & World, 1966.

Sitkoff, Harvard. *The Struggle for Black Equality, 1954–1992.* New York: Hill and Wang, 1993.

Skates, John Ray. *Mississippi: A Bicentennial History.* New York: W. W. Norton, 1979.

Sokol, Jason. *There Goes My Everything: White Southerners in the Age of Civil Rights, 1945–1975.* New York: Alfred A. Knopf, 2006.

Sugarman, Tracy. *Stranger at the Gates: A Summer in Mississippi.* New York: Hill and Wang, 1966.

Tucker, Shirley. *Mississippi from Within.* New York: Arco, 1965.

Von Hoffman, Nicholas. *Mississippi Notebook.* New York: David White, 1964.

Wade, Wyn Craig. *The Fiery Cross: The Ku Klux Klan in America.* New York: Oxford University Press USA, 1998.

Walton, Anthony. *Mississippi: An American Journey.* New York: Alfred A. Knopf, 1996.

Ward, Geoffrey C., Ric Burns, and Ken Burns. *The Civil War: An Illustrated History.* New York: Alfred A. Knopf, 1990.

Wendt, Simon. *The Spirit and the Shotgun: Armed Resistance and the Struggle for Civil Rights.* Gainesville: University Press of Florida, 2007.

Whalen, John. *Maverick Among the Magnolias: The Hazel Brannon Smith Story.* Bloomington, Ind.: Xlibris, 2000.

White, Theodore. *The Making of the President, 1964.* New York: Atheneum, 1965.

Whitehead, Don. *Attack on Terror: The FBI Against the Ku Klux Klan in Mississippi.* New York: Funk & Wagnalls, 1970.

Wilkie, Curtis. *Dixie: A Personal Odyssey Through Events That Shaped the Modern South.* New York: Simon & Schuster, 2003.

Williams, Juan. *Eyes on the Prize: America's Civil Rights Years, 1954–1965.* New York: Penguin Books, 2002.

Winter, William F. *The Measure of Our Days: The Writings of William F. Winter.* Jackson: University Press of Mississippi, 2006.

Wirt, Frederick M. *Politics of Southern Equality: Law and Social Change in a Mississippi County.* Chicago: Aldine, 1970.

Woods, Randall B. *LBJ: Architect of American Ambition.* New York: Free Press, 2006.

Woodward, C. Vann. *The Strange Career of Jim Crow.* 3d rev. ed. New York: Oxford University Press, 1974.

Yates, Gayle Graham. *Mississippi Mind: A Personal Cultural History of an American State.* Knoxville: University of Tennessee Press, 1990.

Youth of the Rural Organizing and Cultural Center. *Minds Stayed on Freedom: The Civil Rights Struggle in the Rural South, an Oral History.* Boulder, Colo.: Westview Press, 1991.

Zellner, Robert. *The Wrong Side of Murder Creek: A White Southerner in the Freedom Movement*. With Constance Curry. Montgomery, Ala.: NewSouth Books, 2008.

Zinn, Howard, ed. *The Power of Nonviolence: Writings by Advocates of Peace*. Boston: Beacon Press, 2002.

———. *SNCC: The New Abolitionists*. Boston: Beacon Press, 1964.

Film and Video

Beymer, Richard. *A Regular Bouquet*. Self-produced, 1965.

Hampton, Henry, dir. "Mississippi—Is This America?" Episode 5 of *Eyes on the Prize: America's Civil Rights Movement*. Boston: Blackside, 1987.

Mulford, Marilyn, and Connie Field, dirs. *Freedom on My Mind*. Berkeley, Calif.: Clarity Film Productions, 1994.

Potter, Anthony, dir. *Murder in Mississippi: The Price of Freedom*. New York: ABC News, 1994.

"Students Asked Not to Say Obama's Name." WAPT, Channel 16, Jackson, Miss. http://www.wapt.com/video/17928161/index.html.

Williams, Marco, dir. *Ten Days That Unexpectedly Changed America—Freedom Summer*. New York: History Channel, 2006.

Personal Interviews (in chronological order)

Gloria Clark, volunteer
Heather Booth Tobis, volunteer
Nancy Schlieffelin, volunteer
Chris Williams, volunteer
Robert Fullilove, volunteer
Fran O'Brien, volunteer
Chude Pamela Allen, volunteer
Karen Hoberman, volunteer
Fred Bright Winn, volunteer
Muriel Tillinghast, volunteer/SNCC staff
Jay Shetterly, volunteer
Geoff Cowan, volunteer
Claire O'Connor, volunteer
Jim Kates, volunteer
Ira Landess, volunteer
Jimmie Travis, SNCC staff
Dr. Stacey White
Robert Miles Jr.
Jack Bishop, cofounder, Association of Tenth Amendment Conservatives
Elaine Baker, volunteer
Kathie Sarachild, volunteer
John Howell, newspaper publisher
Ray Raphael, volunteer
Linda Wetmore, volunteer

Nancy Samstein, volunteer
Arelya Mitchell, Freedom School student
Julius Lester, folksinger
Gary Brooks, McComb, Mississippi, native
Hollis Watkins, SNCC staff
Congressman Barney Frank, volunteer
Richard Beymer, volunteer
Alan Schiffman, volunteer
Michael Thelwell, SNCC staff, Washington, D.C.
Charlie Cobb, SNCC staff
Curtis (Hayes) Muhammad, SNCC staff
Charles Capps Jr., sheriff
Jim Dann, volunteer
Congressman John Lewis, SNCC staff
Margaret Block, volunteer
Otis Brown, SNCC staff
Dennis Flannagan, volunteer
Stephen Bingham, volunteer
Jerry Mitchell, *Jackson Clarion-Ledger* reporter
Charles McLaurin, SNCC staff
Len Edwards, volunteer
Governor William F. Winter
Bob Moses, SNCC staff
Sue Thrasher, volunteer
Bob Zellner, SNCC staff

E-mail Interviews (in chronological order)

Casey Hayden, SNCC staff
Hodding Carter III, editor, *Delta Democrat-Times*
Franklin Delano Roosevelt III

Web Sites

American Radio Works. http://americanradioworks.publicradio.org/.
American Rhetoric. http://www.americanrhetoric.com.
Cambridge Encyclopedia. Vol. 1. http://encyclopedia.stateuniversity.com/pages/.
Cardcow.com, Vintage Postcards and Collectibles. http://www.cardcow.com.
Civil Rights Movement Veterans Web site. http://www.crmvet.org.
"Democracy Now!" http://www.alternet.org.
Meikeljohn Civil Liberties Institute Archives, Bancroft Library, University of Califor-
    nia, Berkeley. http://sunsite.berkeley.edu/meiklejohn/meik-10_1/meik-10_1-6.html
    #580.7.
"Mississippi Burning Trial: Selected Klan Documents." *Famous Trials:* U.S. vs. Cecil
    Price et al. (*"Mississippi Burning" Trial*) Web site. http://www.law.umkc.edu/
    faculty/projects/ftrials/price&bowers/Klan.html.
The Nina Simone Web. http://boscarol.com/nina/html/where/mississipigoddamn
    .html.

Port Gibson Heritage Trust Web site. http://www.portgibsonheritagetrust.org/port
    _gibson.
The Sixties Project. http://www2.iath.virginia.edu/sixties/HTML_docs/Sixties.html.
Digital Library, University of California at Berkeley. http://sunsite.berkeley.edu.
"Wednesdays in Mississippi: Civil Rights as Women's Work." http://www.vcdh
    .virginia.edu/WIMS/.

Index